WESTERN
HOME LANDSCAPING

From the Rockies to the Pacific Coast,
from the Southwestern US to British Columbia

CRE**A**TIVE
HOMEOWNER®

WESTERN

HOME LANDSCAPING

*From the Rockies to the Pacific Coast,
from the Southwestern US to British Columbia*

CREATIVE HOMEOWNER®, Upper Saddle River, New Jersey

WESTERN HOME LANDSCAPING

CONSULTANTS	Roger Holmes, Lance Walheim, Greg Grant, Don Marshall, Rita Buchanan, Deborah Fillion
EDITOR	Lisa Kahn
JUNIOR EDITOR	Angela Hanson
INDEXER	Schroeder Indexing Services
PHOTO COORDINATOR	Mary Dolan
ILLUSTRATORS	Steve Buchanan, Jeff Grunewald, Claude Thivierge, Alain Salesse/contactjupiter.com, Polygone Studio/contactjupiter.com (Portfolio of Designs); Michelle Angle Farrar, Lee Hov, Robert LaPointe, Rick Daskam, Teresa Nicole Green (Guide to Installation)
COVER DESIGN / INTERIOR LAYOUT	Glee Barre
DIGITAL IMAGING SPECIALIST	Frank Dyer

CREATIVE HOMEOWNER

VICE PRESIDENT AND PUBLISHER	Timothy O. Bakke
MANAGING EDITOR	Fran J. Donegan
ART DIRECTOR	David Geer
PRODUCTION COORDINATOR	Sara M. Markowitz

Manufactured in the United States of America

Current Printing (last digit)
10 9 8 7 6 5 4 3 2 1

Western Home Landscaping, First Edition
Library of Congress Control Number: 2009933058
ISBN-10: 1-58011-486-5
ISBN-13: 978-1-58011-486-8

CREATIVE HOMEOWNER®
A Division of Federal Marketing Corp.
24 Park Way
Upper Saddle River, NJ 07458
www.creativehomeowner.com

Planet Friendly Publishing
✓ Made in the United States
✓ Printed on Recycled Paper
Text: 10%   Cover: 10%
Learn more: www.greenedition.org

GREEN EDITION

At Creative Homeowner we're committed to producing books in an earth-friendly manner and to helping our customers make greener choices.

Manufacturing books in the United States ensures compliance with strict environmental laws and eliminates the need for international freight shipping, a major contributor to global air pollution.

And printing on recycled paper helps minimize our consumption of trees, water, and fossil fuels. *Western Home Landscaping* was printed on paper made with 10% post-consumer waste. According to the Environmental Defense Fund Paper Calculator, by using this innovative paper instead of conventional papers we achieved the following environmental benefits:

Trees Saved: 45

Water Saved: 20,691 gallons

Solid Waste Eliminated: 1,256 pounds

Greenhouse Gas Emissions Eliminated: 4,296 pounds

For more information on our environmental practices, please visit us online at www.creativehomeowner.com/green

Safety First

Though all concepts and methods in this book have been reviewed for safety, it is not possible to overstate the importance of using the safest working methods possible. What follows are reminders—do's and don'ts for yard work and landscaping. They are not substitutes for your own common sense.

- *Always* use caution, care, and good judgment when following the procedures described in this book.

- *Always* determine locations of underground utility lines before you dig, and then avoid them by a safe distance. Buried lines may be for gas, electricity, communications, or water. Start research by contacting your local building officials. Also contact local utility companies; they will often send a representative free of charge to help you map their lines. In addition, there are private utility locator firms that may be listed in your Yellow Pages. Note: previous owners may have installed underground drainage, sprinkler, and lighting lines without mapping them.

- *Always* read and heed the manufacturer's instructions for using a tool, especially the warnings.

- *Always* ensure that the electrical setup is safe; be sure that no circuit is overloaded and that all power tools and electrical outlets are properly grounded and protected by a ground-fault circuit interrupter (GFCI). Do not use power tools in wet locations.

- *Always* wear eye protection when using chemicals, sawing wood, pruning trees and shrubs, using power tools, and striking metal onto metal or concrete.

- *Always* read labels on chemicals, solvents, and other products; provide ventilation; heed warnings.

- *Always* wear heavy rubber gloves rated for chemicals, not mere household rubber gloves, when handling toxins.

- *Always* wear appropriate gloves in situations in which your hands could be injured by rough surfaces, sharp edges, thorns, or poisonous plants.

- *Always* wear a disposable face mask or a special filtering respirator when creating sawdust or working with toxic gardening substances.

- *Always* keep your hands and other body parts away from the business ends of blades, cutters, and bits.

- *Always* obtain approval from local building officials before undertaking construction of permanent structures.

- *Never* work with power tools when you are tired or under the influence of alcohol or drugs.

- *Never* carry sharp or pointed tools, such as knives or saws, in your pockets. If you carry such tools, use special-purpose tool scabbards.

The Landscape Designers

For more information about the landscape designers whose work is featured in the Portfolio of Designs, see page 318.

John Ahrens designs appear on pp. 92–95, 120–123.

Mark Bowen designs appear on pp. 20–23, 80–83.

Michael Buccino designs appear on pp. 152–155, 160–163.

Lee Buffington designs appear on pp. 72–75.

Laura Crockett designs appear on pp. 104–107.

Rosa Finsley designs appear on pp. 64–67, 100–103, 116–119.

Lucy Hardiman designs appear on pp. 108–111.

Daniel Lowery designs appear on pp. 32–35.

Curtis Manning designs appear on pp. 44–47, 128–131, 148–151.

Richard Marriotti designs appear on pp. 96–99, 156–159, 172–175.

Michael Parkey designs appear on pp. 36–39.

Susan Romiti and **Ross Holmquist** designs appear on pp. 48–51.

Jana Ruzicka designs appear on pp. 76–79, 140–143.

Carolyn Singer designs appear on pp. 56–59, 68–71, 112–115.

John S. Troy designs appear on pp. 136–139, 180–183.

John Valentino and **Bob Truxell** designs appear on pp. 24–27, 32–35, 40–43, 84–87, 124–127, 164–167, 168–171, 176–179.

Jenny Webber designs appear on pp. 88–83, 133–135.

Mary Wilhite and **Sharon Lee Smith** designs appear on pp. 60–63.

Richard William Wogisch designs appear on pp. 16–19, 144–147.

Phil Wood designs appear on pp. 52–55.

Contents

14 Portfolio of Designs

About This Book

Of all the home improvement projects homeowners tackle, few offer greater rewards than landscaping. Paths, patios, fences, arbors, and—most of all—plantings can enhance home life in countless ways, large and small, functional and pleasurable, every day of the year. At the main entrance, an attractive brick walkway flanked by eye-catching shrubs and perennials provides a cheerful send-off in the morning and welcomes you home from work in the evening. A carefully placed grouping of small trees, shrubs, and fence panels creates privacy on the patio or screens a nearby eyesore from view. An island bed showcases your favorite plants, while dividing the backyard into several areas for a variety of activities.

Unlike some home improvements, the rewards of landscaping are as much in the activity as in the result. Planting and caring for lovely shrubs, perennials, and other plants can afford years of enjoyment. And for those who like to build things, outdoor construction projects can be a special treat.

While the installation and maintenance of plants and outdoor structures are within the means and abilities of most people, few of us are as comfortable determining exactly which plants or structures to use and how best to combine them. It's one thing to decide to dress up the front entrance or patio, another to come up with a design for doing so.

That's where this book comes in. Here, in the Portfolio of Designs, you'll find inspiration for nearly two dozen common home landscaping situations, created by landscape professionals who live and work in the Western region of the country. Drawing on years of experience, they balance functional requirements and aesthetic possibilities, choosing the right plant or structure for the task based on its proven performance in similar situations.

The book's second section, Plant Profiles, provides information on all the plants used in the book. The third section, the Guide to Installation, will help you to install and maintain the plants and structures described in the previous two sections.

The discussions that follow here take a closer look at each section. We've also printed representative pages of the sections on pp. 9 and 10 and pointed out their features.

Portfolio of Designs

This section is the heart of the book, providing examples of landscaping situations and solutions that are at once inspiring and accessible. Some are simple, others more complex, but each one can be installed in a few weekends by homeowners with no special training or experience.

For each situation, we present one or more pairs of designs. In each pair, the second is a variation of the first. As the sample pages on the facing page show, the first design of each pair is displayed on a two-page spread. A perspective illustration (called a "rendering") depicts what the design will look like several years after installation, when the perennials and many of the shrubs have reached mature size. (For more on how plantings change as they age, see "As Your Landscape Grows," pp. 12–13.) The rendering also shows the planting as it will appear at a particular time of year. A site plan indicates the positions of the plants and structures on a scaled grid. Text introduces the situation and the design and describes the plants and projects used.

The second design, presented on the second two-page spread, addresses the same situation as the first but differs in one or more important aspects. It might show a planting suited for a shady rather than a sunny site, or it might incorporate different structures or kinds of plants to create a different look. As for the first design, we present a rendering, site plan, and written information, but in briefer form. The second spread also includes photographs. For some designs, the photos are of plants used in the design; for others, they are of landscapes in situations similar to those featured in the two designs. The landscape photos showcase noteworthy variations or details that you may wish to use in the designs we show or in designs of your own.

Installed exactly as shown here, these designs will provide years of enjoyment. But individual needs and properties will differ, and we encourage you to alter the designs to suit your site and desires. Many types of alterations are easy to make. You can add or remove plants and adjust the sizes of paths, patios, and arbors to accommodate larger or smaller sites. You can rearrange groupings and substitute favorite plants to suit your taste. Or you can integrate the design with your existing landscaping. If you are uncertain about how to solve specific problems or about the effects of changes you'd like to make, consult with staff at a local nursery or with a landscape designer in your area.

PORTFOLIO OF DESIGNS

FIRST DESIGN OPTION

Summary
An overview of the situation and the design.

Concept Box
Summarizes an important aspect of the design; tells whether the site is sunny or shady and what season is depicted in the rendering.

Rendering
Shows how the design will look when plants are well established.

Plants & Projects
Noteworthy qualities of the plants and structures and their contributions to the design.

Site Plan
Positions all plants and structures on a scaled grid.

Site Plan
Plants and structures on a scaled grid.

Variations on a Theme
Photos of inspiring designs in similar situations.

SECOND DESIGN OPTION

Summary
Addressing the same situation as the first design, this variation may differ in design concept, site conditions, or plant selection.

Concept Box
Site, season, and design summary.

Rendering
Depicts the design when plants are well established.

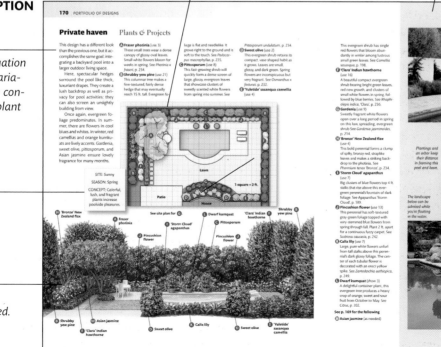

Horicultural nomenclature

The two scientific Latin names identifying a plant are based on the *genus* and *species*. A genus is a group of plants marked by common characteristics. For example, plants from the yarrow genus are all named *Achillea* after the Greek hero Achilles who, according to legend, used yarrow to heal his soldiers' wounds during the Trojan war.

The species is a subdivision of the genus, and refers to more specific qualities of the plant. *Achillea mille-folium* is a species of yarrow with leaves divided into a thousand tiny parts. (*Mille* refers to thousands, and *folium* refers to leaves or foliage.) Another species, woolly yarrow, in Latin is *Achillea tomentosa; tomentosa* refers to its hairy leaves.

The word identifying the genus always comes first and is capitalized as a proper noun. The species name is a descriptive word used as an adjective to modify and further describe the noun; it is always lower case.

Occasionally, there is a third Latin name denoting a *variety* or subdivision of a species that arises in nature spontaneously. For example, the beach or shore pine is *Pinus contorta*. The lodgepole pine, a variety of that species, is *Pinus contorta* var. *latifolia*. *Pinus* indicates both are from the pine family; contorta describes the twisted form in which the trees grow, and—in the case of the lodgepole pine—the variety name *latifolia* explains that the leaves (needles) are broader than those of beach pine.

If a plant is of garden origin—that is, it doesn't exist in the wild—it will have an additional name listed after its Latin name in single quotes; this is the *cultivar*. The geranium cultivar 'Johnson's Blue' has become a staple in the perennials section of nurseries, as has the yarrow 'Moonshine'.

Although the scientific names may seem confusing, they are valuable. Common plant names are charming but they often vary from place to place. In addition, several plants with different characteristics may share the same common name. The scientific name is precise and descriptive.

You can learn a lot about a plant just from its name. For example, if a plant has *officinalis* in its name, you can be sure it was at one time used for medicinal purposes. A *sempervirens* will stay green throughout the year in most climates; *semperflorens* is ever-flowering.

Plant Profiles

The second section of the book includes a description of each of the plants featured in the Portfolio. These profiles outline the plants' basic preferences for environmental conditions—such as soil, moisture, and sun or shade—and provide advice about planting and ongoing care.

Working with the book's landscape designers, we selected plants carefully, following a few simple guidelines: Every plant should be a proven performer in the region; once established, it should thrive without pampering. All plants should be available from a major local nursery or garden center; if they're not in stock, they could be ordered, or you could ask the nursery staff to recommend suitable substitutes.

In the Portfolio section, you'll note that plants are referred to by their common name but are cross-referenced to the Plant Profiles section by their Latinized scientific name. While common names are familiar to many people, they can be confusing. Distinctly different plants can share the same common name, or one plant can have several different common names. Scientific names, therefore, ensure greatest accuracy and are more appropriate for a reference section such as this. (See "Horticultural nomenclature," left.) Although you can confidently purchase most of the plants in this book from local nurseries using the common name, knowing the scientific name allows you to ensure that the plant you're ordering is the same one shown in our design.

Guide to Installation

In this section you'll find detailed instructions and illustrations covering all the techniques you'll need to install any design from start to finish. Here we explain how to think your way through a landscaping project and anticipate the various steps. Then you'll learn how to do each part of the job: readying the site; laying out the design; choosing materials; addressing basic irrigation needs; building paths, trellises, or other structures; preparing the soil for planting; buying the recommended plants and putting them in place; and caring for the plants to keep them healthy and attractive year after year.

We've taken care to make installation of built elements simple and straightforward. The paths, trellises, and arbors all use basic, readily available materials, and they can be assembled by people who have no special skills or tools beyond those commonly used for home maintenance. The designs can easily be adapted to meet specific needs or to fit in with the style of your house or other landscaping features.

Installing different designs requires different techniques. You can find the techniques that you need by following the cross-references in the Portfolio to pages in the Guide to Installation, or by skimming the Guide. You'll find that many basic techniques are reused from one project to the next. You might want to start with one of the smaller, simpler designs. Gradually you'll develop the skills and confidence to do any project you choose.

PLANT PROFILES

Choices
Selections here help you choose from the many varieties of certain popular plants.

Plant Portraits
Photos of selected plants.

Detailed Plant Information
Descriptions of each plant's noteworthy qualities and requirements for planting and care.

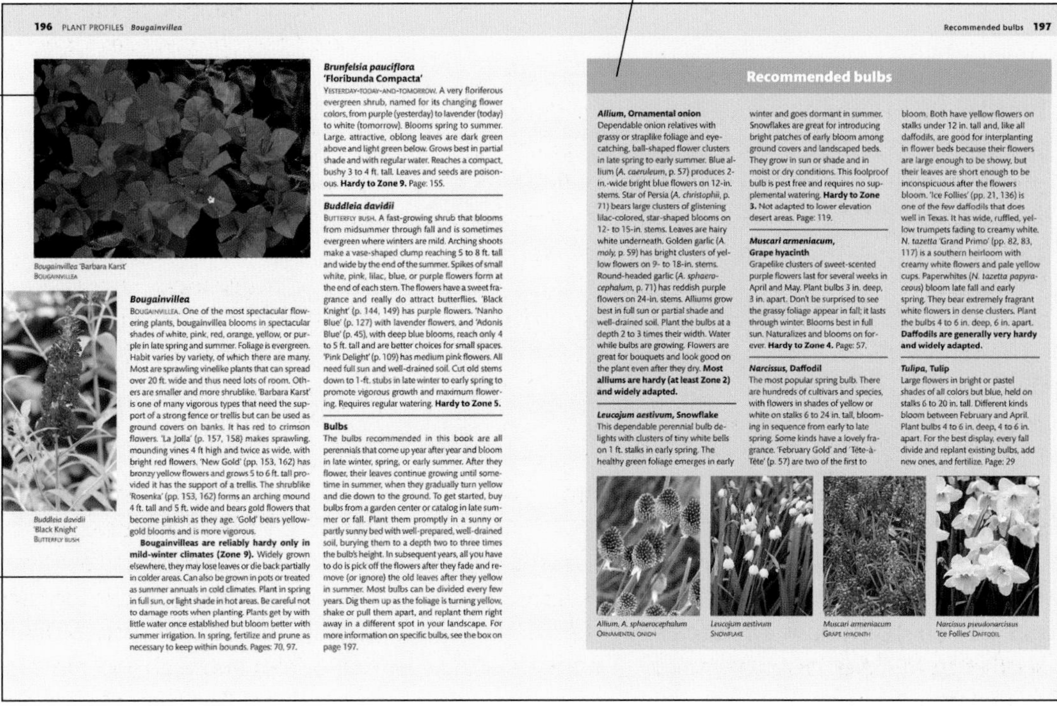

196 PLANT PROFILES *Bougainvillea* — Recommended bulbs 197

Bougainvillea 'Barbara Karst' BOUGAINVILLEA

Buddleia davidii 'Black Knight' BUTTERFLY BUSH

Bougainvillea
BOUGAINVILLEA. One of the most spectacular flowering plants, bougainvillea blooms in spectacular shades of white, pink, red, orange, yellow, or purple in late spring and summer. Foliage is evergreen. Habit varies by variety, of which there are many. Most are sprawling vinelike plants that can spread over 20 ft. wide and thus need lots of room. Others are smaller and more shrublike. 'Barbara Karst' is one of many vigorous types that need the support of a strong fence or trellis but can be used as ground covers on banks. It has red to crimson flowers. 'La Jolla' (p. 157, 158) makes sprawling, mounding vines 4 ft high and twice as wide, with bright red flowers. 'New Gold' (pp. 153, 162) has bronzy yellow flowers and grows 5 to 6 ft. tall provided it has the support of a trellis. The shrublike 'Rosenka' (pp. 153, 162) forms an arching mound 4 ft. tall and 5 ft. wide and bears gold flowers that become pinkish as they age. 'Gold' bears yellow-gold blooms and is more vigorous.
Bougainvilleas are reliably hardy only in mild-winter climates (Zone 9). Widely grown elsewhere, they may lose leaves or die back partially in colder areas. Can also be grown in pots or treated as summer annuals in cold climates. Plant in spring in full sun, or light shade in hot areas. Be careful not to damage roots when planting. Plants get by with little water once established but bloom better with summer irrigation. In spring, fertilize and prune as necessary to keep within bounds. Pages: 70, 97.

***Brunfelsia pauciflora* 'Floribunda Compacta'**
YESTERDAY-TODAY-AND-TOMORROW. A very floriferous evergreen shrub, named for its changing flower colors, from purple (yesterday) to lavender (today) to white (tomorrow). Blooms spring to summer. Large, attractive, oblong leaves are dark green above and light green below. Grows best in partial shade and with regular water. Reaches a compact, bushy 3 to 4 ft. tall. Leaves and seeds are poisonous. **Hardy to Zone 9.** Page: 155.

Buddleia davidii
BUTTERFLY BUSH. A fast-growing shrub that blooms from midsummer through fall and is sometimes evergreen where winters are mild. Arching shoots make a vase-shaped clump reaching 5 to 8 ft. tall and wide by the end of the summer. Spikes of small white, pink, lilac, blue, or purple flowers form at the end of each stem. The flowers have a sweet fragrance and really do attract butterflies. 'Black Knight' (p. 144, 149) has purple flowers. 'Nanho Blue' (p. 127) with lavender flowers, and 'Adonis Blue' (p. 45), with deep blue blooms, reach only 4 to 5 ft. tall and are better choices for small spaces. 'Pink Delight' (p. 109) has medium pink flowers. All need full sun and well-drained soil. Cut old stems down to 1-ft. stubs in late winter to early spring to promote vigorous growth and maximum flowering. Requires regular watering. **Hardy to Zone 5.**

Bulbs
The bulbs recommended in this book are all perennials that come up year after year and bloom in late winter, spring, or early summer. After they flower, their leaves continue growing until sometime in summer, when they gradually turn yellow and die down to the ground. To get started, buy bulbs from a garden center or catalog in late summer or fall. Plant them promptly in a sunny or partly sunny bed with well-prepared, well-drained soil, burying them to a depth two to three times the bulb's height. In subsequent years, all you have to do is pick off the flowers after they fade and remove (or ignore) the old leaves after they yellow in summer. Most bulbs can be divided every few years. Dig them up as the foliage is turning yellow, shake or pull them apart, and replant them right away in a different spot in your landscape. For more information on specific bulbs, see the box on page 197.

Recommended bulbs

***Allium*, Ornamental onion**
Dependable onion relatives with grassy or straplike foliage and eye-catching, ball-shaped flower clusters in late spring to early summer. Blue allium (*A. caeruleum*, p. 57) produces 2-in.-wide bright blue flowers on 12-in. stems. Star of Persia (*A. christophii*, p. 71) bears large clusters of glistening lilac-colored, star-shaped blooms on 12- to 15-in. stems. Leaves are hairy white underneath. Golden garlic (*A. moly*, p. 59) has bright clusters of yellow flowers on 9- to 18-in. stems. Round-headed garlic (*A. sphaerocephalum*, p. 71) has reddish purple flowers on 24-in. stems. Alliums grow best in full sun or partial shade and well-drained soil. Plant the bulbs at a depth 2 to 3 times their width. Water while bulbs are growing. Flowers are great for bouquets and look good on the plant even after they dry. **Most alliums are hardy (at least Zone 2) and widely adapted.**

***Leucojum aestivum*, Snowflake**
This dependable perennial bulb delights with clusters of tiny white bells on 1 ft. stalks in early spring. The healthy green foliage emerges in early winter and goes dormant in summer. Snowflakes are great for introducing bright patches of early bloom among ground covers and landscaped beds. They grow in sun or shade and in moist or dry conditions. This foolproof bulb is pest free and requires no supplemental watering. **Hardy to Zone 3.** Not adapted to lower elevation desert areas. Page: 119.

***Muscari armeniacum*, Grape hyacinth**
Grapelike clusters of sweet-scented purple flowers last for several weeks in April and May. Plant bulbs 3 in. deep, 3 in. apart. Don't be surprised to see the grassy foliage appear in fall; it lasts through winter. Blooms best in full sun. Naturalizes and blooms on forever. **Hardy to Zone 4.** Page: 57.

***Narcissus*, Daffodil**
The most popular spring bulb. There are hundreds of cultivars and species, with flowers in shades of yellow or white on stalks 6 to 24 in. tall, blooming in sequence from early to late spring. Some kinds have a lovely fragrance. 'February Gold' and 'Tête-à-Tête' (p. 57) are two of the first to bloom. Both have yellow flowers on stalks under 12 in. tall and, like all daffodils, are good for interplanting in flower beds because their flowers are large enough to be showy, but their leaves are short enough to be inconspicuous after the flowers bloom. 'Ice Follies' (pp. 21, 136) is one of the few daffodils that does well in Texas. It has wide, ruffled, yellow trumpets fading to creamy white. *N. tazetta* 'Grand Primo' (pp. 82, 83, 117) is a southern heirloom with creamy white flowers and pale yellow cups. Paperwhites (*N. tazetta papyraceous*) bloom late fall and early spring. They bear extremely fragrant white flowers in dense clusters. Plant the bulbs 4 to 6 in. deep, 6 in. apart. **Daffodils are generally very hardy and widely adapted.**

***Tulipa*, Tulip**
Large flowers in bright or pastel shades of all colors but blue, held on stalks 6 to 20 in. tall. Different kinds bloom between February and April. Plant bulbs 4 to 6 in. deep, 4 to 6 in. apart. For the best display, every fall divide and replant existing bulbs, add new ones, and fertilize. Page: 29

Allium, A. sphaerocephalum ORNAMENTAL ONION — *Leucojum aestivum* SNOWFLAKE — *Muscari armeniacum* GRAPE HYACINTH — *Narcissus pseudonarcissus* 'Ice Follies' DAFFODIL

GUIDE TO INSTALLATION

Sidebars
Detailed information on special topics, set within ruled boxes.

Step-by-Step
Illustrations show process; steps are keyed by number to discussion in the main text.

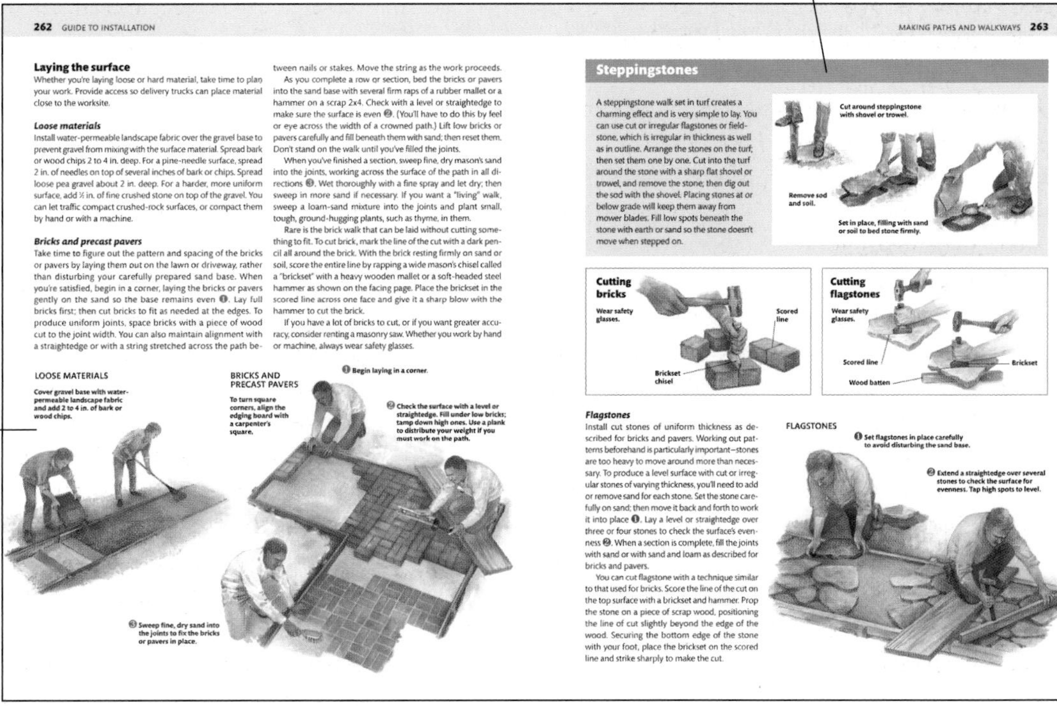

262 GUIDE TO INSTALLATION — MAKING PATHS AND WALKWAYS 263

Laying the surface
Whether you're laying loose or hard material, take time to plan your work. Provide access so delivery trucks can place material close to the worksite.

Loose materials
Install water-permeable landscape fabric over the gravel base to prevent gravel from mixing with the surface material. Spread bark or wood chips 2 to 4 in. deep. For a pine-needle surface, spread 2 in. of needles on top of several inches of bark or chips. Spread loose pea gravel about 2 in. deep. For a harder, more uniform surface, add ½ in. of fine crushed stone on top of the gravel. You can let traffic compact crushed-rock surfaces, or compact them by hand or with a machine.

Bricks and precast pavers
Take time to figure out the pattern and spacing of the bricks or pavers by laying them out on the lawn or driveway, rather than disturbing your carefully prepared sand base. When you're satisfied, begin in a corner, laying the bricks or pavers gently on the sand so the base remains even ❶. Lay full bricks first; then cut bricks to fit as needed at the edges. To produce uniform joints, space bricks with a piece of wood cut to the joint width. You can also maintain alignment with a straightedge or with a string stretched across the path between nails or stakes. Move the string as the work proceeds.
As you complete a row or section, bed the bricks or pavers into the sand base with several firm raps of a rubber mallet or a hammer on a scrap 2x4. Check with a level or straightedge to make sure the surface is even ❷. (You'll have to do this by feel or eye across the width of a crowned path.) Lift low bricks or pavers carefully and fill beneath them with sand; then reset them. Don't stand on the walk until you've filled the joints.
When you've finished a section, sweep fine, dry mason's sand into the joints, working across the surface of the path in all directions ❸. Wet thoroughly with a fine spray and let dry; then sweep in more sand if necessary. If you want a "living" walk, sweep a loam-sand mixture into the joints and plant small, tough, ground-hugging plants, such as thyme, in them.
Rare is the brick walk that can be laid without cutting something to fit. To cut brick, mark the line of the cut with a dark pencil all around the brick. With the brick resting firmly on sand or soil, score the entire line by rapping a wide mason's chisel called a "brickset" with a heavy wooden mallet or a soft-headed steel hammer as shown on the facing page. Place the brickset in the scored line across one face and give it a sharp blow with the hammer to cut the brick.
If you have a lot of bricks to cut, or if you want greater accuracy, consider renting a masonry saw. Whether you work by hand or machine, always wear safety glasses.

LOOSE MATERIALS
Cover gravel base with water-permeable landscape fabric and add 2 to 4 in. of bark or wood chips.
BRICKS AND PRECAST PAVERS
To turn square corners, align the edging board with a carpenter's square.
❶ Begin laying in a corner.
❷ Check the surface with a level or straightedge. Fill under low bricks; tamp down high ones. Use a plank to distribute your weight if you must work on the path.
❸ Sweep fine, dry sand into the joints to fix the bricks or pavers in place.

Steppingstones
A steppingstone walk set in turf creates a charming effect and is very simple to lay. You can use cut or irregular flagstones or fieldstone, which is irregular in thickness as well as in outline. Arrange the stones on the turf; then set them one by one. Cut into the turf around the stone with a sharp flat shovel or trowel, and remove the stone; then dig out the sod with the shovel. Placing stones at or below grade will keep them away from mower blades. Fill low spots beneath the stone with earth or sand so the stone doesn't move when stepped on.

Cut around steppingstone with shovel or trowel.
Remove sod and soil.
Set in place, filling with sand or soil to bed stone firmly.
Cutting bricks
Wear safety glasses.
Scored line
Brickset chisel
Cutting flagstones
Wear safety glasses.
Scored line
Brickset
Wood batten

Flagstones
Install cut stones of uniform thickness as described for bricks and pavers. Working out patterns beforehand is particularly important—stones are too heavy to move around more than necessary. To produce a level surface with cut or irregular stones of varying thickness, you'll need to add or remove sand for each stone. Set the stone carefully on sand; then move it back and forth to work it into place ❶. Lay a level or straightedge over three or four stones to check the surface's evenness ❷. When a section is complete, fill the joints with sand or with sand and loam as described for bricks and pavers.
You can cut flagstone with a technique similar to that used for bricks. Score the line of the cut on the top surface with a brickset and hammer. Prop the stone on a piece of scrap wood, positioning the line of cut slightly beyond the edge of the wood. Securing the bottom edge of the stone with your foot, place the brickset on the scored line and strike sharply to make the cut.

FLAGSTONES
❶ Set flagstones in place carefully to avoid disturbing the sand base.
❷ Extend a straightedge over several stones to check the surface for evenness. Tap high spots to level.

As Your Landscape Grows

AT PLANTING

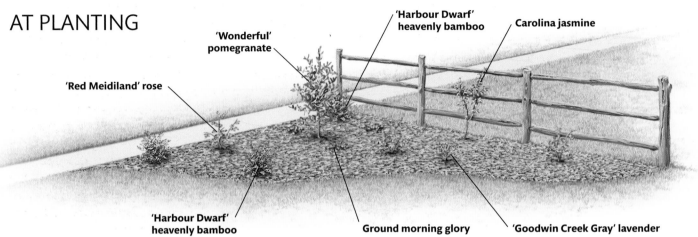

'Wonderful' pomegranate

'Red Meidiland' rose

'Harbour Dwarf' heavenly bamboo

Carolina jasmine

'Harbour Dwarf' heavenly bamboo

Ground morning glory

'Goodwin Creek Gray' lavender

Landscapes change over the years. As plants grow, the overall look evolves from sparse to lush. Trees cast cool shade where the sun used to shine. Shrubs and hedges grow tall and dense enough to provide privacy. Perennials and ground covers spread to form colorful patches of foliage and flowers. Meanwhile, paths, arbors, fences, and other structures gain the comfortable patina of age.

Constant change over the years—sometimes rapid and dramatic, sometimes slow and subtle—is one of the joys of landscaping. It is also one of the challenges. Anticipating how fast plants will grow and how big they will eventually get is difficult, even for professional designers, and was a major concern in formulating the designs for this book.

To illustrate the kinds of changes to expect in a planting, these pages show one of the designs at three different "ages." Even though a new planting may look sparse at first, it will soon fill in. And because of careful spacing, the planting will look as good in 10 to 15 years as it does after 3 to 5. It will, of course, look different, but that's part of the fun.

THREE TO FIVE YEARS

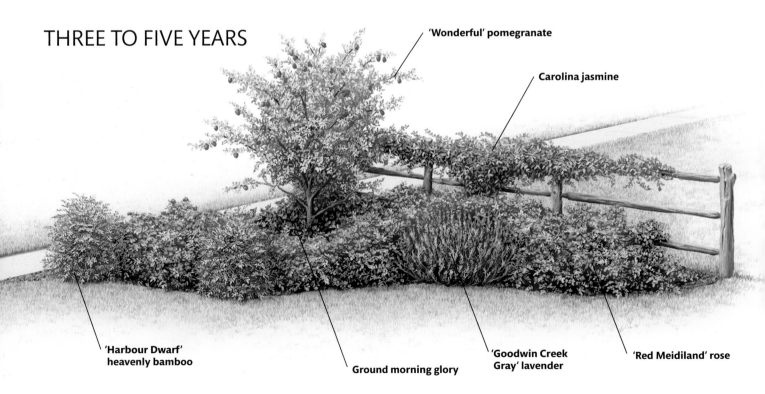

'Wonderful' pomegranate

Carolina jasmine

'Harbour Dwarf' heavenly bamboo

Ground morning glory

'Goodwin Creek Gray' lavender

'Red Meidiland' rose

At Planting—Here's how the corner planting (pp. 48–51) might appear in spring immediately after planting. The branches of the Carolina jasmine, 2 to 3 ft. long, have been tied to the fence. The roses are about 18 in. tall, their canes already beginning to arch. Bought in 1-gal. containers, the lavender and heavenly bamboo have yet to reach a foot in height. The pomegranate is 3 to 4 ft. tall; the ground morning glories are little tufts about 6 in. tall. In addition to mulch, you can fill the spaces between the small plants with some short annuals during the first few growing seasons.

Three to Five Years—As shown here in fall, the planting has filled out nicely. The Carolina jasmine creeps along much of the fence. The roses sprawl, covered now (and much of the year) with red flowers. The lavender and heavenly bamboo have become bushy plants, with handsome foliage, flowers, and berries. At about 6 to 8 ft. tall, the pomegranate displays colorful foliage and a crop of edible fruits in fall. The ground morning glory has filled in beneath the tree and the planting no longer has space, or need, for annuals.

Ten to Fifteen Years—Shown again in fall, the pomegranate, now 10 to 12 ft. tall, is the focal point of the planting. Its lower limbs have been removed as the tree has grown, making room for the roses, which have been allowed to overtake some of the ground morning glory under the tree as well as the two heavenly bamboos at the corner (which have been replanted elsewhere on the property). The third heavenly bamboo has been removed to allow the ground morning glory to spread. Annual pruning has kept the height of the roses in check and prevented them from overgrowing the lavender. Judicious pruning has also kept some of the fence visible around the vigorous Carolina jasmine.

TEN TO FIFTEEN YEARS

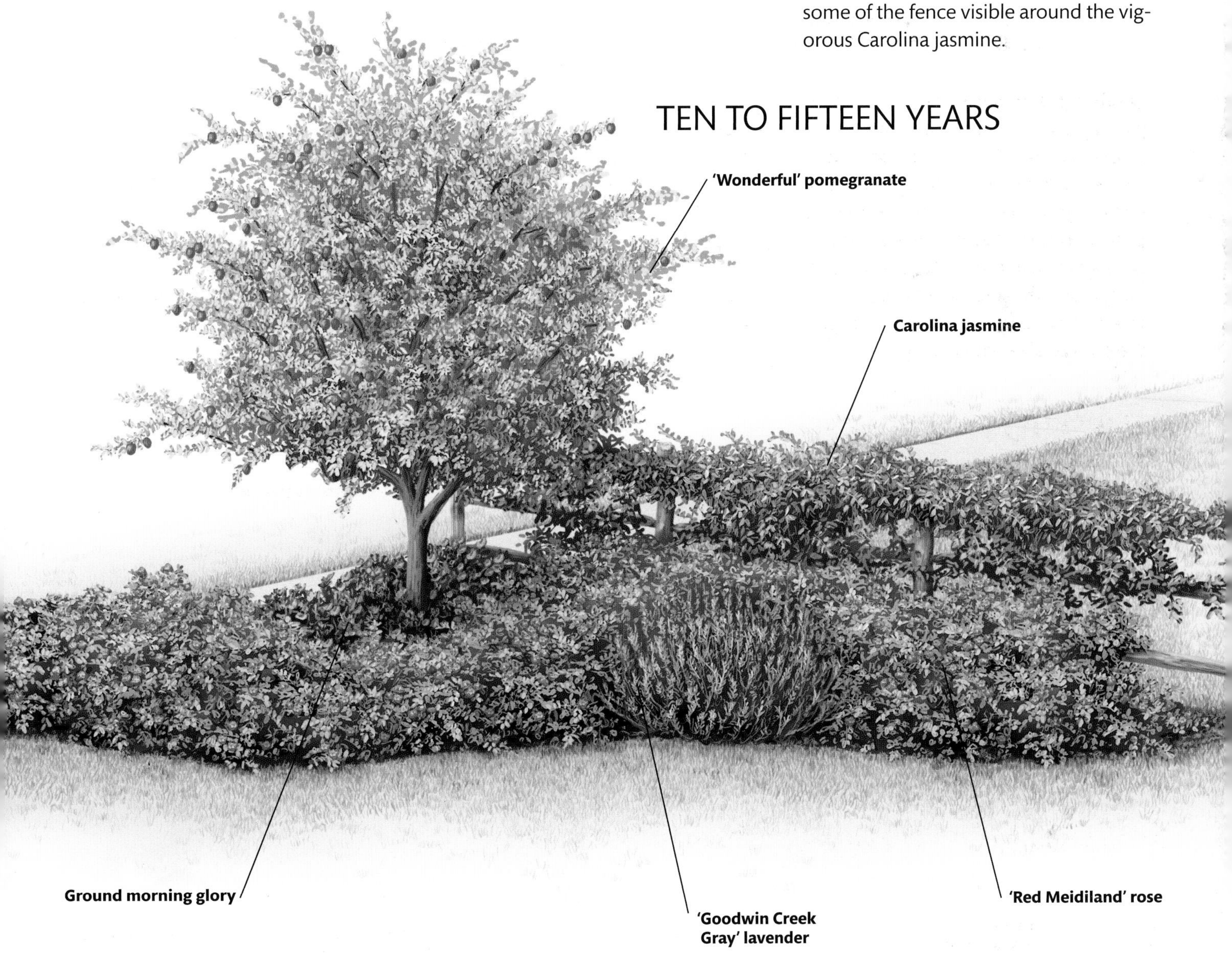

'Wonderful' pomegranate

Carolina jasmine

Ground morning glory

'Goodwin Creek Gray' lavender

'Red Meidiland' rose

Portfolio *of* Designs

This section presents 42 designs for situations common in home landscapes. You'll find designs to enhance entrances, decks, and patios. There are gardens of colorful perennials and shrubs, as well as structures and plantings that create shady hideaways, dress up nondescript walls, and even make a centerpiece of a neglected side yard. Large color illustrations show what the designs will look like, and site plans delineate the layout and planting scheme. The accompanying text explains the designs and describe the plants and projects appearing in them. Installed as shown or adapted to meet your site and personal preferences, these designs can make your property more attractive, more useful, and—most important—more enjoyable for you, your family, and your friends.

A Welcoming Entry

MAKE A PLEASANT PASSAGE TO YOUR FRONT DOOR

Why wait until a visitor reaches the front door to extend a cordial greeting? An entryway landscape of well-chosen plants and a revamped walkway not only make the short journey a pleasant one, they can also enhance your home's most public face and help settle it comfortably in its surroundings.

The flagstone paving here creates a walkway with the feel of a cozy courtyard, an atmosphere enhanced by the small trees and bench. Extending along the driveway, the paving makes it easier for passengers to get in and out of a car. A semicircular garden makes the stroll to the door inviting, while providing interest to viewers inside the house and on the street.

Flowering trees and shrubs bloom throughout the spring and summer in pinks and lavenders. Attractive foliage, much of it evergreen, and striking bark ensure interest all year.

Chaste tree **B**

G 'Sundowner' New Zealand flax

Blue oat grass **J**

'Sundowner' **G** New Zealand flax

Annuals **L**

'Sunset Gold' **I** pink breath of heaven

Plants & Projects

Preparing the planting beds and laying the flagstone walkway are the main tasks in this design. With low-water-use plants, this design requires only seasonal cleanup and pruning once plants are established.

A **'Marina' arbutus** (use 3 plants)
These small trees provide interest year-round, with pink flowers in fall, red berries, and shiny evergreen leaves. Prune to show off the colorful bark and handsome multi-trunk form. See *Arbutus* 'Marina', p. 192.

B **Chaste tree** (use 1)
This deciduous tree arches beautifully over the walk, displaying airy foliage and, in summer and fall, long spikes of violet flowers. See *Vitex agnus-castus*, p. 247.

C **'Zuni' crape myrtle** (use 1)
A deciduous multitrunked tree with striking clusters of papery flowers in summer and colorful fall foliage. Flaking bark provides winter interest. See *Lagerstroemia indica*, p. 224..

D **Dwarf Indian hawthorn** (use 6)
Low masses of glossy dark evergreen foliage show off spring flowers and blue berries from summer into fall. Choose a pink cultivar. See *Rhaphiolepis indica*, p. 236.

E **'Winter Gem' boxwood** (use 8)
These evergreen shrubs form a loosely trimmed low hedge that contrasts with the flowing grasses near the house. See *Buxus microphylla* var. *japonica*, p. 198.

F **Purple fountain grass** (use 7)
This smallish ornamental grass features eye-catching reddish brown leaves that turn gold or tan in fall. Fluffy bronze seed heads arch

above the foliage from midsummer to fall. See *Pennisetum setaceum* 'Rubrum', p. 230.

G **'Sundowner' New Zealand flax** (as needed)
The swordlike, colorfully striped foliage of this evergreen perennial provides bold accents as you approach the door. Tall, airy flower spikes heighten the effect in summer. See *Phormium tenax*, p. 234.

H **'Otto Quast' Spanish lavender** (use 17)
Spikes of blue flowers cover these mounding shrubs in early summer. Fragrant silver-gray foliage is evergreen and looks good all year. See *Lavandula stoechas*, p. 226.

I **'Sunset Gold' pink breath of heaven** (use 5)
A loose, airy evergreen shrub, it has colorful fragrant foliage and tiny pink flowers for months in winter and spring. Shear to maintain a compact shape near the walkway. See *Coleonema pulchrum*, p. 204.

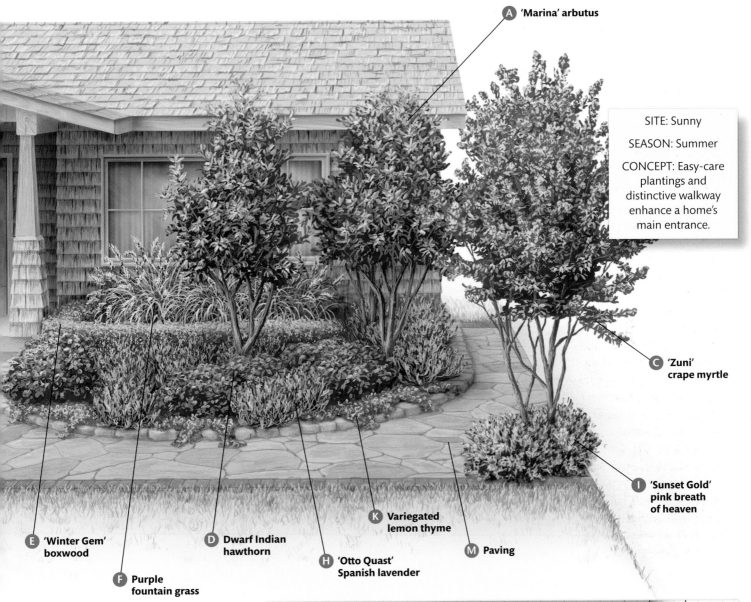

A 'Marina' arbutus

SITE: Sunny

SEASON: Summer

CONCEPT: Easy-care plantings and distinctive walkway enhance a home's main entrance.

C 'Zuni' crape myrtle

I 'Sunset Gold' pink breath of heaven

K Variegated lemon thyme

E 'Winter Gem' boxwood

D Dwarf Indian hawthorn

M Paving

F Purple fountain grass

H 'Otto Quast' Spanish lavender

J **Blue oat grass** (use 8)

Fine-textured blue foliage of this mounding ornamental grass complements the colors and forms of nearby plants. See *Helictotrichon sempervirens*, p. 230.

K **Variegated lemon thyme** (use 10)

A low-growing perennial ground cover, its attractive yellow-and-green foliage sprawls out over the edge of the walkway. See *Thymus x citriodorus* 'Aureus', p. 245.

L **Annuals** (as needed)

A pot of colorful annuals marks the turn toward the front door. Try a mix of salvia, lobelia, phlox, alyssum, and zinnia. Page 190.

M **Paving**

Irregular flagstones are edged by brick next to the lawn, while cobblestones outline the semicircular planting bed. A simple bench provides a comfortable perch. See p. 258.

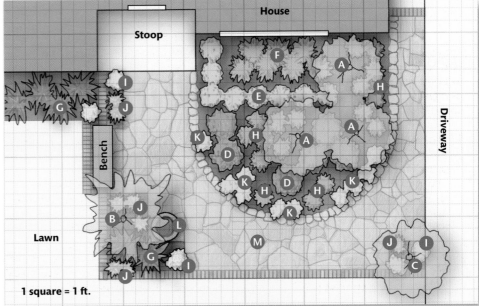

House

Stoop

Bench

Driveway

Lawn

1 square = 1 ft.

VARIATIONS ON A THEME

In addition to extending a splendid welcome to your home, each of these plantings can be enjoyed as a garden.

In this design, a flagstone path set in gravel leads through the yard to the front door. Lined with ornamental grasses and other foliage plants, the design is at once natural and tastefully composed.

Here, a small front yard accommodates a richly planted entry garden. The wide flagstone walkway and colorful foliage complement this bungalow-style home.

A picket fence, brick path, poppies, and other gaily colored perennials create a charming entry to this home.

A shadier welcome

If your entry is lightly shaded, getting less than six hours of sun a day, try this planting scheme. The configuration remains the same as that of the previous design, but here we've used plants that do well in shadier conditions. Overall, the emphasis is still on year-round good looks.

Near the drive, the walkway is framed by a columnar yew pine and the semicircular garden bed. At the opposite corner, a Japanese maple shelters a bench where you can sit and enjoy the plantings. Shrubs and perennials provide flowers in spring and summer as well as attractive foliage throughout the year. The Tasmanian tree ferns add an exotic flavor, with distinctive arching foliage that is echoed by grasses and perennials elsewhere in the planting.

Plants & Projects

Ⓐ Coralbark maple (use 1 plant)
An eye-catching accent for many months, this small deciduous tree has fine-textured foliage that is light green in summer and yellow in fall. Bright red twigs stand out in winter. See *Acer palmatum* 'Sango Kaku', p. 188.

Ⓑ Shrubby yew pine (use 1)
This evergreen tree is a sentinel at the beginning of the walk. Needlelike leaves give it a fine texture. See *Podocarpus macrophyllus* 'Maki', p. 235.

Ⓒ Tasmanian tree fern (use 3)
These Australian natives will eventually form an exotic grove of small "trees" with long arching fronds and thick fuzzy trunks. See Ferns: *Dicksonia antarctica*, p. 212.

Ⓓ 'Gumpo White' evergreen azalea (use 7)
Low, spreading mounds of dark evergreen foliage are a handsome backdrop for a late-spring display of striking large white flowers. Foliage is attractive for the remainder of the year. See *Rhododendron*, p. 237.

Ⓔ Dwarf heavenly bamboo (use 7)
Airy and upright, this shrub provides a leafy accent and companion for nearby plants. Evergreen foliage changes color with the seasons. See *Nandina domestica* 'Gulf Stream', p. 229.

Ⓕ Variegated eulalia grass (use 4)
Graceful clumps of long, arching white-and-green striped leaves rustle in the breeze beneath the window. Tall, fluffy seed heads last

Shrubby
yew
pine **B**

Coralbark **A**
maple

G Agapanthus

Bloody **I**
cranesbill

Agapanthus **G**

Annuals **L**

Lilyturf **K**

Dwarf **E**
heavenly
bamboo

N Paving

H Japanese
anemone

D 'Gumpo White'
evergreen azalea

F Variegated
eulalia grass

E Dwarf
heavenly
bamboo

M 'Winter Gem'
boxwood

J Ajuga

C Tasmanian
tree fern

---

from fall through winter. See *Miscanthus sinensis* 'Variegatus', p. 230.

G **Agapanthus** (as needed)
Tall stalks bearing ball-shaped clusters of small blue flowers strike a welcoming note near the door in late spring and summer. This perennial's straplike foliage is attractive year-round. See *Agapanthus orientalis*, p. 189.

H **Japanese anemone** (use 21)
This perennial's airy white flowers add color in late summer and fall. Soft-textured foliage contrasts nicely with nearby azaleas. See *Anemone* x *hybrida*, p. 191.

I **Bloody cranesbill** (use 5)
A low-growing perennial with finely cut leaves and small pink flowers from spring into summer. A nice accent plant. See *Geranium sanguineum* var. *striatum*, p. 216.

J **Ajuga** (as needed)
Use this perennial evergreen ground cover to fill in open spaces; maturing shrubs will shade some out. See *Ajuga reptans* 'Bronze Beauty', p. 190.

K **Lilyturf** (use 13)
The grassy white-striped evergreen leaves of this perennial edge the walkway and echo the larger ornamental grasses in the planting. See *Liriope muscari* 'Silver Dragon', p. 226.

L **Annuals** (as needed)
A pot of pink annual vinca brightens the walkway here. page. Page 190.

See pp. 16–17 for the following:
M **'Winter Gem' boxwood** (use 8)
N **Paving**

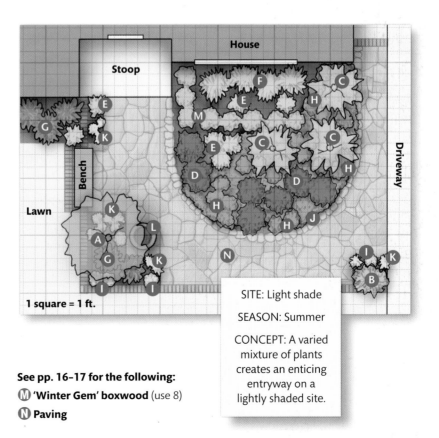

1 square = 1 ft.

House

Stoop

Bench

Lawn

Driveway

SITE: Light shade

SEASON: Summer

CONCEPT: A varied mixture of plants creates an enticing entryway on a lightly shaded site.

First Impressions

OFFER A GRACIOUS WELCOME YEAR ROUND

In this design a flagstone walkway curves gracefully to the front door, creating a roomy planting bed near the house. Where the paving widens out at the front stoop, there's room for a welcoming bench sheltered by a small tree. Sit for a moment with your visitors and enjoy fragrant flowers and eye-catching foliage.

The plants here are selected for a shady entry, one that gets less than six hours of sun a day. Flowers and foliage will keep the entry both colorful and fragrant throughout the year. Redbud blossoms will join daffodils and dianthus in early spring, followed by columbine, plumbago, Mexican petunia, and gardenia. All but the gardenia continue to bloom well into fall. White daffodils and red camellias arrive in November and stay through the winter holidays.

SITE: Shady

SEASON: Spring

CONCEPT: An attractive selection of plants showcases a home's entrance.

1 square = 1 ft.

'Yuletide' **C** sasanqua camellia

Tropical **H** plumbago

Dwarf **D** yaupon holly   Walkway **K**   Holly **G** fern

Plants & Projects

This low-maintenance planting will thrive with just a regular refurbishing of the mulch to control weeds and conserve water. Trim the shrubs if necessary and divide the bulbs if they become crowded.

A **Redbud** (use 1 plant)
Beginning with a splurge of tiny pink blossoms in early spring, this small deciduous tree is an eye-catching accent for many more months. Heart-shaped leaves are light green in summer and yellow in fall. See *Cercis canadensis,* p. 201.

B **'Daisy' gardenia** (use 2)
This desirable shrub will scent the entry with sweet white blossoms in May and June. Foliage stays fresh and glossy all year. See *Gardenia jasminoides* 'Daisy', p. 214.

C **'Yuletide' sasanqua camellia** (use 1)
This evergreen shrub or small tree grows 5 ft. tall and wears a thick coat of shimmering dark green leaves. Fragrant red flowers bloom in time for Christmas. See *Camellia sasanqua* 'Yuletide', p. 198.

D **Dwarf yaupon holly** (use 5)
These shrubs form neat low mounds of tiny, oval, evergreen leaves in front of the windows. Showy clusters of red berries decorate the foliage in winter. See *Ilex vomitoria* 'Nana', p. 222.

E **Dwarf Mexican petunia** (use 22)
The large lush leaves of this low-growing perennial emerge just in time to cover fading spring bulbs. Purple flowers bloom from the center of each plant all season. See *Ruellia brittoniana* 'Katie', p. 240.

F **Texas gold columbine** (use 3)
This perennial forms neat mounds of lacy foliage. Slender stalks bear delicate golden flowers in spring and summer. See *Aquilegia chrysantha hinckleyana,* p. 192.

G **Holly fern** (use 16)
An unusual evergreen fern with leathery, rather than lacy, fronds. The dark green glossy leaves add coarse-textured sheen under the redbud and along the walk. See Ferns: *Cyrtomium falcatum,* p. 212.

H **Tropical plumbago** (use 5)
Ideal as a ground cover beside the drive, this trouble-free perennial creates compact tufts of small, pointed, pale green leaves. Its clear blue flowers look cool and inviting next to the pavement, especially in summer heat. See *Plumbago auriculata,* p. 234.

I **'Bath's Pink' dianthus** (use 9)
This perennial creates a pretty border of fine-textured blue-green foliage topped in spring with masses of delicate and fragrant pink flowers. Leaves look fresh all year. See *Dianthus* 'Bath's Pink', p. 207.

J **'Ice Follies' daffodil** (use 27)
Scatter these bulbs on both sides of the walk for white flowers in spring. The spiky leaves are a nice blue-green. See Bulbs: *Narcissus pseudonarcissus* 'Ice Follies', p. 196.

K **Walkway**
Flagstones of random size and shape are perfect for the curved front walk and for the steppingstones into the front lawn. See p. 259.

L **Bench**
Extend your welcome beyond the front door with a comfortable bench next to the stoop.

B **'Daisy' gardenia**

A **Redbud**

L **Bench**

G **Holly fern**

J **'Ice Follies' daffodil**

I **'Bath's Pink' dianthus**

J **'Ice Follies' daffodil**

F **Texas gold columbine**

See site plan for **E** .

PLANT PORTRAITS

The attractive flowers and foliage of these shrubs and perennials will welcome visitors year-round.

● = First design, pp. 20–21
▲ = Second design, pp. 22–23

Althea (*Hibiscus syriacus*, p. 220) ▲

'Daisy' gardenia (*Gardenia jasminoides* 'Daisy', p. 214) ●

'Yuletide' sasanqua camellia (*Camellia sasanqua*, p. 198) ●

'Apple Blossom' yarrow (*Achillea millefolium* 'Apple Blossom', p. 188) ▲

A sunny welcome

For a site with a sunny exposure, consider this design. Here, flagstone walkways invite visitors to stroll from the driveway to the front door along a choice of paths lined with eye-catching flowers and attractive foliage.

Many of these perennials bloom nonstop from spring to frost. Viburnum's fragrant white bouquets arrive early in March, and the lavender blossoms of aster appear in the fall, extending an already long season of bloom well into November. Handsome foliage, much of it evergreen, ensures interest all year. Like the planting in the previous design, this one needs only seasonal care.

Plants & Projects

Ⓐ Althea (use 1 plant)
A lavish floral display greets visitors when this deciduous shrub blooms in summer and fall. A cultivar with large lavender flowers suits this design well. Trim up about 3 ft. to make room for nearby plants. See *Hibiscus syriacus*, p. 220.

Ⓑ 'Spring Bouquet' viburnum (use 2)
This compact shrub has deep green foliage that stays attractive all year. Clusters of lightly scented white flowers open from pink buds in early spring. See *Viburnum tinus* 'Spring Bouquet', p. 246.

Ⓒ 'Belinda's Dream' rose (use 1)
This rose forms a lovely vase of glossy leaves and exquisite pink flowers. See *Rosa* x 'Belinda's Dream', p. 238.

Ⓓ 'Edward Goucher' glossy abelia (use 3)
Small sparkling leaves line the arching branches of this evergreen shrub, turning from dark green to purple-bronze in winter. From spring to fall, clusters of honeysuckle-like pink blossoms dangle from all of the branches. See *Abelia* x *grandiflora*, 'Edward Goucher', p. 187.

Ⓔ Rosemary (use 3)
This low-growing evergreen shrub produces tiny pungent gray-green leaves. Whorls of equally aromatic blue flowers dot the shrub in late winter and early spring. See *Rosemarinus officinalis*, p. 240.

Ⓕ Daylily (use 16)
This mounding perennial trims the walk with slender grassy leaves and large trumpet-shaped flowers. There are many flower colors to choose from. We've shown a pale coral pink with a yellow throat. A soft yellow variety would work as well. See *Hemerocallis* hybrids, p. 218.

Ⓖ Fall aster (use 1)
Just one of these perennials will fill the space near the walkway with a dense stand of tiny gray-green leaves, blanketed all fall with small lavender daisylike flowers. See *Aster oblongifolius*, p. 193.

Ⓗ 'Apple Blossom' yarrow (use 7)
Fine feathery leaves and a lacework of tiny pink flowers that bloom for months makes this perennial an especially lovely companion for pink roses. See *Achillea millefolium* 'Apple Blossom', p. 188.

Ⓘ 'Homestead Purple' verbena (use 3)
This perennial forms a bright green mat of foliage that is covered from spring through fall with clusters of violet-purple flowers. See *Verbena* x *hybrida* 'Homestead Purple', p. 246.

Ⓙ 'Confetti' lantana (use 3)
A bushy perennial, it offers pink and yellow flowers during the growing season. Shear after bloom cycles. See *Lantana camara* 'Confetti', p. 225.

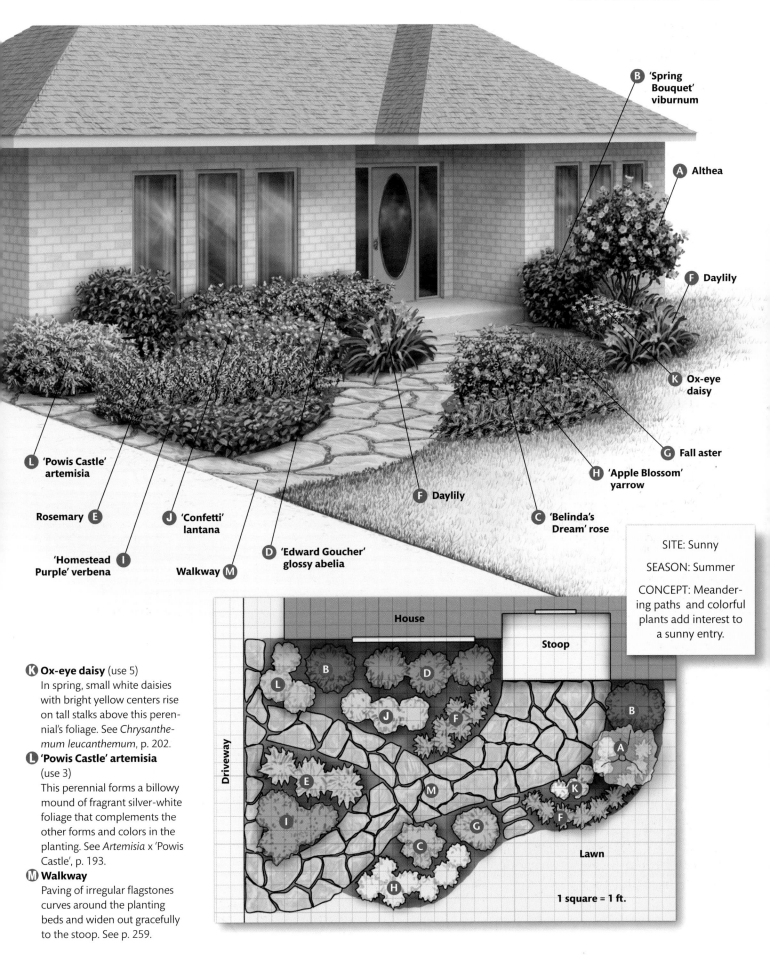

B 'Spring Bouquet' viburnum

A Althea

F Daylily

K Ox-eye daisy

G Fall aster

H 'Apple Blossom' yarrow

F Daylily

C 'Belinda's Dream' rose

L 'Powis Castle' artemisia

Rosemary **E**

'Homestead Purple' verbena **I**

J 'Confetti' lantana

Walkway **M**

D 'Edward Goucher' glossy abelia

SITE: Sunny

SEASON: Summer

CONCEPT: Meandering paths and colorful plants add interest to a sunny entry.

K **Ox-eye daisy** (use 5)
In spring, small white daisies with bright yellow centers rise on tall stalks above this perennial's foliage. See *Chrysanthemum leucanthemum*, p. 202.

L **'Powis Castle' artemisia** (use 3)
This perennial forms a billowy mound of fragrant silver-white foliage that complements the other forms and colors in the planting. See *Artemisia* x 'Powis Castle', p. 193.

M **Walkway**
Paving of irregular flagstones curves around the planting beds and widen out gracefully to the stoop. See p. 259.

House

Stoop

Driveway

Lawn

1 square = 1 ft.

A Courtyard Entry

MAKE AN ENTRY COURTYARD WITHOUT WALLS

This design offers another functional and attractive alternative to the often abrupt and utilitarian suburban front entry. An expanded walkway and plantings form a small "virtual" courtyard for greeting visitors; a bench allows you to sit and enjoy the little garden.

The flagstone circle is the hub of the design, around which the plants and paving create an integrated whole. The sweet bay anchors the design and offers some welcome cooling shade in hot weather. Its evergreen foliage is a presence year round.

In spring, shown here, banks of flowers in blue, pink, and white brighten the planting, with the striking red blooms of the potted calistemon as an exclamation point. Foliage, much of it evergreen in warm-winter areas, provides an attractive accompaniment to your entry in other seasons.

It's easy to integrate a planting like this with existing landscape or extend it farther along the house facade. Here we've shown a low hedge of nandina under the windows beyond the bench.

Plants & Projects

While requiring attention to get them established, these plants are easy to maintain with just seasonal pruning and cleanup.

Ⓐ 'Peter Pan' agapanthus (use 16)
Forming a skirt around the sweet bay, this perennial's strap-like, dark green leaves are evergreen in warm-winter areas. Bears clusters of ball-shaped blue flowers from late spring into summer. See *Agapanthus* 'Peter Pan', p. 189.

Ⓑ 'Little John' calistemon (use 1)
Making a striking accent in a large pot, this small, dense shrub has arching branches clothed in narrow evergreen leaves. Blood-red, bottle brush-like flowers bloom at the ends of the branches throughout the year. See *Callistemon viminalis* 'Little John', p.198.

Ⓒ Blue fescue grass (use 9)
Tufts of thin blue-green leaves form a border between the lawn and paving. A perennial grass, it produces narrow flower spikes in early summer. See *Festuca ovina* var. *glauca*, p. 230.

Ⓓ Lantana (use 10)
This spreading evergreen perennial ground cover flowers from spring through fall or year-round where winters are mild. A lilac-flowered cultivar suits this planting. See *Lantana montevidensis*, p. 225.

Ⓔ Saratoga sweet bay (use 1)
This small round-headed tree with deep-green leaves, provides some shade but won't outgrow its space. See *Laurus nobilis* 'Saratoga', p. 225.

Ⓕ 'Minor' Indian hawthorn (use 10).
A compact shrub with dense leathery foliage, turning from bronzy red when new to deep green. Large clusters of small white flowers bloom in spring. See *Rhaphiolepis umbellata* 'Minor', p. 236.

Ⓖ Japanese cleyera (use 1)
Planted near the door, this evergreen shrub welcomes visitors with shiny leaves ranging over the year from green to red. Fragrant white flowers in late spring and early summer are followed by small colorful fruits. See *Ternstroemia gymnanthera*, p. 245.

Ⓗ 'Crimson Pygmy' Japanese barberry (use 8)
This dwarf deciduous shrub has a spreading habit and showy leaves, purple-red from spring to summer; bright crimson in the fall. See *Berberis thunbergii* 'Crimson Pygmy', p. 194.

Ⓘ Paving
A central circle of flagstones nicely complements the expanded concrete walkway. The combination of flagstone and concrete is somewhat complicated to install; confident do-it-yourselfers can tackle installation. Others will be more comfortable leaving the job to an experienced hardscape installer.

'Crimson Pygmy' Ⓗ
Japanese barberry

Japanese cleyera Ⓖ

Blue fescue grass Ⓒ

SITE: Sunny

SEASON: Late spring

CONCEPT: Attractive low-maintenance plantings and paving create a simple entry courtyard

House

Stoop

Driveway

Lawn

1 square = 1 ft.

E Saratoga sweet bay

D Lantana

B 'Little John' calistemon

F 'Minor' Indian hawthorn

A 'Peter Pan' agapanthus

I Paving

PLANT PORTRAITS

These plants add fresh foliage and bright spots of color to a lightly shaded courtyard.

● = First design, pp. 24–25
▲ = Second design, pp. 26–27

Red Japanese maple (*Acer palmatum* 'Atropurpureum' p. 188) ▲

'Crimson Pygmy' Japanese barberry (*Berberis thunbergii* 'Crimson Pygmy' p. 194) ●

Bugleweed (*Ajuga reptans* p. 190) ▲

'Veitchii' Gardenia (*Gardenia jasminoides* 'Veitchii', p. 214) ▲

A shadier courtyard

This design creates a similar small, wall-less courtyard with plants chosen for a site that is lightly shaded.

The centerpiece is still a tree, but this Japanese maple is chosen for the visual appeal of its spreading branches and finely cut leaves rather than for shade. Flowers in a palette of blue, pink and white are eye pleasing in late spring and summer. A mixture of evergreen and deciduous foliage keeps the area looking fresh all year.

In the background of the rendering, beyond the bench, the design can be extended with low-growing shrubs; we've shown compact Gumpo azaleas, which fit neatly beneath the windows.

Plants & Projects

Ⓐ Red Japanese maple (use 1)
The delicate leaves of this small deciduous tree are red in spring turning greenish in summer. See *Acer palmatum* 'Atropurpureum', p. 188.

Ⓑ Bugleweed (use two flats)
In early summer, small spikes of blue flowers rise above the compact mat of dark evergreen leaves formed by this perennial ground cover. See *Ajuga reptans*, p. 190.

Ⓒ 'Veitchii' gardenia (use 10)
This evergreen shrub features handsome foliage that showcases very fragrant white flowers from spring through fall. See *Gardenia jasminoides* 'Veitchii', p. 214.

Ⓓ Coral bells (use 20)
Tall spikes of pink flowers float above this perennial's mounding deeply cut, ruffled foliage from spring into summer. See *Heuchera sanguninea*, p. 219.

Ⓔ Large-leaf hosta (use 17)
A perennial available in many

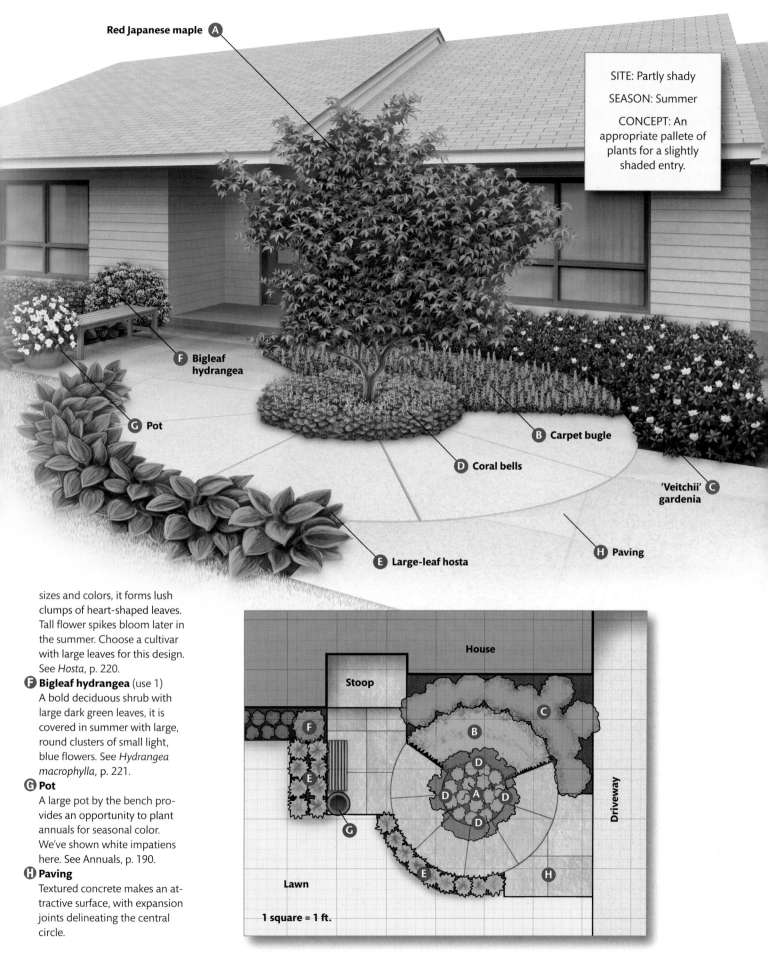

Red Japanese maple Ⓐ

SITE: Partly shady

SEASON: Summer

CONCEPT: An appropriate pallete of plants for a slightly shaded entry.

Ⓕ **Bigleaf hydrangea**

Ⓖ **Pot**

Ⓑ **Carpet bugle**

Ⓓ **Coral bells**

'Veitchii' gardenia Ⓒ

Ⓗ **Paving**

Ⓔ **Large-leaf hosta**

sizes and colors, it forms lush clumps of heart-shaped leaves. Tall flower spikes bloom later in the summer. Choose a cultivar with large leaves for this design. See *Hosta*, p. 220.

Ⓕ **Bigleaf hydrangea** (use 1)
A bold deciduous shrub with large dark green leaves, it is covered in summer with large, round clusters of small light, blue flowers. See *Hydrangea macrophylla*, p. 221.

Ⓖ **Pot**
A large pot by the bench provides an opportunity to plant annuals for seasonal color. We've shown white impatiens here. See Annuals, p. 190.

Ⓗ **Paving**
Textured concrete makes an attractive surface, with expansion joints delineating the central circle.

House

Stoop

Ⓒ

Ⓕ

Ⓔ

Ⓑ

Ⓓ

Ⓓ Ⓐ Ⓓ

Ⓖ

Ⓓ

Driveway

Ⓔ

Ⓗ

Lawn

1 square = 1 ft.

A Foundation with Flair

CREATE A FRONT GARDEN OF STRIKING FOLIAGE

Rare is the home without foundation plantings. These simple skirtings of greenery hide unattractive underpinnings and help integrate a house with its surroundings. Useful as these plantings are, they are too frequently no more than monochromatic expanses of clipped evergreens. But, as this design shows, a foundation planting can be easy, colorful, and fun.

The planting enhances the house as seen from the street, frames the walkway to the front door, and can be enjoyed when viewed from inside the house as well. Extending the planting beyond the ends of the house helps "settle" an upright, boxy house more comfortably on its site.

The design combines trees and shrubs in a deep, gently curving bed. Small maples and a plume cedar lend height and presence, while providing some screening and privacy from the street. Lower evergreen shrubs and ferns add a variety of leaf textures and colors that make an eye-catching display for much of the year, peaking in fall, the season shown here. In addition to woody plants, carefully chosen perennials accent the entry and, in spring, swaths of tulips brighten the scene.

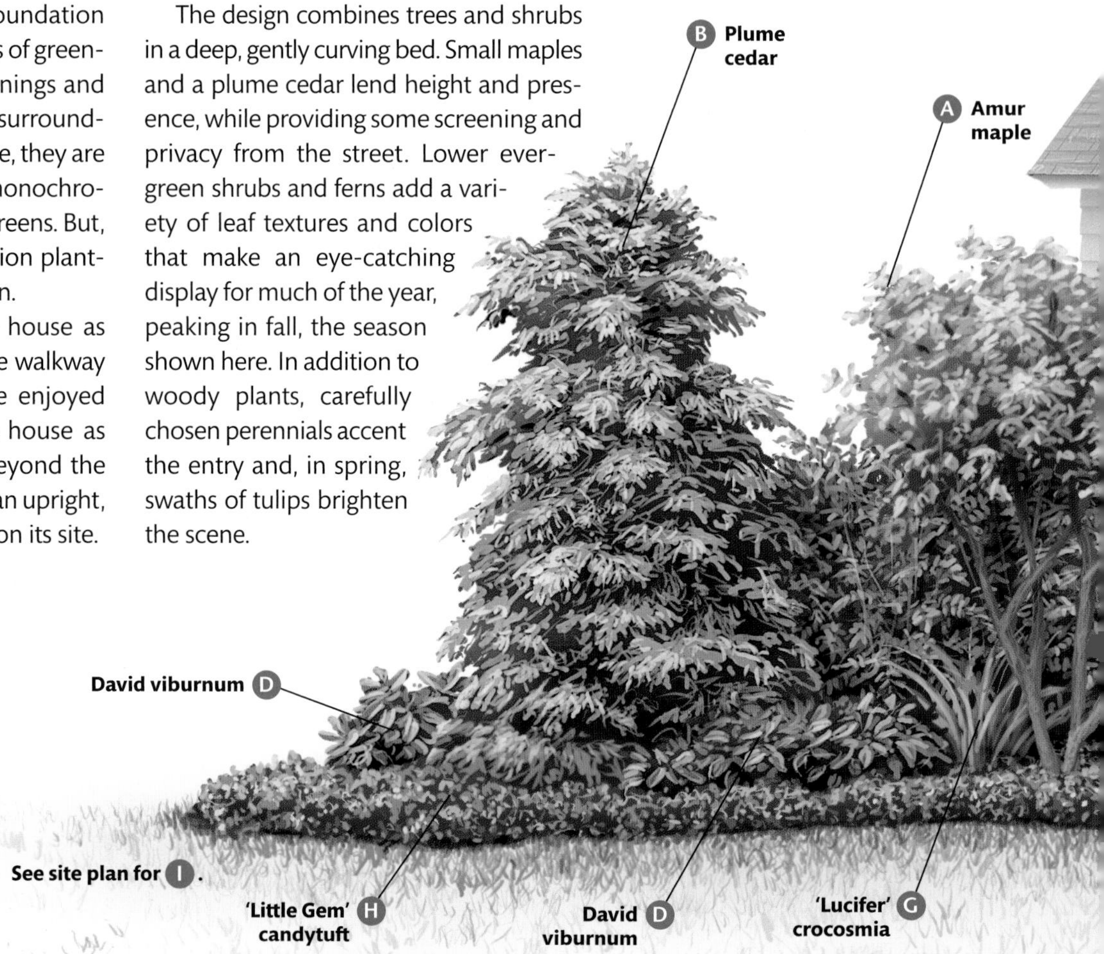

Plants & Projects

This is a low-care planting. Once established, the plants will thrive without much more attention than seasonal cleanup and renewing the mulch in the summer to conserve water. Shear the candytuft after bloom and divide and refurbish the tulips every fall.

A **Amur maple** (use 3 plants)
This small multitrunked deciduous tree offers months of interest. In spring, fragrant yellow flowers are followed by bright red, winged seeds. Summer's glossy green leaves cast a dappled shade and turn striking colors in fall. See *Acer ginnala*, p. 188.

B **Plume cedar** (use 1)
Making a neat cone, this evergreen tree contrasts nicely with the nearby maples. Needlelike blue-green foliage turns bronze in winter. Peeling, cinnamon-colored bark is also attractive. See *Cryptomeria japonica* 'Elegans', p. 206.

C **Dwarf Hinoki cypress** (use 2)
Flanking the steps, a pair of

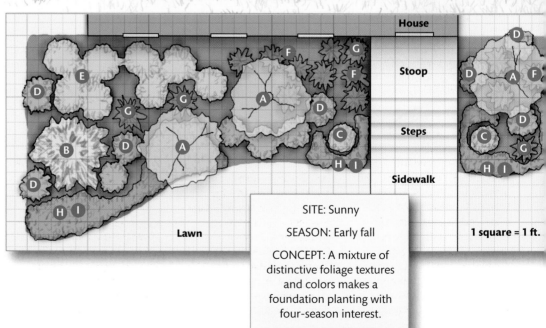

B Plume cedar

A Amur maple

David viburnum **D**

See site plan for **I** .

'Little Gem' **H** candytuft

David **D** viburnum

'Lucifer' **G** crocosmia

House

Stoop

Steps

Sidewalk

Lawn

SITE: Sunny

SEASON: Early fall

CONCEPT: A mixture of distinctive foliage textures and colors makes a foundation planting with four-season interest.

1 square = 1 ft.

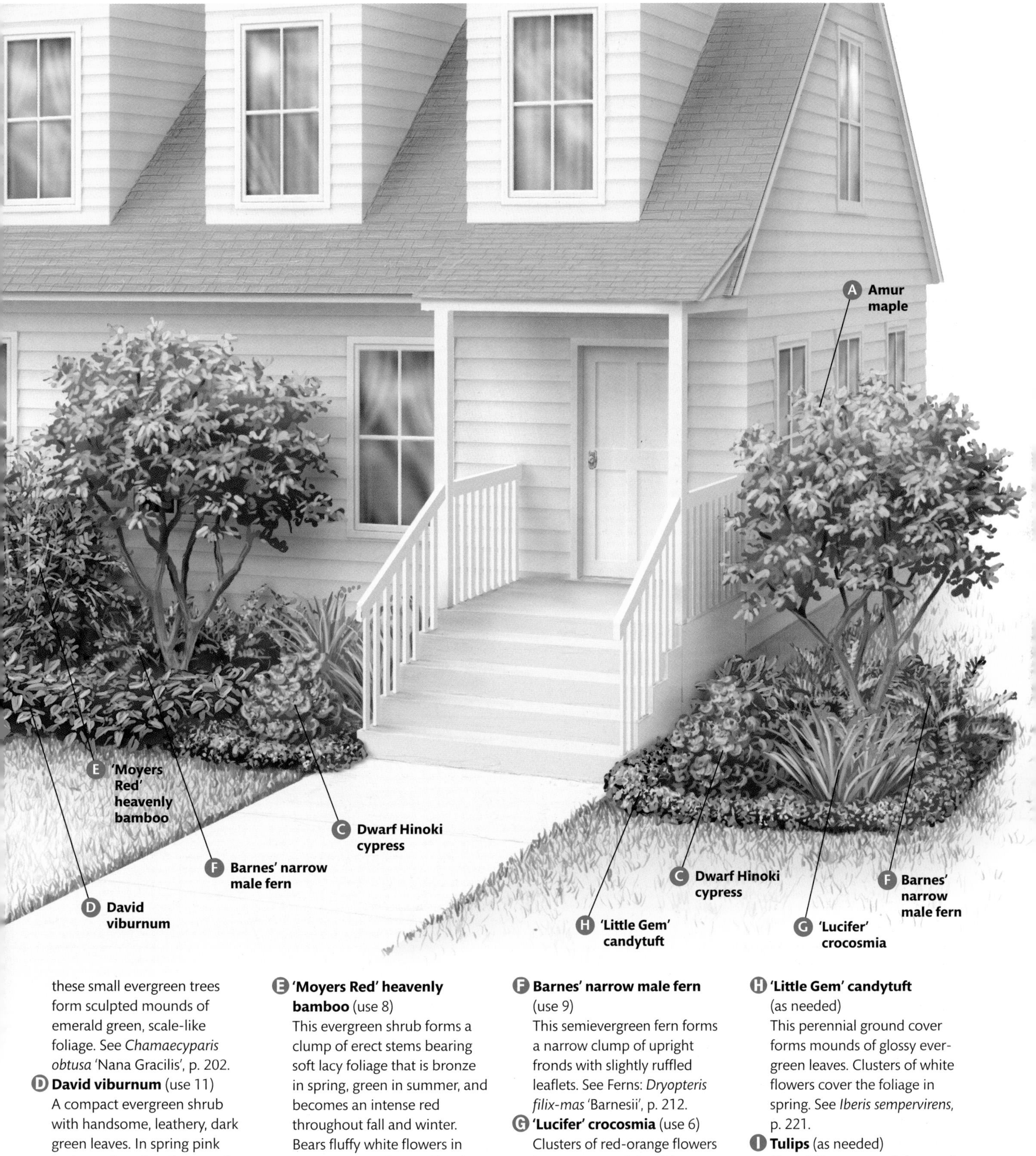

A Amur maple

E 'Moyers Red' heavenly bamboo

F Barnes' narrow male fern

C Dwarf Hinoki cypress

D David viburnum

C Dwarf Hinoki cypress

H 'Little Gem' candytuft

G 'Lucifer' crocosmia

F Barnes' narrow male fern

these small evergreen trees form sculpted mounds of emerald green, scale-like foliage. See *Chamaecyparis obtusa* 'Nana Gracilis', p. 202.

D **David viburnum** (use 11)
A compact evergreen shrub with handsome, leathery, dark green leaves. In spring pink buds produce flat clusters of small white flowers. It bears metallic blue fruits in fall. See *Viburnum davidii*, p. 247.

E **'Moyers Red' heavenly bamboo** (use 8)
This evergreen shrub forms a clump of erect stems bearing soft lacy foliage that is bronze in spring, green in summer, and becomes an intense red throughout fall and winter. Bears fluffy white flowers in summer, sometimes off and on throughout the year, and orange-red berries. See *Nandina domestica*, p. 229.

F **Barnes' narrow male fern** (use 9)
This semievergreen fern forms a narrow clump of upright fronds with slightly ruffled leaflets. See Ferns: *Dryopteris filix-mas* 'Barnesii', p. 212.

G **'Lucifer' crocosmia** (use 6)
Clusters of red-orange flowers hover on graceful arching stems among this perennial's swordlike leaves from summer into fall. See *Crocosmia*, p. 206.

H **'Little Gem' candytuft** (as needed)
This perennial ground cover forms mounds of glossy evergreen leaves. Clusters of white flowers cover the foliage in spring. See *Iberis sempervirens*, p. 221.

I **Tulips** (as needed)
Plant 100 or more of these colorful bulbs in the candytuft for a striking spring display. See Bulbs: *Tulipa*, p. 196.

PLANT PORTRAITS

These plants will dress up the most nondescript foundation or front porch while requiring little care.

● = First design, pp. 28–29
▲ = Second design, pp. 30–31.

Weeping hemlock (*Tsuga canadensis* 'Pendula', p. 246) ▲

Tulips (*Tulips*, p. 197) ●

'Setsugekka' sasanqua camellia (*Camellia sasanqua*, p. 198) ▲

Amur maple (*Acer ginnala*, p. 188) ●

Bird's-nest Norway spruce (*Picea abies* 'Nidiformis', p. 234) ▲

Setting for a shady porch

This foundation planting graces a front porch on a site shaded from the afternoon sun. Like the previous design, this one mixes the year-round attractions of evergreens with deciduous trees and perennials. From spring through fall, many-stemmed vine maples screen porch sitters from activity on the street. In late winter, fragrant flowers entice visitors to linger on the porch.

Here again, foliage is the key. Conifers, ferns, broadleaved evergreens, and leafy hostas combine a pleasing variety of forms, leaf textures, and colors. Unlike many plantings, this one reaches its flowering peak in late winter, which is shown here. Seasonally planted hanging baskets and containers add accents during the rest of the year.

Plants & Projects

Ⓐ Vine maple (use 6 plants)
This deciduous Northwest native tree forms an open thicket of stems that is interesting year-round. Green leaves turn red, yellow, and purple in fall. See *Acer circinatum*, p. 188.

Ⓑ Weeping hemlock (use 1)
A slow-growing evergreen tree, its arching branches forming a wide mound of soft blue-green foliage. A striking contrast to the vine maples. See *Tsuga canadensis* 'Pendula', p. 246.

Ⓒ Bird's-nest Norway spruce (use 3)
Another slow-growing evergreen tree. It makes a hassock-like mound of dark green needles. Commonly has a slight depression on top, which gives rise to its name. See *Picea abies* 'Nidiformis', p 234.

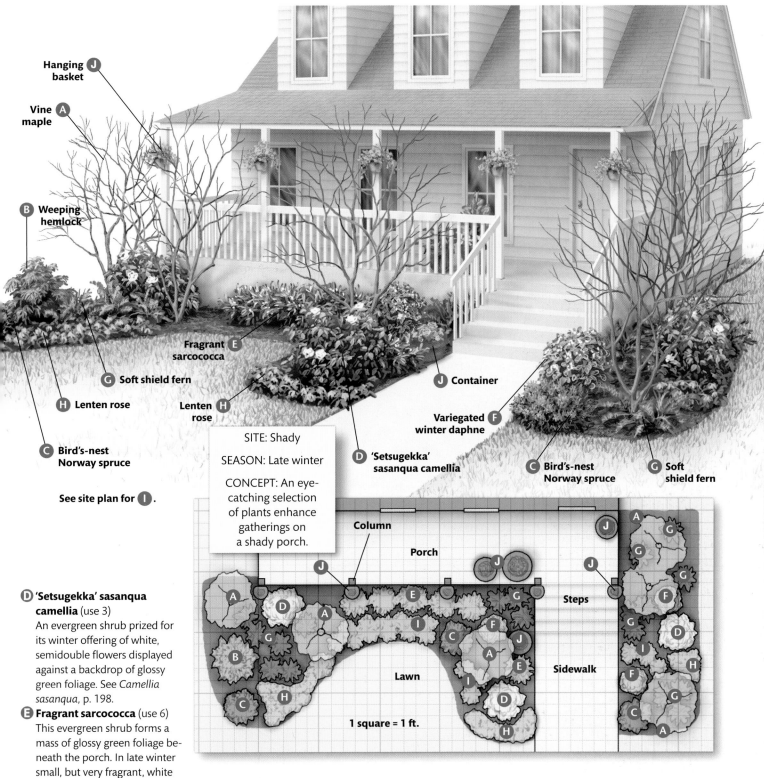

Hanging basket **J**

Vine maple **A**

Weeping hemlock **B**

Fragrant sarcococca **E**

Soft shield fern **G**

Lenten rose **H**

Lenten rose **H**

Bird's-nest Norway spruce **C**

See site plan for **I**.

Container **J**

Variegated winter daphne **F**

'Setsugekka' sasanqua camellia **D**

Bird's-nest Norway spruce **C**

Soft shield fern **G**

SITE: Shady

SEASON: Late winter

CONCEPT: An eye-catching selection of plants enhance gatherings on a shady porch.

Column

Porch

Steps

Sidewalk

Lawn

1 square = 1 ft.

D **'Setsugekka' sasanqua camellia** (use 3)
An evergreen shrub prized for its winter offering of white, semidouble flowers displayed against a backdrop of glossy green foliage. See *Camellia sasanqua*, p. 198.

E **Fragrant sarcococca** (use 6)
This evergreen shrub forms a mass of glossy green foliage beneath the porch. In late winter small, but very fragrant, white flowers cluster among the leaves. See *Sarcococca ruscifolia*, p. 242.

F **Variegated winter daphne** (use 3)
The glossy green leaves of this evergreen shrub are edged in gold. Fragrant, rose-tinged white flowers bloom from late winter into spring. See *Daphne odora* 'Aureomarginata', p. 207.

G **Soft shield fern** (use 18)
Clumps of lacy bright green fronds accent the planting in several spots. The foliage is evergreen and soft to the touch. See Ferns: *Polystichum setiferum*, p. 213.

H **Lenten rose** (use 12)
A popular late-winter-blooming perennial with distinctive fleshy flowers and shiny ever-green leaves. See *Helleborus orientalis*, p. 217.

I **Hosta** (use 20)
A popular perennial that is prized for its foliage. To complement this planting, choose a medium-size cultivar with variegated white-and-green leaves. See *Hosta*, p. 220.

J **Pots and hanging baskets** (as needed)

For winter we've shown trailing glacier ivy and primroses in the baskets hanging on the porch columns. For the large pots on the porch and by the steps, use a tall plant (such as a dwarf conifer, evergreen fern, or spike plant) underplanted with seasonal annuals. Here we've shown winter pansies and kale.

A Pleasant Welcome

FIT A PLEASING "GREEN" SKIRT TO YOUR HOME

This colorful planting eases the transition from an upright house to its lawn while providing a lot of attractive garden to enjoy.

Liberal inclusion of evergreen foliage ensures interest all year. Where winters are warm, the 'Iceberg' rose provides a year-round floral bonus. There's plenty of seasonal change, too. Spring displays include pink thrift and Indian hawthorn flowers as well as the deliciously sweet blooms of lilac. Summer provides flowers in yellow, white, and deep pink.

Complementing the evergreen foliage are colorful transformations of the heavenly bamboo leaves from bronze to green to red as the seasons progress. In fall, the crape myrtle will chip in with red, orange, or yellow foliage.

Plants & Projects

If, as is likely, your house differs from this one, the design is easy to adapt. The main consideration is to make sure that plants placed near windows will not, as the plants mature, unintentionally obscure a desired view or light source.

Ⓐ Thrift (use 15)
This compact grassy perennial forms tufts of narrow evergreen leaves, topped in spring with small, round, powder puff-like flowers. See *Armeria maritima*, p. 192.

Ⓑ Euryops (use 3)
A large perennial with finely cut gray green leaves, its yellow daisylike flowers bloom from summer into autumn. See *Euryops pectinatus*, p. 211.

Ⓒ 'Iceberg' rose (use 2)
This upright shrub bears clusters of bright white flowers in dark green leaves off and on all year where winters are warm. See *Rosa* 'Iceberg', p. 238.

Ⓓ 'Nana' heavenly bamboo (use 12)
The soft, feathery evergreen leaves of this dwarf shrub change colors from season to season and are fiery red fall and winter. White summer flowers are followed by red berries. See *Nandina* 'Nana', p. 229.

Ⓔ Crape myrtle (use 1)
This small deciduous tree offers pink or white flowers in summer and eye-catching foliage and bark in fall and winter. See *Lagerstroemia indica*, p. 224.

Ⓕ Tropical plumbago (use 1)
Trained flat on a trellis, this vining shrub has light green leaves and clusters of powder blue flowers from summer to frost. See *Plumbago auriculata*, p. 234.

Ⓖ 'Pinkie' Indian hawthorn (use 6)
From spring into summer, large clusters of light pink flowers are showcased by this compact shrub's glossy evergreen leaves. See *Rhaphiolepis* 'Pinkie', p. 236.

Ⓗ Common lilac (use 1)
A long-favored shrub, prized for its fragrant spring display of flowers in shades of lavender, purple, pink, and white. One of the smaller cultivars will work well in this design. See *Syringa vulgaris*, p. 244.

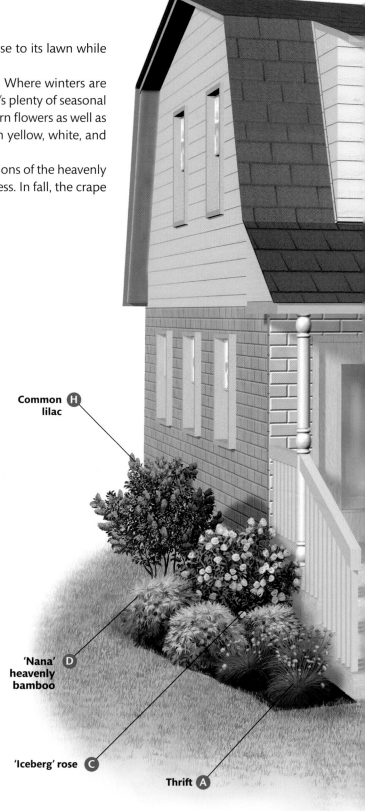

Common lilac Ⓗ

'Nana' heavenly bamboo Ⓓ

'Iceberg' rose Ⓒ

Thrift Ⓐ

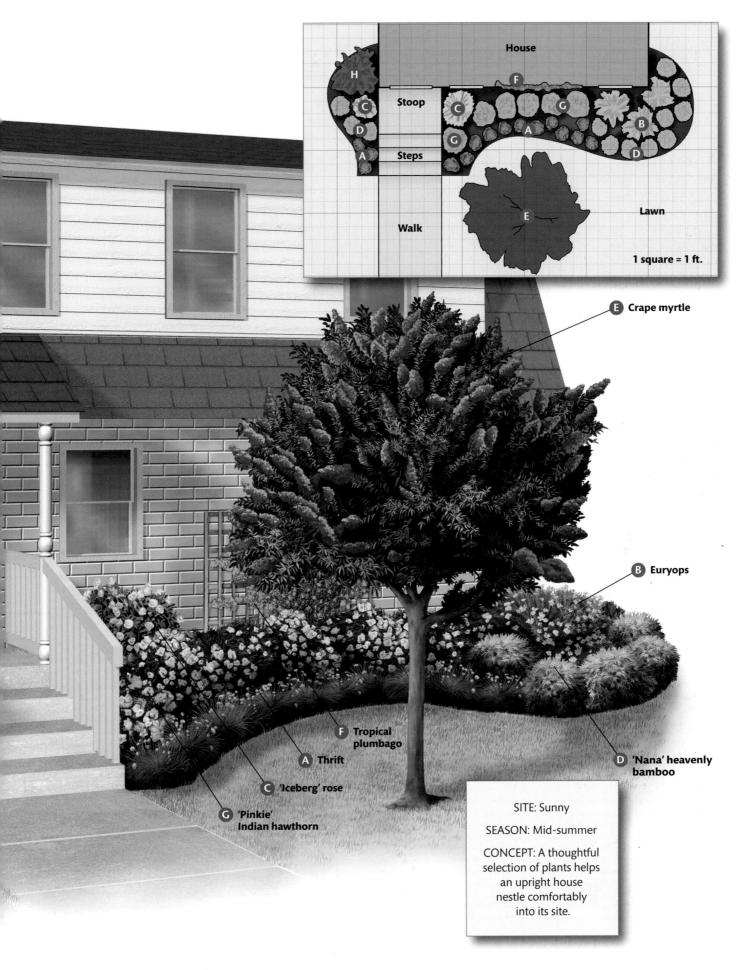

House

H

C

D

A

Stoop

Steps

Walk

F

C

G

A

G

B

D

E

Lawn

1 square = 1 ft.

E Crape myrtle

B Euryops

D 'Nana' heavenly bamboo

F Tropical plumbago

A Thrift

C 'Iceberg' rose

G 'Pinkie' Indian hawthorn

SITE: Sunny

SEASON: Mid-summer

CONCEPT: A thoughtful selection of plants helps an upright house nestle comfortably into its site.

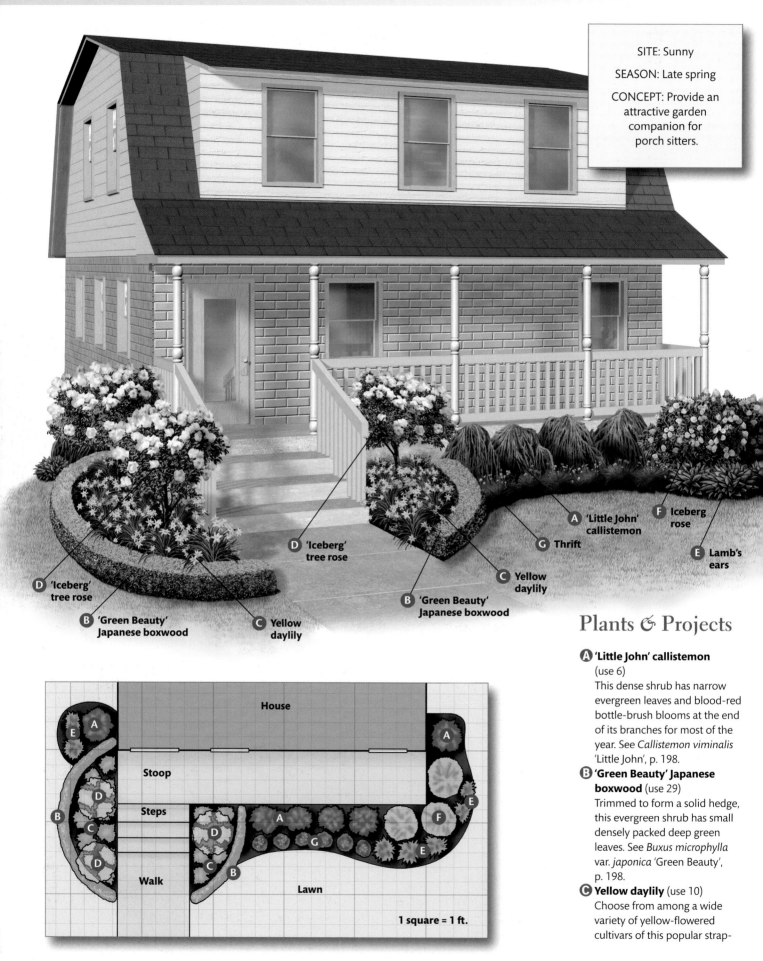

SITE: Sunny

SEASON: Late spring

CONCEPT: Provide an attractive garden companion for porch sitters.

A 'Little John' callistemon

F Iceberg rose

G Thrift

C Yellow daylily

E Lamb's ears

D 'Iceberg' tree rose

B 'Green Beauty' Japanese boxwood

D 'Iceberg' tree rose

B 'Green Beauty' Japanese boxwood

C Yellow daylily

House

Stoop

Steps

Walk

Lawn

1 square = 1 ft.

Plants & Projects

A **'Little John' callistemon** (use 6)
This dense shrub has narrow evergreen leaves and blood-red bottle-brush blooms at the end of its branches for most of the year. See *Callistemon viminalis* 'Little John', p. 198.

B **'Green Beauty' Japanese boxwood** (use 29)
Trimmed to form a solid hedge, this evergreen shrub has small densely packed deep green leaves. See *Buxus microphylla* var. *japonica* 'Green Beauty', p. 198.

C **Yellow daylily** (use 10)
Choose from among a wide variety of yellow-flowered cultivars of this popular strap-

Porchside pleasures

Many older homes have front porches that rise several feet above the ground. A planted skirt around the porch base hides unsightly structure and provides an opportunity to enhance the view for porch sitters as well as passersby on the street.

This design includes a small hedged garden flanking the entry steps, featuring cheerful daylilies and lovely "tree" or "standard" roses, which carry their bright white flowers well above ground level.

Elsewhere in the planting, evergreen leaves and a selection of colorful and long-blooming flowers provide porchside pleasure throughout the year.

PLANT PORTRAITS

These brightly hued plants provide a cheerful "skirt" for a drab foundation.
- ● = First design, pp. 32–33.
- ▲ = Second design, pp. 34–35.

'Little John' callistemon (*Callistemon viminalis* 'Little John', p. 198) ▲

Yellow daylily (*Hemerocallis*, p. 218) ▲

'Nana' heavenly bamboo (*Nandina* 'Nana', p. 229) ●

leaved perennial. See *Hemerocallis*, p. 218.

D **'Iceberg' tree rose** (use 3)
Nurseries sell this lovely shrubby rose grafted to a sturdy stem, providing a chest-high display of lovely white flowers. See *Rosa* 'Iceberg', p. 238.

E **Lamb's ears** (use 7).
Loved by children for its soft silvery leaves, this perennial produces small purple flowers on thick stalks that rise above the foliage in early summer. See *Stachys byzantina*, p. 244.

See p. 32 for the following:

F **Iceberg rose** (use 3)

G **Thrift** (use 6)

Lamb's ears (*Stachys byzantina*, p. 244) ▲

Thrift (*Armeria maritima*, p. 192) ●

Up Front Informal

TURN A SMALL FRONT YARD INTO A WELCOMING GARDEN

With a little imagination and a host of pleasing plants, front yards can be transformed into inviting front gardens. Replacing the existing lawn and concrete walkways with colorful plantings and decorative paving will not only reduce mowing and watering, it will also provide a pleasant setting for welcoming guests or watching the world go by.

The transformation from yard to garden begins here with an oversized front walk that widens into a space for sitting. The front walk and patio are tightly laid flagstone to accommodate heavy foot traffic and furniture. A more casual path to the drive is set with wide joints that are planted with a grasslike ground cover.

Bordering the seating area is an informal planting of trees and shrubs. The small red oak and two large hollies will create a cozy atmosphere around the entry, and the tree will provide shade as it matures. Beneath these taller plants are colorful shrubs, grasses, perennials, and a durable carpet of evergreen ground covers. While the ground covers won't stand up to much traffic, they will look good year-round with less water and maintenance than a turfgrass lawn.

The planting is illustrated here at its showiest—during the cooler months of fall—when the weather invites lingering outdoors. But each season holds attractions. An abundance of emerging foliage will give the garden a fresh look in spring, the Turk's cap blooms will invite hummingbirds in summer, and evergreen foliage and purple and red berries will keep color in the garden through winter.

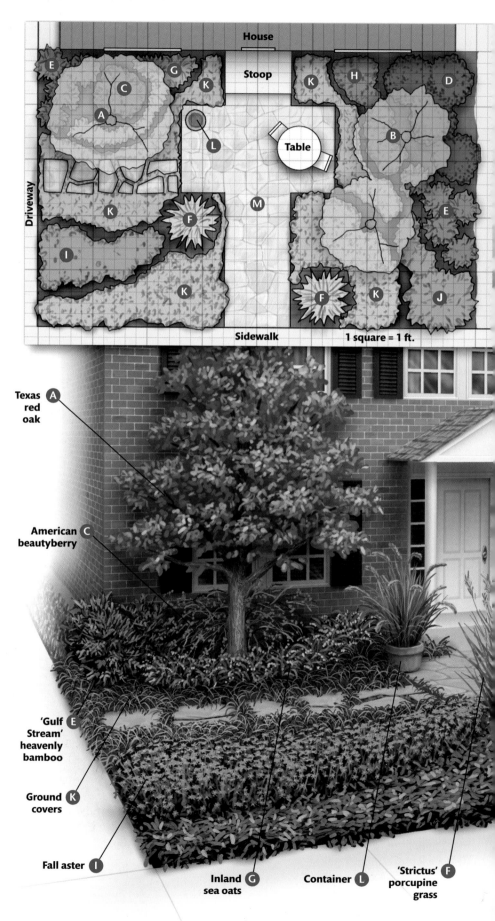

Texts on the diagram:
House · Stoop · Table · Driveway · Sidewalk · 1 square = 1 ft.

Labels:
Texas red oak **A**
American beautyberry **C**
'Gulf Stream' heavenly bamboo **E**
Ground covers **K**
Fall aster **I**
Inland sea oats **G**
Container **L**
'Strictus' porcupine grass **F**

Plants & Projects

Once established, the plants in this design are not particularly demanding. Prune trees and shrubs as needed to maintain size and shape. Seasonal cleanup will keep the planting tidy.

A **Texas red oak** (use 1 plant)
Growing 30 ft. high and wide after many years, this red oak is a fitting shade tree for a small garden. It has silvery bark and lacy leaves that turn from green to red and orange in fall. See *Quercus buckleyi*, p. 236.

B **'Warren's Red' possumhaw holly** (use 2)
These multitrunked deciduous hollies have small lustrous dark green leaves. They bear countless showy red berries in fall that persist on bare silver-gray branches into the winter season. See *Ilex decidua* 'Warren's Red', p. 222.

C **American beautyberry** (use 1)
Prized for its bright clusters of violet berries that hang on the plant through the winter season , this deciduous shrub spreads into a loose thicket of green leaves under the red oak. See *Callicarpa americana*, p.198.

D **Dwarf Burford holly** (use 4)
This durable shrub's glossy evergreen foliage and dense round shape create a handsome screen for the heavenly bamboo. Red berries peek through the foliage in winter. See *Ilex cornuta* 'Burfordii Nana', p.222.

E **'Gulf Stream' heavenly bamboo** (use 9)
Fine-textured foliage turns from bronze to green to red. See *Nandina domestica* 'Gulf Stream', p. 229.

F **'Strictus' porcupine grass** (use 2)
This ornamental grass forms a graceful vase of yellow-striped emerald green leaves. Silvery tan flower plumes wave above the plant in fall. The foliage and flowers stay showy even in winter. See *Miscanthus sinensis* 'Strictus', p. 230.

G **Inland sea oats** (use 12)
A clump-forming grass grown for long, dangling, oatlike seedheads that dance above the foliage in late summer, turning from light green to bronze and then to tan. See *Chasmanthium latifolium*, p. 230.

H **Turk's cap** (use 8)
These bushy perennials make an attractive flowering hedge near the patio. Deep green foliage is speckled from late spring to fall with red blossoms resembling small turbans. See *Malvaviscus arboreus drummondii*, p. 228.

I **Fall aster** (use 16)
These carefree perennials form a solid mass of fine-textured foliage completely covered in autumn with lavender-purple daisylike blossoms. See *Aster oblongifolius*, p. 193.

J **Mexican bush sage** (use 7)
From late summer to frost, this grayish green bushy perennial bristles with long spikes of purple and white flowers. See *Salvia leucantha*, p. 241.

K **Ground covers** (as needed)
Two low-growing evergreen perennials make durable "welcome mats" along the paths and around the patio. Asian jasmine (*Trachelospermum asiaticum*, p. 246) spreads to form a thick glossy carpet of small green leaves on both sides of the front walk. Mondo grass (*Ophiopogon japonicus*, p. 229) has fine dark green foliage that adds grassy texture around the patio and between the flagstones on the narrow walk to the driveway.

L **Container**
Plant a patio pot with purple fountain grass for a fountain of foliage topped with foxtail-like flowers. See Annuals, p. 190.

M **Paving**
A wide front walk of flagstone handles heavy foot traffic and outdoor furniture. A more casual flagstone path to the drive has wide joints filled with prepared soil and planted with mondo grass. See p. 259.

D Dwarf Burford holly

B 'Warren's Red' possumhaw holly

E 'Gulf Stream' heavenly bamboo

J Mexican bush sage

M Paving

H Turk's cap

F 'Strictus' porcupine grass

K Ground covers

K Ground covers

SITE: Sunny

SEASON: Fall

CONCEPT: Well-chosen plants and paving create an entry garden of comfortable informality.

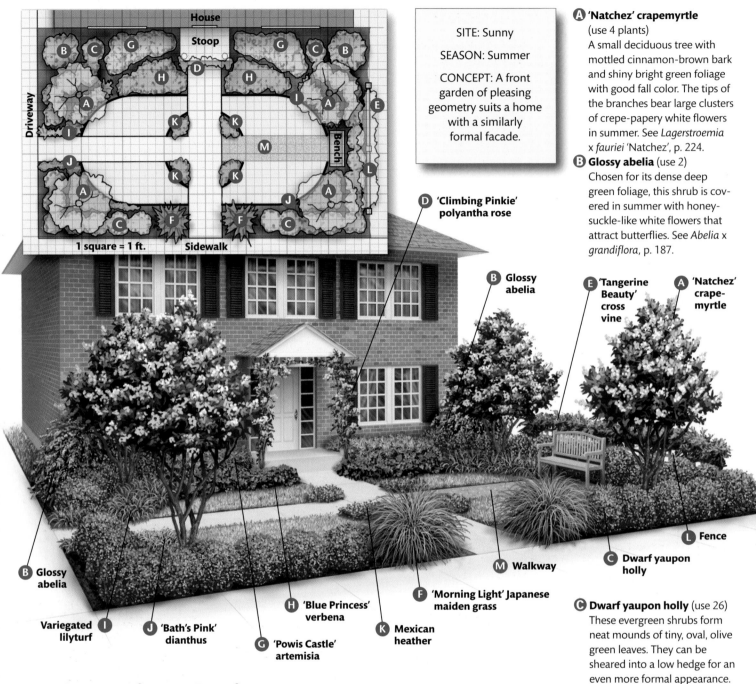

SITE: Sunny

SEASON: Summer

CONCEPT: A front garden of pleasing geometry suits a home with a similarly formal facade.

Ⓓ 'Climbing Pinkie' polyantha rose

Ⓑ Glossy abelia

Ⓔ 'Tangerine Beauty' cross vine

Ⓐ 'Natchez' crape-myrtle

Ⓑ Glossy abelia

Ⓛ Fence

Ⓒ Dwarf yaupon holly

Ⓜ Walkway

Ⓕ 'Morning Light' Japanese maiden grass

Ⓗ 'Blue Princess' verbena

Ⓘ Variegated lilyturf

Ⓙ 'Bath's Pink' dianthus

Ⓖ 'Powis Castle' artemisia

Ⓚ Mexican heather

Plants & Projects

Ⓐ 'Natchez' crapemyrtle (use 4 plants)
A small deciduous tree with mottled cinnamon-brown bark and shiny bright green foliage with good fall color. The tips of the branches bear large clusters of crepe-papery white flowers in summer. See *Lagerstroemia x fauriei* 'Natchez', p. 224.

Ⓑ Glossy abelia (use 2)
Chosen for its dense deep green foliage, this shrub is covered in summer with honey-suckle-like white flowers that attract butterflies. See *Abelia x grandiflora*, p. 187.

Ⓒ Dwarf yaupon holly (use 26)
These evergreen shrubs form neat mounds of tiny, oval, olive green leaves. They can be sheared into a low hedge for an even more formal appearance. See *Ilex vomitoria* 'Nana', p. 222..

Ⓓ 'Climbing Pinkie' polyantha rose (use 2)
A mannerly, thornless, climbing rose that bears loose clusters of pink, semi-double flowers from April through November. See *Rosa x polyantha* 'Climbing Pinkie', p. 238.

Ⓔ 'Tangerine Beauty' cross vine (use 3)
This twining vine will cover the fence with lustrous, dark green

A formal introduction

If your taste, and your house facade, runs to symmetry, a formal approach to landscaping your front yard may appeal to you.

This design offers a simpler makeover than the first by retaining existing concrete walks. The symmetrical layout features a central oval of lawn flanked by almost mirror image plantings on each side of the main walk. A loose-surface path extends the cross walk to a garden bench, a perfect perch for enjoying the view.

Whether approaching from the street or the drive, visitors get an attractive welcome. Small flowering trees and a hedge of low-growing shrubs give the garden its structure. A variety of contrasting foliage textures and colors provide considerable interest year-round. And there are abundant roses and other flowers in spring and summer.

leaves all year. Bears red-or-ange trumpet-shaped flowers in late spring and again in fall. See *Bignonia capreolata* 'Tangerine Beauty', p. 195.

F **'Morning Light' Japanese maiden grass** (use 2)
This lovely grass has slender foliage and a fountainlike shape. See *Miscanthus sinensis* 'Morning Light', p. 230.

G **'Powis Castle' artemisia** (use 14)
Silvery mounds of lacy foliage make this evergreen perennial an outstanding choice next to the lavender-blue verbena and the pink-blooming climbing rose. See *Artemisia* x 'Powis Castle', p. 193.

H **'Blue Princess' verbena** (use 16)
This perennial forms a fine mat of deep green leaves topped with masses of tiny lavender-blue flowers. Especially showy in spring. See *Verbena* x *hybrida* 'Blue Princess', p. 246.

I **Variegated lilyturf** (use 50)
This evergreen ground cover forms grassy clumps of slender leaves striped bright green and creamy yellow. Bears spikes of very small lavender flowers in June. See *Liriope muscari* 'Variegata', p. 226.

J **'Bath's Pink' dianthus** (use 44)
A fine-textured perennial that forms a mat of silver-gray foliage all year. Topped in spring with pretty pink flowers. See *Dianthus* 'Bath's Pink', p. 207.

K **Mexican heather** (use 12)
For texture as well as color, plant in the circular bed where the walks intersect. This tender perennial forms a low bush of tiny leaves in fernlike fans and delicate lavender-pink flowers. See *Cuphea hyssopifolia*, p. 206.

L **Fence**
Interlaced with flowering vines, the lattice-panel fence behind the bench creates a sense of privacy. See p. 280.

M **Walkway**
A loose surface of decomposed granite extends the existing walkway to the bench and provides a level surface beneath it. See p. 262.

PLANT PORTRAITS

These well-behaved plants require little care while garnering lots of attention.
● = First design, pp. 36–37.
▲ = Second design, pp. 38–39.

Variegated lilyturf (*Liriope muscari* 'Variegata', p. 226) ▲

'Strictus' porcupine grass (*Miscanthus sinensis* 'Strictus', p. 230) ●

'Natchez' crapemyrtle (*Lagerstroemia* x *fauriei* 'Natchez', p. 224) ▲

'Climbing Pinkie' polyantha rose (*Rosa* x *polyantha* 'Climbing Pinkie', p. 238) ▲

Dwarf Burford holly (*Ilex cornuta* 'Burfordii Nana', p.222) ●

'Warren's Red' possumhaw holly (*Ilex decidua* 'Warren's Red', p. 222) ●

An Elegant Entry

GARDEN GEOMETRY TRANSFORMS A SMALL FRONT YARD

Formal gardens have a special appeal. Their simple geometry can be soothing in a hectic world, and the look is timeless, never going out of style. Homes with symmetrical facades are especially suited to formal makeovers, which complement and accent the architecture.

This design enhances both approaches to a front door—from the sidewalk and the driveway—while echoing the symmetry of the house facade when viewed from the street. The result is more playful and unpredictable than a "classic" formal landscape design.

Visitors approaching from street or drive are drawn toward the leafy crape myrtle canopy at the intersection of the two walkways. From

SITE: Sunny

SEASON: Late spring

CONCEPT: Subtle geometry and well-chosen plants create an entry garden of comfortable, low-key formality.

Crape myrtle Ⓐ

Saucer Ⓑ magnolia

Wax leaf Ⓖ privet

Common Ⓒ lilac

Daylily Ⓘ

'Veitchii' Ⓓ gardenia

Dwarf Ⓙ periwinkle

'Winter Gem' Ⓗ boxwood

Ⓚ Walkway extension

'Iceberg' Ⓔ rose

here, you can proceed to the door, or enjoy a few minutes of conversation and relaxation in a grassy semicircular courtyard nearby, with its central birdbath or fountain and bench tucked into an evergreen hedge.

Overcrowded, intricate plantings can make a small space seem smaller. So here, a limited palette of plants is arrayed in bold masses to impart a comfortably spacious feel to a small garden. Flowers are abundant from late winter through fall, and the balance of deciduous and evergreen foliage ensures a year-round presence. For much of the year, fragrant lilacs, gardenias, and roses reward a stroll around the garden.

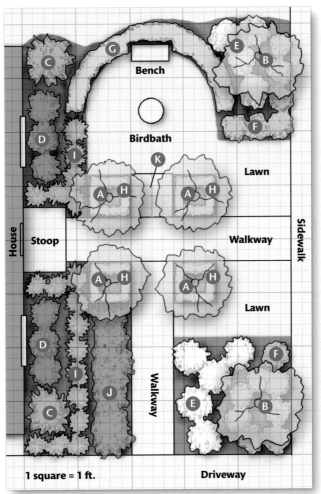

1 square = 1 ft.

B Saucer magnolia

F 'Ballerina' Indian hawthorn

Plants & Projects

Once established, the plants in this design are not particularly demanding. Clip the hedges regularly to keep them tidy. Prune trees and shrubs as needed to maintain size and shape.

A **Crape myrtle** (use 4 plants)
This deciduous tree offers something in every season: pink, red, or white flowers in summer; colorful foliage in fall; eye-catching bark in winter. See *Lagerstroemia indica*, p. 224.

B **Saucer magnolia** (use 2)
This handsome deciduous tree

accents the front corners with bold foliage and striking flowers. Blooms appear in spring on bare branches before the leaves expand. See *Magnolia* x *soulangiana*, p. 228.

C **Common lilac** (use 2)
Marking the corners of the house, this upright deciduous shrub produces sweet-scented flowers in spring. See *Syringa vulgaris*, p. 244.

D **'Veitchii' gardenia** (use 6)
These compact evergreen shrubs won't outgrow the space under the windows. Dark foliage showcases very fragrant white flowers from spring through fall. See *Gardenia jasminoides*, p. 214.

E **'Iceberg' rose** (use 9)
A floribunda rose, it bears clusters of fragrant white flowers all year. It forms upright clumps and makes a fine mid-height ground cover. See *Rosa*, p. 238.

F **'Ballerina' Indian hawthorn** (use 14)
This low evergreen shrub is another excellent ground cover. It bears numerous clusters of pink flowers in spring. See *Rhaphiolepis indica*, p. 236.

G **Wax leaf privet** (use 9)
The glossy leaves of this evergreen shrub make a handsome formal hedge. Though clipping as a hedge diminishes their numbers, scented white flowers will draw you to the bench in early summer. See *Ligustrum japonicum* 'Texanum', p. 226.

H **'Winter Gem' boxwood** (use 48)
The small leaves and dense habit of this evergreen shrub are ideal for a small clipped hedge like this. See *Buxus microphylla* var. *japonica*, p. 198.

I **Daylily** (use 18)
The grassy foliage of this perennial contrasts pleasantly with the clipped hedges and bushy shrubs nearby. Choose cultivars with flower colors and bloom times to suit your taste. See *Hemerocallis*, p. 218.

J **Dwarf periwinkle** (as needed)
The glossy dark green leaves of this low, spreading perennial ground cover are evergreen. Lilac-colored flowers bloom in late spring. Plant 6 in. apart. See *Vinca minor*, p. 247.

K **Walkway extension**
Made of precast pavers (see p. 262) or poured concrete, this short extension creates symmetry at the crossing of the two front walkways.

Formal and fresh

In this design, a paved courtyard and a planting of handsome trees, shrubs, and ground covers have transformed a site typically given over to lawn and a concrete walkway. The result is a more dramatic entry, but also one where you can happily linger with guests.

Like the previous design, this one is simple, comprising mass plantings of a limited number of plants. Small trees shade the paving and, with the low hedge and underplanting of shrubs, create a cozy atmosphere in the courtyard without walling out the street. A birdbath garnished with colorful annuals provides a focal point in the courtyard. A pair of benches offer perches for enjoying the results of your landscaping labors.

Replacing the lawn with an evergreen perennial ground cover completes the transformation from front yard to front garden. While the ground cover will not stand up to games of touch football, it will look good year-round with less water and maintenance than a turfgrass lawn. The deep green foliage adds an attractive texture to the garden. And, as a bonus, in early spring it becomes a carpet of small white flowers.

SITE: Sunny

SEASON: Late spring

CONCEPT:
A courtyard garden of elegant simplicity complements a home with a symmetrical facade.

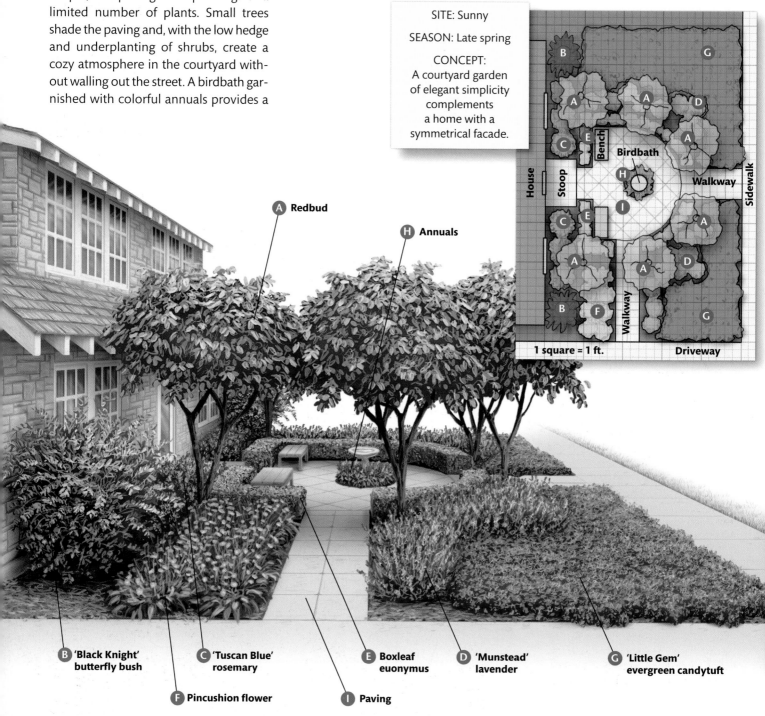

1 square = 1 ft.

A Redbud

H Annuals

B 'Black Knight' butterfly bush

C 'Tuscan Blue' rosemary

F Pincushion flower

E Boxleaf euonymus

I Paving

D 'Munstead' lavender

G 'Little Gem' evergreen candytuft

Plants & Projects

Ⓐ Redbud (use 6 plants)
Branches of this small deciduous tree are covered with tiny bright purple flowers in early spring before the leaves appear. The leaves turn gold in fall. Tracery of bare branches is handsome in winter. See *Cercis canadensis*, p. 201.

Ⓑ 'Black Knight' butterfly bush (use 2)
The arching stems of this deciduous shrub bear long spikes of fragrant dark purple flowers from midsummer through fall. Butterflies love them. See *Buddleia davidii*, p. 196.

Ⓒ 'Tuscan Blue' rosemary (use 6)
This evergreen Mediterranean shrub is prized for its aromatic foliage and attractive upright form. It bears small dark blue flowers in spring. See *Rosmarinus officinalis*, p. 240.

Ⓓ 'Munstead' lavender (use 19)
Bushy mounds of silver-gray aromatic foliage make an attractive mid-height ground cover beneath the redbuds. Spikes of lavender-blue flowers scent the air in late spring. See *Lavandula angustifolia*, p. 226.

Ⓔ Boxleaf euonymus (use 23)
Neatly clipped to form a low formal hedge, this evergreen shrub reinforces the geometry of the design. See *Euonymus japonicus* 'Microphyllus', p. 210.

Ⓕ Pincushion flower (use 8)
Planted as a ground cover next to the walkway, this perennial offers airy foliage covered with light blue flowers from late spring through fall. See *Scabiosa caucasica*, p. 242.

Ⓖ 'Little Gem' evergreen candytuft (as needed)
Replacing lawn grass, this perennial ground cover forms a low mat of fine dark green leaves. Bears bright white flowers for a few weeks in early spring. Space plants on 2-ft. centers. Lightly trim plants with a weed whacker after bloom and whenever the foliage needs rejuvenation. See *Iberis sempervirens*, p. 221.

Ⓗ Annuals
Plant seasonal annuals at the foot of the birdbath (or other garden ornament) in the center of the paving. For spring, try combinations of salvia, phlox, snapdragons, alyssum, and purple basil. See Annuals, p. 190.

Ⓘ Paving
We've shown square precast concrete pavers here. Poured concrete, scored to form the gridwork patterns, is a more expensive but very durable alternative. See p. 259.

VARIATIONS ON A THEME

A formal design can serve intimacy or expansiveness. It may be open, light, and gay, or subdued and contemplative.

This serene courtyard entry is a pleasing combination of simplicity and subtle detail.

In this large, cheerful garden, the lawn forms paths around planting beds of tree roses, shrub roses, and perennials.

This is a formal entryway garden in the classical tradition, complete with a fountain and stone benches.

Frontyard Makeover

A FRONT GARDEN INVITES RELAXATION

This design transforms a front yard into a multipurpose space: an attractive and welcoming entry; a setting for a glass of wine in the evening or a morning cup of coffee.

Framed by well-chosen plantings, wide walkways guide visitors to your door, allowing them to enjoy the scenery along the way. The layout creates several comfortable niches where you or your guests can linger.

There is an abundance of shade under the the hawthorns. A substantial hedge screens one side of the property, enhancing privacy in one of the niches. Along the front of the house, butterfly bushes, a mugo pine, and ornamental grasses contrast with the vertical facade. A large perennial bed anchors a front corner, providing lively colors from spring through fall. The three other corners feature smaller displays.

Plants & Projects

Any planting this size requires attention throughout the year, but the low-care plants chosen here ensure that maintenance is not onerous. Other than keeping the hedge tidy, seasonal cleanup and pruning cover most of the tasks.

A **Washington hawthorn** (use 6) This dense, twiggy, deciduous tree bears glossy green leaves that turn red in fall. White spring flowers are followed by red fruits that last into the winter. See *Crataegus phaenopyrum*, p. 206.

A **Washington hawthorn**

C **Adonis Blue' buddleia**

Bench O

M Pot

Lady in Black' G calico aster

E 'Munstead' English lavender

B 'Big Tuna' mugo pine

J Blue oat grass

'Boulder Blue' fescue I

B **'Big Tuna' mugo pine** (use 2)
A large evergreen shrub, it has dense fine-textured needles. Slow growing, but worth the time. See *Pinus mugo* 'Big Tuna', p. 234.

C **'Adonis Blue' buddleia** (use 3)
This upright branching shrubby perennial has narrow, gray-green leaves that can be evergreen where winters are mild. Spikes of deep blue, fragrant flowers adorn the ends of the stems from midsummer through fall. See *Buddleia davidii* 'Adonis Blue', p. 196.

D **Curl-leaf mountain mahogany** (use 6)
This broadleaf evergreen's small leathery foliage is well suited to training and maintaining as a clipped hedge. See *Cercocarpus ledifolius*, p. 201.

E **'Munstead' English lavender** (use 9)
An evergreen perennial ideal for dry-summer climates. Its mounding gray-green foliage is covered in early summer with spikes of pale lavender flowers. See *Lavandula angustifolia* 'Munstead', p. 226.

F **Basket of Gold** (one to two flats of 4-in. pots)
This perennial features spreading evergreen foliage and bright yellow flowers from spring through summer. See *Aurinia saxatilis*, p.194.

G **'Lady in Black' calico aster** (use 7)
An upright, mounding perennial with dark green leaves on purple stems, it blooms profusely in fall, its small white flowers dotted by raspberry-colored centers. See *Aster lateriflorus* 'Lady in Black', p. 193.

H **Yellow columbine** (use 10)
This perennial is prized for its distinctive spur-shaped flowers that float above finely cut light green leaves in spring. See *Aquilegia chrysantha*, p. 192.

I **'Boulder Blue' fescue** (use 13)
A perennial grass, it forms a small neat mound of spiky blue-gray foliage. See *Festuca ovina* var. *glauca* 'Boulder Blue', p. 230.

J **Blue oat grass** (use 7)
This is an evergreen perennial, forming a fountain of wiry, upright pale blue leaves. Its thin flower spikes turn tan in late summer and fall. See *Helictotrichon sempervirens*, p. 230.

K **White coneflower** (use 5)
This is a white-flowered version of the popular purple coneflower. Bears daisylike flowers on stiff stalks above a neat mound of narrow, dark green leaves. See *Echinacea purpurea* 'White Swan', p. 208.

L **'Goldsturm' black-eyed Susan** (use 3).
From summer into fall, this perennial bears numerous black-centered yellow flowers atop a mound of dark green leaves. See *Rudbeckia fulgida*, p. 240.

M **Pots**
Potted plants can provide accents and seasonal variety. Here we've shown large pots planted with feather reed grass (*Calamagrostis* 'Overdam', p. 230).

N **Paving**
Choose paving that suits your taste, your house and your budget. Those shown here can be laid on a sand and gravel base. Paving an area this large is an undertaking; consider hiring a professional if you're uncertain of your stamina or skill. See p. 259.

O **Bench**
A traditional teak garden bench is shown here; choose something comfortable for enjoying your plantings.

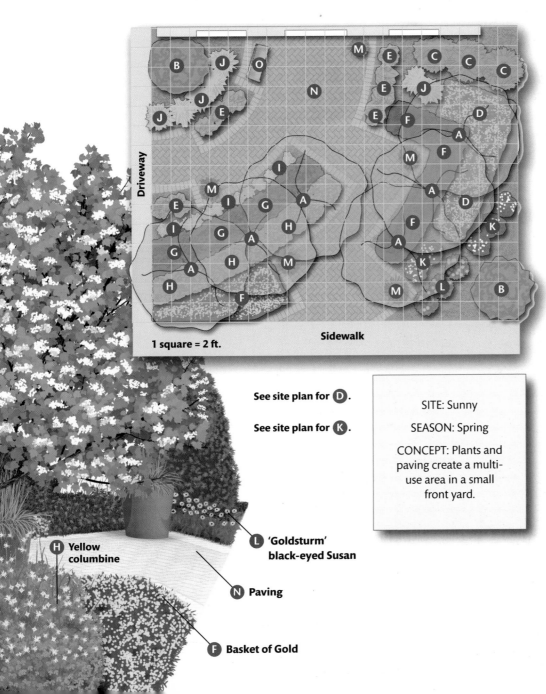

1 square = 2 ft.

Driveway

Sidewalk

See site plan for **D**.

See site plan for **K**.

SITE: Sunny

SEASON: Spring

CONCEPT: Plants and paving create a multi-use area in a small front yard.

H Yellow columbine

L 'Goldsturm' black-eyed Susan

N Paving

F Basket of Gold

More private space

This design has a more straightforward geometry, but accomplishes the same goals as the previous one. The screened paving provides more privacy, perhaps for conversations around the small table.

Two golden raintrees offer shade and a fine display of dangling yellow panicles in spring. An assortment of shrubs, perennials, and ornamental grasses hug the screens and soften their woody presence. The plants produce a colorful display of flowers and foliage for many months.

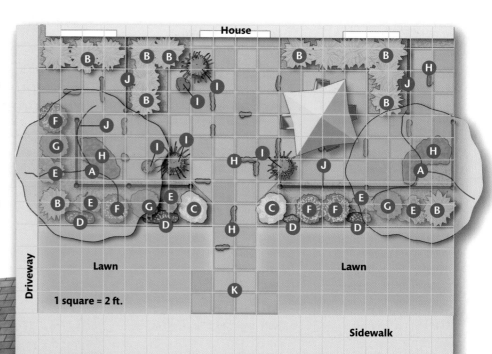

House

Driveway

Lawn

Lawn

1 square = 2 ft.

Sidewalk

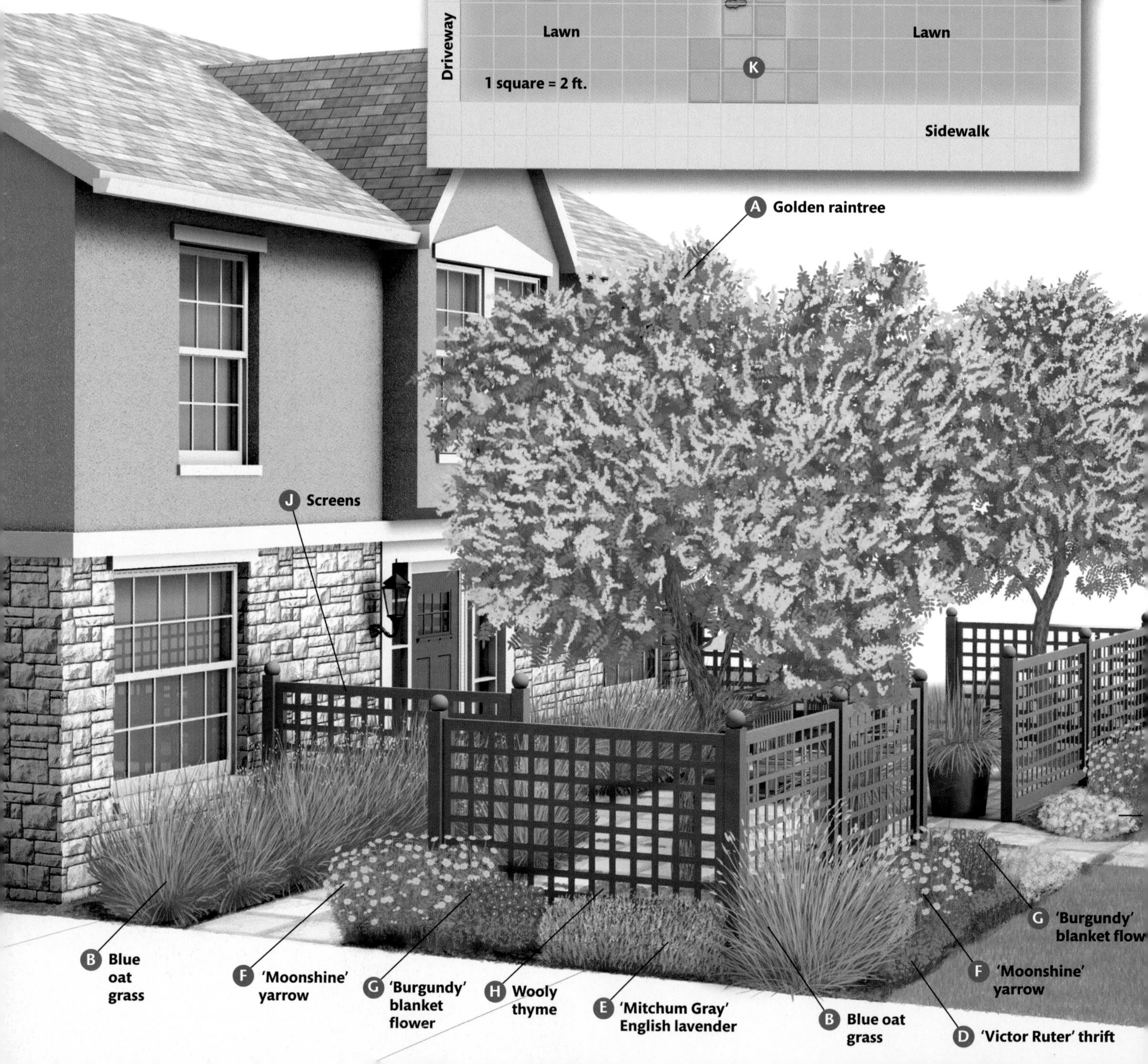

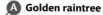

A Golden raintree

J Screens

B Blue oat grass

F 'Moonshine' yarrow

G 'Burgundy' blanket flower

H Wooly thyme

E 'Mitchum Gray' English lavender

B Blue oat grass

D 'Victor Ruter' thrift

G 'Burgundy' blanket flow

F 'Moonshine' yarrow

Plants & Projects

A Golden raintree (use 2)
This round-topped deciduous tree has fine-textured, divided green leaves that turn (rather undependably) golden yellow in fall. In summer large panicles of yellow flowers hang from the branches. See *Koelreuteria paniculata*, p. 224.

B Blue oat grass (use 16)
Forms an upright mound of grassy blue foliage with thin, wiry pale blue evergreen leaves. Tan seedheads appear in midsummer. See *Helictotrichon sempervirens*, p. 230.

C 'Seafoam' artemisia (use 2)
This perennial forms a wide, airy mound of curly silver leaves. See *Artemisia versicolor* 'Seafoam', p. 193.

D 'Victor Ruter' thrift (use 8)
This perennial bears pink puffball flowers on thin stalks atop a mound of narrow grassy evergreen foliage. Blooms in spring and intermittently through fall. See *Armeria* 'Victor Ruter', p. 192.

E 'Mitchum Gray' English lavender (use 11)
A bushy evergreen shrub with fragrant gray-green leaves. Fragrant blue flowers perch above the foliage on stiff stalks in summer. See *Lavandula angustifolia* 'Mitchum gray', p. 226.

F 'Moonshine' yarrow (use 4)
Lemon yellow flowers cover this perennial's mound of feathery, silver-blue foliage for months in the summer. See *Achillea* 'Moonshine', p.188.

G 'Burgundy' blanket flower (use 3)
Large red daisylike flowers carpet this perennial's gray-green foliage in summer. See *Gaillardia* x *grandiflora* 'Burgundy', p. 214.

H Wooly thyme (use 1 to 2 flats of six-packs)
Planted randomly between the pavers, the aromatic gray-green foliage of this perennial is topped by small pink flowers in summer. See *Thymus pseudolanginosus*, p. 245.

I Pots
Potted plants accent the design. We've shown two sizes. In the larger are feather reed grass, *Calamagrostis* 'Overdam', p. 230; the smaller pots contain the annuals lilac verbena and *Osteospermum* 'Lemon Symphony'. See Annuals, p. 190.

J Lattice Screens
Creating a sense of enclosure and privacy, these lattice-covered screens are made of cedar. See p. 280.

K Paving
Here we've shown large cement pavers set on a base of sand and gravel; the gaps between pavers are filled with fine gravel and, where thyme is planted, enough soil to root it in. See p. 259.

SITE: Sunny

SEASON: Summer.

CONCEPT: Plants and hardscape make a welcoming entry as well as a space for outdoor living.

B Blue oat grass

G 'Burgundy' blanket flower

D 'Victor Ruter' thrift

C 'Seafoam' artemisia

K Paving

See site plan for I.

PLANT PORTRAITS

A simple but lovely combination of plants, paving, and lattice-work screens lends beauty, shade, and privacy to this welcoming entry space.
- ● = First design, pp. 44–45.
- ▲ = Second design, pp. 46–47.

'Goldsturm' black-eyed Susan (*Rudbeckia fulgida*, p. 240) ●

Washington hawthorn (*Crataegus phaenopyrum*, p. 206) ●

Yellow columbine (*Aquilegia chrysantha*, p. 192) ●

'Burgundy' blanket flower (*Gaillardia* x *grandiflora* 'Burgundy', p. 214) ▲

An Eye-Catching Corner

BEAUTIFY A BOUNDARY WITH EASY-CARE PLANTS

The corner where your property meets your neighbor's and the sidewalk is often a kind of grassy no-man's-land. This design defines that boundary with a planting that can be enjoyed by both property owners, as well as by passersby. Good gardens make good neighbors, so we've used well-behaved, low-maintenance plants that won't make extra work for the person next door—or for you.

Because of its exposed location, remote from the house and close to the street, this is a less personal planting than those in more private and frequently used parts of your property. It is meant to be appreciated from a distance. Anchored by a small multitrunked tree, the planting is a bold patchwork of leaf colors and bright flowers. An existing fence provides scaffolding for a vigorous vine. While not intended as a barrier, the planting also provides a modest psychological, if not physical, screen from activity on the sidewalk and street.

Something is in bloom almost every month, producing flowers in red, orange, yellow, blue, or lavender. The foliage is nearly as colorful, with yellows, maroon, reds, and grays as well as green. Scented flowers and tasty fruit make a stroll to the planting worthwhile, too.

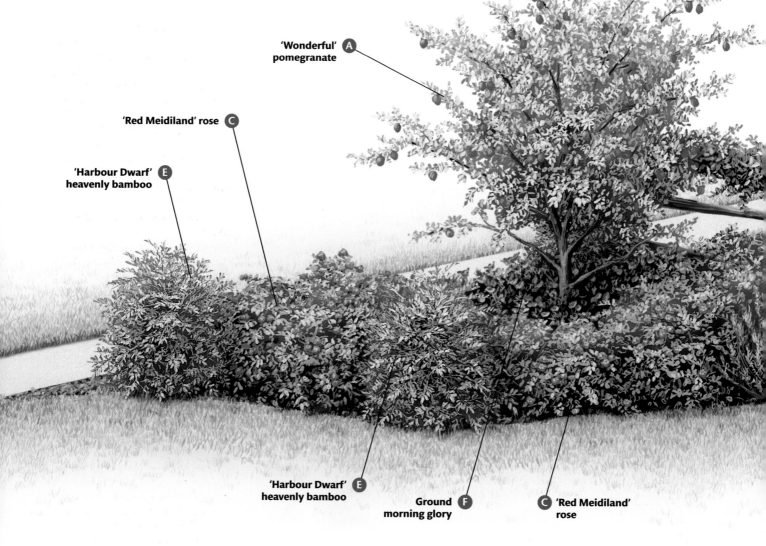

'Wonderful' pomegranate **A**

'Red Meidiland' rose **C**

'Harbour Dwarf' heavenly bamboo **E**

'Harbour Dwarf' heavenly bamboo **E**

Ground morning glory **F**

C 'Red Meidiland' rose

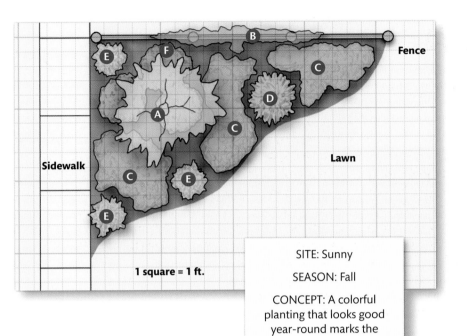

SITE: Sunny

SEASON: Fall

CONCEPT: A colorful planting that looks good year-round marks the property line in a neighborly fashion.

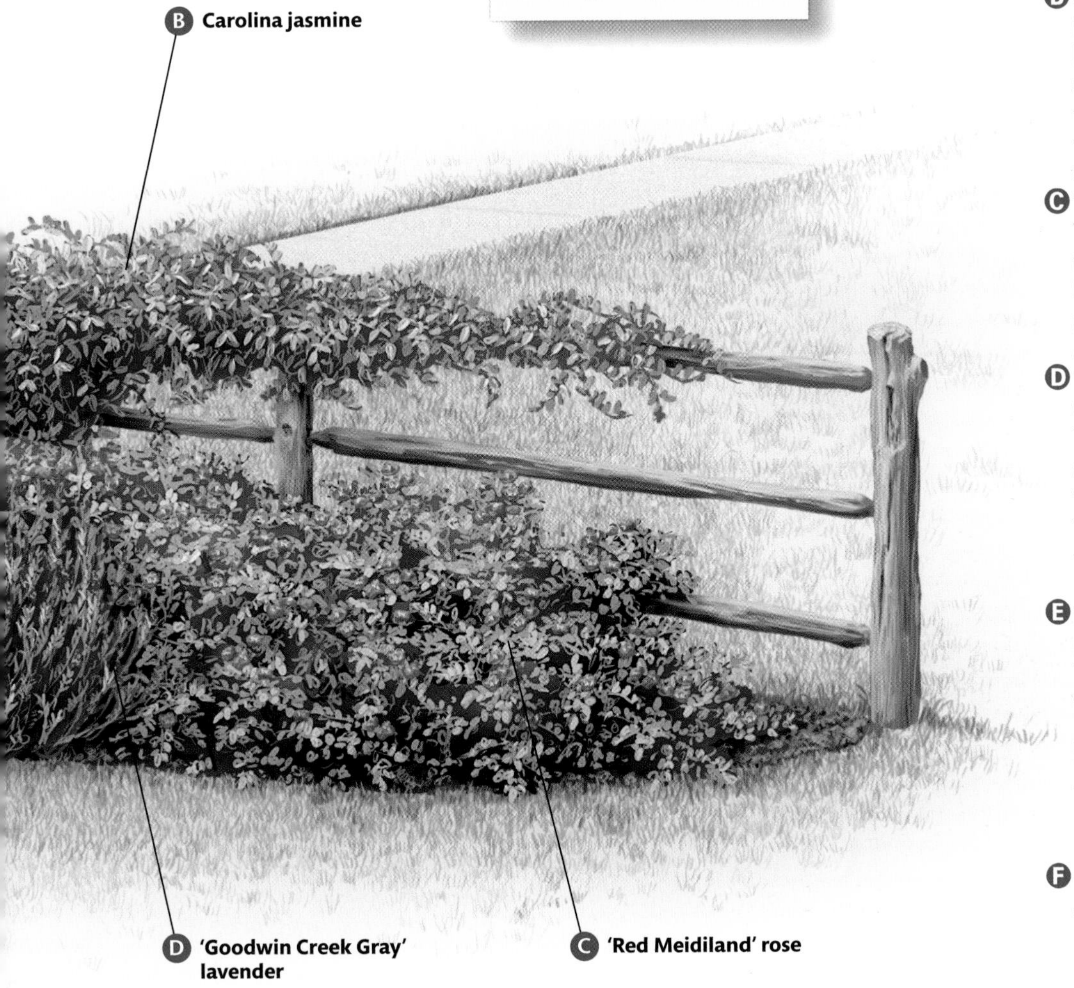

B Carolina jasmine

D 'Goodwin Creek Gray' lavender

C 'Red Meidiland' rose

Plants & Projects

As befits a planting some distance from the house, these durable, reliable plants require little care beyond seasonal pruning. Shear the morning glory and lavender after bloom to keep plants neat and compact. Trim the Carolina jasmine to control its size. Remove spent flowers from the roses. The plants withstand dry spells but do best with regular watering.

A 'Wonderful' pomegranate
(use 1 plant)
This popular deciduous fruit tree provides months of enjoyment. Spring's eye-catching orange-red flowers produce bright red edible fruits in fall. The fine-textured green foliage of summer turns yellow in autumn. The tree's multitrunked fountain shape is handsome in winter. See *Punica granatum*, p. 236.

B Carolina jasmine (use 1)
Draped over the fence, the evergreen leaves of this vigorous vine form a shiny dark green backdrop in summer, turning maroon in winter. Fragrant yellow flowers bloom in early spring. See *Gelsemium sempervirens*, p. 215.

C 'Red Meidiland' rose (use 3)
This sprawling shrub rose makes an effective and colorful ground cover. It bears white-centered red flowers in profusion for much of the year. See *Rosa*, p. 238.

D 'Goodwin Creek Gray' lavender
(use 1)
The gray-green leaves of this evergreen shrub are set off handsomely by the surrounding roses. In summer and fall, the foliage bristles with spikes of deep blue flowers. See *Lavandula*, p. 226.

E 'Harbour Dwarf' heavenly bamboo
(use 3)
This evergreen shrub bears fine-textured leaves that change from gold, to green, to red from spring through fall. Fluffy white flowers appear in summer, followed by a long-lasting crop of red berries. See *Nandina domestica*, p. 229.

F Ground morning glory (use 3)
A perennial ground cover, its soft gray-green leaves echo those of the lavender. It's sprinkled with cheerful lavender-blue flowers from summer through fall. See *Convolvulus mauritanicus*, p. 204.

VARIATIONS ON A THEME

These photos show a few of the numerous ways a planting, or an element in a planting, can catch the eye.

Large masses of brightly colored flowers don't so much catch the eye as grab it.

Set among fuzzy lamb's ears and fine-textured eulalia grass, a large terra-cotta pot makes a handsome accent.

A white picket fence is an ideal backdrop for the play of foliage color and texture in this planting.

Roses set the tone

The backbone of this planting is the popular 'Iceberg' rose, which provides clusters of beautiful and fragrant white flowers for months. Backed by an evergreen vine on the fence, the roses are at the center of a selection of colorful and durable perennials.

Once again, there are flowers for many months. Panicles of pinkish purple blossoms drape the vine-covered fence in late winter. The summer offers the most variety. Blanketflowers, daylilies, and salvias combine bold oranges, reds, yellows, and blues—a display that is eye-catching whether viewed at a distance or close up.

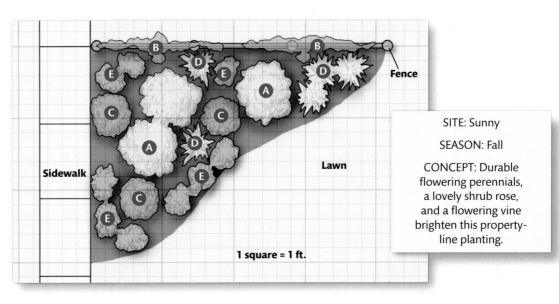

SITE: Sunny

SEASON: Fall

CONCEPT: Durable flowering perennials, a lovely shrub rose, and a flowering vine brighten this property-line planting.

1 square = 1 ft.

Plants & Projects

Ⓐ 'Iceberg' rose (use 3 plants) Fragrant white flowers are displayed against mounds of light green foliage. Blooms from spring through fall; off and on throughout the year in warm-winter areas. See *Rosa*, p. 238.

Ⓑ 'Happy Wanderer' hardenbergia (use 2) This vigorous vine engulfs the fence in fine-textured evergreen foliage. Bears pinkish purple flowers in late winter and early spring. See *Hardenbergia violacea*, p. 217.

Ⓒ Blanketflower (use 3) The cheerful red-and-orange daisylike blooms of this perennial wildflower accent the planting all summer. See *Gaillardia* x *grandiflora*, p. 214.

Ⓓ Daylily (use 5) Distinctive flowers rise on tall stems above the grassy foliage of these popular perennials. Choose varieties that bloom at different times to extend the season. Foliage is attractive when the plants aren't blooming. See *Hemerocallis*, p. 218.

Ⓔ Salvia (use 9) This perennial forms a patch of upright, dark green, leafy stems topped all summer with spikes of dark bluish purple flowers. See *Salvia* x *superba*, p. 241.

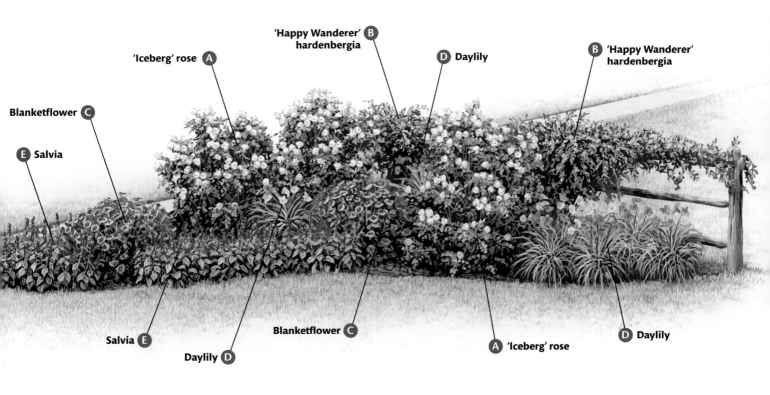

A Neighborly Corner

ADD INTEREST TO A VERY PUBLIC PART OF YOUR PROPERTY

This planting also addresses the requirements of a site usually located some distance from the house. Its plants are large enough to be enjoyed from a front-room window, while requiring relatively few visits each season to keep them looking their best.

Something is in bloom from spring through fall. The blue flowers of the rosemary start things off in late winter, followed by blooms in white, deep blue, and yellow from the serviceberry, lilac, and honeysuckle.

From early summer on, flowers of woadwaxen, senecio, coneflower and crocosmia mingle with foliage in an attractive variety of colors and textures. The serviceberry leaves provides a blaze of color in fall, while evergreen plants ensure a year-round presence.

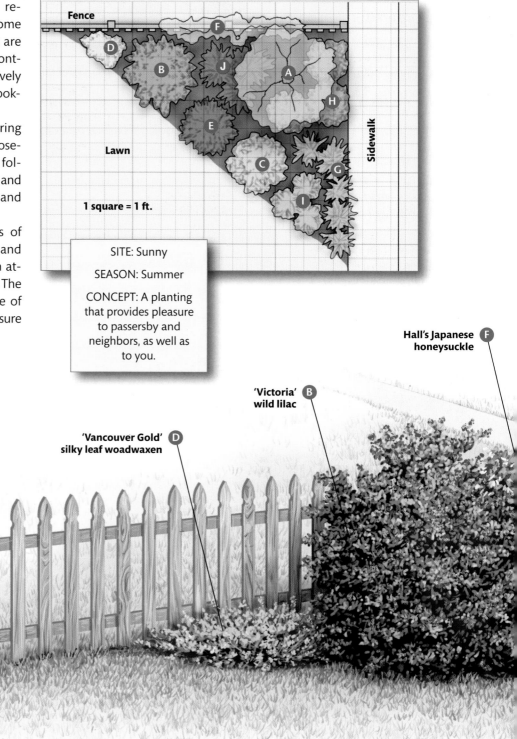

Fence

Lawn

1 square = 1 ft.

Sidewalk

SITE: Sunny

SEASON: Summer

CONCEPT: A planting that provides pleasure to passersby and neighbors, as well as to you.

Hall's Japanese honeysuckle F

'Victoria' wild lilac B

'Vancouver Gold' silky leaf woadwaxen D

Plants & Projects

Site preparation and planting account for most of the effort you'll spend on this planting over the years. As they reach maturity, the shrubs and vine may need occasional pruning to control size.

Ⓐ 'Autumn Brilliance' service-berry (use 1 plant)
This small deciduous tree is a three-season performer, with white flowers in spring, blue berries in summer, and colorful foliage in fall. See *Amelanchier* x *grandiflora*, p. 191.

Ⓑ 'Victoria' wild lilac (use 1)
In spring, this evergreen shrub displays small deep blue flowers at the ends of its branches. Small, glossy dark green leaves make an effective background. See *Ceanothus*, p. 200.

Ⓒ Grey's senecio (use 1)
Grown primarily for its soft gray foliage, this evergreen shrub bears pretty yellow flowers in summer. Bloom is unreliable. Flowers are sometimes sheared off, as shown here, to emphasize the foliage. See *Senecio greyi*, p. 242.

Ⓓ 'Vancouver Gold' silky leaf woadwaxen (use 1)
A low deciduous ground cover whose twiggy matlike stems are covered with tiny green leaves. In late spring and early summer it bears a mass of bright yellow pealike flowers. See *Genista pilosa*, p. 216.

Ⓔ 'Tuscan Blue' rosemary (use 3)
This evergreen shrub has fragrant gray-green leaves. Periwinkle blue flowers bloom in late winter and sporadically the rest of the year. See *Rosmarinus officinalis*, p. 240.

Ⓕ Hall's Japanese honeysuckle (use 1)
A vigorous semievergreen vine with dull green leaves. Late-spring flowers are trumpet-shaped and turn from yellow to white with age. See *Lonicera japonica* 'Halliana', p. 227.

Ⓖ Blue oat grass (use 5)
This evergreen grass forms a clump bristling with thin pale blue leaves. Trim off the sparse flower spikes, as shown here, if you wish. See *Helictotrichon sempervirens*, p. 230.

Ⓗ 'Powis Castle' artemisia (use 3)
A perennial, this forms a spreading mound of deeply cut silvery leaves that adds a striking accent to the planting. See *Artemisia*, p. 193.

Ⓘ 'Goldsturm' coneflower (use 3)
From summer into fall this perennial's daisylike flowers rise on sturdy stems above clumps of green leaves. Flowers are yellow with dark centers. See *Rudbeckia*, p. 240.

Ⓙ 'Lucifer' crocosmia (use 3)
This perennial forms attractive clumps of sword-shaped leaves. In summer, bright red-orange flowers line the ends of tall branched stems. See *Crocosmia*, p. 206.

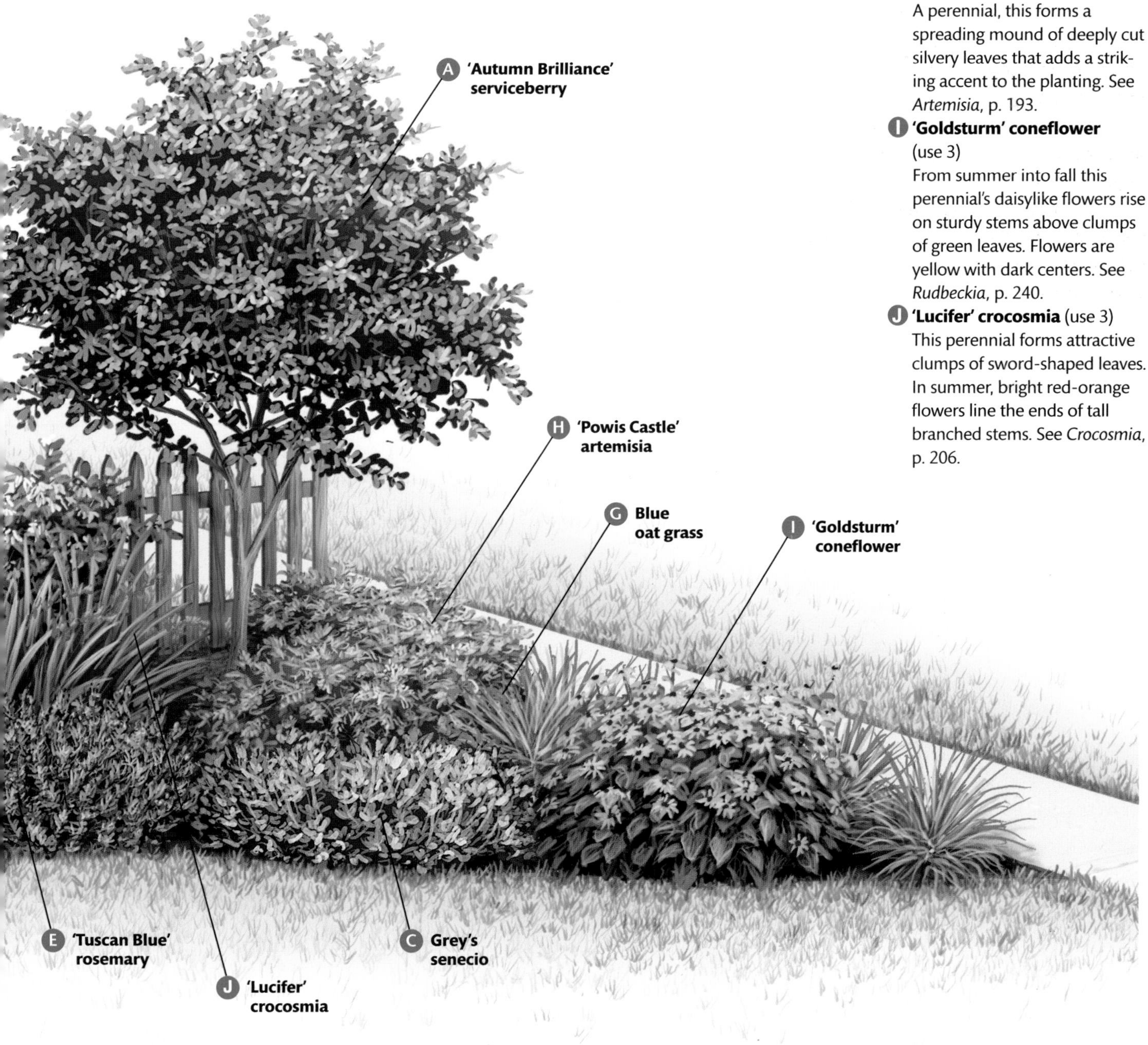

Ⓐ 'Autumn Brilliance' serviceberry

Ⓗ 'Powis Castle' artemisia

Ⓖ Blue oat grass

Ⓘ 'Goldsturm' coneflower

Ⓔ 'Tuscan Blue' rosemary

Ⓙ 'Lucifer' crocosmia

Ⓒ Grey's senecio

A winter full of flowers

Like the previous design, this one provides a handsome mix of foliage and flowers, but for a shady site. Again, low maintenance and year-round interest are priorities. To relieve the dreary days of the rainy season, this planting offers a lovely, often fragrant, array of flowers from fall to spring.

A large deciduous viburnum anchors the design, while evergreen or nearly evergreen plants fill out the space. Foliage colors and textures take center stage from late spring through fall. Mounding and spreading shrubs are accented by lacy fern fronds and sword-leaved irises. The dominant flower colors are pink and white. Adding highlights are splashes of yellow barrenwort and magenta geranium blossoms, along with the bright orange-red seedpods of the Gladwin irises.

Plants & Projects

A 'Dawn' viburnum (use 1 plant)
A large deciduous shrub with very fragrant pink flowers from fall into spring, peaking in late winter. Its dark green leaves turn scarlet in fall. See *Viburnum* x *bodnantense*, p. 246.

B David viburnum (use 1)
This compact evergreen shrub has leathery dark green leaves. In spring, pink buds open into flat-topped clusters of white flowers. See *Viburnum davidii*, p. 246.

C 'Apple Blossom' sasanqua camellia (use 1)
Trained along the fence, this shrub displays pink-and-white flowers against a backdrop of glossy evergreen leaves from late fall into winter. See *Camellia sasanqua*, p. 198.

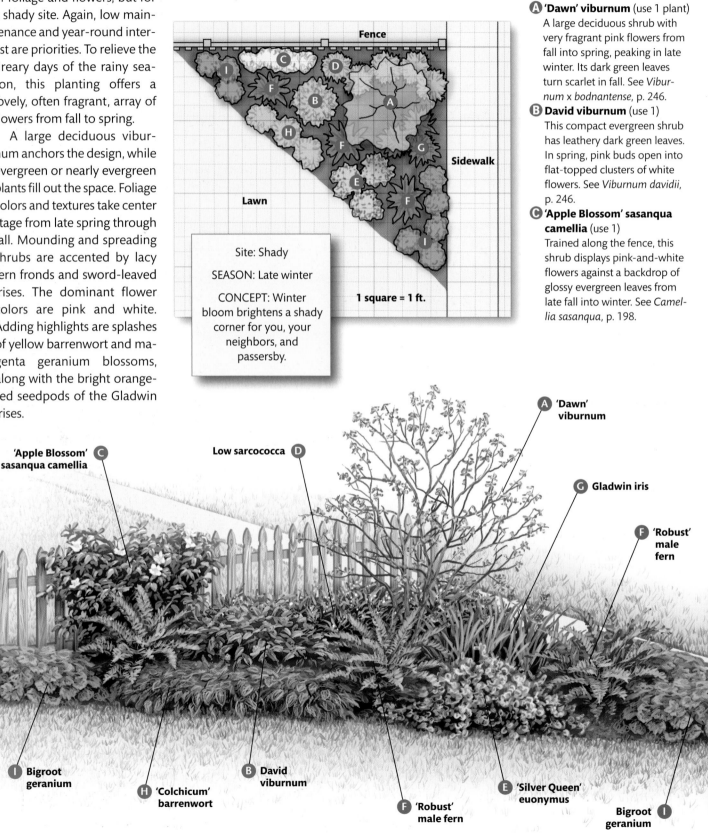

Fence

Sidewalk

Lawn

1 square = 1 ft.

Site: Shady

SEASON: Late winter

CONCEPT: Winter bloom brightens a shady corner for you, your neighbors, and passersby.

'Apple Blossom' C
sasanqua camellia

Low sarcococca D

A 'Dawn' viburnum

G Gladwin iris

F 'Robust' male fern

I Bigroot geranium

H 'Colchicum' barrenwort

B David viburnum

F 'Robust' male fern

E 'Silver Queen' euonymus

Bigroot I geranium

D Low sarcococca (use 5)
This low, spreading evergreen shrub bears tiny white flowers that nestle at the base of its green lancelike leaves. Blooms in late winter. See *Sarcococca humilis*, p. 242.

E 'Silver Queen' euonymus (use 3)
Another low-growing evergreen, this shrub has small, white-edged green leaves that take on a pink tinge in winter. See *Euonymus fortunei*, p. 210.

F 'Robust' male fern (use 3)
A graceful bright green fern. Its lacy evergreen fronds do well in winter conditions. See Ferns: *Dryopteris* x *complexa*, p. 212.

G Gladwin iris (use 3)
This perennial forms a clump of glossy upright leaves and bears clusters of purple flowers in summer. Long-lasting pods follow, splitting to reveal bright orange-red seeds. See *Iris foetidissima*, p. 222.

H 'Colchicum' barrenwort (use 3)
This perennial ground cover is prized for its heart-shaped evergreen foliage, which changes color with the seasons. Bears yellow flowers in spring. See *Epimedium pinnatum*, p. 209.

I Bigroot geranium (use 8)
Bushy clumps of colorful and fragrant semievergreen foliage distinguish this perennial. Late-spring flowers are magenta or purple. See *Geranium macrorrhizum*, p. 216.

PLANT PORTRAITS

Viewed from house, sidewalk, or street, these easy-care plants provide good-looking foliage and flowers year-round.
● = First design, pp. 52–53.
▲ = Second design, pp. 54–55.

Apple Blossom' sasanqua camellia (*Camellia sasanqua*, p. 198) ▲

'Dawn' viburnum (*Viburnum* x *bodnantense*, p. 246) ▲

Hall's Japanese honeysuckle (*Lonicera japonica* 'Halliana', p. 227) ●

Blue oat grass (*Helictotrichon sempervirens*, p. 230) ●

Gladwin iris (*Iris foetidissima*, p.222) ▲

'Powis Castle' Artemisia (*Artemisia*, p. 193) ●

On the Street

GIVE YOUR CURBSIDE STRIP A NEW LOOK

Homeowners seldom give a thought to the part of their property adjacent to the street. Often bounded by a sidewalk, this area is at best a tidy patch of lawn and at worst a weed-choked eyesore. Yet this is one of the most public parts of many properties. Filling this strip with attractive plants and paths from street to walkway can give pleasure to passersby and visitors who park next to the curb, as well as enhancing the streetscape you view from the house. (Curbside strips are usually city owned, so check local ordinances for restrictions before you start a remake.)

This can be a difficult site, subject to summer drought and heat, pedestrian and car traffic, and errant dogs. Plants need to be tough and drought tolerant to perform well here. (Water-conserving plantings in curbside areas are encouraged by many towns and cities.)

The plants in this design meet both criteria. And they look good, too. Though there are many flowers from late winter to early summer, foliage is the main event here. In shades of silver, gray, green, blue, and striking purple and an equal variety of textures, the foliage provides interest throughout the year. Two paths afford access from cars parked on the street. If your curbside property doesn't include a sidewalk, you can extend the planting farther into the yard and connect the paths to the walkway to your front door.

> SITE: Sunny
>
> SEASON: Spring
>
> CONCEPT: Plants with striking foliage transform an often neglected area and treat visitors and passersby to a colorful display.

Dwarf daffodil **I**

Creeping thyme **K**

'Tuscan Blue' **B** rosemary

Blue oat grass **E**

Plants & Projects

Once established, these plants require very little care. You can lightly shear the Russian sage and rosemary after bloom and the ground morning glory in midwinter. Trim the thyme to keep it out of the path. In late winter, cut the Russian sage to short stubs and run your fingers through the blue oat grass to remove dead leaves.

A **Feathery cassia** (use 1 plant)
This evergreen shrub forms an airy clump of gray needlelike foliage. Bears small sulphur yellow flowers from late winter through spring. See *Cassia artemisioides*, p. 243.

B **'Tuscan Blue' rosemary** (use 4)
An upright evergreen shrub with aromatic gray-green foliage marks two corners of the planting. Deep blue flowers bloom in late winter. See *Rosmarinus officinalis*, p. 240.

C **'Crimson Pygmy' Japanese barberry** (use 5)
This low-growing deciduous shrub adds color at the curb. Foliage is purple through the summer and turns a rich crimson in fall. See *Berberis thunbergii*, p. 194.

D **Russian sage** (use 6)
With straight stems and small, light gray leaves, this perennial is a wispy presence. Its delicate lavender-blue flowers complement the form and foliage perfectly all summer. See *Perovskia atriplicifolia*, p. 233.

F **Snow-in-summer**

E **Blue oat grass** (use 6)
This evergreen perennial's spiky mounds of thin blue leaves look striking next to nearby foliage. See *Helictotrichon sempervirens*, p. 230.

F **Snow-in-summer** (use 16)
A perennial ground cover, its silvery leaves are covered with small white flowers in late

spring to early summer. See *Cerastium tomentosum*, p. 201.

G **Ground morning glory** (use 7)
Edging the sidewalk, this perennial spreads to form a cushion of soft gray-green leaves. Bears pretty lavender-blue flowers from summer into fall. See *Convolvulus mauritanicus*, p. 204.

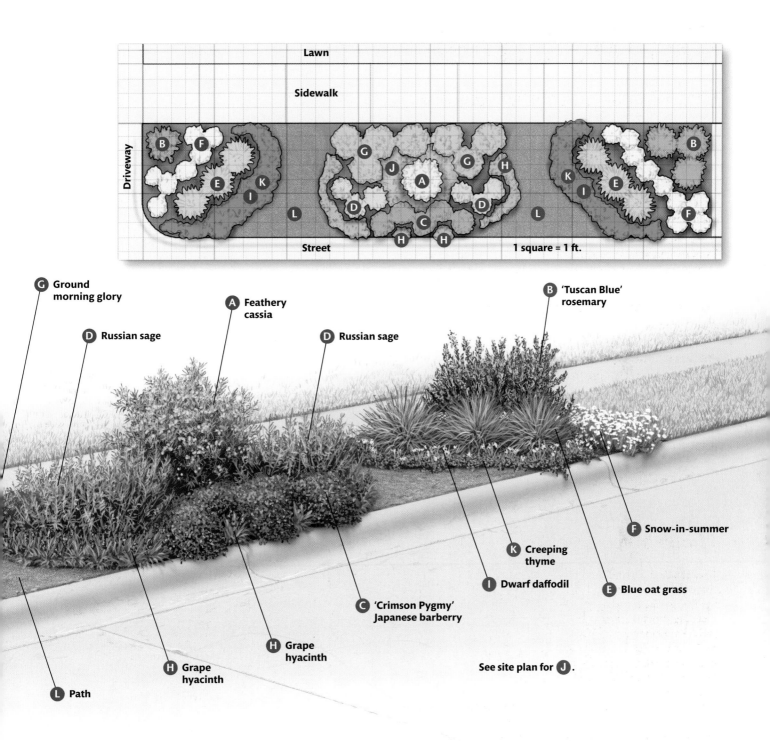

G Ground morning glory

D Russian sage

A Feathery cassia

D Russian sage

B 'Tuscan Blue' rosemary

F Snow-in-summer

K Creeping thyme

I Dwarf daffodil

E Blue oat grass

C 'Crimson Pygmy' Japanese barberry

H Grape hyacinth

H Grape hyacinth

See site plan for **J**.

L Path

H Grape hyacinth (use 180)
The fragrant blue flowers of this little bulb edge the path in spring. Grassy leaves are dormant in summer and appear again in fall. See Bulbs: *Muscari armeniacum*, p. 196.

I Dwarf daffodil (use 120)
A small version of the popular bulb, these perky flowers enliven the path in spring. Choose from a variety of dwarf cultivars, such as the yellow 'Tête-à-Tête' shown here. Foliage will grow through the thyme planted in the same space and die back after bloom. See Bulbs: *Narcissus*, p.196.

J Blue allium (use 28)
Blooming in June, after the daffodils, these bulbs produce balls of blue flowers held on erect stems above grassy foliage. See Bulbs: *Allium caeruleum*, p. 196.

K Creeping thyme (use 20)
This perennial herb spreads to form low-growing mats of pungent dark green foliage along the path. It can bear light foot traffic. See *Thymus praecox* ssp. *arcticus*, p. 245.

L Path
Decomposed granite or crushed rock laid on a sand-and-gravel base makes a durable, easily maintained surface. See p. 258.

VARIATIONS ON A THEME

An attractive selection of readily available low-growing shrubs and perennials is tough enough to thrive in demanding streetside conditions.

Clump-forming ornamental grasses highlight this durable and colorful planting at the curb.

These brightly colored perennials and shrubs are as easy to appreciate when you're going 35 miles per hour as they are at a stroll.

Here, a single planting is split by a sidewalk. Low-growing perennials and spreading shrubs keep sight lines open between the sidewalk and street.

A curbside stroll garden

In this design, paths and steppingstones allow visitors emerging from a car to move directly to the sidewalk or to meander and enjoy the planting. As in the previous design, the evergreen and long-lasting deciduous foliage of small shrubs and perennials is attractive year-round, mixing shades of green, gray, and red. From spring through fall, there are colorful flowers. Those of the English lavender are fragrant and, with its aromatic leaves, will encourage lingering along the path.

This is also a low-maintenance, low-water-use planting, requiring little more than shearing off spent flowers. Or, better yet, cut and dry the flowers and seed heads of yarrow, lavender, and fountain grass for long-lasting arrangements.

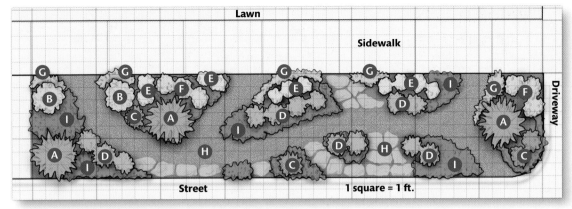

Plants & Projects

A Purple fountain grass (use 3 plants)
This ornamental grass offers reddish brown leaves that turn gold or tan in fall. Bronze seed heads arch above the foliage from midsummer. See *Pennisetum setaceum* 'Rubrum', p. 230.

B 'Moonshine' yarrow (use 2)
Attractive clumps of silvery green foliage give this perennial a year-round interest. Flat clusters of tiny golden yellow flowers top the foliage in summer. See *Achillea*, p. 188.

C 'Otto Quast' Spanish lavender (use 4)
An evergreen shrub with fragrant gray-green foliage and showy spikes of dark lavender flowers in early summer. See *Lavandula stoechas*, p. 226.

D 'Munstead' English lavender (use 13)
Shorter than its nearby relative, this lavender produces spikes of wonderfully fragrant dark blue flowers in early summer. See *Lavandula angustifolia*, p. 226.

E Santa Barbara daisy (use 11)
A perennial with airy low-growing foliage, it bears small whitish pink daisylike flowers from spring through fall. See *Erigeron karvinskianus*, p. 209.

F 'Nana' heavenly bamboo (use 6)
The fine-textured evergreen foliage of this dwarf shrub changes colors with the seasons; its fiery red leaves are particularly striking in winter. See *Nandina domestica*, p. 229.

G Golden garlic (use 68)
Ball-shaped yellow flowers brighten the edges of the sidewalk in spring. This little bulb's grassy foliage looks good long after the flowers are gone. See Bulbs: *Allium moly*, p.196.

H Walkway
Flagstone steppingstones and a path of decomposed granite or crushed rock provide several avenues from street to sidewalk. See p. 258.

See p. 57 for the following:

I Creeping thyme (use 49)

SITE: Sunny

SEASON: Early summer

CONCEPT: Meandering paths encourage more leisurely enjoyment of the curbside planting.

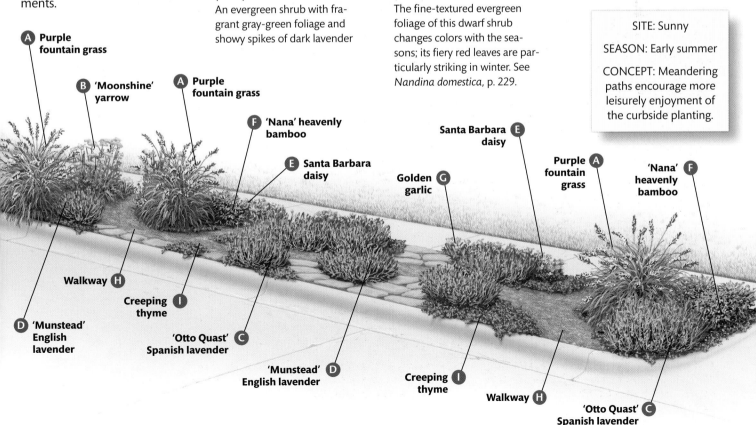

Streetwise and Stylish

MAKE A GEM OF A GARDEN IN AN UNLIKELY SPOT

SITE: Sunny

SEASON: Fall

CONCEPT: Eye-catching foliage and flowers provide enjoyment for arriving visitors and passersby while enhancing your overall landscape.

This curbside planting blazes from late winter to frost in the fall with flowers in rich deep colors. Rosemary, asters and verbena at the blue end of the spectrum are complemented by the red autumn sage and pink gaura. Yellow-flowered santolina and white yarrow round out the palette.

Foliage in a variety of complementary shades and texture, much of it evergreen, keeps the curbside looking attractive through winter. The gray santolina and silvery artemisia provide striking foliage accents.

The 4-ft.-wide path allows ample room for passengers getting in and out of a car. The interlocking pavers shown here are readily available and easy to install. Other surfaces—brick, crushed rock, and concrete—work equally well.

The planting is easily extended beside a longer walk; you can expand the areas covered by each group of plants or repeat the design one or more times.

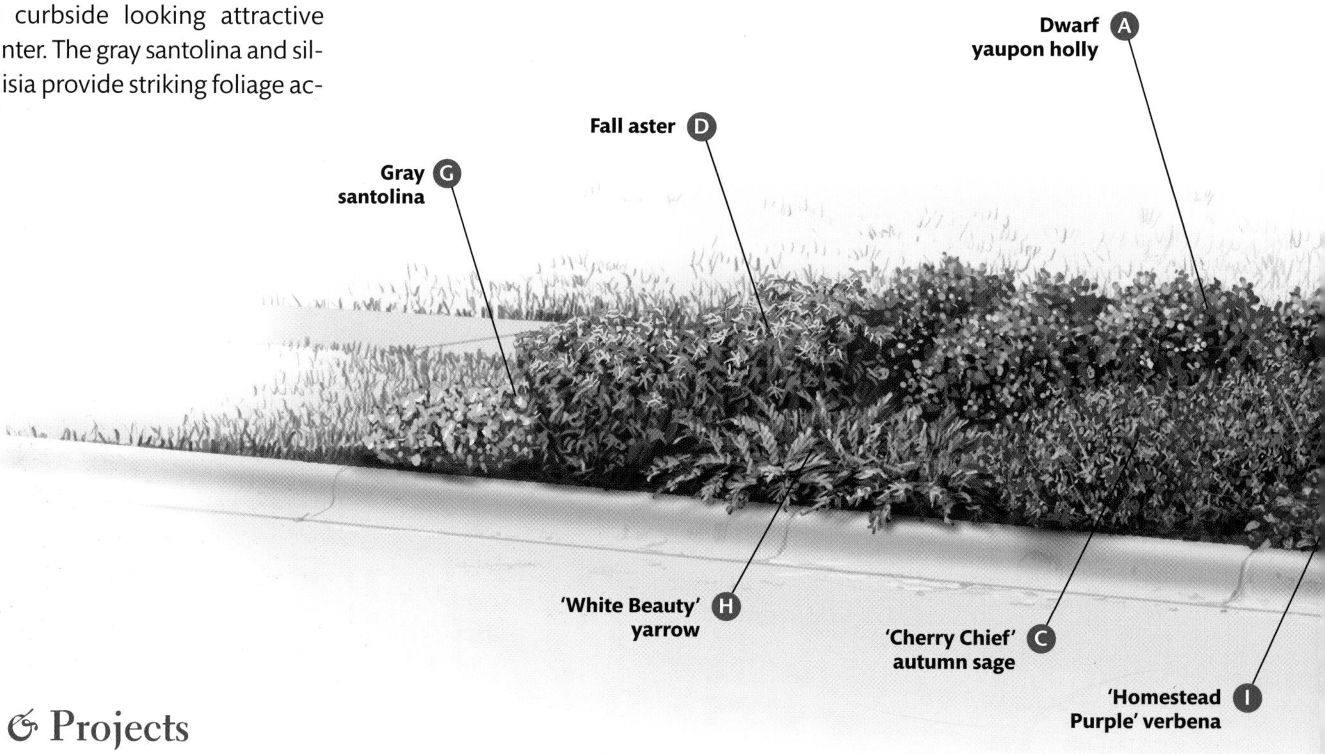

Dwarf yaupon holly (A)

Fall aster (D)

Gray santolina (G)

'White Beauty' yarrow (H)

'Cherry Chief' autumn sage (C)

'Homestead Purple' verbena (I)

Plants & Projects

These plants are easily maintained and easy on water. You can shear off spent flowers, or, better yet, cut and dry the sage, santolina, and rosemary flowers for long-lasting arrangements. An occasional trim will keep the artemisia tidy. Prune the gaura to the ground after a freeze. Cut back the old stems of santolina in early spring.

(A) Dwarf yaupon holly
(use 5 plants)
This evergreen shrub forms a dense, rounded globe of tiny, spineless, oval leaves that never need shearing. See *Ilex vomitoria* 'Nana', p. 222.

(B) 'Hill's Hardy' rosemary (use 2)
Fine texture and fragrance distinguish both the foliage and flowers of this upright evergreen shrub. Blue flowers arrive in early spring. See *Rosmarinus officinalis*, p. 240.

(C) 'Cherry Chief' autumn sage
(use 3)
This bushy perennial's small oval leaves echo the holly's foliage, but are softer and paler. Small red flowers bloom heavily in spring and lightly in summer and fall. See *Salvia greggii* 'Cherry Chief', p. 241.

(D) Fall aster (use 3)
Lavender-purple daisies literally blanket this carefree perennial's small dull green leaves in early summer. See *Aster oblongifolius*, p. 193.

(E) 'Dauphin' gaura (use 3)
With straight stems rising from a base of small pale green leaves and delicate pink and white flowers, this tall perennial adds an airy presence to the planting. See *Gaura lindheimeri* 'Dauphin', p. 215.

(F) 'Powis Castle' artemisia
(use 4)
Prized for its foliage, this peren-

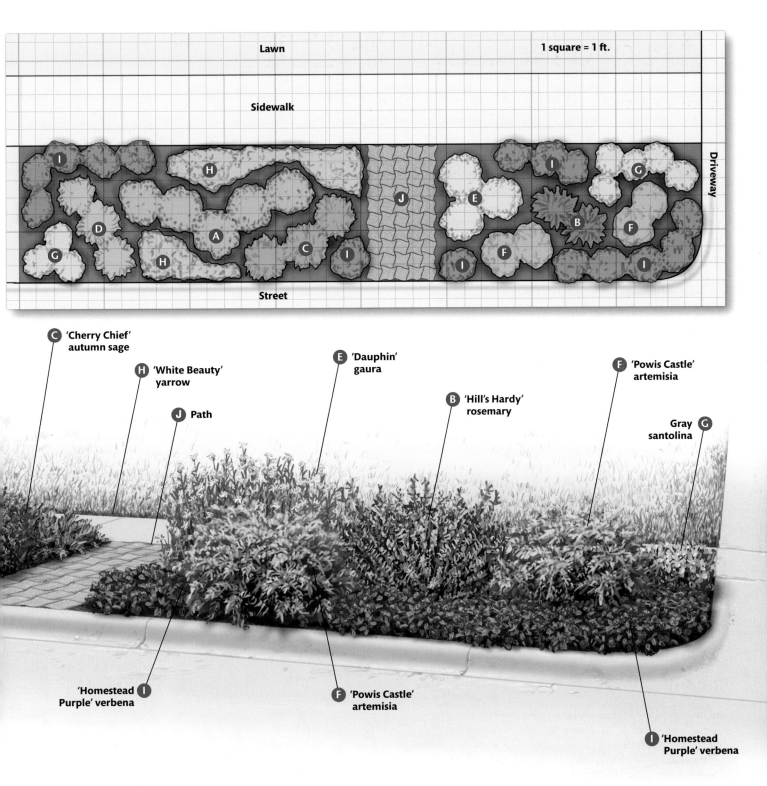

C **'Cherry Chief'** autumn sage

H **'White Beauty'** yarrow

J **Path**

E **'Dauphin'** gaura

B **'Hill's Hardy'** rosemary

F **'Powis Castle'** artemisia

G Gray santolina

'Homestead Purple' verbena I

F **'Powis Castle'** artemisia

I **'Homestead Purple'** verbena

nial forms a dense billowing mound of very fine silvery leaves. See *Artemisia* x 'Powis Castle', p. 193.

G **Gray santolina** (use 8)
This perennial spreads to form a cushion of fragrant leaves along the curb. Bears yellow flowers in summer. See *Santolina chamaecyparissus*, p. 242.

H **'White Beauty' yarrow** (use 13)
Clusters of flat, pure white flowers of this mat-forming perennial edge the walk in spring. Ferny, aromatic leaves are gray-green all year. See *Achillea millefolium* 'White Beauty', p. 188.

I **'Homestead Purple' verbena** (use 15)
This perennial's deeply cut bright green leaves and masses of purple flowers will enliven the curbside from spring to frost. See *Verbena* x *hybrida* 'Homestead Purple', p. 246.

J **Path**
Interlocking pavers create an attractive, durable, and easily maintained surface. The gray paver shown here ties in with the sidewalk, street, and planting. See p. 259.

Branching out

A small tree and a branching path distinguish this design and give it an informal appeal. The evergreen and long-lasting deciduous foliage of the shrubs and perennials is colorful year-round, mixing shades of green, gray, red, and purple. Flowers in white, pink, and yellow complement the foliage and are pretty in their own right.

Like the previous design, this one is a low-maintenance, low-water-use planting. It requires little more than shearing off spent flowers, trimming back the lantana after a freeze, and lightly pruning the spirea and barberry to maintain their size and shape.

Plants & Projects

A **Wax myrtle** (use 1 plant)
A graceful shrub that can be pruned into a shapely multi-trunked tree. In most parts of Texas, foliage stays green through the winter. See *Myrica cerifera*, p. 228.

B **'Anthony Waterer' Japanese spirea** (use 1)
Clusters of pink flowers top the fine-leaved branches of this attractive deciduous shrub in summer. Needs only light shearing to keep its rounded shape. See *Spirea* x *bumalda* 'Anthony Waterer', p. 243.

C **Dwarf Japanese barberry** (use 6)
This compact shrub has arching branches crowded with small oval maroon-red leaves. See *Berberis thunbergii* 'Crimson Pygmy', p. 194.

D **Purple wintercreeper** (use 4)
This evergreen ground cover fills in the space with dark green leaves that turn red in winter. See *Euonymus fortunei* 'Coloratus', p. 210..

E **'Weeping White' trailing lantana** (use 13)
Clusters of pure white flowers cover this vigorous low-growing perennial from spring to fall. In mild-winter areas plant sometimes blooms all year. See *Lantana montevidensis* 'Weeping White', p. 225.

F **St. John's wort** (use 13)
Under the wax myrtle, this evergreen shrub creates a dense, fine-textured carpet, dotted in summer with bright yellow periwinkle-like flowers. Small oval leaves turn reddish purple in winter. See *Hypericum calycinum*, p. 221.

G **'Bath's Pink' dianthus** (use 7)
Delightfully fragrant pink flowers greet visitors in spring. The rest of the year this perennial's fine blue-green foliage attracts all the attention. See *Dianthus* 'Bath's Pink', p. 207.

See p. 61 for the following:

H **Path**

SITE: Sunny

SEASON: Summer

CONCEPT: Two streetside paths join up with colorful plantings to welcome visitors.

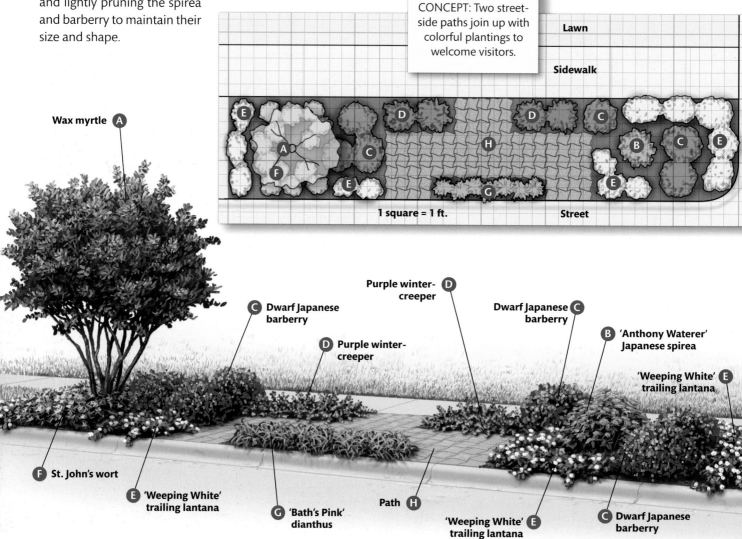

1 square = 1 ft.

PLANT PORTRAITS

These low-maintenance plants will improve any curbside area, while withstanding the rigors of life by the street.

● = First design, pp. 60–61.

▲ = Second design, pp. 62–63.

'Weeping White' Trailing lantana
(*Lantana montevidensis*, p.225) ▲

'Dauphin' Gaura
(*Gaura lindheimeri*, p. 215) ●

Dwarf Japanese barberry
(*Berberis thunbergii*, p. 194) ▲

'Anthony Waterer' Japanese spirea
(*Spirea* x *bumalda*, p. 243) ▲

'Bath's Pink' Dianthus
(*Dianthus*, p. 207) ▲

'Powis Castle' Artemisia
(*Artemisia*, p. 193) ●

Fall aster
(*Aster oblongifolius*, 193) ●

Landscape a Low Wall

A TWO-TIERED GARDEN REPLACES A BLAND SLOPE

Retaining wall Ⓙ
and steps

Some things may not love a wall, but plants and gardeners do. For plants, walls offer warmth for an early start in spring and good drainage for roots. Gardeners appreciate the rich visual potential of composing a garden on two levels, as well as the practical advantage of working on two relatively flat surfaces instead of a single sloping one.

This design places complementary plantings above and below a wall bounded at one end by a set of steps. While each bed is relatively narrow, when viewed from the lower level the two combine to form a border more than 10 ft. deep. Two other design features add depth to the display. A jog in the wall cre-

ates a niche for a splashy fountain grass, and the beds are rounded rather than linear. Together with a selection of billowy plants, these features soften the face of the wall and offer pleasing views from many vantage points.

Building the wall that makes this impressive sight possible doesn't require the time or skill it once did. Nor is it necessary to scour the countryside for tons of fieldstone or to hire an expensive contractor. Thanks to precast retaining-wall systems, anyone with a healthy back (or access to energetic teenagers) can install a knee-high do-it-yourself wall in as little as a weekend or two.

Plants & Projects

This planting showcases colorful flowers against curtains of soft, silvery green foliage. All the plants tolerate heat and drought and need little care to keep them at their best. Trim the autumn and mealycup sages lightly through summer to encourage new bloom. The Mexican bush sage and mint marigold will benefit from pruning in late spring and midsummer to keep them dense and full.

Ⓐ **'Gracillimus' Japanese maiden grass** (use 1 plant)
This perennial grass graces the steps with narrow arching leaves. Flowers rise another foot above the foliage in late summer. See *Miscanthus sinensis* 'Gracillimus', p. 230.

Ⓑ **Compact Texas sage** (use 3)
A native evergreen shrub with a billowy shape. It bears masses of orchid pink flowers in summer. See *Leucophyllum frutescens* 'Compactum', p.226.

Ⓒ **Mexican bush sage** (use 1)
This big bushy perennial anchors the end of the border and echoes the arching habit of the fountain grass. Slender branches bear gray-green foliage. In autumn, long wands of small purple and white flowers bloom from branch tips. See *Salvia leucantha*, p. 241.

Ⓓ **White autumn sage** (use 3)
This perennial forms a mat of small oval leaves that usually stay green all winter. A profusion of pure white flowers greets visitors at the steps from spring to fall. See *Salvia greggii* 'Alba', p. 241.

Ⓔ **Mealycup sage** (use 6)
A fringe of blue flower spikes top the narrow grayish leaves of this compact bushy perennial throughout the growing season. Bumblebees will buzz among the blooms. See *Salvia farinacea*, p. 241.

Ⓕ **Soft-tip yucca** (use 1)
This perennial forms an attractive rosette of succulent gray-blue leaves. It puts on a dazzling display of bloom in summer, when clusters of large creamy white bells rise from the center on sturdy stalks. See *Yucca gloriosa*, p. 249.

Ⓖ **Mexican mint marigold** (use 1)
This compact perennial has narrow, emerald green leaves topped with a profusion of small gold flowers. See *Tagetes lucida*, p. 245.

Ⓗ **Fall aster** (use 3)
In autumn, a solid mass of purple daisylike flowers makes this perennial a knockout in front of the gray foliage and white flow-

ers of the sage. See *Aster oblongifolius*, p. 193.

Ⓘ **'Blue Princess' verbena** (use 2)
Lavender-blue flowers blanket this low-growing perennial from spring through fall. It will spread wide enough to surround the yucca in a sea of bloom. See *Verbena* x *hybrida* 'Blue Princess', p. 246.

Ⓙ **Retaining wall and steps**
Prefabricated wall systems make this project easy to install. See p. 270.

Ⓚ **Path**
We've shown gravel here, but use any materials that complement the wall. See p. 259.

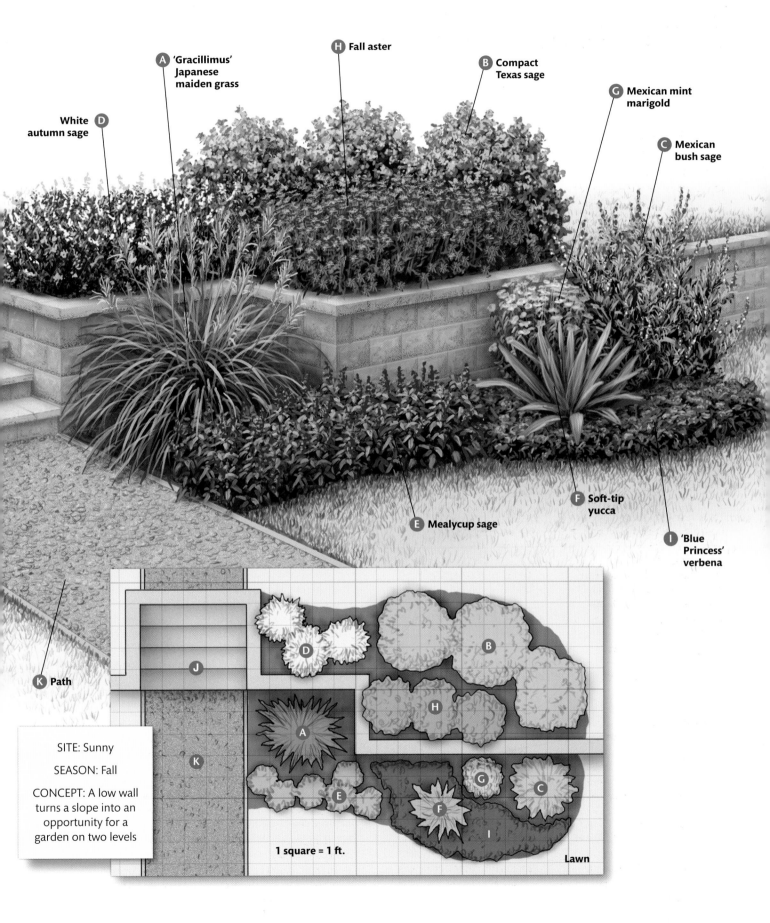

D White autumn sage

A 'Gracillimus' Japanese maiden grass

H Fall aster

B Compact Texas sage

G Mexican mint marigold

C Mexican bush sage

F Soft-tip yucca

E Mealycup sage

I 'Blue Princess' verbena

K Path

J

K

D

B

H

A

E

G

C

F

I

1 square = 1 ft.

Lawn

SITE: Sunny

SEASON: Fall

CONCEPT: A low wall turns a slope into an opportunity for a garden on two levels

PLANT PORTRAITS

These plants double the pleasure of a retaining wall with eye-catching flowers and handsome foliage.

● = First design, pp. 64–65.

▲ = Second design, pp. 66–67.

'Gracillimus' Japanese maiden grass (*Miscanthus sinensis,* p. 230) ●

Black mondo grass (*Ophiopogon planiscapus* 'Ebony Knight', p. 229) ▲

Soft-tip yucca (*Yucca gloriosa,* p. 249) ●

White autumn sage (*Salvia greggii* 'Alba', p. 241) ●

Two tiers in the shade

A retaining-wall planting can be equally alluring in a shady yard. This design uses the same wall-and-step system but keeps the wall straight and nestles the steps into the lawn. Bold shrubs on both levels break up the retaining wall's horizontal plane while bringing the garden together as a whole. The shade-loving plants are chosen for their colorful foliage and flowers in a contrasting palette of rosy purples, cool blues, and cheerful yellows.

Plants & Projects

Ⓐ Chinese fringe flower (use 1 plant)
This evergreen shrub is valued for its luxuriant fringe of dainty pink flowers and its layers of small purple leaves. Where soils are alkaline, substitute American beautyberry. See *Loropetalum chinense rubrum,* p.227.

Ⓑ Fatsia (use 1)
A bold and beautiful tropical-looking shrub. Glossy evergreen leaves will drape over the wall and nearby plants. See *Fatsia japonica,* p. 211.

Ⓒ American beautyberry (use 1)
This shrub wears a thick coat of pale green foliage most of the year. Clusters of eye-popping purple berries line the branches in late summer. See *Callicarpa americana,* p. 198.

Ⓓ Cast-iron plant (use 3)
An unusual and striking evergreen perennial, it has dark, strappy leaves that jut directly from the ground like giant exclamation points. See *Aspidistra elatior,* p. 193.

Ⓔ Holly fern (use 9)
These glossy stands of evergreen fronds will keep the garden lit up through dull winter months. See Ferns: *Cyrtomium falcatum,* p. 212.

Ⓕ Carolina jasmine (use 1)
In no time at all this vine will twine under the redbud and trail over the wall. Tiny lance-like evergreen leaves are almost hidden in spring by sweet-scented yellow flower bells. See *Gelsemium sempervirens,* p. 215.

Ⓖ Louisiana iris (use 3)
This perennial forms an erect clump of narrow arching leaves. Large flowers rise above the foliage in spring. Choose a complementary blue or lavender variety. See *Iris x Louisiana* hybrids, p. 222.

Ⓗ Texas gold columbine (use 3)
Plant this evergreen perennial at the front of the border to show off the attractive ferny foliage. Delicate yellow flowers with long spurs bloom in spring. See *Aquilegia chrysantha hinckleyana,* p. 192.

Ⓘ St. John's wort (use 3)
This semi-evergreen perennial makes a thick mat of miniature leaves that cascade over the wall. Small yellow flowers decorate the plant in summer. See *Hypericum calycinum,* p. 221.

Ⓙ Black mondo grass (use 15)
Slender purple-black leaves give this distinctive plant a bold look that also accents the other purples in the planting. See *Ophiopogon planiscapus* 'Ebony Knight', p. 229.

Ⓚ Dwarf Mexican petunia (use 6)
This low-growing perennial produces tufts of narrow, long, dark green leaves that are ideal for an informal edging. Slow to emerge in spring, this plant makes up time with a long season of purple bloom. The flowers are funnel-shaped and light purple. See *Ruellia brittoniana* 'Katie', p. 240.

Ⓛ Purple heart (use 1)
Given a chance, the succulent purple foliage of this mat-forming perennial will tumble decorously over the wall. See *Setcreasea pallida,* p. 243.

See p. 64 for the following:

Ⓜ Retaining wall and steps

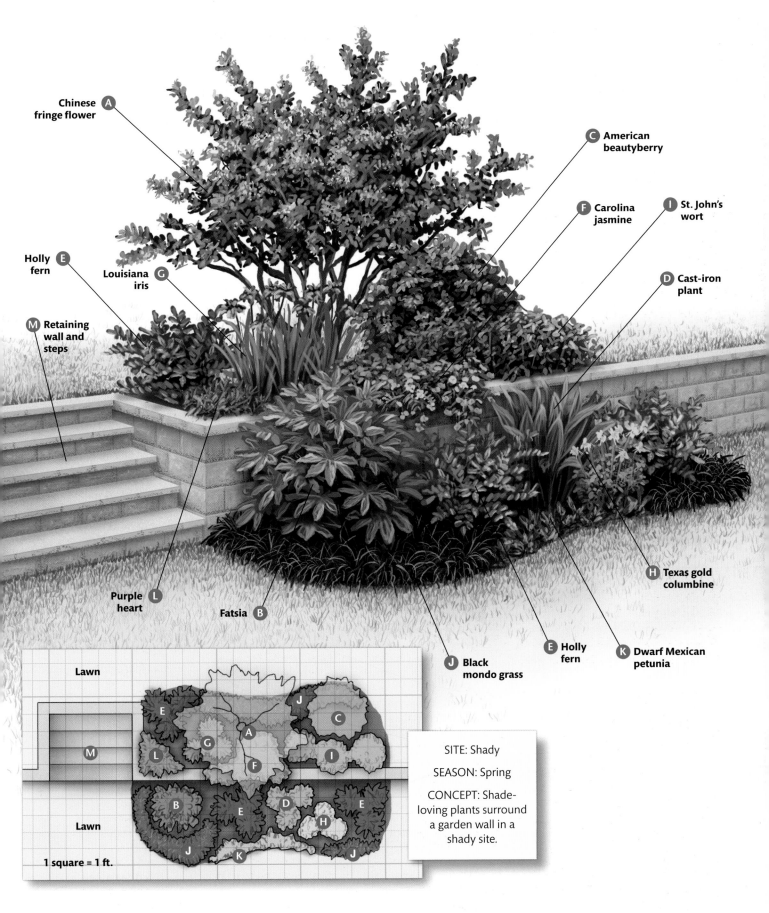

Chinese **A** fringe flower

C American beautyberry

F Carolina jasmine

I St. John's wort

Holly **E** fern

Louisiana **G** iris

D Cast-iron plant

M Retaining wall and steps

Purple **L** heart

Fatsia **B**

J Black mondo grass

E Holly fern

K Dwarf Mexican petunia

H Texas gold columbine

Lawn

Lawn

1 square = 1 ft.

SITE: Shady

SEASON: Spring

CONCEPT: Shade-loving plants surround a garden wall in a shady site.

Beautify a Blank Wall

A VERTICAL GARDEN MAKES THE MOST OF A NARROW SITE

Just as you can enhance a wall in your home with a painting, you can decorate a blank wall outdoors with plants. The design shown here transforms a nondescript front entrance by showcasing perennials, ferns, shrubs, and a small tree against an adjacent garage wall. Such entrances are common in suburban homes, but a vertical garden like this is ideal for other spots where yard space is limited.

Selected for a shady site, these plants offer something in every season. Most are evergreen, with foliage that looks fresh year-round. In fall, the maple's yellow leaves brighten the entrance.

The garden is at its flowering peak in early spring. The fragrant white flowers of tobira in spring and gardenia in summer greet visitors by the corner of the garage and at the front door. Adorning the wall are lovely camellias. The wall also serves as a backdrop for the striking red twigs of the coralbark maple, which highlight the graceful patterns of the tree's branches.

Camellia Ⓑ

'Cream de Mint' Ⓓ
tobira

SITE: Shady

SEASON: Early spring

CONCEPT: Handsome plants arrayed against a blank wall make a picture that pleases year-round.

Plants & Projects

Training the coralbark maple and the camellia are the most demanding aspects of this planting. As the maple grows, select horizontal branches that grow parallel to the wall and arch over the other plants. Prune to restrict growth toward the walk until the tree is tall enough that you can select branches to arch over the walkway. Train the camellia by attaching it to wire supports fixed to the wall. Prune the foliage so that it extends about 18 in. from the wall.

Ⓐ **Coralbark maple** (use 1 plant)
The fine-textured foliage of this small deciduous tree is light green in summer and yellow in fall. Its bright red twigs are eye-catching in winter and spring before the tree leafs out. See *Acer palmatum* 'Sango Kaku', p. 188.

Ⓑ **Camellia** (use 1)
Trained flat against the wall, the glossy foliage of this popular evergreen shrub is an ideal backdrop for its lovely flowers. Choose a cultivar with flower color and bloom time you like. Here we've shown the pink-flowered, early-spring-blooming 'Debutante'. See *Camellia japonica*, p. 198.

Ⓒ **'August Beauty' gardenia** (use 1)
This evergreen shrub's intensely fragrant white flowers perfume the entry in summer. Its shiny dark green foliage looks good year-round. See *Gardenia jasminoides*, p. 214.

Ⓓ **'Cream de Mint' tobira** (use 3)
Low-growing, with white-edged leaves, this dwarf evergreen shrub bears small clusters of fragrant creamy white flowers in early spring. See *Pittosporum tobira*, p. 234.

Ⓔ **Sword fern** (use 2)
A native of redwood forests, this evergreen fern forms a neat mound of shiny dark green fronds, just right for this narrow space. See Ferns: *Polystichum munitum*, p. 212.

Ⓕ **Hosta** (use 3)
Prized for its handsome foliage, this perennial also produces lavender, purple, or white flowers in summer. For this spot, choose a small cultivar with green or variegated foliage. See *Hosta*, p. 220.

Ⓖ **Lenten rose** (use 1)
This perennial has attractive toothed evergreen leaves and bears pink, rose, green, or white flowers on branched stems in early spring. See *Helleborus orientalis*, p. 217.

Ⓗ **Lamium** (use 21)
Two cultivars of this perennial ground cover are used here. Both have green-and-white foliage that is evergreen where winters are mild. 'White Nancy', with white flowers in summer, edges the front and end of the bed. 'Roseum' is planted at the back, between the sword ferns, where its rose-colored flowers catch the eye from late winter through fall. See *Lamium maculatum*, p. 224.

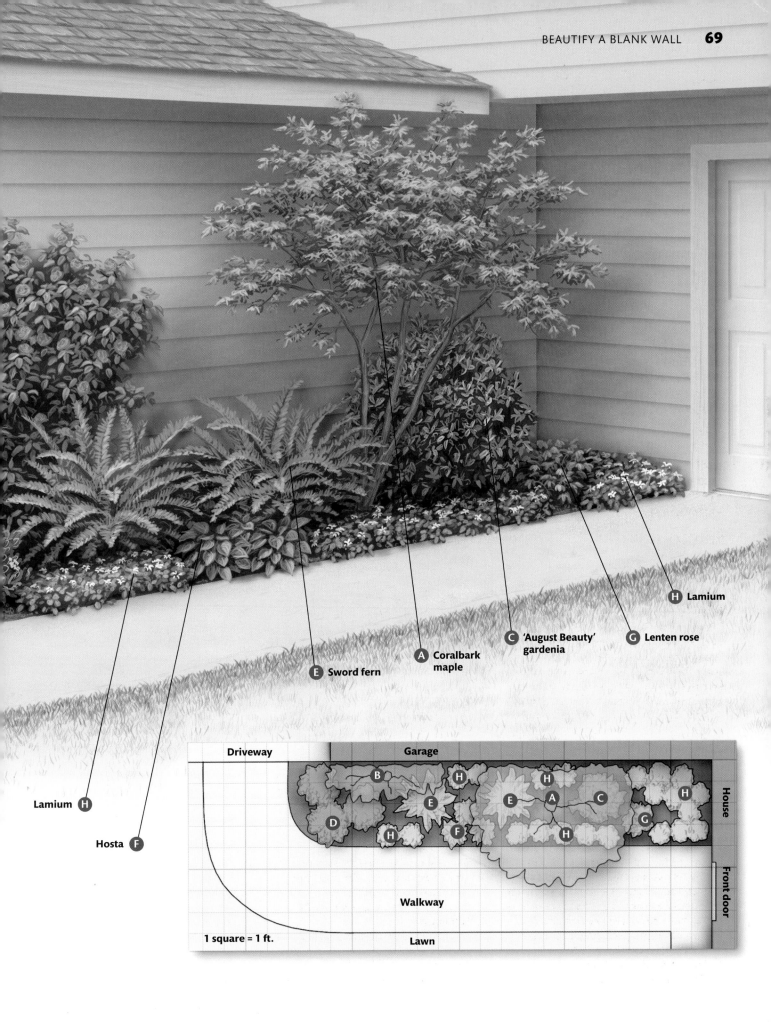

H Lamium

C 'August Beauty' gardenia

G Lenten rose

A Coralbark maple

E Sword fern

Lamium **H**

Hosta **F**

Driveway

Garage

House

Front door

Walkway

Lawn

1 square = 1 ft.

VARIATIONS ON A THEME

Running out of garden space? Here are some ideas to help you garden up as well as out.

Some climbing roses are capable of scaling great heights with the help of a trellis. Notice how the trellis continues above the windows. The roses will soon follow.

A giant stand of sunflowers is a playful way to decorate a wall. And birds can feast on the sunflower seeds in the fall.

Climbing pink and red roses produce a colorful abstract pattern on a clapboard wall.

Dressing up a sunny wall

A sunnier, hotter site, such as a south- or west-facing wall, calls for a different palette of plants. The basic idea of this design remains the same as before: incorporate wall space to make the best use of a narrow plot.

Arrayed on a handsome wooden trellis, the star of this planting is a vigorous bougainvillea. From spring through summer its hot pink flowers glow against the dense green foliage. The supporting cast of plants holds its own with a summerlong display of flowers in yellow, lilac, purple, and white. In spring and fall a dwarf pomegranate takes center stage with bright orange flowers and yellow foliage. After all this color, the planting offers enough foliage that is evergreen, or nearly evergreen, to make a handsome display in winter.

Plants & Projects

Ⓐ Fortnight lily (use 3 plants)
This striking perennial forms a clump of straplike evergreen leaves. Wiry stems bear white flowers with colorful markings from spring through fall. See *Dietes vegeta*, p. 208.

Ⓑ Dwarf pomegranate (use 1)
A dwarf deciduous tree, it makes a mound of shiny green leaves that turn yellow in autumn. Bright orange flowers in spring produce small inedible red fruits. See *Punica granatum* 'Nana', p. 236.

Ⓒ Bougainvillea (use 1)
A vigorous vine with hot pink flowers against a dense backdrop of evergreen. Train a vining type to a trellis. (In colder areas, substitute *Clematis montana*, pg. 204.) See *Bougainvillea*, p. 196.

Ⓓ Garden penstemon (use 3)
This perennial forms a patch of leafy upright stems topped from late spring to frost by distinctive tubular flowers that are available in a wide range of colors; coordinate your choice with the color of your wall. (In colder areas, substitute *Echium fatuosum*.) See *Penstemon gloxinioides*, p. 233.

Garden penstemon **D**

'Moonbeam' coreopsis **E**

G Star of Persia

B Dwarf pomegranate

I Trellis

C Bougainvillea

Fortnight lily **A**

F Snow-in-summer

See site plan for **H**.

E **'Moonbeam' coreopsis** (use 8)
A perennial, its neat mound of fine-textured, dark green foliage is covered for months in summer and fall with small bright yellow flowers. See *Coreopsis verticillata*, p. 205.

F **Snow-in-summer** (use 11)
The silvery evergreen foliage of this perennial will brighten the corner by the door. In early summer, small white flowers completely cover the low-growing foliage. See *Cerastium tomentosum*, p. 201.

G **Star of Persia** (use 12)
Eye-catching spherical clusters of rich lilac flowers hover above this bulb's straplike leaves in early summer. See Bulbs: *Allium christophii*, p. 196.

H **Round-headed garlic** (use 72)
With long, thin leaves and smaller clusters of red-purple flowers, this bulb is attractive but less spectacular than star of Persia. See Bulbs: *Allium sphaerocephalum*, p. 196.

I **Trellis**
You can support the bougainvillea with the homemade trellis shown here, or buy one at a garden center. See p. 280.

SITE: Sunny

SEASON: Summer

CONCEPT: Basking against a sunny wall, a vine, perennials, and shrubs offer a warm welcome at the front door.

Driveway   Garage

Walkway

Lawn   1 square = 1 ft.   House

Front door

The Vertical Garden

CLIMBING PLANTS AND IMAGINATION MAKE A LOT OF GARDEN IN A LITTLE SPACE

Gardening space is often limited in new housing developments and in condominiums. Growing plants up, rather than out is often the best solution for a frustrated gardener with too little space. An entryway garden like this one satisfies the gardening urge and provides a friendly welcome at your front door.

Selected for a sunny site, these plants produce flowers spring through fall, and evergreen shrubs provide fresh-looking foliage year-round. The garden is at its flowering peak in early and midsummer, with blooms in yellow, blue, purple, and red. The flowers and foliage of the two lavenders offer fragrance as well. Two trellises laden with clematis flowers draw the eye upward, making a canvas of an otherwise blank wall. When flowers fade, the planting's varied foliage colors, shapes, and textures provide interest on the walk to the front door.

Plants & Projects

Once established, these plants require little more than seasonal maintenance. As they mature, the shrubs will need to be pruned to limit their size. In late fall, cut down the perennials along the walk to keep the bed tidy. Or, instead, let the escallonia expand to displace the perennials and fill their space during the winter.

Ⓐ Clematis hybrid (use 2 plants)
Trained up matching trellises, the generous foliage of these deciduous vines is covered with eye-catching flowers for months. Choose from numerous cultivars. For winter presence, try an evergreen type. See *Clematis*, p. 204.

Ⓑ 'Sunshine' Grey's senecio (use 1)
An evergreen shrub, this makes a loose mound of soft paddle-shaped green leaves. Bears yellow flowers in summer. See *Senecio greyi*, p. 242.

Ⓒ 'Newport Dwarf' escallonia (use 4)
Shading the roots of the clematis, this evergreen shrub has a tight, compact form. Shiny green leaves have red margins. Red flowers cluster at the ends of stems in summer. See *Escallonia rubra*, p. 210.

Ⓓ 'Tuscan Blue' rosemary (use 1)
The upright stems of this evergreen shrub are lined with fragrant blue-green leaves. Bears deep blue flowers sporadically throughout the year. See *Rosmarinus officinalis*, p. 240.

Ⓔ 'Flower Carpet White' rose (use 3)
This shrub forms a low, spreading ground cover of reddish green leaves. From spring through autumn it bears clusters of single white flowers. See *Rosa*, p. 238.

Ⓕ 'Provence' lavender (use 1)
This evergreen shrub's spikes of fragrant deep purple flowers and fragrant gray-green foliage combine well with the nearby roses. It blooms in early summer. See *Lavandula* x *intermedia*, p. 226.

Ⓖ 'Hidcote' English lavender (use 6)
An evergreen shrub, it forms a compact clump of upright stems bearing small gray-green leaves. Spikes of deep purple flowers rise above the foliage in summer. See *Lavandula angustifolia*, p. 226.

Ⓗ 'Moonbeam' coreopsis (use 3)
A perennial, this forms a neat patch of lacy green foliage covered from summer to fall with sunny yellow flowers. See *Coreopsis verticillata*, p. 205.

Ⓘ 'Vera Jameson' sedum (use 3)
The floppy stems of this perennial bear succulent blue-gray and purple leaves. From summer to fall, flat clusters of tiny flowers turn from pinkish green to rose pink to rust. See *Sedum*, p. 242.

Ⓙ 'Johnson's Blue' geranium (use 3)
This perennial makes a sprawling mass of pretty lobed green leaves. Bears periwinkle blue flowers in early summer. See *Geranium*, p. 216.

Ⓚ Trellis
This pair of simple trellises provide support for the clematis and look good in winter, too. See p. 280.

'Provence' lavender Ⓕ

'Flower Carpet White' rose Ⓔ

SITE: Sunny

SEASON: Summer

CONCEPT: Growing up, rather than out, these plants offer the same attractions as a much larger garden.

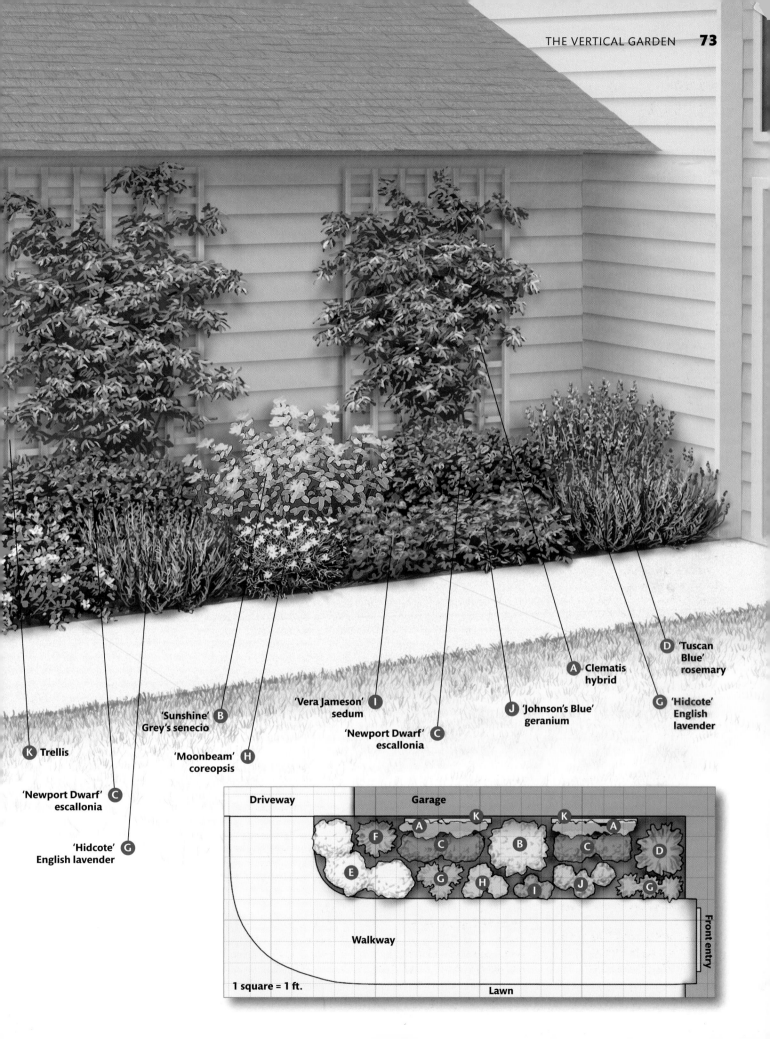

Ⓓ 'Tuscan Blue' rosemary

Ⓐ Clematis hybrid

Ⓙ 'Johnson's Blue' geranium

Ⓖ 'Hidcote' English lavender

Ⓒ 'Newport Dwarf' escallonia

Ⓘ 'Vera Jameson' sedum

Ⓑ 'Sunshine' Grey's senecio

Ⓗ 'Moonbeam' coreopsis

Ⓚ Trellis

Ⓒ 'Newport Dwarf' escallonia

Ⓖ 'Hidcote' English lavender

Driveway　　Garage

Ⓚ　Ⓐ　Ⓚ　Ⓐ

Ⓕ　Ⓒ　Ⓑ　Ⓒ　Ⓓ

Ⓔ　Ⓖ　Ⓗ　Ⓘ　Ⓙ　Ⓖ

Front entry

Walkway

1 square = 1 ft.

Lawn

PLANT PORTRAITS

These perennials and shrubs enhance a blank wall and narrow entry walk with handsome foliage and pretty flowers all year.

● = First design, pp. 72-73

▲ = Second design, pp. 74-75

'Moonbeam' Coreopsis (*Coreopsis verticillata*, p. 205) ●

Barrenwort (*Epimedium*, p. 209) ▲

'Provence' lavender (*Lavandula* x *intermedia*, p. 226) ●

'Tuscan Blue' Rosemary (*Rosmarinus officinalis*, p. 240) ●

'Bressingham White' Bergenia (*Bergenia cordifolia*, p.195) ▲

Growing on a shady wall

Narrow, shady areas are common where houses or condos are close together. The planting shown here, for morning sun and afternoon shade, accomplishes the same thing as the previous design but with a different selection of plants.

Arrayed on a wooden trellis, the star of this planting is a striking camellia. It graces the late-winter to early-spring floral display (shown here) with soft white flowers. At its feet, a supporting cast of plants adds flowers in pink, white, and blue. And the powerful scent of winter daphne welcomes visitors on the entry walk. After the spring show has faded, the remaining foliage creates a pleasant scene through summer, fall, and winter.

Plants & Projects

Ⓐ Sasanqua camellia (use 1 plant)
Trained to the trellis, this shrub displays lovely flowers against glossy evergreen foliage from late fall through early spring. Choose a white-flowered cultivar suitable for trellis training. See *Camellia sasanqua*, p. 198.

Ⓑ 'Cilpinense' evergreen rhododendron (use 1)
Branching low to the ground, this shrub forms a handsome mound of small evergreen leaves. In late winter and early spring, it bears pale pink flowers that fade to white. See *Rhododendron*, p. 237.

Ⓒ Variegated winter daphne (use 1)
An evergreen shrub with shiny green leaves edged in yellow. In

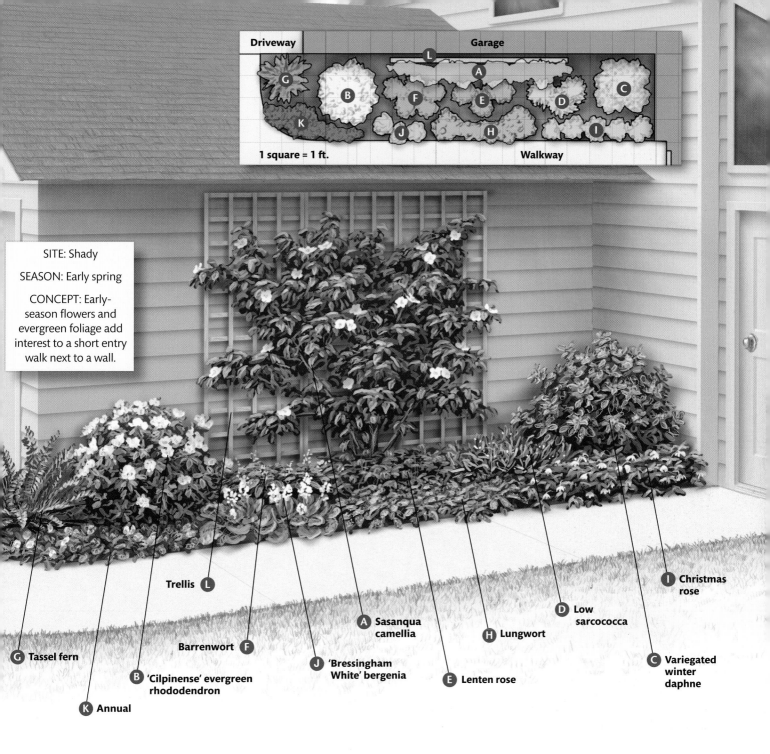

Driveway

Garage

1 square = 1 ft.

Walkway

SITE: Shady

SEASON: Early spring

CONCEPT: Early-season flowers and evergreen foliage add interest to a short entry walk next to a wall.

Trellis **L**

A Sasanqua camellia

H Lungwort

I Christmas rose

D Low sarcococca

Barrenwort **F**

G Tassel fern

J 'Bressingham White' bergenia

E Lenten rose

C Variegated winter daphne

B 'Cilpinense' evergreen rhododendron

K Annual

spring, purple buds open into clusters of rose-tinged white flowers near the ends of the branches and perfume the entire area. See *Daphne odora* 'Aureomarginata', p. 207.

D **Low sarcococca** (use 3)
A spreading evergreen shrub with glossy green, leathery leaves. Bears clusters of very fragrant, tiny white flowers in late winter. See *Sarcococca humilis*, p. 242.

E **Lenten rose** (use 3)
Grown for its distinctive flowers

and shiny evergreen leaves, this perennial blooms in late winter and early spring. See *Helleborus orientalis*, p. 217.

F **Barrenwort** (use 5)
This perennial's evergreen leaves change from bronze to green to maroon from spring to winter. Bears flowers in yellow, pink, red, or white in spring. See *Epimedium*, p. 209.

G **Tassel fern** (use 1)
This evergreen fern forms an attractive clump of stiff, finely divided, and glossy fronds. See

Ferns: *Polystichum polyblepharum*, p. 212.

H **Lungwort** (use 6)
The fuzzy gray-green leaves of this perennial are sprinkled with white spots. Spikes of tiny blue, red, or pink flowers appear in early spring. See *Pulmonaria saccharata*, p. 235.

I **Christmas rose** (use 5)
This perennial closely resembles Lenten rose but bears showy white flowers in winter and early spring. See *Helleborus niger*, p. 217.

J **'Bressingham White' bergenia** (use 3)
A perennial with large green leaves and white flowers that bloom on stalks in spring. See *Bergenia cordifolia*, p. 195.

K **Annuals** (as needed)
Use seasonal annuals, such as the pansies shown here. See Annuals, pg. 190.

L **Trellis**
You can make this trellis using the same construction as in the previous design. See p. 280.

A Shady Hideaway

BUILD A COZY RETREAT IN A CORNER OF YOUR YARD

One of life's little pleasures is sitting in a shady spot reading a book or newspaper or just looking out onto your garden, relishing the fruits of your labors. If your property is long on lawn and short on shade, a chair under a leafy arbor can provide a cool respite from the heat or the cares of the day. Tucked into a corner of the yard and set among attractive trees, shrubs, vines, and perennials, the arbor shown here is a desirable destination even when the day isn't sizzling.

Picturesque redbuds help create a cozy enclosure, affording privacy as well as shade. Plantings in front of the arbor and extending along the property lines integrate the hideaway with the lawn and make a handsome scene when viewed from the house. The design is equally effective in an open corner or backed by a property-line fence. The arbor is small; if you'd like more company beneath it, it's easy to make it wider and longer.

Flowers and foliage contribute color and fragrance around the arbor throughout the year. The redbuds, clematis, roses, and columbines bloom in spring. The roses carry on blooming through the summer, joined by lavender and plumbago. Camellias grace the fall and winter. Leaves in a range of greens, purple, maroon, and silver-gray provide background and balance to the floral display and are eye catching in their own right.

Plants & Projects

The arbor and plants can be installed in a few weekends. Plant dwarf plumbago between the new shrubs. It will be shaded out as the shrubs mature, but you'll enjoy its summerlong blue carpet of flowers in the meantime. Once the plants are established, seasonal pruning and cleanup should keep this durable planting looking good for years.

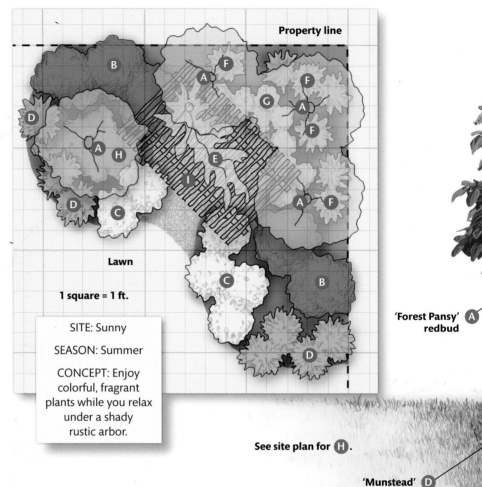

Property line

Lawn

1 square = 1 ft.

SITE: Sunny

SEASON: Summer

CONCEPT: Enjoy colorful, fragrant plants while you relax under a shady rustic arbor.

'Forest Pansy' redbud **A**

See site plan for **H**.

'Munstead' lavender **D**

A **'Forest Pansy' redbud** (use 4 plants)
The heart-shaped purple leaves of this small deciduous tree shade the arbor in summer and early fall. Eye-catching tiny red flowers line bare branches in spring. See *Cercis canadensis*, p. 201.

B **'Setsugekka' camellia** (use 5)
A compact low-growing form of this popular evergreen shrub. White flowers are showcased against the glossy green foliage in late fall and winter. See *Camellia sasanqua*, p. 198.

C **'Margaret Merril' rose** (use 6)
Fragrant white roses welcome visitors to the arbor from spring to fall. This floribunda rose has attractive dark green leaves and a bushy habit. See *Rosa*, p. 238.

D **'Munstead' lavender** (use 7)
The silver-gray foliage of this evergreen shrub contrasts handsomely with its neighbors. Bears spikes of blue flowers in summer. See *Lavandula angustifolia*, p. 226.

E **Anemone clematis** (use 1)
This vigorous deciduous vine covers the arbor. Choose from cultivars offering generous displays of white or pink flowers in early spring. Some are strongly scented. See *Clematis montana*, p. 204.

F **Leatherleaf fern** (use 7)
The finely cut, glossy foliage of this evergreen fern makes a lush patch beneath the redbuds. See Ferns: *Rumohra adiantiformis*, p. 213.

G **Rocky Mountain columbine** (use 9)
Elegant blue-and-white flowers sway on thin stalks in late spring and early summer. This perennial's delicate lacy foliage complements nearby ferns. See *Aquilegia caerulea*, p. 192.

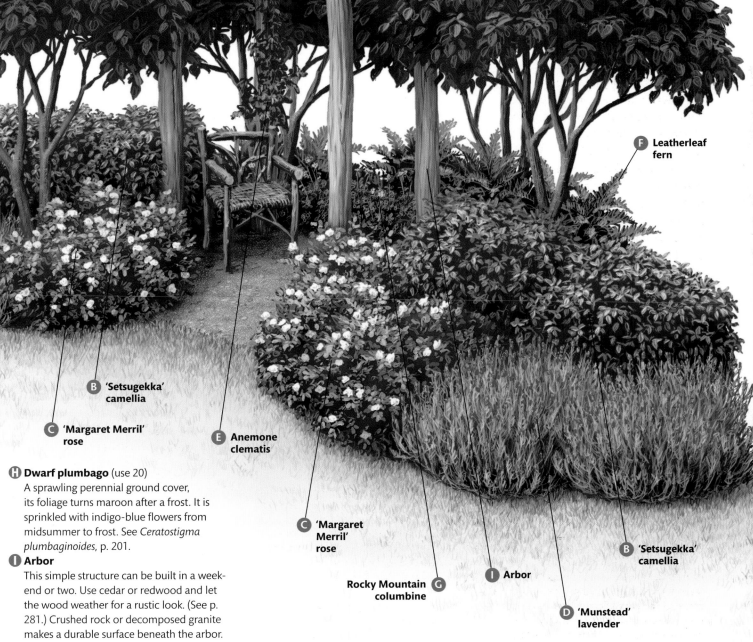

F Leatherleaf fern

B 'Setsugekka' camellia

C 'Margaret Merril' rose

E Anemone clematis

H Dwarf plumbago (use 20)
A sprawling perennial ground cover, its foliage turns maroon after a frost. It is sprinkled with indigo-blue flowers from midsummer to frost. See *Ceratostigma plumbaginoides*, p. 201.

I Arbor
This simple structure can be built in a week-end or two. Use cedar or redwood and let the wood weather for a rustic look. (See p. 281.) Crushed rock or decomposed granite makes a durable surface beneath the arbor. (See p. 259.)

C 'Margaret Merril' rose

B 'Setsugekka' camellia

I Arbor

Rocky Mountain columbine **G**

D 'Munstead' lavender

VARIATIONS ON A THEME

What a treat to steal a quiet moment in a shady spot surrounded by lovely plants.

An arched arbor frames a cozy hide-away just large enough for a bench. The canopy of a tree provides a screen behind and shade overhead.

This "hideaway" is located on an island bed in the center of a shady garden. Though in plain view, its trellised walls and leafy surround give the impression of a hidden retreat. A bench swing hangs from the covered roof.

The fieldstone patio beneath this vine-covered rustic arbor has ample room for a gathering of friends and family.

Another cozy corner

Small fruit trees combined with midsize shrubs provide a sense of enclosure and privacy in this shady retreat. The pomegranate and tangerine may reach 10 ft. or so, but without the grovelike feel of the previous design.

There are flowers for many months. In spring, the back of the planting blooms in red, pink, blue, and white, complementing the fragrant yellow blossoms of the jasmine. The front of the planting comes on from summer through fall with flowering perennials and shrubs in red, yellow, and purple. And much of it is evergreen for year-round good looks.

The design works equally well in the open or against a fence. If your site is fenced, you might omit the small clumps of blue fescue along the back edge.

Plants & Projects

Ⓐ 'Wonderful' pomegranate
(use 1 plant)
A small multitrunked deciduous tree with orange-red flowers in spring and bright yellow leaves and edible fruit in fall. See *Punica granatum*, p. 236.

Ⓑ 'Clementine' dwarf tangerine
(use 1)
This small tree has evergreen foliage, fragrant flowers in spring, and tasty fruit in late fall and winter. See *Citrus*, p. 202.

Ⓒ 'Julia Phelps' ceanothus (use 3)
This native shrub provides deep blue flowers in spring and dark evergreen foliage year-round. See *Ceanothus*, p. 200.

Ⓓ Shrub marigold (use 3)
Small yellow flowers are scattered on this shrubby perennial throughout the year. The fine-textured leaves are fragrant. See *Tagetes lemmonii*, p. 244.

Ⓔ Carolina jasmine (use 1)
The evergreen foliage of this vine is

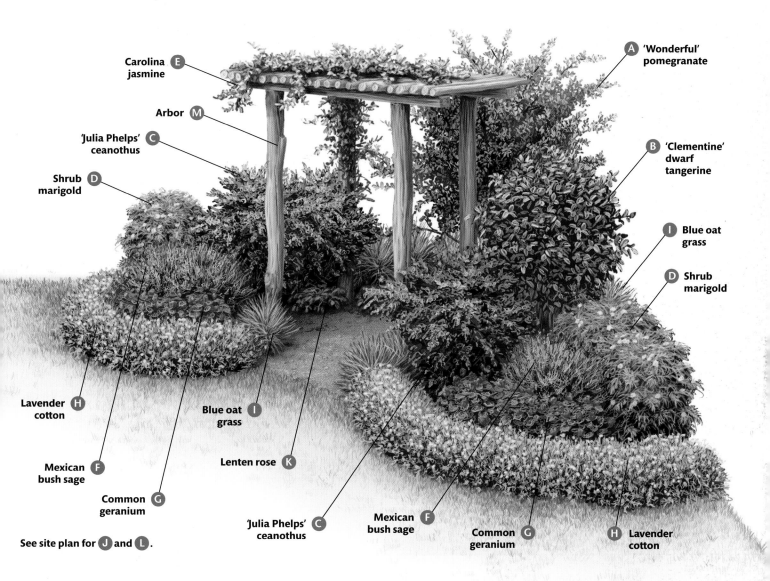

Carolina jasmine **E**

Arbor **M**

'Julia Phelps' ceanothus **C**

Shrub marigold **D**

Lavender cotton **H**

Mexican bush sage **F**

Common geranium **G**

Blue oat grass **I**

Lenten rose **K**

'Julia Phelps' ceanothus **C**

Mexican bush sage **F**

Common geranium **G**

Lavender cotton **H**

A 'Wonderful' pomegranate

B 'Clementine' dwarf tangerine

I Blue oat grass

D Shrub marigold

See site plan for **J** and **L**.

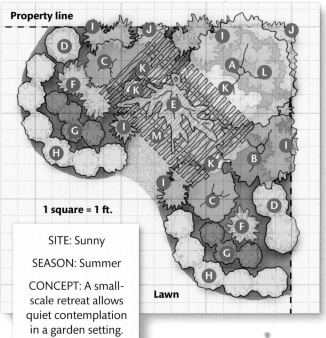

Property line

1 square = 1 ft.

Lawn

SITE: Sunny

SEASON: Summer

CONCEPT: A small-scale retreat allows quiet contemplation in a garden setting.

dark green in summer and maroon in winter. Bears fragrant yellow flowers in late winter to early spring. See *Gelsemium sempervirens*, p. 215.

F **Mexican bush sage** (use 3)
This perennial forms mounds of gray-green foliage that bristle with spikes of deep purple flowers from late spring into fall. See *Salvia leucantha*, p. 241.

G **Common geranium** (use 7)
Pick a red-flowered cultivar of this popular perennial to complement nearby foliage and flowers. Blooms from spring through fall. See *Pelargonium* x *hortorum*, p. 233.

H **Lavender cotton** (use 11)
A small evergreen shrub with silver-gray foliage and yellow flowers in midsummer. See *Santolina chamaecyparissus*, p. 242.

I **Blue oat grass** (use 13)

Clumps of this evergreen perennial's bluish foliage add texture and color to the planting. See *Helictotrichon sempervirens*, p.230.

J **Blue fescue grass** (use 16)
Choose a dwarf cultivar (such as 'Blausilber') of this evergreen perennial to form little pincushions of blue-gray foliage. See *Festuca ovina* var. *glauca*, p. 230.

K **Lenten rose** (use 17)
A perennial with distinctive pink, rose, or white flowers and evergreen leaves. See *Helleborus orientalis*, p. 217.

L **Bearded iris** (use 8)
Choose your favorites among these popular perennials with elegant spring-blooming flowers and swordlike leaves. See *Iris*, p. 222.

See p. 77 for the following:

M **Arbor**

A Garden Getaway

CREATE A CHARMING SPOT IN YOUR YARD

Surrounded by plants, the arbor in this design offers more seclusion than versions on previous pages. Tuck yourself away with a good book in the shade of the holly tree and honeysuckle vine for a welcome respite from a hot or hectic day.

Flowers contribute warm colors throughout the growing season. Festive yellows, pinks, and reds start the year off and continue until the first frost. Along with a canopy of honeysuckle blossoms, there will be showy hibiscus flowers and lantanas by the bench. Masses of black-eyed Susans and red pomegranate flowers join up in summer. And in fall, deciduous foliage adds to the colorful mix. This is primarily a warm-season planting, but pomegranate fruits and holly berries will make the hideaway well worth a winter visit.

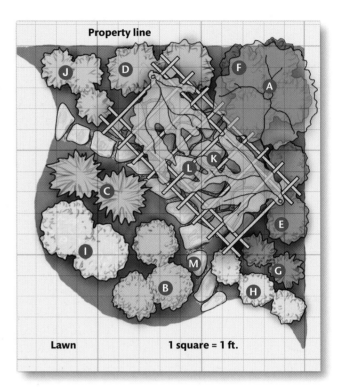

Plants & Projects

The arbor, bench, and plants can be installed in a few weekends. Once the plants are established, seasonal pruning and cleanup should keep this durable planting looking good.

A **Possumhaw holly** (use 1 plant)
This fast-growing deciduous tree makes a handsome screen for the hideaway. Smooth oval leaves turn yellow in fall. When they drop, they expose silvery branches with bright red, orange, or yellow berries, the color depending on the cultivar you select. See *Ilex decidua*, p. 222.

B **Compact pomegranate** (use 3)
A low-growing form of a popular deciduous shrub. Lustrous foliage showcases red carnation-like flowers in summer and small ornamental fruits in fall. See *Punica granatum* 'Nana', p. 236.

C **Dwarf Japanese maiden grass** (use 2)
One of the most compact fountain grasses. Abundant cream-colored flowers rise above long leaves in summer. Foliage turns tawny in winter. See *Miscanthus sinensis* 'Adagio', p. 230.

D **Texas star hibiscus** (use 2)
This perennial forms a large airy clump of slender, deeply divided, glossy leaves borne on red-tinged stems. Brilliant red five-petaled flowers open daily during the summer and fall. See *Hibiscus coccineus*, p. 220.

E **Firebush** (use 2)
Small slender flowers dangle at the ends of this perennial's many branches from summer to frost. Dull green leaves turn red in fall. See *Hamelia patens*, p. 216.

F **Turk's cap** (use 4)
This shrubby perennial will tolerate the eventual shade under the tree canopy, providing a lush screen of dark green leaves studded with small red turban-like flowers. See *Malvaviscus arboreus drummondii*, p. 228.

G **Cigar plant** (use 2)
Adding a vertical element to the planting, this perennial spreads to form a patch of upright stems topped with long narrow leaves. Thin orange and yellow flowers complement the firebush blossoms in summer. See *Cuphea micropetala*, p. 206.

H **'Goldstrum' black-eyed Susan** (use 3)
This popular perennial's abundant, golden, dark-eyed daisies bloom abundantly in summer, with plenty to spare for flower arrangements. See *Rudbeckia fulgida* 'Goldsturm', p. 240.

I **'New Gold' lantana** (use 2)
Tiny golden flowers in tight round clusters cover the foliage of this spreading perennial from late spring to frost. See *Lantana x hybrida* 'New Gold', p. 225.

J **Mexican mint marigold** (use 3)
Plant this perennial next to the bench for fragrant foliage and a fall display of rich yellow flowers. On your way into the house, snip a few anise-flavored leaves for cooking and a handful of flowers for fall bouquets. See *Tagetes lucida*, p. 245.

K **Coral honeysuckle** (use 2)
Whorls of scarlet flowers decorate this popular vine from late spring to fall. Attractive blue-green foliage is evergreen. See *Lonicera sempervirens*, p. 227.

L **Arbor**
This simple structure can be built in a weekend or two. See p. 282.

M **Paving**
Flat fieldstones in tones of gray complement the arbor and the planting. See p. 259.

SITE: Sunny

SEASON: Summer

CONCEPT: Flowers and foliage envelop you as you relax under a shady arbor.

Possumhaw holly **A**

Coral honeysuckle **K**

Arbor **L**

Texas star hibiscus **D**

See site plan for **F**.

Mexican mint marigold **J**

Dwarf Japanese maiden grass **C**

'New Gold' lantana **I**

Compact pomegranate **B**

Paving **M**

Firebush **E**

Cigar plant **G**

'Goldsturm' black-eyed Susan **H**

PLANT PORTRAITS

Privacy, shade, flowers, foliage, and fragrance—these plants provide all the necessities for a relaxing backyard retreat.

● = First design, pp. 80-81

▲ = Second design, pp. 82-83

Compact pomegranate (*Punica granatum* 'Nana', p. 236) ●

Narcissus
(Bulbs: *Narcissus tazetta* 'Grand Primo', p. 196) ▲

Mexican mint marigold
(*Tagetes lucida*, p. 245) ●

Homegrown hideaway

Instead of building your garden retreat, you can grow it. A small tree and midsize shrubs replace the arbor in the previous design. Their lush greenery provides a sense of enclosure and privacy year-round, and the cool flower colors (blues, pinks, and whites) will soothe the senses even as the temperature rises.

Reliably evergreen, the wax myrtle's deliciously scented leaves will cast dappled shade over the bench all year. The camellias, viburnums, and abelias are evergreen too, their dark glossy foliage a perfect foil for pink and white blossoms. There will be flowers in every season: sweet-scented viburnum in early spring, roses from May to October, camellias in November, and narcissus for snow-white blooms in winter.

Plants & Projects

Ⓐ **Wax myrtle** (use 1 plant)
This small evergreen tree offers a fragrant and shady canopy for bench-sitters. Leaves are smooth and slender. See *Myrica cerifera*, p. 228.

Ⓑ **'Shi Shi Gashira' camellia** (use 3)
This low, compact, and lustrous evergreen shrub bears double rose-colored flowers in late fall. See *Camellia sasanqua* 'Shi Shi Gashira', p. 198.

Ⓒ **'Spring Bouquet' viburnum** (use 1)
Pink buds open into scented white flowers when this evergreen shrub blooms in early spring. See *Viburnum tinus* 'Spring Bouquet', p. 246.

Polyantha rose (*Rosa* x *polyantha* 'Marie Daly', p. 238) ▲

Property line

SITE: Sunny

SEASON: Fall

CONCEPT: Planting your own retreat can be as therapeutic as sitting and enjoying the results.

Lawn

1 square = 1 ft.

D 'Edward Goucher' glossy abelia (use 3)
This evergreen shrub forms a low mound of small, pointed, glossy leaves tinged purple-bronze in winter. Pink flowers in summer lead to creamy pink seedheads later on. See *Abelia grandiflora* 'Edward Goucher', p. 187.

E Polyantha rose (use 3)
Apple green foliage topped with pale pink semi-double flowers make this dwarf rose a standout next to the path. See *Rosa* x *polyantha* 'Marie Daly', p. 238.

F Tropical plumbago (use 4)
The clear blue flowers of this shrubby perennial add cool color to the planting in hot summer months. See *Plumbago auriculata*, p. 234.

G 'Indigo Spires' salvia (use 1)
This lush, vigorous perennial makes a bushy mound of triangular leaves topped all season with long spikes of blue-purple flowers. See *Salvia* x 'Indigo Spires,' p. 241.

H 'Blue Princess' verbena (use 2)
Plant this low-growing perennial up front for a season-long border of lavender-blue flowers. See *Verbena* x *hybrida* 'Blue Princess', p. 246.

I 'Bath's Pink' dianthus (use 5)
This evergreen perennial's pincushion-like blue-gray foliage adds texture and color to the border. Masses of small pink flowers blanket the plant in spring. See *Dianthus* 'Bath's Pink', p. 207.

J 'Grand Primo' narcissus (use 40)
Scatter bulbs of this small daffodil around the planting, especially the plumbago and salvia, for grassy foliage and white flowers after the perennials freeze back. See Bulbs: *Narcissus tazetta* 'Grand Primo', p. 196.

See p. 80 for the following:

K Paving

See site plan for **J**.

Wax myrtle **A**

'Spring Bouquet' viburnum **C**

Tropical plumbago **F**

Polyantha rose **E**

'Blue Princess' verbena **H**

'Indigo Spires' salvia **G**

Paving **K**

'Shi Shi Gashira' camellia **B**

'Edward Goucher' glossy abelia **D**

'Bath's Pink' dianthus **I**

A Cozy Retreat

BUILD A COZY GETAWAY IN A CORNER OF YOUR YARD

Backed by dense shrubs and sheltered by a vigorous climbing vine, this design will work well in an open corner or in a niche created by a fence on your property line.

Tucked inside the low curving wall, the sitting area is big enough for chairs and a small table. The wall itself provides overflow seating.

The larger plants are all evergreen and most bear fragrant flowers—an ideal combination for a secluded bower. The kumquat even provides tasty snacks.

It is easy to expand the planting along the property line. If your yard's orientation requires it, shift the arrangement to block or enhance views. Add a planting in front of the arbor for increased privacy or interest.

Arbor **G**

Dwarf **B**
heavenly
bamboo

Fortnight **E**
lily

'Peter Pan' **F**
agapanthus

Plants & Projects

Installing the arbor, wall, and paving require time and effort; if you choose a concrete wall, a skilled landscape contractor will be invaluable. After the hard work is done, however, the planting is very easy to maintain.

A Sweet olive (use 2)
This compact, upright evergreen shrub bears very small, very fragrant white flowers in spring and summer. See *Osmanthus fragrans*, p. 232.

B Dwarf heavenly bamboo (use 4)
An upright multi-stemmed shrub, its soft, feathery foliage is evergreen (new leaves are bronze toned). In summer there are fluffy clusters of white flowers followed by long-lasting red berries. See *Nandina domestica* 'Compacta', p. 229.

C Dwarf kumquat (use 1 in planter)
A small version of a prized citrus tree, this evergreen shrub bears fragrant flowers and sweet-tasting fruit. See *Kumquat*, p.202.

D Star jasmine (use 2)
This evergreen vine twines up posts and over top of the arbor, covering it with dark, shiny leaves and, in early summer, clusters of small sweet-smelling creamy white flowers. See *Trachelospermum jasminoides*, p. 246..

E Fortnight lily (use 5)
A perennial, its stiff, upright, straplike, green leaves are topped intermittently from spring to fall with white and yellow flowers. See *Dietes vegeta*, p. 208.

F 'Peter Pan' agapanthus (use 5)
A dwarf form of a popular perennial, its ball-shaped clusters of blue flowers float on stalks above strap-like, dark green leaves in late spring and summer. See *Agapanthus* 'Peter Pan', p.189.

G Arbor
This simple arbor is easy to build; its posts can be set into a poured-concrete wall and planter or built in conjunction

with a precast wall system. See p. 282.

H Low wall and planter
Creating a comfy sitting area beneath the arbor, the wall and planter can be made using a precast concrete wall system or poured concrete. See p. 270.

I Paving
Laid on a sand and gravel base, flagstone makes an attractive "floor" for your hideaway. See p. 264.

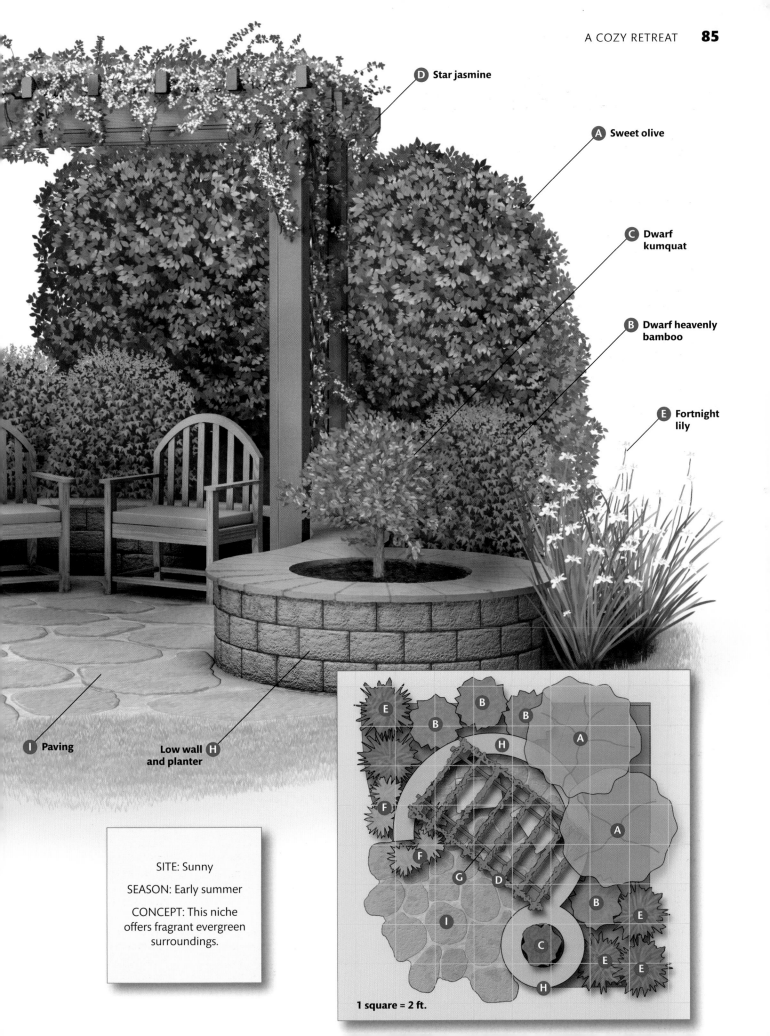

D Star jasmine

A Sweet olive

C Dwarf kumquat

B Dwarf heavenly bamboo

E Fortnight lily

I Paving

H Low wall and planter

SITE: Sunny

SEASON: Early summer

CONCEPT: This niche offers fragrant evergreen surroundings.

1 square = 2 ft.

Old-fashioned hideaway

If your tastes are traditional, this design evokes a more formal era of gardening: trimmed privet hedges frame a bed of roses. Neatly shaped topiaries flank a rose-covered trellis. Old bricks in a herringbone pattern underpin a teak bench. Surrounded by seasonal annuals, a bird bath provides entertainment for feathered friends and those observing them.

The plant palette is limited but packs a punch, primarily because the roses will bloom for many months; year round if you live where winters are mild.

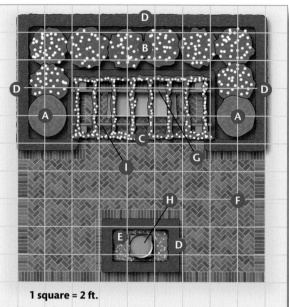

1 square = 2 ft.

SITE: Sunny

SEASON: Summer

CONCEPT: An old-style design provides simple pleasures.

Arbor **I**

Climbing 'Iceberg' rose **C**

Climbing **C** 'Iceberg' rose

Japanese **A** privet

Japanese **A** privet

'Iceberg' **B** rose

Water **H** feature

D 'Green Beauty' boxwood

Bench **G**

E Annuals

D 'Green Beauty' boxwood

F Paving

D 'Green Beauty' boxwood

Plants & Projects

(A) Japanese privet (use 2)
Sheared to a cone shape, this fast-growing evergreen shrub with glossy, bright green leaves makes an excellent potted topiary. See *Ligustrum japonicum*, p. 226.

(B) 'Iceberg' rose (use 8)
This popular upright shrub rose produces clusters of bright white flowers among dark green leaves off and on all year where winters are warm. See *Rosa* 'Iceberg', p. 238.

(C) Climbing 'Iceberg' rose (use 2)
Trained up and over the arbor, the climbing form of the shrub rose above provides shade and charming flowers. See *Rosa* 'Iceberg', p. 238.

(D) 'Green Beauty' boxwood (use 61)
Its small, densely packed glossy evergreen leaves make this shrub an ideal hedge plant. See *Buxus microphylla* var. *japonica* 'Green Beauty', p. 198.

(E) Annuals
Change this planting with the seasons. White verbena is shown here. See Annuals, p. 190.

(F) Paving
Old terra-cotta paving brick laid on sand and gravel is shown here. Note that it extends under bench. See p. 258.

(G) Bench
A traditional teak bench with a slat back suits this design.

(H) Water feature
We've shown a bird bath; you might try something more ambitious, too.

See p. 84 for the following:

(I) Arbor

PLANT PORTRAITS

These flowering plants and shrubs lend a nostalgic and slightly formal appeal to this architectural planting design.

● = First design, pp. 84-85
▲ = Second design, pp. 86-87

'Iceberg' rose (*Rosa* 'Iceberg', p. 238) ▲

Fortnight lily (*Dietes vegeta*, p. 208) ●

'Green Beauty' boxwood (*Buxus microphylla* var. *japonica* 'Green Beauty', p.198) ▲

Star jasmine (*Trachelospermum jasminoides*, p. 246) ●

An Outdoor "Living" Room

PATIO AND SHADY ARBOR PROVIDE OPEN-AIR OPPORTUNITIES

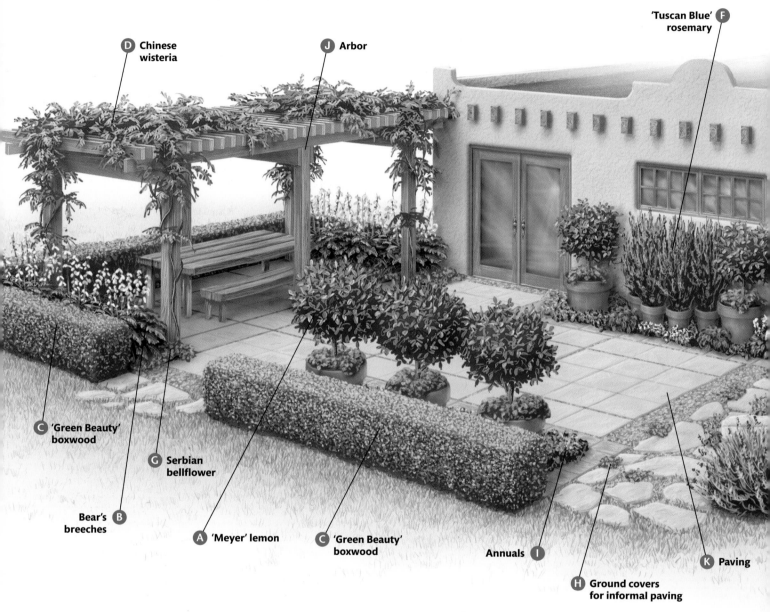

D Chinese wisteria

J Arbor

F 'Tuscan Blue' rosemary

C 'Green Beauty' boxwood

G Serbian bellflower

B Bear's breeches

A 'Meyer' lemon

C 'Green Beauty' boxwood

I Annuals

K Paving

H Ground covers for informal paving

In the West, opportunities for year-round outdoor living abound. This design demonstrates how a patio next to the house can become a true extension of your living space with the addition of an arbor and plants that create an attractive setting.

At one end of a formal patio, a vine-covered arbor provides a shady, cool spot for dining or relaxing. At the opposite end, random paving and a seat-height curved wall invite informal gatherings when the heat of the day has passed.

A neatly trimmed boxwood hedge, clipped trees, and shrubs in terra-cotta pots reinforce the formality of the gridwork paving, while annuals and ground covers spilling onto the pavement soften the effect. Backing the curved seating wall, a loose hedge of rosemary is an informal echo of its boxwood counterpart. Easily accessed and viewed from the house, the arbor, patio, and plants nicely mingle the "indoors" with the "outdoors."

Scale is particularly important when you're landscaping near the house. This design can be adapted to suit houses and properties in a range of sizes. The gridwork patio can be altered by adding or removing rows of pavers. And the plantings can be extended or reduced along the edges.

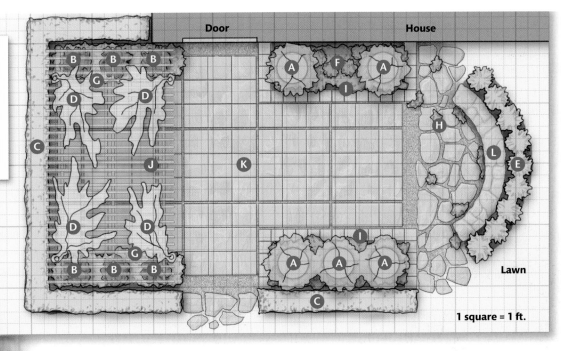

SITE: Sunny

SEASON: Summer

CONCEPT: Arbor, paving, and plants provide shade and a pleasant ambiance for outdoor relaxation and entertaining.

Door   House

Lawn

1 square = 1 ft.

L Seating wall

E 'Goodwin Creek Gray' lavender

Plants & Projects

The patio and arbor are sizable projects, but their rewards are large, too. Grow the lemon trees in 3-ft.-diameter terra-cotta pots, and the rosemary in deep pots, 12 in. in diameter. Prune these plants to emphasize their natural shapes: a loose ball for the lemons, a narrow column for the rosemary. Keep the boxwood hedge neatly clipped. Train a single stem of each wisteria to twist up its arbor post.

A **'Meyer' lemon** (use 5 plants)
The evergreen foliage of these small trees showcases fragrant white flowers and tangy yellow fruits borne on and off all year. Bellflowers planted in the pots provide additional interest. See *Citrus*, p. 202.

B **Bear's breeches** (use 6)
As if this perennial's big, bold, deeply divided green leaves aren't striking enough, in late spring spikes of white or deep pink flowers rise several feet above the foliage. See *Acanthus mollis*, p. 187.

C **'Green Beauty' boxwood** (use 20)
The small leaves and dense, compact habit of this evergreen shrub make it ideal for the formal, clipped hedge edging the arbor. See *Buxus microphylla* var. *japonica*, p.198.

D **Chinese wisteria** (use 4)
A vigorous deciduous vine with lacy leaves and clusters of fragrant purple, lavender, or white flowers in spring. See *Wisteria sinensis*, p. 249.

E **'Goodwin Creek Gray' lavender** (use 9)
This evergreen shrub's mounding gray foliage makes an attractive informal hedge. Bears spikes of blue flowers in early summer. See *Lavandula*, p. 226.

F **'Tuscan Blue' rosemary** (use 4)
Trim this evergreen shrub to a tall, narrow column. Foliage is aromatic; light blue flowers bloom in winter and spring, sometimes in fall. See *Rosmarinus officinalis*, p. 240.

G **Serbian bellflower** (use 31)
This spreading perennial is used as a ground cover and as an underplanting in the lemon tree pots (3 per pot). In spring and early summer, blue flowers float about a foot above the foliage on slender stalks. See *Campanula poscharskyana*, p. 199.

H **Ground covers for informal paving** (as needed)
Planted in the gaps between the flagstones, these perennials accent the informality of this end of the design. Snow-in-summer (*Cerastium tomentosum*, p. 201) has silver leaves and bears white

flowers in early spring. Coralbells (*Heuchera*, p. 219) features neat tufts of round leaves topped from spring to late summer by red flowers. Creeping thyme (*Thymus praecox* sp. *arcticus*, p. 245) withstands light foot traffic and smells good when you step on it.

I **Annuals** (as needed)
Change the plantings of annuals in the beds around the potted trees and shrubs for seasonal interest. In summer, (shown here) try phlox, snapdragons, alyssum, and purple basil. See Annuals, pg. 190.

J **Arbor**
This large arbor is designed to serve as a sunscreen for the area beneath even without a foliage canopy. See p. 282.

K **Paving**
Use flagstone pavers, 24 in. square, in the formal area. Press rounded pebbles into the gaps between pavers for added interest. Irregular flagstones pave the informal area. See p. 259.

L **Seating wall**
This low wall provides seating and should be constructed with mortared fieldstone. If your budget doesn't allow hiring a mason, buy commercially made curved wooden or precast concrete benches.

VARIATIONS ON A THEME

Each of these outdoor rooms takes inspiration from our sunny region's distinctive architecture.

Several patio rooms extend along the side of this house. Crushed rock lined with flagstones makes a stunning centerpiece to the design.

Reminiscent of a desert oasis, this free-form pond is a wonderful addition to an extensive naturalistic southwestern patio.

Cut-stone paving and steps set off mounds of striking plants.

A patio oasis

This design creates an outdoor room with the feel of a lush southern California oasis. A small "grove" of queen palms is the most striking element. With their long arching fronds, the palms provide dappled shade as well as character. A tall yew hedge screens the patio from neighboring properties and creates a sense of enclosure, aided by a low mortared stone wall that doubles as casual seating. The flagstone paving is roomy enough for several groups of tables, chairs, and shade umbrellas. If you're ambitious, add a small pond and fountain to enhance the oasis theme.

Free-form beds wrap around the patio. Foliage is a year-round attraction here. Swaths of yellow daylilies, with their broad, grassy leaves, complement the palm fronds. Mounding shrubs and perennials and carpet-forming ground covers add softer outlines. Flowers bloom for many months in a range of colors, including white, pale yellow, and blue. The fragrant flowers of the Natal plum are a heady enticement to linger on the patio.

Plants & Projects

Ⓐ Queen palm (use 5 plants)
Glossy green fronds arch from atop this fast-growing South American palm. See Palms: *Syagrus romanzoffianus*, p. 232.

Ⓑ 'Tuttle' Natal plum (use 5)
This evergreen shrub offers shiny dark green leaves, fragrant star-shaped flowers that bloom throughout the year, and bright red edible fruits. See *Carissa macrocarpa*, p. 200.

Ⓒ Irish yew (use 11)
A dense upright evergreen with small needles, it is clipped to form a solid dark green hedge-about 6 ft. tall. See *Taxus baccata* 'Stricta', p. 245.

Ⓓ Santa Barbara daisy (use 7)
The airy foliage of this sprawling perennial is covered from late spring to fall with small white flowers. See *Erigeron karvinskianus*, p. 209.

Ⓔ Daylily (use 17)
A popular perennial with grassy foliage and short-lived but plentiful flowers. There are many lovely cultivars; the apricot and pale yellow varieties look good with this design. See *Hemerocallis*, p. 218.

Ⓕ Alstroemeria (use 8)
This perennial forms a patch of erect leafy stems that bear striking azalea-like flowers from spring to midsummer. Choose from the long-blooming evergreen Meyer hybrids. See *Alstroemeria*, p. 191.

G **'Bronze Beauty' ajuga** (use 30)
This durable perennial ground cover forms a bronzy green mat of evergreen leaves covered in spring and early summer with short spikes of tiny deep blue flowers. See *Ajuga reptans*, p. 190.

H **Thrift** (as needed)
Planted between flagstones at the edges of the paving, this perennial offers grassy evergreen leaves topped with rose, pink, or white flowers. Blooms heaviest in spring, scattered blooms until fall. See *Armeria maritima*, p. 192.

I **Paving**
Irregular flagstones on a sand-and-gravel base form the patio. See p. 258.

J **Mowing strip**
Flat, random-size fieldstones make a durable mowing strip around the beds. See p. 289.

See p. 89 for the following:

K **Serbian bellflower** (use 22)

L **Creeping thyme** (as needed)

M **Seating wall**

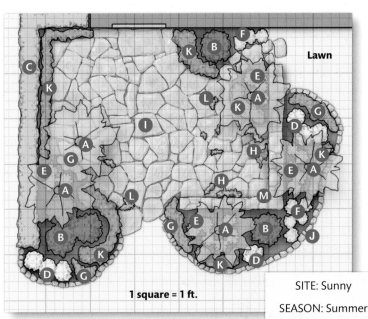

1 square = 1 ft.

SITE: Sunny

SEASON: Summer

CONCEPT: Palms set the tone for an outdoor room with a tropical feel.

A Patio Garden

MAKE A FRESH-AIR FAMILY CENTER WITH PLANTINGS AND PRIVACY

As the term implies, a patio garden provides fresh air and plantings. This design offering a sense of enclosure and privacy. A tall fence and vine-covered arbor allow the family to enjoy outdoor gatherings without having to make them neighborhood event—and the plants attract hummingbirds as well.

Sheltered by the trumpet-vine-covered arbor and a small tree, a table and chairs occupy a cool shady spot for dining or relaxing. In addition to privacy, the wooden fence and its border of flowers offer a colorful display to be enjoyed from the patio or the house.

From early spring to late fall, the plantings will provide colorful accompaniments to your patio activities. Blossoms of fragrant jasmine open first. By May the patio will be in full swing with long-lasting flowers and nectar-seeking hummingbirds.

As with the previous designs, this one can be adapted to suit houses and properties in a range of sizes. The flagstone patio can be altered by adding or removing irregular pavers. And the plantings can be extended or reduced along the edges.

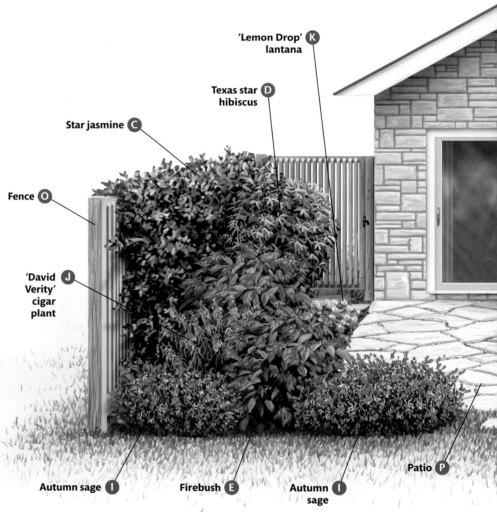

'Lemon Drop' lantana **K**

Texas star **D** hibiscus

Star jasmine **C**

Fence **O**

'David Verity' cigar plant **J**

Autumn sage **I**

Firebush **E**

Autumn sage **I**

Patio **P**

Plants & Projects

This design will keep your yard busy with winged creatures. Hummingbirds are drawn to the trumpet creeper, Texas star hibiscus, firebush, red yucca, Turk's cap, autumn sage, and the cigar plant. Butterflies are fond of Turk's cap and the two lantanas.

Ⓐ 'Bubba' desert willow (use 1 plant)
The willowy foliage of this deciduous tree showcases orchid-like purple flowers on and off throughout the summer. See *Chilopsis linearis* 'Bubba', p. 202.

Ⓑ 'Mme. Galen' trumpet creeper (use 1)
A vigorous, leafy deciduous vine laden from summer to fall with clusters of showy salmon red flowers. A dense canopy of foliage provides shade for the patio in warm months. See *Campsis* x *tagliabuana* 'Mme. Galen', p. 199.

Ⓒ Star jasmine (use 6)
An evergreen vine bearing dark green glossy leaves and clusters of sweetly fragrant blossoms in springtime. The white flowers resemble small stars or pin-

wheels. See *Trachelospermum jasminoides*, p. 246.

Ⓓ Texas star hibiscus (use 1)
Dazzling star-shaped red flowers bloom at the tips of this bushy perennial's leafy green branches all season long. See *Hibiscus coccineus*, p. 220.

Ⓔ Firebush (use 3)
This perennial forms a neat mound of dark green foliage. Numerous small firecracker red flowers bloom from summer to frost. Stems and new growth are tinged red. See *Hamelia patens*, p. 216.

Ⓕ 'Dallas Red' lantana (use 3)
Swirls of tight-knit tiny red-and-orange blossoms create a fine-textured backdrop for the holly fern. New flower clusters are yellowish orange inside and red outside. See *Lantana camara* 'Dallas Red', p. 225.

Ⓖ Red yucca (use 1)
A bold year-round accent, this yucca relative forms a large clump of narrow succulent leaves. It is especially striking when in summer and fall bloom under the desert willow tree shown here. Flowers are

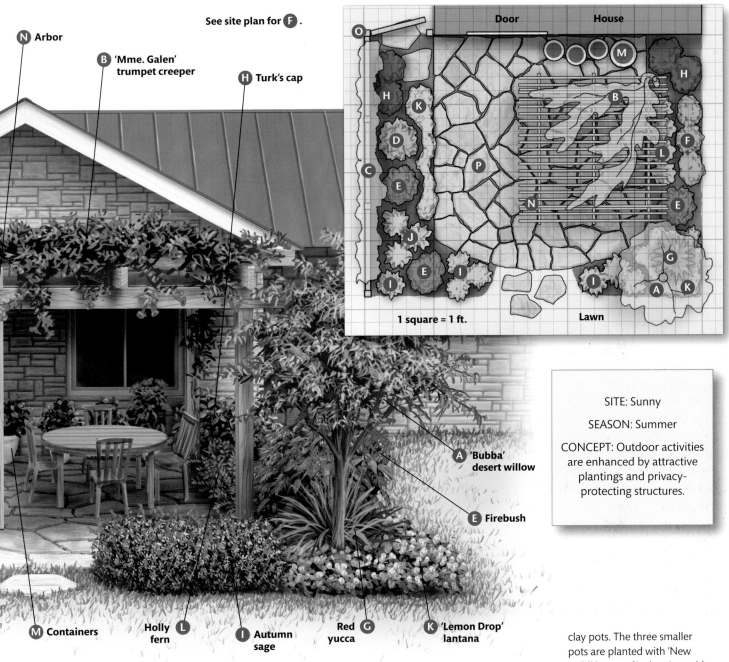

See site plan for **F**.

N Arbor

B 'Mme. Galen' trumpet creeper

H Turk's cap

Door House

A 'Bubba' desert willow

E Firebush

M Containers

L Holly fern

I Autumn sage

G Red yucca

K 'Lemon Drop' lantana

1 square = 1 ft. Lawn

SITE: Sunny

SEASON: Summer

CONCEPT: Outdoor activities are enhanced by attractive plantings and privacy-protecting structures.

coral pink. See *Hesperaloe parviflora*, p. 218.

H **Turk's cap** (use 4)
Plant this perennial near the patio to enjoy its summer-to-frost display of unusual red flowers. Dense and upright, it will fill the corner with handsome dark green palmate leaves. See *Malvaviscus arboreus drummondii*, p.228.

I **Autumn sage** (use 7)
Plant this well-behaved perennial by the flagstones. Branch tips bear red blooms the size and shape of lipsticks. Flowers are especially abundant in spring and fall. See *Salvia greggii*, p. 241.

J **'David Verity' cigar plant** (use 3)
A perfect perennial companion for sage and firebush. Upright stems are topped with narrow leaves and a profusion of orange flowery "cigars" all summer long. See *Cuphea* x 'David Verity', p. 206.

K **'Lemon Drop' lantana** (use 6)
This vigorous spreading perennial lays out a thick carpet of cheery yellow flowers next to the patio from late spring to late fall. See *Lantana* x hybrida 'Lemon Drop', p. 225.

L **Holly fern** (use 4)
An unusual fern with coarse-textured evergreen fronds resembling holly leaves. Provides a dense, durable, knee-high border on the shady side of the patio. See Ferns: *Cyrtomium falcatum*, p. 212.

M **Containers** (as needed)
Bring butterflies right on to your patio with colorful plants in handsome pots. We suggest using Texas-made Grub's white-clay pots. The three smaller pots are planted with 'New Gold' lantana (1 plant in each) and the larger pot with 'Ruby Glow' red penta (3 plants for full effect). Both flowers are magnets for butterflies.

N **Arbor**
This large arbor will serve as a sunscreen for the patio even before the trumpet vine fills in. See p. 282.

O **Fence**
A simple structure creates an attractive screen for flowers as well as for privacy. See p. 276.

P **Patio**
Flagstones set on a sand-and-gravel base make a durable informal patio. See p. 264.

PLANT PORTRAITS

While lending privacy, shade, color, and fragrance to your outdoor room, this selection of plants attracts butterflies and other wildlife on the wing.

● = First design, pp. 92-93
▲ = Second design, pp. 94-95

'Dallas Red' Lantana
(*Lantana camara*, p. 230) ●

'David Verity' Cigar plant
(*Cuphea*, p. 206) ●

'Bubba' Desert willow
(*Chilopsis linearis*, p. 202) ●

'Mme. Galen' Trumpet creeper
(*Campsis* x *tagliabuana*, p. 199) ●

'Whirling Butterflies' Gaura
(*Gaura lindheimeri*, p. 215) ▲

Butterfly viewing

This design creates an outdoor room that beckons butterflies along with friends and family. The live oak will provide pleasant shade for a portion of the patio, while playing host to duskywings, hairstreaks, and many other butterfly species. Long-blooming flowers are a feast for the eye and for skippers, swallowtails, and roving monarchs. Other plants play their part too. Texas sage and holly fern shelter butterflies from storms; maiden grasses serve as nurseries for eggs and larvae; and pots of leafy edibles, such as dill, parsley, and fennel, give the pupa (caterpillars) something to munch.

Here are a few tips to increase your butterfly population once they discover your patio. Place decorative rocks or logs in the flower beds for them to rest on and spread their wings. Butterflies need to soak up warmth from the sun to become active. Protect their life stages, eggs, larva, and pupa by avoiding the use of pesticides on plants. And remember, some leaf eating is desirable and beneficial in a butterfly garden.

Plants & Projects

Ⓐ **Live oak** (use 1 plant)
This large native tree forms a thick canopy of small hollylike evergreen leaves that will eventually shade the whole patio. If you'd like less shade, plant a smaller oak, such as Texas red oak or lacey oak. See *Quercus virginiana*, p. 236.

Ⓑ **Butterfly rose** (use 1)
This delicate bush rose flowers all season. The profusion of sin-

gle silky blossoms change color as they bloom, turning from pale yellow to orange to pink. New shoots and leaves are flushed purple; mature leaves are dark green. See *Rosa chinensis* 'Mutabilis', p. 238.

C Compact Texas sage (use 3)
This native evergreen shrub is grown for striking purple bell-shaped flowers that open after summer rains. Woolly silver-gray leaves make a handsome, informal year-round screen. See *Leucophyllum frutescens* 'Compactum', p. 226.

D Dwarf Japanese maiden grass (use 3)
The foliage of this small, fine-textured grass spills over like a fountain. These distinct yet overlapping clumps create a smooth transition to the lawn. See *Miscanthus sinensis* 'Adagio', p. 230.

E 'Whirling Butterflies' gaura (use 4)
From spring through fall, this graceful perennial sends up many slender stems of delicate "floating" flowers. They both resemble and attract butterflies. See *Gaura lindheimeri* 'Whirling Butterflies', p. 215.

F Fall aster (use 2)
This carefree native perennial puts on a dazzling show of lavender-purple "daisies" from early fall to frost. Their nectar draws roving monarchs. See *Aster oblongifolius*, p. 193.

G 'Homestead Purple' verbena (use 1)
This sprawling perennial forms a lacy mat of evergreen leaves and bright purple flowers. It blooms nonstop from spring to fall if deadheaded regularly. See *Verbena* x *hybrida* 'Homestead Purple', p. 246.

H Purple verbena (use 3)
This perennial's lavender-purple flowers are borne aloft tall, stiff stems. A magnet for butterflies from spring to frost. See *Verbena bonariensis*, p. 246.

I Coreopsis (use 5)
Plant these perennials to weave a gold "daisy" chain through the border in spring. See *Coreopsis lanceolata*, p. 204.

J 'Trailing Lavender' lantana (use 5)
This evergreen shrub's weeping branches are laden with clusters of small lavender-purple flowers in summer. See *Lantana montevidensis* 'Trailing Lavender', p. 225.

K Containers (as needed)
Plant dill, parsley, carrots, fennel, and anise to attract swallowtail butterflies; abutilons, hibiscus, and mallows for skipper butterflies.

L Water basin
A shallow dish makes an ideal birdbath for butterflies. Place some sand in the bottom, add a few pebbles for butterflies to land on, fill it with water, and watch what happens.

M Paving
Shown here is a brick patio laid in a simple basketweave pattern. See p. 259.

See p. 93 for the following:

N Holly fern (use 20)

O Autumn sage (use 4)

SITE: Sunny

SEASON: Spring

CONCEPT: A butterfly garden brings this outdoor room to life.

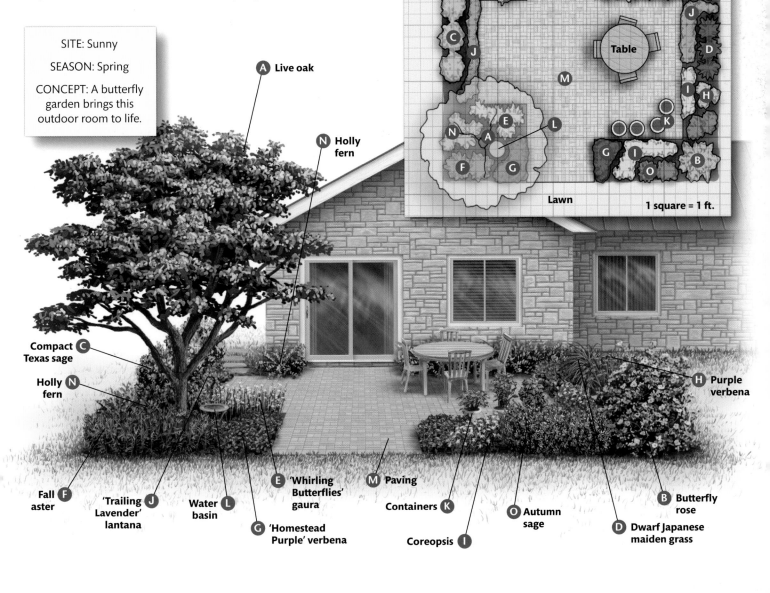

A Live oak
N Holly fern
Compact C Texas sage
Holly N fern
Fall F aster
J 'Trailing Lavender' lantana
Water L basin
E 'Whirling Butterflies' gaura
G 'Homestead Purple' verbena
M Paving
Containers K
Coreopsis I
O Autumn sage
H Purple verbena
B Butterfly rose
D Dwarf Japanese maiden grass
Door
Table
Lawn
1 square = 1 ft.

Arbor-Covered Patio

A DOUBLE ARBOR MULTIPLIES OPEN-AIR POSSIBILITIES

This distinctive design provides a large space for gatherings, both in the sun or under vine-covered arbors. Carefully chosen and placed plantings screen the area from certain vantage points, while offering avenues of connection to the yard beyond.

Shrubs and perennials with striking foliage line the walls of the house, marking an effective transition between indoor and outdoor rooms. The curved planting along the lawn screens activities in the backyard from those on the patio and makes an attractive background for the fire pit. Flowers and foliage of bougainvillea overhead make it a pleasure to relax beneath the arbor.

Late spring into summer is the peak time for flowers, with agapanthus and bougainvillea joined by fragrant lavender and pittosporum blossoms. Foliage, much of it evergreen, in shades of red, green, gray, and blue provides interest the rest of the year.

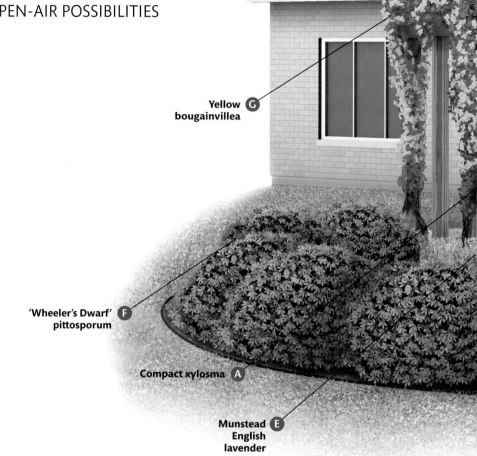

Yellow bougainvillea G

'Wheeler's Dwarf' pittosporum F

Compact xylosma A

Munstead English lavender E

SITE: Sunny

SEASON: Summer

CONCEPT: Create transitions from houise to patio to backyard to provide outdoor opportunities

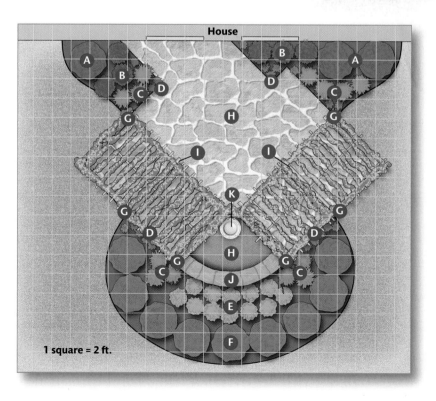

House

1 square = 2 ft.

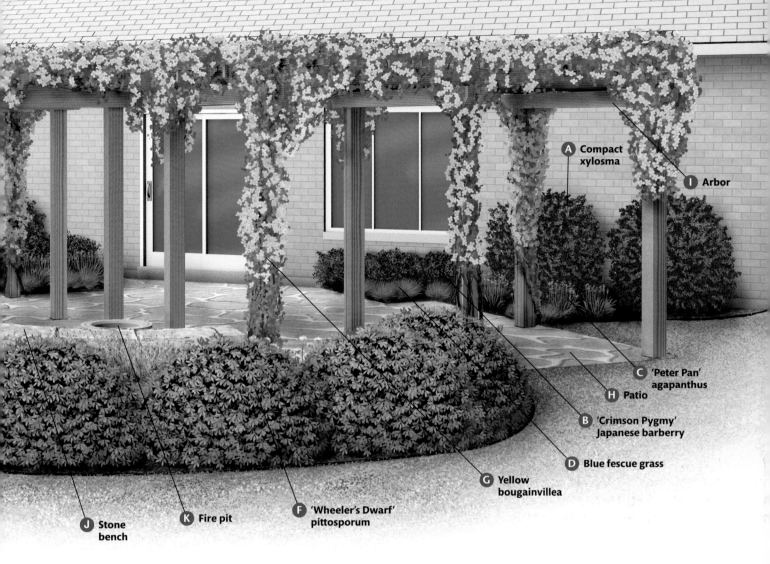

A Compact xylosma
I Arbor
C 'Peter Pan' agapanthus
H Patio
B 'Crimson Pygmy' Japanese barberry
D Blue fescue grass
G Yellow bougainvillea
F 'Wheeler's Dwarf' pittosporum
K Fire pit
J Stone bench

Plants & Projects

The lion's share of the work on this design is constructing the hardscape. Planting may take a weekend. Once established, the plants need only seasonal maintenance and pruning.

A Compact xylosma (use 3)
This evergreen shrub forms a dense mound of glossy green leaves. Grown for its foliage, the flowers are insignificant. See *Xylosma congestum* 'Compacta', p. 249.

B 'Crimson Pygmy' Japanese barberry (use 6)
A deciduous shrub, this is a compact, slightly spreading dwarf prized for its foliage. Its small leaves are a showy purple-red spring and summer and crimson red in fall. See *Berberis thunbergii* 'Crimson Pygmy', p. 194.

C 'Peter Pan' agapanthus (use 13)
This perennial forms mounds of strap-like, dark green leaves topped with tall, ball-shaped clusters of blue flowers in late spring and summer. See *Agapanthus* 'Peter Pan', p. 189.

D Blue fescue grass (use 21)
A perennial, its tufts of thin blue-green leaves produce narrow spikes of flowers in early summer; as season progresses, spikes turn tan. See *Festuca ovina* var. *glauca* p. 230.

E Munstead English lavender (use 12)
Tall stalks topped by fragrant, deep purple flower spikes rise above the fragrant gray-green foliage of this evergreen shrub in early summer. Plant in full sun. See *Lavandula angustifolia* 'Munstead', p. 226.

F 'Wheeler's Dwarf' pittosporum (use 9)
Whorls of dark glossy evergreen leaves showcase the fragrant white flowers of this dense, mounding shrub. Blooms in early summer. See *Pittosporum tobira* 'Wheeler's Dwarf', p. 234.

G Yellow bougainvillea (use 6)
This vigorous evergreen vine thrives on a trellis, producing spectacular masses of yellow flowers in late spring and summer. See *Bougainvillea*, p. 196.

H Patio
Bold flagstone paving complements this design. In the firepit area, decomposed granite contrasts nicely. See p. 264.

I Arbor
The double arbor is large, but not complicated or difficult to construct. See p. 274.

J Stone bench
For ease of construction and comfort when sitting, make the bench of relatively flat stones or precast wall blocks.

K Fire pit
We show a free standing, commercially available fire pit here. If you want to build your own, be sure to consult a landscape contractor or your city's codes department to ensure safety.

PLANT PORTRAITS

These flowering plants and shrubs provide cool greenery in the heat of a desert landscape.

● = First design, pp. 96-97

▲ = Second design, pp. 98-99

Red yucca (*Hesperaloe parviflora*, p. 218) ▲

Carolina jasmine (*Gelsemium sempervirens*, p. 215) ▲

Angelita daisy (*Hymenoxys acaulis*, p. 221) ▲

Compact xylosma (*Xylosma congestum* 'Compacta', p. 249) ●

'Furman's Red' autumn sage (*Salvia greggii* 'Furmans Red', p. 241) ▲

A patio oasis

If you live in one of the West's hot arid spots, this design creates a cool outdoor room furnished with attractive desert plants.

Using the same concept and hardscape (paving, arbor, fire pit and stone bench) as the previous design, this planting provides shade from two desert native tree—desert willow from America, and mulga, an Australian native.

Evergreen plants offer leafy surroundings year-round. And many of the plants bloom for months on end, providing bright yellows and reds, lavender, white, and rose-pink. Overhead, fragrant Carolina jasmine perfumes a gathering in the arbor.

Mulga Ⓑ

Plants & Projects

Ⓐ **'Rio Salado' desert willow** (use 2)
This small deciduous tree has willowy gray-green leaves. From spring to fall, it bears fragrant clusters of large, ruffled, deep burgundy flowers. See *Chilopsis linearis* 'Rio Salado', p. 202.

Ⓑ **Mulga** (use 3)
An evergreen tree with narrow, pendulous, gray-green to silver leaves. As many as four times a year, yellow rod-like flowers produce tan seed pods. See *Acacia aneura*, p. 187.

Ⓒ **'Furman's Red' autumn sage** (use 3)
This fine-textured perennial herb is covered with slender spikes of bright red flowers from early summer through fall. See *Salvia greggii* 'Furmans Red', p. 241.

Ⓓ **'New Gold' lantana** (use 6)
A spreading evergreen shrub, it bears golden yellow flowers for months, year-round in mild-winter areas. See *Lantana* 'New Gold', p. 225.

Ⓔ **Red yucca** (use 13)
This evergreen shrub forms a tight clump of narrow, grasslike, silver green leaves. From early summer through fall, tall stalks support rosy pink flowers. See *Hesperaloe parviflora*, p.218.

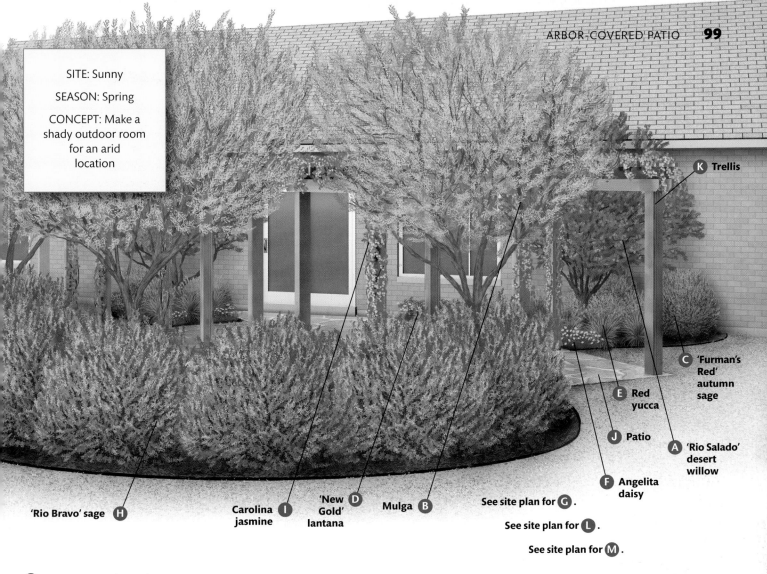

SITE: Sunny

SEASON: Spring

CONCEPT: Make a shady outdoor room for an arid location

K Trellis

C 'Furman's Red' autumn sage

E Red yucca

J Patio

A 'Rio Salado' desert willow

F Angelita daisy

'Rio Bravo' sage H

Carolina jasmine I

'New Gold' lantana

D

Mulga B

See site plan for G .

See site plan for L .

See site plan for M .

F Angelita daisy (use 21)
A neat, rounded perennial with narrow dark green leaves, it bears bright yellow, daisylike flowers on long stems from late spring through fall. See *Hymenoxys acaulis,* p.221.

G 'Holly's White' penstemon (use 12)
This evergreen perennial has upright branches and dark green leaves. White flowers bloom from late spring through fall. See *Penstemon gloxinoides,* p. 233.

H 'Rio Bravo' sage (use 9)
An upright evergreen shrub with dark blue-green leaves, its lavender-blue flowers last all summer. See *Leucophyllum langmaniae* 'Rio Bravo', p. 226.

I Carolina jasmine (use 6)
Covering the arbor with narrow, dark green leaves, this evergreen vine produces fragrant yellow flowers in late winter and spring. See *Gelsemium sempervirens,* p. 215.

See p. 97 for the following:

J Patio

K Trellis

L Stone bench

M Fire pit

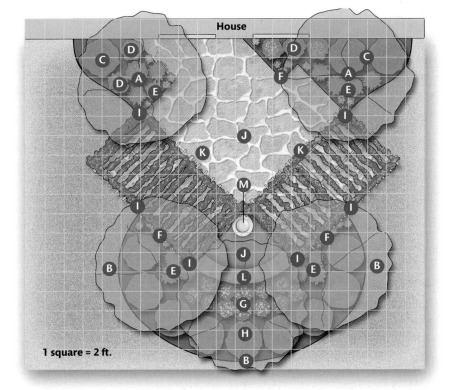

House

1 square = 2 ft.

Splash Out

MAKE A HANDSOME WATER GARDEN IN A FEW WEEKENDS

SITE: Sunny

SEASON: Summer

CONCEPT: Water is a welcome presence in the landscape, especially when surrounded by lovely plants.

A water garden adds a new dimension to a home landscape. It can be the eye-catching focal point of the entire property or a quiet out-of-the-way retreat. A pond can be a hub of activity—a place to garden, watch birds and wildlife, raise ornamental fish, or stage an impromptu paper-boat race. It just as easily affords an opportunity for some therapeutic inactivity; a few minutes contemplating the ripples on the water's surface provides a welcome break in a busy day.

A pond can't be moved easily, so choose your site carefully. Practical considerations are outlined on pp. 000-000 (along with instructions on installation and on planting water plants). In addition to those considerations, think about how the pond and its plantings relate to the surroundings. Before plopping a pond down in the middle of the backyard, imagine how you might integrate it visually with nearby plantings and structures.

The plantings in this design are intended to settle the pond comfortably into an expanse of lawn. Flagstone paving invites visitors to stroll up to the pond's edge. Framing the pond and path are a small broadleaf evergreen tree and perennial ground covers planted in contrasting waves of color and texture. A full season of flowers in complementary blues, purples, and golds will draw hummingbirds and butterflies as surely as they delight the eye.

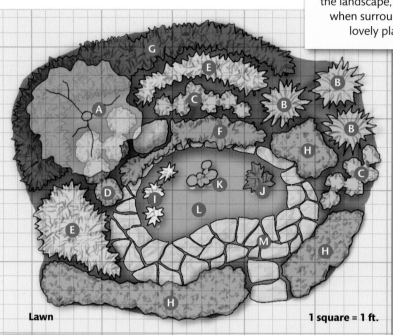

Lawn   1 square = 1 ft.

'Big Blue' lilyturf G

'Stella d'Oro' daylily E

Plants & Projects

Installing a pond is arduous but simple work, requiring several weekends of energetic digging. Lay out and install the paving at the same time as the pond. Once established, the plants require only seasonal care. The pond will need regular attention to keep a healthy balance of water plants and fish (if you have them) in order to maintain oxygen levels and to keep algae in check. Consult local or mail-order suppliers to help you determine the right mix.

Ⓐ Wax myrtle (use 1 plant)
This small tree adds graceful height to the pond planting. Fragrant leaves are fairly small, smooth, leathery, and evergreen; they won't litter the pond in fall. See *Myrica cerifera*, p. 228.

Ⓑ 'Gracillimus' Japanese maiden grass (use 3)
An ornamental grass with a weeping habit. Flower plumes rise high above the foliage in late summer and last through winter. See *Miscanthus sinensis* 'Gracillimus', p. 230.

Ⓒ Mealycup sage (use 12)
This perennial's grayish green foliage is topped with many blue flower spikes visited by hummingbirds and butterflies. To keep it blooming all season, remove flowers as they fade. But don't discard them—they make wonderful dried flowers. See *Salvia farinacea*, p. 241.

Ⓓ St. John's wort (use 5)
Bright yellow flowers with showy stamens top this dense, mounding shrub in summer. Some of them will eventually cascade over the edge of the pond. The overlapping evergreen leaves are small and oval. They turn reddish purple in fall and last through winter. See *Hypericum calycinum*, p. 221.

Ⓔ 'Stella d'Oro' daylily (use 20)
For small fountains of grassy

foliage near water's edge, plant these perennials en masse. Clusters of golden trumpets open daily in spring and often repeat in fall. See *Hemerocallis* 'Stella d'Oro', p. 218.

F **'Blue Pacific' shore juniper** (use 3)
An evergreen shrub bearing bright blue-green trailing fo-

liage that will fall softly over the flagstone edging and into the pond. See *Juniperus conferta* 'Blue Pacific', p. 223.

G **'Big Blue' lilyturf** (use 30)
Evergreen and lush-looking, this perennial's foliage makes an attractive grassy outer edge to the planting. Bears lavender flowers in summer, followed by black berries in fall. See *Liriope muscari* 'Big Blue', p. 226.

H **'Homestead Purple' verbena** (use 6)
This perennial spreads out to form an edging of felty leaves interlaced with bright purple

flowers. Cut back occasionally to encourage a new flush of bloom. See *Verbena* x *hybrida* 'Homestead Purple', p. 246.

I **Louisiana iris** (use 3)
This plant forms a tall clump of pale green swordlike leaves that can survive half-submerged in water. Bright yellow flowers rise a foot above the leaves in spring. Foliage is attractive year-round. See *Iris* x Louisiana hybrids, p. 222.

J **Umbrella sedge** (use 2)
Plant this bold grasslike water plant for its many unusual green stalks topped with rib-

bons of foliage, arranged like the spokes of an umbrella. See *Cyperus alternifolius*, p. 207.

K **Water lily** (use 1)
No pond is complete without these lovely floating flowers. Pointed petals open in layers above saucer-shaped leaf pads. We've shown a pink-flowering cultivar here. See Water plants: *Nymphaea*, p. 248.

L **Pond**
You can make this pond with a commercially available flexible liner. See p. 266.

M **Paving**
A flagstone edge widens into a natural path around the front of the pond. See p. 258.

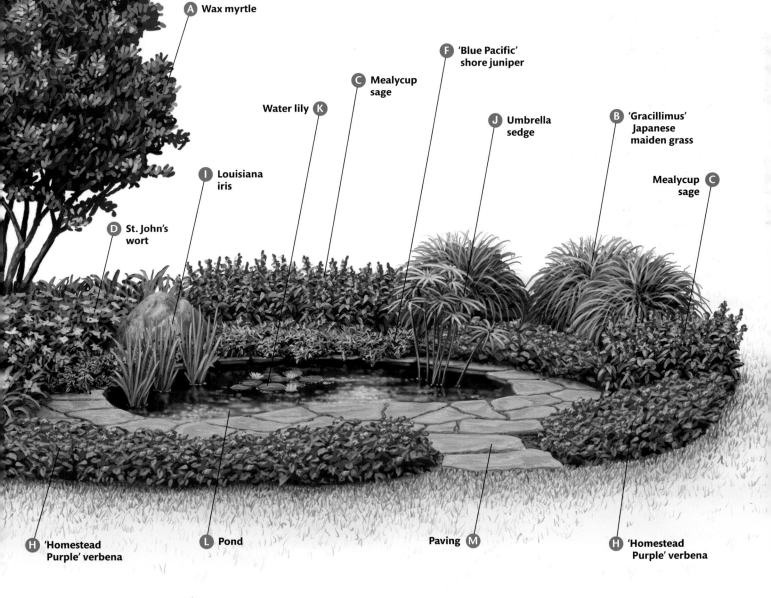

A Wax myrtle

F 'Blue Pacific' shore juniper

C Mealycup sage

J Umbrella sedge

B 'Gracillimus' Japanese maiden grass

K Water lily

I Louisiana iris

C Mealycup sage

D St. John's wort

H 'Homestead Purple' verbena

L Pond

Paving **M**

H 'Homestead Purple' verbena

Patio pool

A little pond can make a big splash in a well-chosen setting. And it provides all the pleasures of water gardening but without the energy or space required to install and maintain a larger pond. Within its confines you can enjoy one or more water plants and a few fish, or even a small fountain.

The scale of this pond is just right for a small patio or as a part of a larger patio planting. We've included a low fence along the patio perimeter, but the design would work just as well without it. The pond is simple and inexpensive. We recommend a 4-ft.-diameter fiberglass tub sunk into the ground and planted to the edge.

The planting displays an exuberant collection of foliage and flowers. We've selected plants that mound and arch, dangle and droop to create billowy contours around the small pool. The soft tones of the foliage also serve to complement the pinks and blues of the many blossoms.

Plants & Projects

A **'Pink Dawn' chitalpa**
(use 1 plant)
This small fast-growing deciduous tree provides an open airy backdrop for the patio planting as well as decorative gray bark, attractive pale green leaves, and pink ruffled flowers. See x *Chitalpa tashkentensis* 'Pink Dawn', p. 202.

B **Compact Texas sage** (use 4)
Silver-gray foliage suffused with orchid pink blooms distinguish this evergreen shrub. It provides a soft background for the flower display in summer and a privacy screen during winter. See *Leucophyllum frutescens* 'Compactum', p. 226.

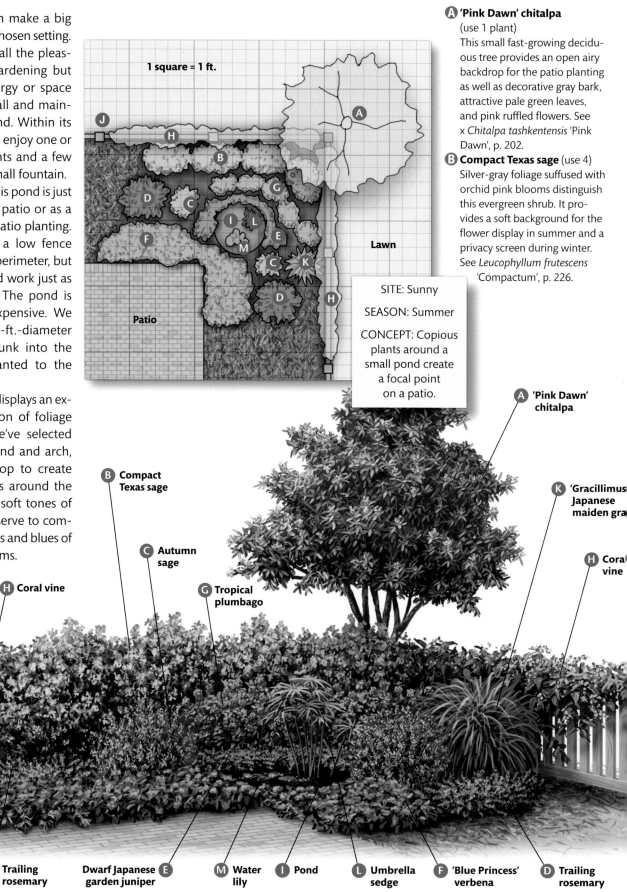

1 square = 1 ft.

Lawn

Patio

SITE: Sunny

SEASON: Summer

CONCEPT: Copious plants around a small pond create a focal point on a patio.

A 'Pink Dawn' chitalpa

K 'Gracillimus' Japanese maiden gra[ss]

H Cora[l] vine

B Compact Texas sage

C Autumn sage

G Tropical plumbago

J Low fence

H Coral vine

D Trailing rosemary

E Dwarf Japanese garden juniper

M Water lily

I Pond

L Umbrella sedge

F 'Blue Princess' verbena

D Trailing rosemary

C **Autumn sage** (use 2)
Loose clusters of pretty flowers bloom at the tips of this bushy perennial's branches all season. Choose a cultivar with pink flowers for this planting. See *Salvia greggii*, p. 241.

D **Trailing rosemary** (use 2)
An attractive evergreen shrub, it forms a sprawling mound of needle-thin leaves that are both fragrant and tasty. Small blue flowers appear in spring and off and on through the year. See *Rosmarinus officinalis* 'Prostratus', p. 240.

E **Dwarf Japanese garden juniper** (use 3)
This beautiful compact shrub forms a blue-green mat of dense evergreen needles, layered sprays of which will eventually spill over the edge of the pond. See *Juniperus procubens* 'Nana', p. 223.

F **'Blue Princess' verbena** (use 5)
This perennial produces clusters of small flowers from spring through fall (year-round in areas with mild winters). See *Verbena* x *hybrida* 'Blue Princess', p. 246.

G **Tropical plumbago** (use 5)
This perennial contributes baby blue flowers and fresh green foliage to the planting. See *Plumbago auriculata*, p. 234.

H **Coral vine** (use 2)
Grown for its showy panicles of tiny heart-shaped pink blossoms. Plant two of these vines and train them along the fence. They will cover it quickly. See *Antigonon leptopus*, p. 192.

I **Pond**
Bury a 4-ft.-diameter watertight tub and add water plants or a fountain, as you wish. See p. 266.

J **Low fence**
This variation on a picket fence frames the pond and patio nicely. See p. 274.

See pp. 100-101 for:
K **'Gracillimus' Japanese maiden grass** (use 1)

L **Umbrella sedge** (use 1)

M **Water lily** (use 1)

PLANT PORTRAITS

Whether growing in the water or nearby, these plants combine fresh foliage and lovely flowers for your poolside pleasure.
● = First design, pp. 100-101
▲ = Second design, p. 102-103

Coral vine
(*Antigonon leptopus*, p. 192) ▲

'Blue Pacific' Shore juniper
(*Juniperus conferta*, p. 223) ●

Dwarf Japanese garden juniper
(*Juniperus procubens* 'Nana', p. 223) ▲

Water lily
(Water plants: *Nymphaea*, p. 248) ▲

'Pink Dawn' Chitalpa
(x *Chitalpa tashkentensis*, p. 202) ▲

A Garden Pond

MAKE A WATER GARDEN THE FOCUS OF A NATURAL LANDSCAPE

A small pond can be a striking companion to an informal patio. The design shown here, with a "shore" of gravel and larger stones and a border of shrubs and perennials offers a slice of natural habitat alongside a crushed-rock patio.

Foliage is the star of the planting and gives it year-round appeal. Fall and winter are the most colorful seasons, with the bronzy red plume cedar and curly sedge, yellow ocher heather, tawny Japanese silver grass, and bright red dogwood stems. In spring and summer, the season shown here, flowers accent foliage that comes in a pleasing range of greens.

You can, of couse, expand the planting to border the patio as well as the pond. If you're a naturalist at heart, consider making over your entire backyard as a haven for birds, butterflies and other wildlife. Substitute or augment the design with plants native to your area.

SITE: Sunny

SEASON: Summer

CONCEPT: A pond is at the center of a versatile and exciting outdoor nature area.

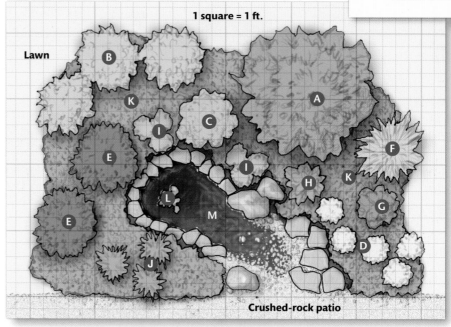

1 square = 1 ft.

Lawn

Crushed-rock patio

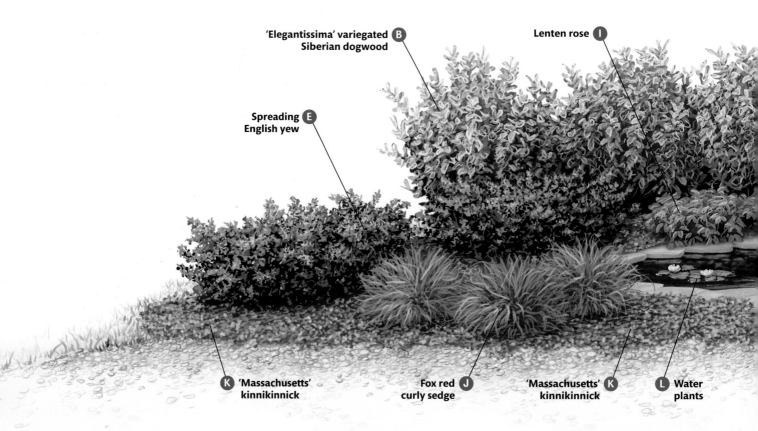

'Elegantissima' variegated B Siberian dogwood

Lenten rose I

Spreading E English yew

K 'Massachusetts' kinnikinnick

Fox red J curly sedge

'Massachusetts' K kinnikinnick

L Water plants

Plants & Projects

If your pond is part of a larger project, construct it at the same time as the adjoining hardscape. This will allow you to ensure that grade levels and drainage issues are addressed comprehensively.

A **Plume cedar** (use 1 plant)
This fine-textured evergreen tree is soft gray-green in summer and bronzy red in winter. Peeling cinnamon-colored bark is attractive. See *Cryptomeria japonica* 'Elegans', p. 206.

B **'Elegantissima' variegated Siberian dogwood** (use 3)
An all-season performer, this deciduous shrub displays red stems in winter, white flowers in spring, green-and-white leaves in summer, and blue berries in late summer. See *Cornus alba*, p. 205.

C **Winter hazel** (use 1)
A wispy open deciduous shrub, this bears yellow flowers on bare wood in early spring that are followed by bronze leaves that turn green in summer. See *Corylopsis pauciflora*, p. 205.

D **'Robert Chapman' Scotch heather** (use 5)
This evergreen shrub forms a low mass of ascending stems. Tiny scalelike leaves are bright red when new and then turn golden. In summer, small white flowers bloom up and down the stems. See *Calluna vulgaris*, p. 198.

E **Spreading English yew** (use 2)
This low evergreen shrub has large dark green needles. Spreads to make a good ground cover. See *Taxus baccata* 'Repandens', p. 245.

F **'Morning Light' Japanese silver grass** (use 1)
The slender arching leaves of this perennial are green with a white midrib that gives the clump a silvery sheen. In late summer and fall it bears tall fluffy flower and seed heads. See *Miscanthus sinensis*, p. 230.

G **Bear's breeches** (use 1)
This striking perennial forms a clump of large, deeply cut leaves from which arise tall spikes of white-and-purple flowers. Blooms in late spring. See *Acanthus mollis*, p. 187.

H **Hosta** (use 1)
A perennial grown primarily for its foliage. For this design, choose a cultivar that forms a big mound of large blue leaves. See *Hosta*, p. 220.

I **Lenten rose** (use 6)
An evergreen perennial that bears distinctive purple, pink, white, or green flowers in early spring. Its leathery green leaves are attractive all year. See *Helleborus orientalis*, p.217.

J **Fox red curly sedge** (use 3)
This perennial makes a clump of thin reddish bronze leaf blades that keep their color year-round. The summer flowers are insignificant. See *Carex buchananii*, p. 199.

K **'Massachusetts' kinnikinnick** (as needed)
Plant this tough evergreen ground cover in open spaces between other plants. Deep green leaves have a burgundy cast. The small white-to-pink spring flowers produce red berries. See *Arctostaphylos uva-ursi* 'Massachusetts', p. 192.

L **Water plants** (as desired)
You can grow a variety of plants in the pond. We've shown a water lily. See Water plants, p. 248.

M **Pond**
You can make this pond with a commercially available liner. The deep end is edged with flagstones. The other rises gradually until water and surrounding "land" are joined by a miniature shore of river rock and large stones. See p. 266.

C Winter hazel

I Lenten rose

A Plume cedar

F 'Morning Light' Japanese silver grass

G Bear's breeches

M Pond

H Hosta

K 'Massachusetts' kinnikinnick

D 'Robert Chapman' Scotch heather

PLANT PORTRAITS

Set off by nearby water, these plants combine fresh foliage and lovely flowers for your poolside pleasure.

● = First design, pp.104–105

▲ = Second design, pp. 106–107

Black mondo grass (*Ophiopogon planiscapus* 'Ebony Knight', p. 229) ▲

'Morning Light' Japanese Silver grass (*Miscanthus sinensis*, p. 230) ●

Fox red curly sedge (*Carex buchananii*, p. 199) ●

'Robert Chapman' Scotch heather (*Calluna vulgaris*, p. 198) ●

'Sulphureum' Barrenwort (*Epimedium* x *versicolor*, p. 209) ▲

Water lily (Water plants: *Nymphaea*, p. 248) ●

Sweet woodruff (*Galium odoratum*, p. 214) ▲

Mini-pond

This little pond takes an entirely different direction than the previous. Here, pond and planting have a geometric, architectural inclination, rather than mimicking nature's design. You might leave it as a reflecting pool, as shown here.

Pond and plantings can stand alone in an expanse of lawn, but they will look best integrated into a larger scheme. The scale is just right for use as the focal point of a small patio, as shown here, or as part of a larger patio planting.

Though its style is different than the previous design, this planting also displays a delightful collection of foliage textures and colors chosen to complement or contrast with those of their nearby neighbors. Spring is brightened by delicate flowers. And the leaves of the black mondo grass and the colorful pavers are a striking sight throughout the year.

Plants & Projects

Ⓐ Red-vein enkianthus (use 1 plant)
The blue-green leaves of this slow-growing deciduous shrub turn orange-red in fall. Small white bell-shaped flowers that are veined with red bloom in late spring. See *Enkianthus campanulatus*, p. 209.

Ⓑ Soft shield fern (use 7)
This evergreen fern forms a dense mass of upright green fronds, each rising from its own brown crown. See Ferns: *Polystichum setiferum*, p. 213.

Ⓒ 'Krossa Regal' hosta (use 1)
This perennial makes a vase-shaped clump of wide, powdery blue-green leaves. Tall stalks bear pale lilac flowers in summer. See *Hosta*, p. 220.

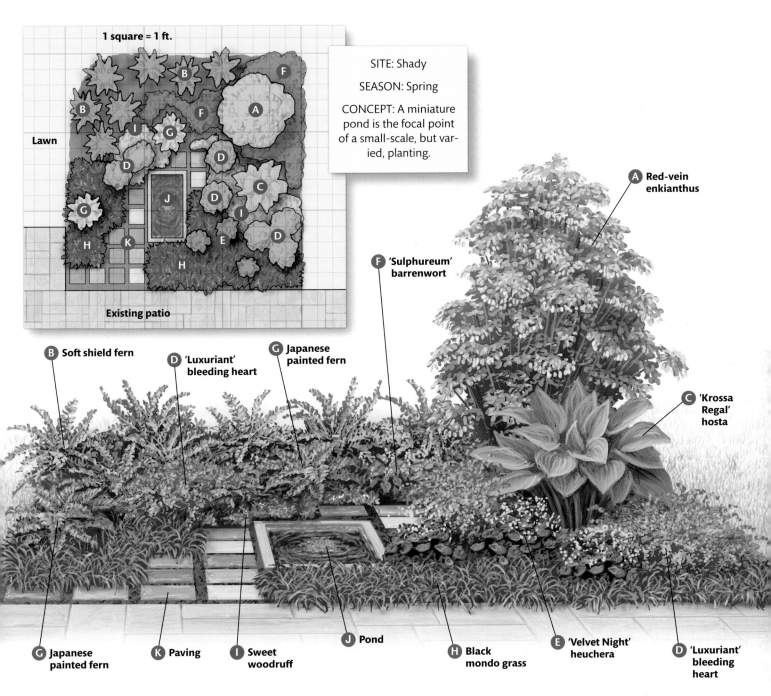

1 square = 1 ft.

Lawn

Existing patio

SITE: Shady

SEASON: Spring

CONCEPT: A miniature pond is the focal point of a small-scale, but varied, planting.

A Red-vein enkianthus

F 'Sulphureum' barrenwort

B Soft shield fern

D 'Luxuriant' bleeding heart

G Japanese painted fern

C 'Krossa Regal' hosta

G Japanese painted fern

K Paving

I Sweet woodruff

J Pond

H Black mondo grass

E 'Velvet Night' heuchera

D 'Luxuriant' bleeding heart

D 'Luxuriant' bleeding heart
(use 7)
Lines of dainty heart-shaped pink flowers dangle from thin curving stalks above this perennial's soft, fernlike blue-green foliage. Blooms in late spring. See *Dicentra*, p. 208.

E 'Velvet Night' heuchera
(use 3)
A semievergreen perennial prized for its striking purple foliage. Tiny brown-green flowers float on thin stalks above the foliage in spring. See *Heuchera americana*, p. 219.

F 'Sulphureum' barrenwort
(use 12)
This evergreen perennial bears purple-tinted green, heart-shaped foliage leaves on wiry stems. Yellow flowers rise above the leaves in spring. See *Epimedium* x *versicolor*, p. 209.

G Japanese painted fern
(use 2)
A small deciduous fern with lacy fronds of silver, green, and maroon. See Ferns: *Athyrium nipponicum* 'Pictum', p. 212.

H Black mondo grass (as needed)
This perennial ground cover spreads to form a patch of wide, grassy, purple-black leaves. See *Ophiopogon planiscapus* 'Ebony Knight', p. 229.

I Sweet woodruff (as needed)
Planted around the bleeding heart and hosta, this perennial carpets the ground with bright green foliage that is covered with tiny clusters of white flowers in spring. See *Galium odoratum*, p. 214.

J Pond
It's easy to make this shallow reflecting pond with a rectangular fiberglass shell available at garden centers and some elbow grease. See p. 266.

K Paving
Set bright-colored pavers on a sand-and-gravel base after you have installed the shallow pond. See p. 258.

A Beginning Border

FLOWERS AND A FENCE OFFER A TRADITIONAL DESIGN

A mixed border can be one of the most delightful of all gardens. Indeed, that's usually its sole purpose. Unlike many other types of landscape plantings, a traditional border is seldom yoked to any function beyond that of providing as much beauty as possible. From the first neat mounds of foliage in the spring to the fullness of summer bloom and autumn color, the mix of flowers, foliage, textures, tones, and hues brings pleasure.

This border is designed for a beginning or busy gardener, using durable plants that are easy to establish and care for. Behind the planting, screening out distraction, is a simple fence. The border is meant to be viewed from the front, so tall plants need to go at the back. There are interesting plant combinations to enjoy from every vantage point, near or close-up. It is easy to extend the planting along the fence to suit your site and energy.

The plants here provide months of bloom. To complement the spring flowers of the clematis, plant bulbs that will bloom among the emerging perennials. In summer and fall, the garden is a subtle tapestry of color, with flowers in shades of pink, violet, and blue woven among leaves in many shades of green. Attractive foliage of the grasses, heavenly bamboo, and other plants carries interest through the winter.

Lawn

1 square = 1 ft.

SITE: Sunny

SEASON: Fall

CONCEPT: Even a novice can make this flower border flourish. Attractive plants displayed against a simple fence will provide months of enjoyment.

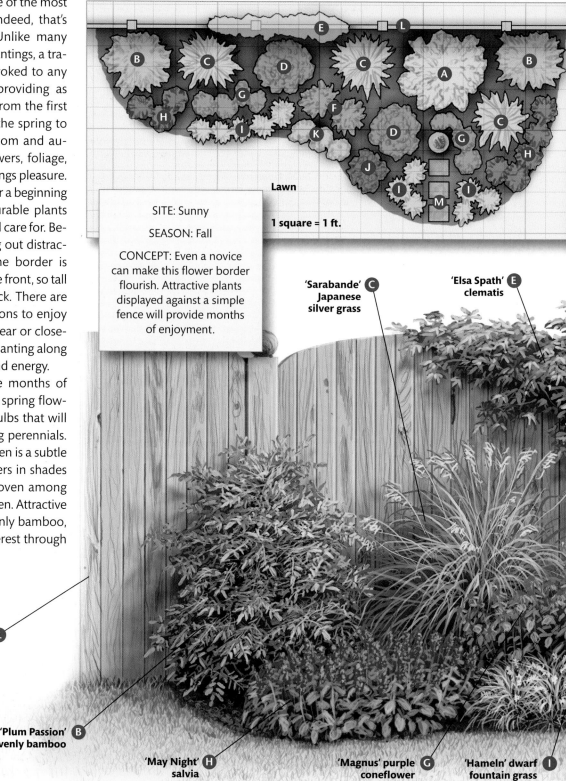

'Sarabande' Japanese silver grass **C**

'Elsa Spath' clematis **E**

Fence **L**

'Plum Passion' heavenly bamboo **B**

'May Night' **H** salvia

'Magnus' purple **G** coneflower

'Hameln' dwarf **I** fountain grass

Plants & Projects

In early spring, cut the butterfly bush, Russian sage, and ornamental grasses close to the ground. Shear spent flowers off the salvia to promote repeat bloom. Prune the clematis to control its size.

A **'Pink Delight' butterfly bush** (use 1 plant)
This deciduous shrub forms a clump of arching stems. From midsummer into fall, long spikes of pink flowers bloom at the ends of the stems. See *Buddleia davidii*, p. 196.

B **'Plum Passion' heavenly bamboo** (use 2)
The foliage of this evergreen shrub is purple when new, blue-green in summer, and purple in fall and winter. White flowers bloom in summer, followed by red berries. See *Nandina domestica*, p. 229.

C **'Sarabande' Japanese silver grass** (use 3)
This perennial forms a fountain of long, thin leaves, each green with a central white stripe. Flower stalks rise above the leaves in late summer or fall. See *Miscanthus sinensis*, p. 230.

D **'Sunset' rockrose** (use 2)
Magenta-pink flowers cover this mounded evergreen shrub for weeks in summer. Wavy-edged gray-green foliage is attractive year-round. See *Cistus* x *pulverulentus*, p. 202.

E **'Elsa Spath' clematis** (use 1)
A deciduous vine with dark green compound leaves. It bears large violet-blue flowers from late spring into fall. See *Clematis hybrids*, p. 204.

F **'Longin' Russian sage** (use 2)
This perennial forms an airy silver-gray clump of upright stems and small leaves. Bears spikes of lavender-blue flowers from summer into fall. See *Perovskia atriplicifolia*, p. 233.

G **'Magnus' purple coneflower** (use 7)
A perennial with tall, sturdy stalks that bear rosy pink flowers with dark centers from summer into fall. See *Echinacea purpurea*, p. 208.

H **'May Night' salvia** (use 8)
From early summer into fall, spikes of dark indigo-purple flowers rise above this perennial's heart-shaped leaves. See *Salvia* x *superba*, p. 241.

I **'Hameln' dwarf fountain grass** (use 11)
A clump-forming grass with thin leaves that are green in summer and gold or tan in fall.

Plumes of buff-colored flowers are borne from midsummer through fall. See *Pennisetum alopecuroides*, p. 230.

J **'Mavis Simpson' geranium** (use 1)
This sprawling perennial has light green leaves and bears small pink flowers in summer. See *Geranium* x *riversleaianum*, p. 216.

K **'Autumn Joy' sedum** (use 3)
A perennial with succulent gray-green foliage. Topped from summer through fall by flat flower heads that turn from greenish pink to deep russet. See *Sedum*, p. 242.

L **Fence**
This easy-to-build fence makes an attractive backdrop for the border. See p. 274.

M **Steppingstones and ornament**
Flagstones lead to an ornamental focal point.

C 'Sarabande' Japanese silver grass

A 'Pink Delight' butterfly bush

B 'Plum Passion' heavenly bamboo

'Autumn Joy' K sedum

F 'Longin' Russian sage

D 'Sunset' rockrose

J 'Mavis Simpson' geranium

I 'Hameln' dwarf fountain grass

M Steppingstones and ornament

A border in the shade

If the best spot for a border on your property receives only morning sun, try this design. Like the previous design, this one arranges carefully chosen combinations of shrubs and perennials against the solid background of the fence. Here, however, the plants are proven performers in the shade.

Nearest the fence are mid-size shrubs offering a mixture of deciduous and evergreen foliage and a variety of eye-catching flowers that bloom late winter through fall. Lower-growing perennials fill out the front of the bed with no less interesting foliage and flowers. The upright, swordlike leaves of the iris and sweet flag are particularly effective accents here.

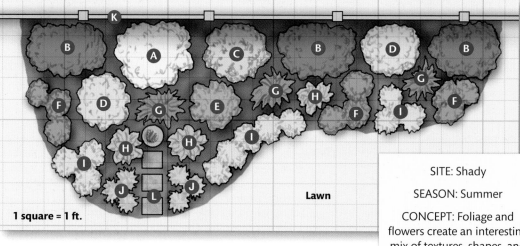

1 square = 1 ft.

Lawn

SITE: Shady

SEASON: Summer

CONCEPT: Foliage and flowers create an interesting mix of textures, shapes, and colors in a border of shade-tolerant plants.

Plants & Projects

Ⓐ Mexican orange (use 1 plant) An evergreen shrub with shiny compound leaves. Clusters of fragrant white flowers bloom in spring and sporadically through summer. See *Choisya ternata*, p. 202.

Ⓑ 'Cleopatra' camellia (use 3) An upright, compact evergreen shrub. In late fall and winter, its glossy green leaves set off rose-

pink flowers. See *Camellia sasanqua*, p. 198.

Ⓒ 'Nikko Blue' hydrangea (use 1) This deciduous shrub offers large round leaves and striking clusters of papery blue flowers in summer. See *Hydrangea macrophylla*, p. 221.

Ⓓ 'Sungold' St. Johns wort (use 2)

A vase-shaped deciduous shrub with chartreuse green leaves. It bears bright yellow flowers in summer, followed by a fall display of bright red fruit. See *Hypericum*, p. 221.

Ⓔ 'Maiden's Blush' fuchsia (use 1) An upright shrub prized for its distinctive pale pink, pendent flowers. Foliage may be ever-

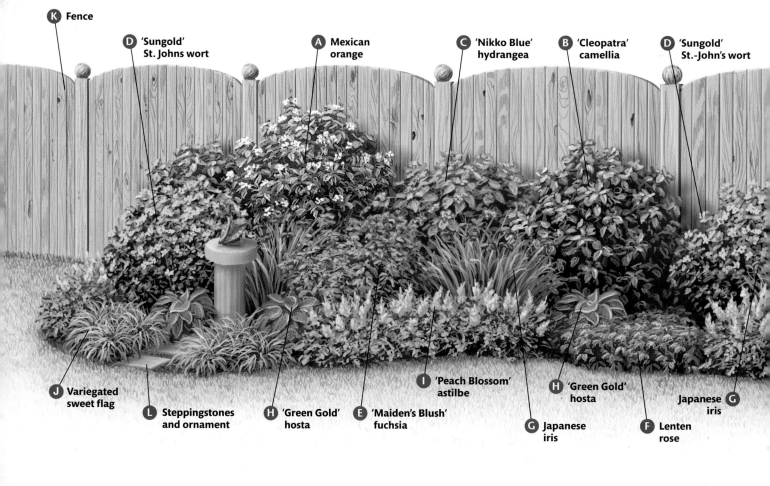

Ⓚ **Fence**

Ⓓ **'Sungold' St. Johns wort**

Ⓐ **Mexican orange**

Ⓒ **'Nikko Blue' hydrangea**

Ⓑ **'Cleopatra' camellia**

Ⓓ **'Sungold' St.-John's wort**

Ⓙ **Variegated sweet flag**

Ⓛ **Steppingstones and ornament**

Ⓗ **'Green Gold' hosta**

Ⓔ **'Maiden's Blush' fuchsia**

Ⓘ **'Peach Blossom' astilbe**

Ⓖ **Japanese iris**

Ⓗ **'Green Gold' hosta**

Ⓕ **Lenten rose**

Ⓖ **Japanese iris**

green in mild winters. See *Fuchsia*, p. 214.

F **Lenten rose** (use 9)
This perennial forms a clump of shiny green leaves with toothed edges. In late winter it bears white, greenish, pink, or purple flowers. See *Helleborus orientalis*, p. 217.

G **Japanese iris** (use 3
A perennial displaying sword-like leaves and spectacular purplish blue flowers in summer. See *Iris ensata*, p. 222.

H **'Green Gold' hosta** (use 3)
This perennial makes a clump of large dark green leaves with yellow borders that fade to cream. In summer, you can remove the lavender flowers to highlight the foliage. See *Hosta*, p. 220.

I **'Peach Blossom' astilbe** (use 11)
Striking plumes of tiny flowers rise above this perennial's feathery foliage in summer. Flowers are peach colored. See *Astilbe* x *japonica*, p. 194.

J **Variegated sweet flag** (use 6)
A perennial, grasslike plant with leaves striped creamy white and green. Spreads to form a patch. See *Acorus gramineus* 'Variegatus', p. 189.

See p. 109 for the following:

K **Fence**

L **Steppingstones and ornament**

B **'Cleopatra' camellia**

F **Lenten rose**

PLANT PORTRAITS

These shrubs and perennials are a welcome sight in borders in sun or shade.

● = First design, pp. 108-109

▲ = Second design, pp. 110-111

'Nikko Blue' Hydrangea (*Hydrangea macrophylla*, p. 221) ▲

'Hameln' Dwarf fountain grass (*Pennisetum alopecuroides*, p. 230) ●

'Peach Blossom' Astilbe (*Astilbe* x *japonica*, p. 194) ▲

'Elsa Spath' Clematis (*Clematis hybrids*, p. 204) ●

Japanese iris (*Iris ensata*, p. 222) ▲

Border for a Garden Wall

FLOWERS AND A WALL MAKE A DISTINCTIVE DISPLAY

A garden wall can serve as a backdrop for a perennial border—one of the most delightful of all gardens. Aside from softening the wall—or fence, if that is what is in your yard— a traditional border is seldom yoked to any function beyond that of providing as much pleasure as possible.

Using durable plants that are easy to establish and care for, this border is designed for a beginning or busy gardener. Behind the planting, providing a solid backdrop, is a simple wall. The border is meant to be viewed from the front, so taller plants go at the back. Draped over the wall, a trumpet vine adds a swath of dark green leaves to the backdrop, dappled for weeks in late summer with lovely deep pink flowers.

The planting offers a selection of flowers in blues, reds, pinks, and purples. Blooming over many months, there are small flowers borne in spiky clusters as well as bright cheerful daisies.

The garden's foliage is at least as compelling as its flowers. A range of textures and colors contrast with and complement one another. At the back of the planting, the striking spiky purple leaves of New Zealand flax contrast with the bushy green mound of the autumn sage. These plants are in turn framed by lacy masses of silver- gray foliage. Similar juxtapositions of color and texture are repeated on a smaller scale at the front of the planting.

If you want a larger border, just plant more of each plant to fit the space, or repeat parts of the design.

'Atropurpureum' New Zealand flax Ⓐ

Mexican bush sage Ⓑ

Sunrose Ⓛ

'Powis Castle' artemisia Ⓖ

Ⓚ 'Burgundy' gazania

Plants & Projects

Removing spent flowers and seasonal pruning are the main chores in this garden. (To allow for maintenance, leave a space between the plants at the front of the border and those at the back, as shown on the site plan.) In winter, cut the gaura and Russian sage almost to the ground, cut the germander sage back by one-third, and prune the trumpet vine to control its size. Once established, the plants require little supplemental water.

Ⓐ **'Atropurpureum' New Zealand flax** (use 1 plant)

A bold, colorful accent, this perennial offers long, reddish purple, straplike leaves. From late spring to midsummer, branched stalks of reddish flowers rise above the foliage. See *Phormium tenax*, p. 234.

Ⓑ **Mexican bush sage** (use 1)
This perennial forms a billowy mass of silver-gray foliage. It bears long spikes of velvety purple-and-white flowers from midsummer into fall. See *Salvia leucantha*, p. 241.

Ⓒ **Gaura** (use 1)
Another wispy perennial, its graceful, arching stems bear small leaves and spikes of small pink and white flowers from spring through fall. See *Gaura lindheimeri*, p. 215.

Ⓓ **Autumn sage** (use 5)
This bushy perennial's green foliage bristles with striking spikes of red flowers from spring into fall. See *Salvia greggii*, p. 241.

Ⓔ **Russian sage** (use 1)
From early summer into fall, small lavender-blue flowers float amidst this perennial's airy clump of stiff gray-green stems and sparse silvery foliage. See *Perovskia atriplicifolia*, p. 233.

Ⓕ **'Mme. Galen' trumpet vine** (use 1)
This vigorous deciduous vine bears large compound leaves on thick stems. Showy clusters of salmon flowers bloom in late summer. Stake it the first year; after that its aerial rootlets will cling to the wall. See *Campsis x tagliabuana*, p. 199.

Ⓖ **'Powis Castle' artemisia** (use 3)
This perennial makes a mound of lacy silver foliage that looks good year-round. It is an excellent companion for the colorful gazania and New Zealand flax. See *Artemisia*, p. 193.

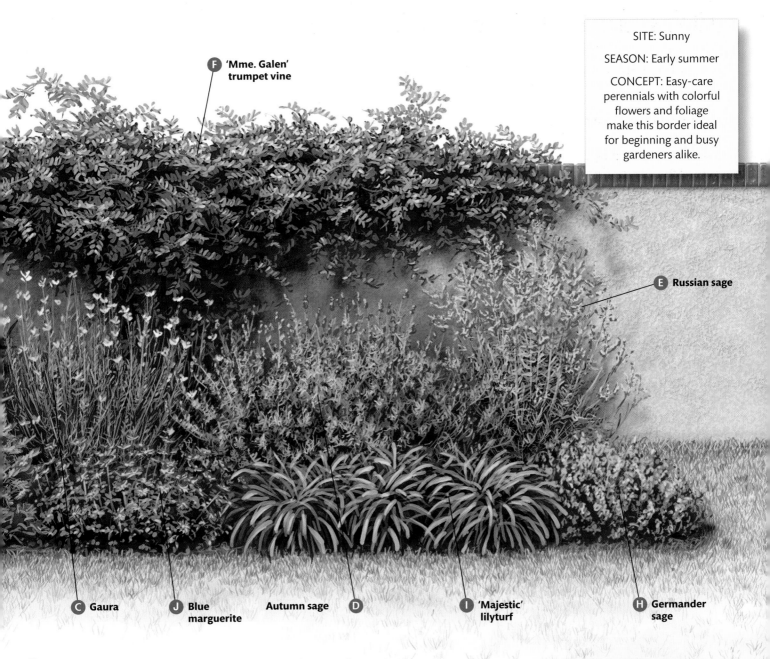

F 'Mme. Galen' trumpet vine

E Russian sage

C Gaura

J Blue marguerite

Autumn sage D

I 'Majestic' lilyturf

H Germander sage

SITE: Sunny

SEASON: Early summer

CONCEPT: Easy-care perennials with colorful flowers and foliage make this border ideal for beginning and busy gardeners alike.

H Germander sage (use 1)
Forming a low, spreading mass of small silvery leaves, this perennial bears wispy spikes of bright blue flowers from summer into fall. See *Salvia chamaedryoides*, p. 241.

I 'Majestic' lilyturf (use 3)
This evergreen perennial makes a clump of grassy dark green leaves topped by tall spikes of purple flowers in summer. See *Liriope muscari*, p. 226.

J Blue marguerite (use 3)
Cheerful blue daisies nod above the spreading foliage of this perennial throughout the

year (if you deadhead them). See *Felicia amelloides*, p. 211.

K 'Burgundy' gazania (use 4)
This perennial produces large reddish purple daisies in late spring and early summer. Dark green foliage looks good for months. See *Gazania*, p. 215.

L Sunrose (use 3)
Small, bright-colored flowers sparkle in spring and early summer on the evergreen foliage of this small shrub. Choose a cultivar with red flowers and green leaves for this design. See *Helianthemum nummularium*, p. 217.

Wall

Lawn

1 square = 1 ft.

Mixing it up

In a mixed border, shrubs join perennials, broadening the plant palette and the border's possibilities. Where winters are cold and perennials die back after hard frosts, shrubs provide interest while the perennials are dormant. However, for gardeners in much of the West, mixing shrubs and perennials in a border simply adds interest to borders that are already year-round performers. This planting shares the color scheme of the preceding design. Flowers in pinks, blues, and purples bloom for many months against a backdrop of handsome foliage in shades of silver, gray, and green. The contrasts in form and texture are perhaps less dramatic than those in the previous design. But the result is no less lovely.

SITE: Sunny

SEASON: Fall

CONCEPT: Mixing perennials and shrubs increases possibilities for a border.

Plants & Projects

Ⓐ 'Edward Goucher' abelia (use 1 plant)
An evergreen shrub with abundant rosy purple flowers from early summer to frost. Glossy foliage turns bronze-purple in winter. Flowers attract butterflies and hummingbirds. See *Abelia* x *grandiflora*, p. 187.

Ⓑ Cape mallow (use 1)
Small pink hollyhock-like flowers grace this fast-growing evergreen shrub for many months (year-round where winters are mild). See *Anisodontea* x *hypomandarum*, p. 191.

Ⓒ 'Rubens' clematis (use 1)
A deciduous vine, trained on wires attached to the wall. Fragrant pink flowers bloom in late spring. See *Clematis montana*, p. 204.

Ⓓ 'Autumn Joy' sedum (use 3)
This perennial forms clumps of fleshy gray-green leaves topped with flat flower clusters that turn from light pinkish green in summer to russet seed heads in fall. See *Sedum*, p. 242.

Ⓔ Siberian iris (use 2)
Prized for its elegant spring flowers, this perennial's graceful narrow leaves look good for many months. A purple-flowered cultivar will look best here. See *Iris sibirica*, p. 222.

Ⓕ Salvia (use 3)
A perennial topped with numerous spikes of tiny flowers from early summer through fall. Flowers range from purple to blue depending on cultivar. See *Salvia* x *superba*, p. 241.

Ⓖ Garden penstemon (use 5)
Prized for leafy spikes of showy tubular flowers, this perennial blooms from late spring to frost if deadheaded. See *Penstemon gloxinioides*, p. 233.

Ⓗ Aster (use 2)
This is a lower-growing long-blooming version of the popular perennial. It bears lilac-blue to purple flowers (depending

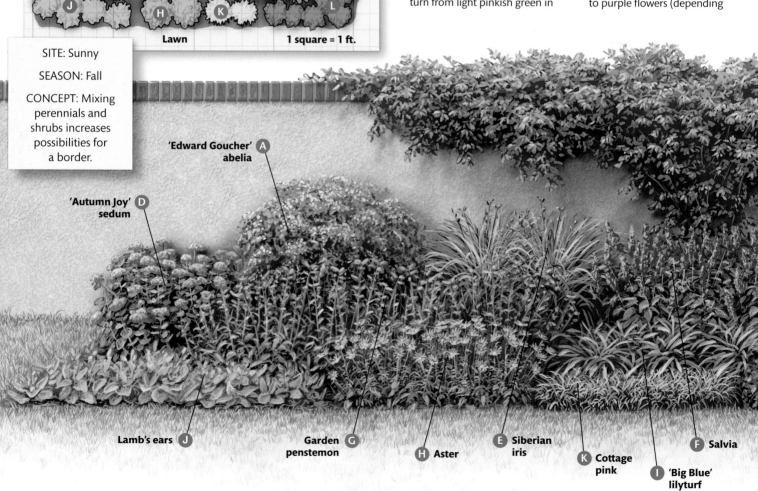

'Edward Goucher' Ⓐ abelia

'Autumn Joy' Ⓓ sedum

Lamb's ears Ⓙ

Garden Ⓖ penstemon

Ⓗ Aster

Ⓔ Siberian iris

Ⓚ Cottage pink

Ⓘ 'Big Blue' lilyturf

Ⓕ Salvia

on the cultivar) from spring through fall if deadheaded. See *Aster* x *frikartii*, p. 193.

I **'Big Blue' lilyturf** (use 4)
This perennial forms a clump of grassy evergreen foliage and bears spikes of small blue flowers in summer. See *Liriope muscari*, p. 226.

J **Lamb's ears** (use 5)
The furry silver-gray leaves of this perennial are favorites of children. Bears stalks of small purple flowers in early summer. See *Stachys byzantina*, p. 244.

K **Cottage pink** (use 2)
From late spring into fall, wonderfully fragrant light pink flowers rise above this perennial's mat of fine-textured, silvery evergreen foliage. See *Dianthus plumarius*, p. 207.

L **Dwarf plumbago** (use 6)
This perennial ground cover is covered with blue flowers in late summer and fall. See *Cerato-stigma plumbaginoides*, p. 201.

C **'Rubens' clematis**

B **Cape mallow**

L **Dwarf plumbago**

VARIATIONS ON A THEME

Whether your taste runs to native plants or formal English perennial gardens, there are countless ways to create an attractive border.

Tall and short, bold and fine-textured plants mingle in this mixed border. Its glory is traditional—the display of beautiful flowers.

Ornamental grasses are a striking addition to a border and provide interest throughout the year.

A Woodland Link

CREATE A SHRUB BORDER FOR NEARBY WOODS

Mature woodlands are sometimes found in urban as well as rural areas. Some newer subdivisions incorporate woodland as communal space or have left it intact on individual properties. And in some older neighborhoods, mature trees on adjacent lots create almost the same woodland feeling.

The planting shown here integrates a domestic landscape with a woodland edge, making a pleasant transition between the open area of lawn and the woods beyond. The design takes inspiration from the buffer zone of small trees and shrubs nature provides at a sunny woodland edge, and it should provide the same attraction for wildlife and people as does the edge of a natural woodland.

Shrubs and perennials of various sizes mingle in the planting, larger ones toward the back, imitating natural layered growth. A small tree anchors one corner, its height echoing the taller trees in the woods behind. A path winds through a "meadow" of flowering shrubs and perennials before entering the woods.

Whether viewed from across the yard or up close, the planting is appealing all year. Spring ushers in nodding narcissus, redbud blossoms, scented viburnum, and stands of delicate, frilly irises; summer produces a rich assortment of red, pink, orange, and yellow flowers; and fall offers up pink-blushed camellias.

SITE: Sunny

SEASON: Summer

CONCEPT: A small tree, shrubs, and perennials make a pleasing transition between lawn and adjacent woodland.

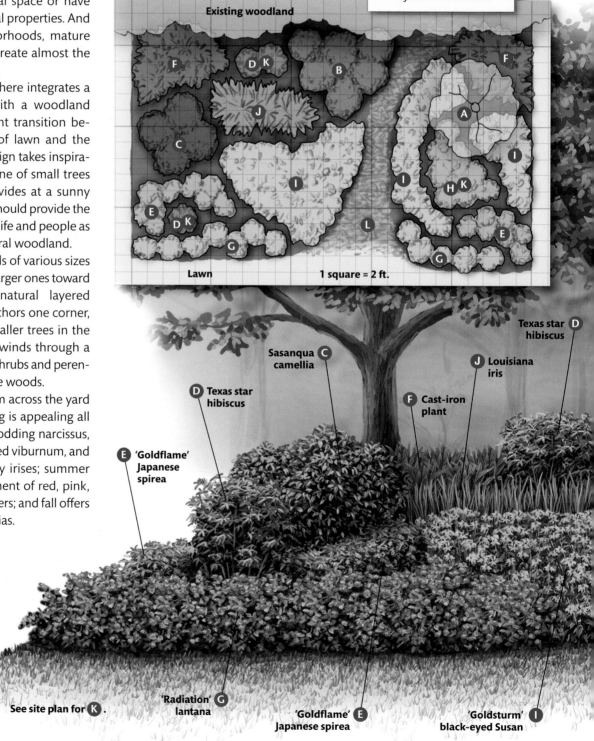

Existing woodland

Lawn

1 square = 2 ft.

Texas star hibiscus **D**

Sasanqua camellia **C**

Louisiana iris **J**

Texas star hibiscus **D**

Cast-iron plant **F**

'Goldflame' Japanese spirea **E**

'Radiation' lantana **G**

See site plan for **K** .

'Goldflame' Japanese spirea **E**

'Goldsturm' black-eyed Susan **I**

Plants & Projects

Before planting, dig and improve the soil throughout the entire area (except under the path) with organic matter. A mulch of compost or wood chips and regular watering the first summer will speed establishment. Other than seasonal maintenance, you'll need to divide the perennials when they become crowded in a few years.

Ⓐ Redbud (use 1 plant)
A graceful native tree for wood's edge. Branches are suffused in spring with pink-purple blossoms followed by heart-shaped leaves, green in summer, gold in fall. Its rounded shape is attractive even when branches are bare of blossoms and leaves. See *Cercis canadensis*, p. 201

Ⓑ 'Spring Bouquet' viburnum (use 6)
Foliage, flowers, and fruit make this plant an outstanding woodland selection. Massed together, these shrubs will provide a grand display of fragrant white blossoms in spring as well as dark blue berries in summer and handsome green foliage the year round. See *Viburnum tinus* 'Spring Bouquet', p. 246.

Ⓒ Sasanqua camellia (use 4)
Beautiful blooms framed by dark glossy foliage give this evergreen shrub a strong presence in the planting. Colors and bloom time vary by cultivar. We've shown 'Hana Jiman', a white-flowering cultivar edged in pink. See *Camellia sasanqua*, p. 198.

Ⓓ Texas star hibiscus (use 3)
This striking perennial will rise above neighboring plants in summer and fall, its leafy stalks showcasing large red flowers that attract butterflies and hummingbirds. See *Hibiscus coccineus*, p. 220.

Ⓔ 'Goldflame' Japanese spirea (use 16)
For sunlit foliage, plant this gold-leafed shrub among the deeper greens. Large, flat clusters of tiny pink flowers give the shrub a lacy appearance from late spring through midsummer. See *Spiraea* x *bumalda* 'Goldflame', p. 243.

Ⓕ Cast-iron plant (use 35)
These evergreen perennials will make an impressive stand of erect, swordlike, dark green leaves at the foot of the woods. See *Aspidistra elatior*, p. 193.

Ⓖ 'Radiation' lantana (use 12)
This bushy perennial spreads to form a wide mound of fuzzy foliage covered from spring to fall with masses of tiny orange flowers. See *Lantana camara* 'Radiation', p. 225.

Ⓗ Turk's cap (use 9)
Another perennial with striking red blooms sought by hummingbirds and butterflies. Deciduous leaves are heart-shaped and deep green. See *Malvaviscus arboreus drummondii*, p. 228.

Ⓘ 'Goldsturm' black-eyed Susan (as needed)
Plant these black-eyed Susans in swaths—a hundred or more for an unbroken sweep of gold daisies the first season; half as many if you're willing to wait a year or so. These vigorous, bushy plants will soon fill the space. See *Rudbeckia fulgida* 'Goldsturm', p. 240.

Ⓙ Louisiana iris (as needed)
This perennial forms an attractive clump of erect foliage. In early spring it sends up showy flowers on 3 ft. stalks. Colors range across the spectrum. For this planting we recommend a yellow-blooming variety. Plant on 2 ft. to 3 ft. centers. See *Iris* x *Louisiana* hybrids, p. 222.

Ⓚ Narcissus (as needed)
Splashes of bright color can be had early in the season with these spring bulbs. Plant them around the Turk's cap and Texas star hibiscus; they'll be in bloom while the two shrubs are dormant. These bulbs come in yellows, whites, and oranges. Choose a yellow flower, as shown here, or your favorite mix of colors, and plant lots of them. See Bulbs: *Narcissus tazetta*, p.196.

Ⓛ Path
This wood-chip path nicely complements the woodland feeling. See p. 258.

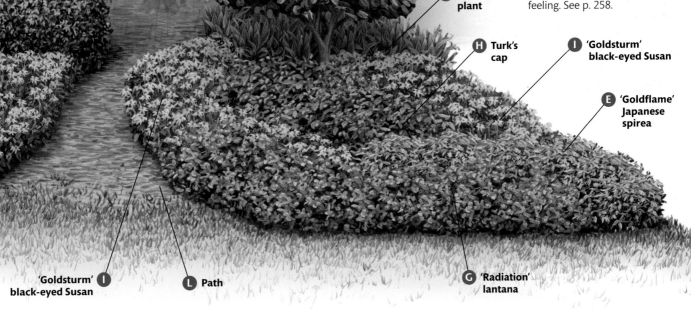

PLANT PORTRAITS

With handsome foliage and flowers, these plants are effective against a woodland backdrop.

● = First design, pp. 116-117
▲ = Second design, pp. 118-119

'Hana Jiman' Sasanqua camellia
(*Camellia sasanqua*, p. 198) ●

Louisiana iris
(*Iris* x *Louisiana hybrids*, p. 222) ●

'Harbour Dwarf' Heavenly bamboo
(*Nandina domestica*, p. 229) ▲

'Manhattan' Euonymus
(*Euonymus kiautschovicus*, p. 210) ▲

'Goldflame' Japanese spirea
(*Spiraea* x *bumalda*, p. 243) ●

Link for a shadier edge

If a woodland adjacent to your property lends a great deal of shade, try this design, which features shade-tolerant plants. The concept is the same as in the previous design—plants increasing in height toward the woods—but the actual layout is somewhat different. A wider path ambles to the right; a flowering trellis marks the entry into the woods; and foliage textures and colors take the place of flowers, providing interest in all seasons.

The planting is at its most colorful in fall and winter, when masses of burnished heavenly bamboo stand out against the light greens of ferns and the deeper greens of holly and euonymous. Fall is also emblazoned with the reds and purples of countless berries.

Plants & Projects

Ⓐ Possumhaw holly (use 2 plants)
This native deciduous shrub has year-round appeal. In season, it wears a thick coat of glossy foliage. When shed, it exposes silver-gray twigs laden with long-lasting red berries. Birds love to eat them. See *Ilex decidua*, p. 222.

Ⓑ 'Manhattan' euonymus (use 12)
These evergreen shrubs will make a handsome framework for the other plantings, eventually growing into a dense, irregular mound 8 to 10 ft. tall. The attractive foliage stays dark green and shiny all year. See *Euonymus kiautschovicus* 'Manhattan', p. 210.

Ⓒ American beautyberry (use 3)
A pest-free shrub with a somewhat open and arching habit.

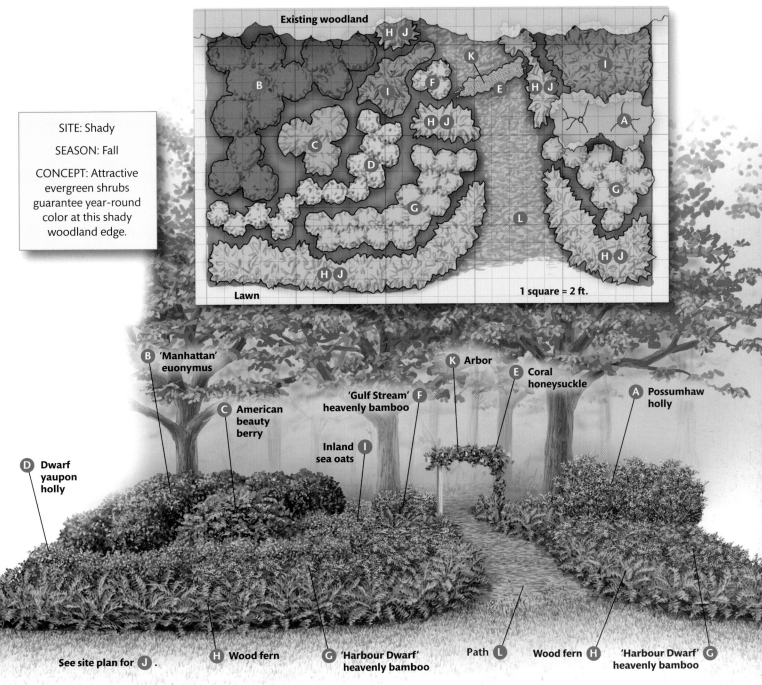

SITE: Shady

SEASON: Fall

CONCEPT: Attractive evergreen shrubs guarantee year-round color at this shady woodland edge.

Existing woodland

Lawn

1 square = 2 ft.

B 'Manhattan' euonymus

C American beauty berry

D Dwarf yaupon holly

K Arbor

E Coral honeysuckle

A Possumhaw holly

F 'Gulf Stream' heavenly bamboo

I Inland sea oats

See site plan for **J**.

H Wood fern

G 'Harbour Dwarf' heavenly bamboo

Path **L**

H Wood fern

G 'Harbour Dwarf' heavenly bamboo

The inconspicuous flowers produce eye-popping purple berries that last long after the leaves drop. See *Callicarpa americana*, p. 198.

D Dwarf yaupon holly (use 14) This shrub's olive-green foliage complements the other leaf colors. See *Ilex vomitoria* 'Nana', p. 222.

E Coral honeysuckle (use 1) A native vine that blooms dependably in shade. It bears showy whorls of red-orange flowers, followed by pretty red berries in fall and winter. Gray-blue leaves are attractive and

usually evergreen. See *Lonicera sempervirens*, p. 227.

F 'Gulf Stream' heavenly bamboo (use 3) This compact evergreen shrub makes a colorful ground cover. Fine-textured leaves are tinged bronze, orange, and purple, turning bright red in winter. See *Nandina domestica* 'Gulf Stream', p. 229.

G 'Harbour Dwarf' heavenly bamboo (use 26) A lower-growing version of heavenly bamboo (wider than tall) with larger, less colorful foliage than 'Gulf Stream'. It pro-

duces small red berries in the center of the plant. See *Nandina domestica* 'Harbour Dwarf', p. 229.

H Wood fern (as needed) A vigorous spreading perennial fern. The fronds are bright green and deeply cut. Plant as many of them as needed on 2-ft. centers. See Ferns: *Thelypteris kunthii*, p. 213.

I Inland sea oats (use 32) This native grass makes a natural transition to the woods. Grows in ever-larger clumps and also spreads from seed. Long seed heads resemble oats

and dangle and dance from arching stems in fall. See *Chasmanthium latifolium*, p. 230.

J Snowflake (as needed) White flowers planted among the ferns are lovely in early spring. Plant several hundred bulbs if possible. See Bulbs: *Leucojum aestivum*, p. 196.

K Arbor Placed at the entry to the woods, this simple cedar arbor invites visitors for a woodland stroll. See p. 283.

See p.117 for the following:

L Path

A No-Mow Slope

A TERRACED GARDEN TRANSFORMS A STEEP SLOPE

SITE: Sunny

SEASON: Fall

CONCEPT: Retaining walls, steps, and plants tame this slope and enhance the home's public face.

F Russian sage

J Coreopsis

C Spineless prickly pear

H Copper canyon daisy

A Texas mountain laurel

B Turk's cap

F Russian sage

H Copper canyon daisy

Dwarf pampas grass **E**

Yucca **K**

Mealycup sage **D**

'Trailing Lavender' lantana **G**

Ox-eye daisy **I**

E Dwarf pampas grass

F Russian sage

Retaining wall and steps **L**

Yucca **K**

Steep slopes can be a landscaping headache. Planted with lawn grass, they're a chore to mow, and they can present problems of erosion and maintenance if you try to establish other ground covers or plantings. One solution to this dilemma is shown here—tame the slope by building a low retaining wall and steps. Then plant the resulting flat (or flatter) beds with an assortment of interesting low-care trees, shrubs, and perennials.

In this design, a narrow steeply sloping front yard has been terraced and walled and the lawn replaced by plantings. The result transforms the home's public face and creates an enticing walk to the front door. You can extend the planting by repeating elements of the design, or leave some lawn for kids to enjoy.

Visitors approaching from the sidewalk pass through colorful shrubs and perennials. A small landing on the steps, introduced at wall height, offers opportunity to pause and enjoy nearby plants before continuing on to the front door. The walk from the drive is no less pleasant. Visitors from both directions will be met with a profusion of blooms in nearly every season, and a few surprises as well: the sweet scent of Texas mountain laurel in spring, the spectacle of large white yucca blossoms in summer, and purple cactus fruit in fall.

Plants & Projects

Reshaping the slope and building the hardscape (retaining walls, steps, and walkways) is a big job. Even if you plan to do much of the work yourself, it is prudent to consult a landscape contractor for advice. Once the plants are established, this design will provide years of enjoyment with little more than seasonal pruning and cleanup.

A Texas mountain laurel (use 1 plant)
A Texas native evergreen tree with gnarly branches, sparkling leaflets, and attractive bark. Wisteria-like clusters of grape-scented flowers in spring are followed by fat bean pods that eventually reveal shiny red seeds. See *Sophora secundiflora*, p. 243.

B Turk's cap (use 9)
This tough perennial makes a velvety patch of foliage that showcases small red flowers all season. See *Malvaviscus arboreus drummondii*, p. 228.

C Spineless prickly pear (use 2)
A bold "sculpture" for the entry, this cactus forms an interesting patchwork of coarse succulent leaf pads. In some years it may produce yellow flowers in summer and purple fruits in the fall. See *Opuntia lindheimeri*, p. 230.

D Mealycup sage (use 11)
The fringe of bright blue flowers borne on this perennial makes a pretty edge around plants and lawn. Shear a few times during the season to refresh their bloom. See *Salvia farinacea*, p. 241.

E Dwarf pampas grass (use 11)
These fountains of fine-textured grass are topped in late summer with feathery creamy-white flowers. Foliage is evergreen. See *Cortaderia selloana* 'Pumila', p. 205.

F Russian sage (use 14)
This erect perennial forms an airy vase of slender, silver-leaved stems tipped with tiny pale blue flowers. Blooms non-stop from midsummer to fall. Cut plant back after frost. See *Perovskia atriplicifolia*, p. 233.

G 'Trailing Lavender' lantana (use 4)
This perennial spreads into a wide mound of fuzzy leaves covered with small domes of lavender-purple flowers. See *Lantana montevidensis* 'Trailing Lavender', p. 225.

H Copper canyon daisy (use 8)
A pretty, lace-leafed perennial marigold bearing bright gold flowers in autumn. See *Tagetes lemmonii*, p. 244.

I Ox-eye daisy (use 8)
White daisies with yellow centers will cheer visitors in spring. The rest of the season this perennial offers a mound of curly green leaves. See *Chrysanthemum leucanthemum*, p. 202.

J Coreopsis (use 15)
A mounding perennial with linear leaves and many slender stalks of single flower heads with sunlike rays. See *Coreopsis lanceolata*, p .204.

K Yucca (use 3)
These spiky evergreen shrubs make striking accents. Spectacular stalks of nodding white flowers rise as high as lampposts in late spring and last through midsummer. See *Yucca filamentosa*, p. 249.

L Retaining wall and steps
The walls and steps are made with a precast concrete retaining-wall system available at garden centers. Choose a color that complements the house. See p. 270.

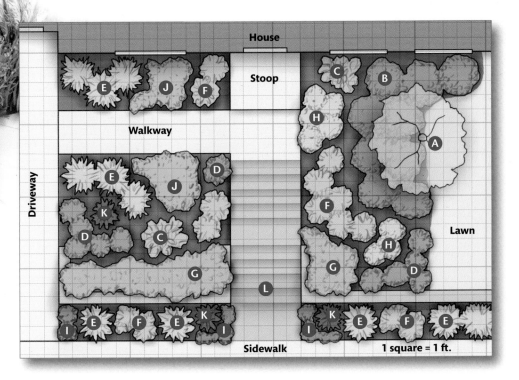

House · Stoop · Walkway · Driveway · Lawn · Sidewalk · 1 square = 1 ft.

PLANT PORTRAITS

These durable, low-care plants will help transform difficult hillsides.

● = First design, pp. 120-121

▲ = Second design, pp. 122-123

'Petite Salmon' Oleander
(*Nerium oleander*, p. 229) ▲

Periwinkle
(*Vinca major*, p. 247) ▲

Yucca (*Yucca filamentosa*, p. 249) ●

'Trailing Lavender' Lantana
(*Lantana montevidensis*, p. 225) ●

'Evergreen Giant' Lilyturf
(*Liriope muscari*, p. 226) ▲

Victoria regina agave
(*Agave victoriae-reginae*, p. 190) ▲

Working with a hillside

If terracing a slope with retaining walls and steps does not appeal to you, or is beyond your budget, consider this design. Here we've worked with the existing hillside, replacing turfgrass with tough, easy-care ground covers. A small tree provides a colorful accent as well as a modest level of privacy from street and sidewalk traffic.

These plants thrive in the poor, dry soil and the heat often found on slopes and hillsides. Their tenacious root systems, particularly those of periwinkle and lilyturf, will hold the soil in place. Without exception, these plants require infrequent watering once they are established.

The planting is as attractive as it is durable. There are flowers blooming nearly all season. And the varied textures and colors of the foliage are pleasing year-round.

Plants & Projects

Ⓐ Chaste tree (use 1 plant)
Well-suited to dry hillside conditions, this small deciduous tree produces showers of blue-purple flowers all season. See *Vitex agnus-castus*, p. 247.

Ⓑ 'Petite Salmon' oleander (use 6)
This compact evergreen shrub bears small glossy leaves. From spring to frost the foliage is flush with salmon pink flowers. See *Nerium oleander* 'Petite Salmon', p. 229.

Ⓒ Periwinkle (as needed)
A vigorously trailing evergreen ground cover. Bears lavender-purple flowers amid heart-shaped foliage in spring. Space plants 1 ft. apart for solid coverage. See *Vinca major*, p. 247.

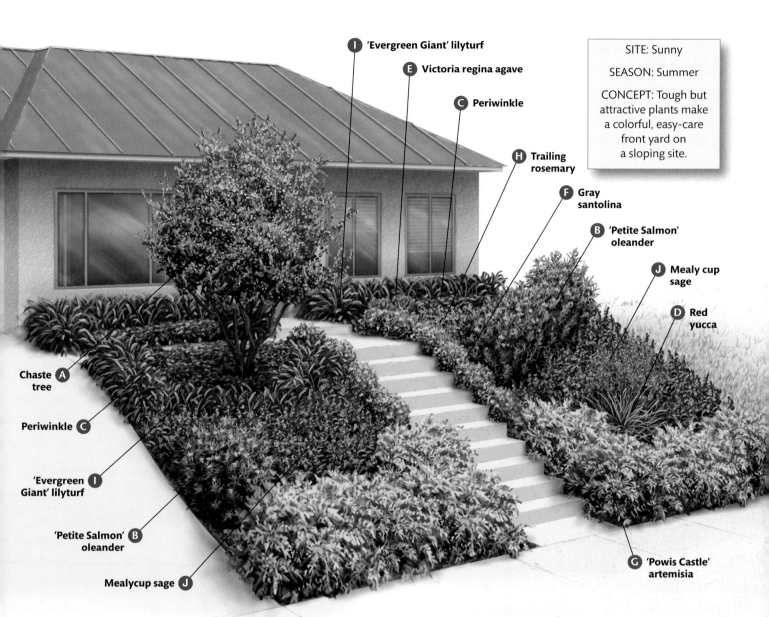

I 'Evergreen Giant' lilyturf

E Victoria regina agave

C Periwinkle

H Trailing rosemary

F Gray santolina

B 'Petite Salmon' oleander

J Mealy cup sage

D Red yucca

SITE: Sunny

SEASON: Summer

CONCEPT: Tough but attractive plants make a colorful, easy-care front yard on a sloping site.

Chaste **A** tree

Periwinkle **C**

'Evergreen **I** Giant' lilyturf

'Petite Salmon' **B** oleander

Mealycup sage **J**

G 'Powis Castle' artemisia

D Red yucca (use 3)
Spiky foliage gives this shrub a striking presence among billowy neighbors. Coral pink flowers echo the color of the oleander blossoms. *Hesperaloe parviflora*, p. 218.

E Victoria regina agave (use 3)
A small but nonetheless bold succulent perennial, it resembles an artichoke bud. See *Agave victoriae-reginae*, p. 190.

F Gray santolina (use 10)
Ideal for edges, this evergreen shrub's low mounds of thick gray leaves bear countless small flowers in summer. See *Santolina chamaecyparissus*, p. 242.

G 'Powis Castle' artemisia (use 11)
A billowy perennial whose

foliage will soften the slope's steep face and act as a foil for the flowers. See *Artemisia* x 'Powis Castle', p. 193.

H Trailing rosemary (use 5)
A low, spreading evergreen shrub bearing tiny fragrant quill-like leaves and equally fragrant blue blossoms. See *Rosmarinus officinalis* 'Prostratus', p. 240.

I 'Evergreen Giant' lilyturf (as needed)
This is the largest version of a popular grassy evergreen ground cover. Plant on 2-ft. centers. See *Liriope muscari* 'Evergreen Giant', p. 226.

See p. 121 for the following:

J Mealycup sage (use 30)

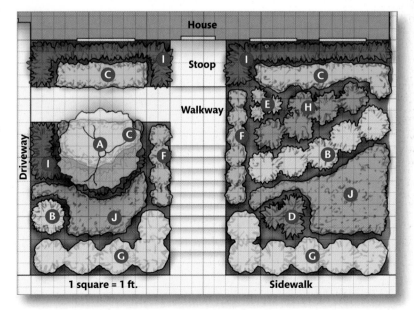

1 square = 1 ft.

Taming a Slope

RETAINING WALLS CREATE GARDENING OPPORTUNITIES

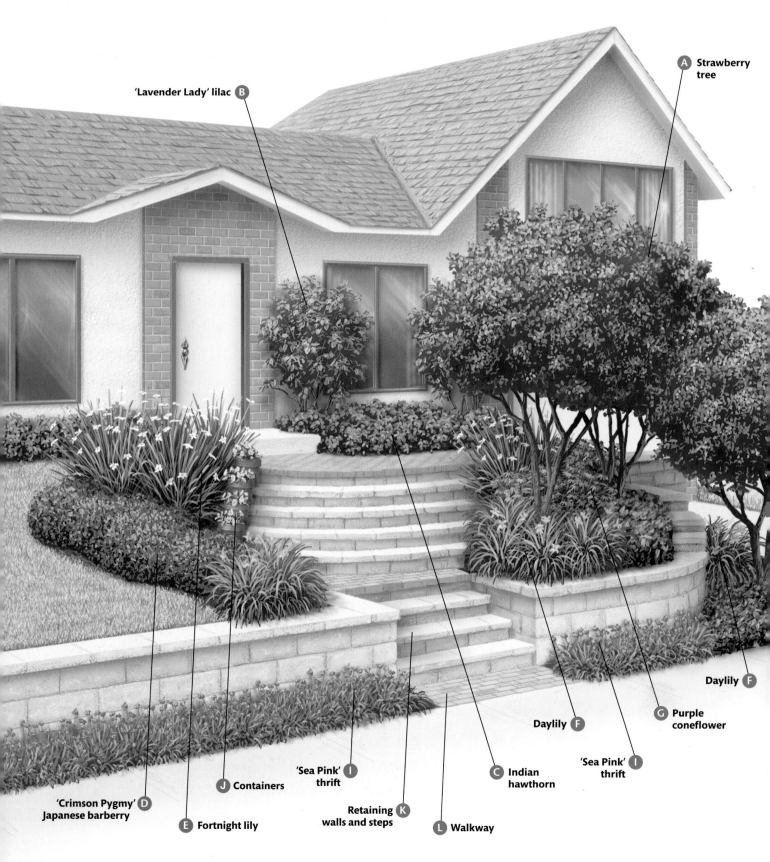

A Strawberry tree

'Lavender Lady' lilac B

F Daylily

G Purple coneflower

I 'Sea Pink' thrift

F Daylily

C Indian hawthorn

J Containers

I 'Sea Pink' thrift

K Retaining walls and steps

L Walkway

D 'Crimson Pygmy' Japanese barberry

E Fortnight lily

Steep slopes pose a true landscaping challenge. Even a small hill planted with lawn grass is difficult to mow and to keep looking its best. And slopes often suffer from erosion problems. One solution is shown here—tame the slope with low retaining walls and steps, and plant the resulting flat (or flatter) beds with attractive trees, shrubs, and perennials.

Steep slopes near the house are common in many newer hillside communities. Here, a narrow steeply sloping front yard has been terraced with low retaining walls and wide steps. The result transforms the home's public face and creates an enticing path that meanders up to the front door from the street.

Visitors approaching from the sidewalk pass through colorful plantings. A set of wide curving steps framed by landings above and below encourages a slow passage, offering time to enjoy the nearby plants. The walk from the drive to the front door is more direct, but no less pleasant. Near the house, you can extend the foundation shrubs along the house or tie them into existing plantings. For houses with steep backyards, the lawn here can provide a play area. Or, you might replace the lawn with an easy-care alternative ground cover.

Plants & Projects

Building retaining walls, steps, and walkways will reshape our yard, but they are all big jobs often left to a contractor. Even if you plan to do much of the work yourself, it is prudent to consult a landscape contractor for advice. Once the plants are established, this design will provide years of enjoyment with little more than seasonal pruning and cleanup.

Ⓐ Strawberry tree (use 3 plants)
This multitrunked evergreen tree with gnarly branches offers shiny leaves and attractive bark. Small bell-shaped white flowers are followed by red fruits in autumn and winter. See *Arbutus unedo*, p. 192.

Ⓑ 'Lavender Lady' lilac (use 2)
Bred to bloom well in mild-winter areas, this deciduous shrub bears sweetly fragrant lavender flowers in spring. See *Syringa vulgaris*, p. 244.

Ⓒ Indian hawthorn (use 10)
From fall to spring, this ever-green shrub showcases small flowers against rich green foliage. Pick a low-growing cultivar such as 'Jack Evans', which bears light pink flowers. See *Rhaphiolepis indica*, p. 236.

Ⓓ 'Crimson Pygmy' Japanese barberry (use 5)
The purple foliage of this low, spreading deciduous shrub turns crimson in fall, making a colorful edge to the planting. See *Berberis thunbergii*, p. 194.

Ⓔ Fortnight lily (use 4)
This perennial forms an eye-catching clump of straplike evergreen leaves. Colorfully marked white flowers top wiry stems from spring through fall. See *Dietes vegeta*, p. 208.

Ⓕ Daylily (use 10)
The cheerful, fresh flowers of this perennial greet visitors. Choose a long-blooming yellow-flowered cultivar such as 'Stella d'Oro'. See *Hemerocallis*, p. 218.

Ⓖ Purple coneflower (use 4)
With coarse green foliage and bold purple daisylike flowers, this perennial is a good companion for the nearby daylilies and fortnight lilies. Blooms many weeks in summer. See *Echinacea purpurea*, p. 208.

Ⓗ Dwarf plumbago (use 7)
A sprawling perennial ground cover, its light green foliage turns maroon after a frost. Bears indigo blue flowers in summer. See *Ceratostigma plumbaginoides*, p. 201.

Ⓘ 'Sea Pink' thrift (use 15)
This perennial forms tufts of grassy evergreen foliage. It produces a spring display of pink flowers and scattered bloom into fall. You can extend the planting along the wall. See *Armeria maritima*, p. 192.

Ⓙ Containers
Make seasonal plantings in four 12-in. terra-cotta pots, one on each curved step. Yellow and blue pansies are shown here for spring.

Ⓚ Retaining walls and steps
The walls and steps are made with a precast concrete retaining-wall system available at garden centers. See p. 270.

Ⓛ Walkway
Choose a surface that complements your house. Here a brick walkway echoes brick details on the house. See p. 259.

SITE: Sunny

SEASON: Late spring

CONCEPT: Retaining walls, steps, and attractive plants tame this slope and enhance the home's public face.

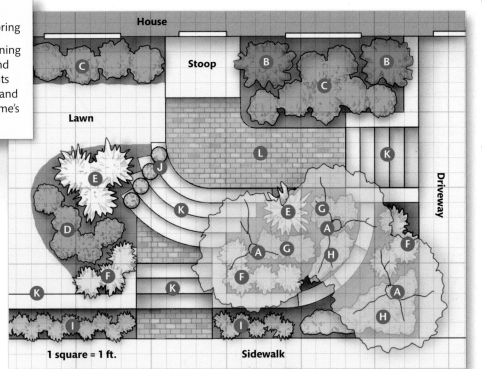

Ⓗ Dwarf plumbago

House

Stoop

Lawn

Driveway

1 square = 1 ft.

Sidewalk

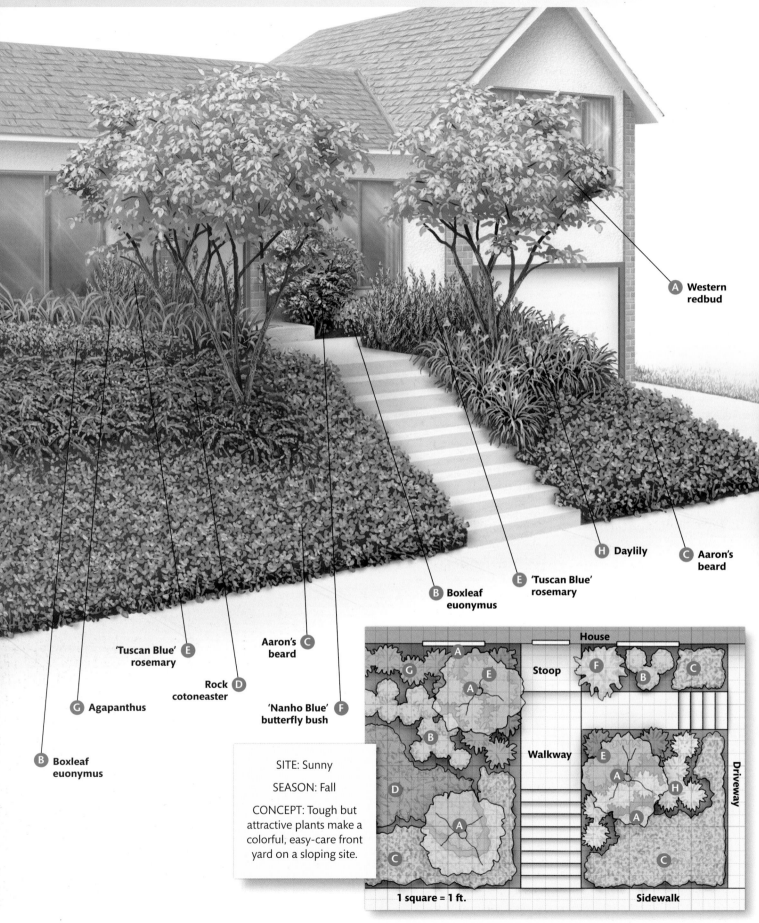

A Western redbud

H Daylily

C Aaron's beard

B Boxleaf euonymus

E 'Tuscan Blue' rosemary

E 'Tuscan Blue' rosemary

C Aaron's beard

D Rock cotoneaster

G Agapanthus

F 'Nanho Blue' butterfly bush

B Boxleaf euonymus

SITE: Sunny

SEASON: Fall

CONCEPT: Tough but attractive plants make a colorful, easy-care front yard on a sloping site.

House

Stoop

Walkway

Driveway

Sidewalk

1 square = 1 ft.

Planting a hillside

Terracing a steep slope with retaining walls and steps is only one option for dealing with a slope. Here we've worked with, rather than change, the existing hillside, replacing turfgrass with tough, easy-care ground covers. Small trees provide dappled shade as well as a modest level of privacy from street and sidewalk traffic.

These plants thrive in the poor, dry soil and the heat often found on slopes. Their tenacious root systems, particularly those of Aaron's beard and rock cotoneaster, will hold the soil in place. With the exception of the butterfly bush by the door, these plants require infrequent supplemental watering once they're established.

The planting is as attractive as it is durable. Flowers bloom almost year-round, beginning with the tiny reddish flowers of the redbuds and extending through a late-winter display of deep blue rosemary blossoms. Butterflies hovering over the butterfly bush are an added treat. The varied textures of the foliage are pleasing year-round. And the fall colors of the redbuds and rock cotoneaster are a delight.

Plants & Projects

Ⓐ Western redbud (use 3 plants)
This small California native deciduous tree is well suited to dry hillside conditions. In spring, leafless branches bear small magenta flowers. Foliage is yellow in fall. See *Cercis occidentalis*, p. 201.

Ⓑ Boxleaf euonymus (use 14)
This compact evergreen shrub has small, glossy green leaves. See *Euonymus japonicus* 'Microphyllus', p. 210.

Ⓒ Aaron's beard (as needed)
A low, vigorously spreading ground cover, this evergreen shrub bears large, bright yellow flowers in summer. Space plants 1½ ft. apart for solid coverage. See *Hypericum calycinum*, p. 221.

Ⓓ Rock cotoneaster (as needed)
This wiry deciduous shrub is another tough ground cover. Dark green leaves turn orange and red in fall. New leaves appear quickly. Bears white to pink flowers in spring. Showy red berries follow. Plant 5 ft. apart, or closer for quicker coverage. See *Cotoneaster horizontalis*, p. 206.

Ⓔ 'Tuscan Blue' rosemary (use 8)
An upright evergreen shrub, it offers fragrant foliage and deep blue flowers in late winter and early spring. See *Rosmarinus officinalis*, p. 240.

Ⓕ 'Nanho Blue' butterfly bush (use 1)
A compact form of the popular deciduous shrub, ideal next to the door. Its arching stems bear spikes of fragrant blue flowers from midsummer to fall. See *Buddleia davidii*, p. 196.

Ⓖ Agapanthus (use 7)
This perennial makes a handsome clump of straplike evergreen leaves topped in late spring and summer with ball-shaped clusters of small blue or white flowers. See *Agapanthus orientalis*, p. 189.

See p. 125 for the following:

Ⓗ Daylily (use 8)

VARIATIONS ON A THEME

The possibilities for attractive plantings on a slope are endless. Similar in approach to the designs shown in the renderings, those shown below employ different plants and hardscape just as effectively.

Low-growing shrubs in shades of gray, green, and purple cover the hillside in this large-scale rock garden. Lavender, santolina, and rosemary are shown here. Narrow evergreen trees provide a vertical accent near the house.

Intermingled with mounding plants, these long, low steps suit the site perfectly.

A Sloping Yard

FRONT YARD EVOKES THE PRAIRIE

The prairie, with its many grasses, silver- and gray-leaved plants adapted to aridity, and striking wildflowers, is brought to mind by this design.

Like the one on p. 124, this design incorporates a curving stair off center from the front door. The landing at the top of the stairs is ideal for welcoming visitors, and it is big enough to accommodate a bench to sit on while enjoying the plantings.

The semicircular planting bed along the sidewalk pleases passersby with its late spring display of red-purple cranesbill and its long-blooming summer show of coneflowers, both set off by silvery gray artemisia.

Flanking the driveway, a colorful spring mixture of purple, red, hot pink, and yellow flowers segues into a foliage display through the summer and fall. Up on the top level, maiden grass, yarrow, and Russian sage reinforce the prairielike feel of the planting. The redbud provides a focal point and, depending on the planting's orientation, some much appreciated shade.

'Blue Spice' Russian sage **D**

'Moonshine' yarrow **C**

'Morning Light' maiden grass **B**

'Magnus' coneflower **G**

'Powis Castle' artemisia **F**

Bloody cranesbill **E**

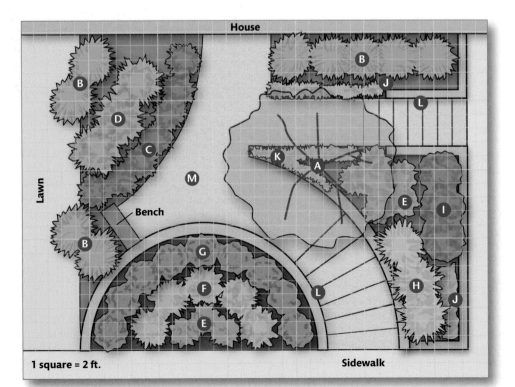

House

Lawn

Bench

1 square = 2 ft.

Sidewalk

Plants & Projects

A Eastern redbud (use 1)
The limbs of this small deciduous tree are covered by a haze of tiny purple flowers in spring. Dark green, heart-shaped leaves turn gold in fall. See *Cercis canadensis,* p. 201.

B 'Morning Light' maiden grass (use 9)
A vase-shaped perennial with slender arching white-striped leaves, it produces tall stalks of fluffy flowers in late summer and fall. See *Miscanthus sinensis* 'Morning Light', p. 231.

C 'Moonshine' yarrow (use 7)
This perennial forms neat mounds of ferny gray-green foliage topped with lots of little

A Eastern redbud

B 'Morning Light' maiden grass

J 'Firewitch' dianthus

I 'Furman's Red' autumn sage

E Bloody cranesbill

J 'Firewitch' dianthus

K 'Boulder Blue' blue fescue

L Retaining wall and steps

H Lydia broom

SITE: Sunny

SEASON: Summer

Concept: A low-water-use planting replaces part of a thirsty lawn and showcases the front entry.

yellow flowers during the summer months. See *Achillea* 'Moonshine', p. 188.

D **'Blue Spice' Russian sage** (use 3)
In summer this perennial produces tiny dark blue flowers on long stiff stalks bearing wispy gray-green foliage. See *Perovskia atripliciolfia* 'Blue Spice' p. 233.

E **Bloody cranesbill** (use 9)
This perennial produces a sprawling mat of finely cut leaves topped in spring and early summer with round, red to purple flowers. See *Geranium sanguineum*, p. 216.

F **'Powis Castle' artemisia** (use 5)
Grown for its distinctive foliage, this perennial forms a billowy mass of finely cut silver-gray leaves. See *Artemisia* 'Powis Castle' p. 193.

G **'Magnus' coneflower** (use 9)
Large daisylike reddish purple flowers with fat, button centers, float above this perennial's narrow, dark green leaves for much of the summer. See *Echinacea purpurea* 'Magnus' p. 208.

H **Lydia broom** (use 3)
Smothered with small yellow flowers in spring, this shrub's tangle of low-arching, twiggy

green stems (it is almost leafless) make a fine ground cover the rest of the year. See *Genista lydia*, p. 216.

I **'Furman's Red' autumn sage** (use 3)
Fine-textured upright perennial covered with slender spikes of bright red flowers from late spring through fall. Light green leaves are evergreen. See *Salvia greggi* 'Furmans Red' p. 241.

J **'Firewitch' dianthus** (use 9)
This perennial forms an airy mass of gray foliage topped in late spring by hot-pink flowers. See *Dianthus gratianopolitanus* 'Firewitch', p. 207.

K **'Boulder Blue' blue fescue** (use 12)
An evergreen perennial, it forms a neat, spiky mound of blue-gray grassy foliage. See *Festuca ovina* var. *glauca* 'Boulder Blue', p. 230.

L **Retaining wall and steps**
The walls and steps shown here are made with a precast concrete retaining-wall system that is available at garden centers. See p. 270.

M **Paving**
A concrete walkway complements the precast concrete steps and retaining walls. See p. 259.

A sloping prairie

If you like your slope but are bored with the lawn (and tired of watering and mowing it), here is a design that will provide months of colorful flowers and foliage in a prairie style.

Near the house, two ornamental pear trees shelter a small bench, and shrubby currants line the foundation. (You can make jam from the currants; the pears are inedible.)

All the hillside plants function beautifully as ground covers, holding the soil, smothering weeds, and requiring little water. And while their greenery and varying textures are attractive in summer, they are most striking in fall, with leaves and seedheads in shades of yellow, red, and tan. Up top, the pears and currants, with leaves of red, purple, and orange, join the autumn show.

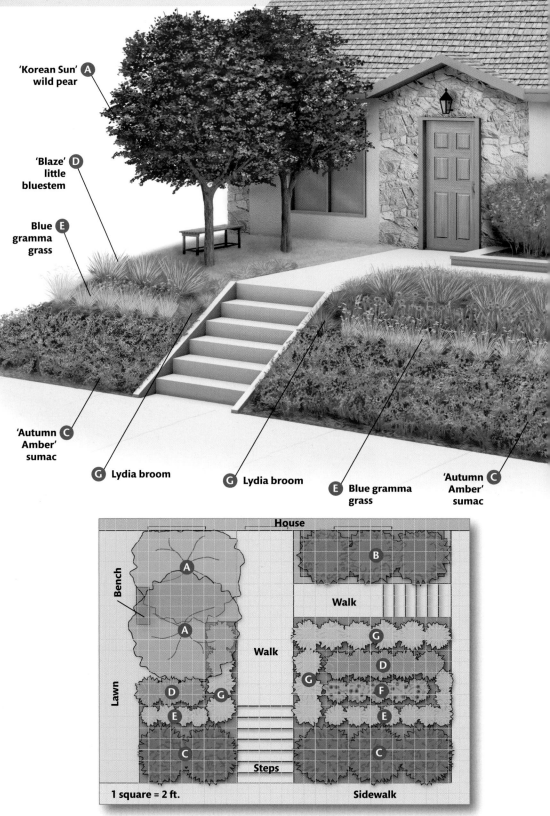

'Korean Sun' Ⓐ wild pear

'Blaze' Ⓓ little bluestem

Blue Ⓔ gramma grass

'Autumn Ⓒ Amber' sumac

Ⓖ Lydia broom

Ⓖ Lydia broom

Ⓔ Blue gramma grass

'Autumn Ⓒ Amber' sumac

Plants & Projects

Ⓐ **'Korean Sun' wild pear** (use 2)
The leaves of this small deciduous tree produce a memorable fall showing of red, purple, and yellow. It bears white flowers in spring, followed by small inedible fruits. See *Pyrus fauriei* 'Korean Sun', p. 235.

Ⓑ **'Crandall' clove-scented currant** (use 3)
A wiry deciduous shrub, it bears deliciously scented yellow flowers in spring and tasty fruit, and striking orange-red foliage in autumn. See *Ribes odoratum* 'Crandall', p. 237.

Ⓒ **'Autumn Amber' sumac** (use 5)
This deciduous shrub forms a dense wide-spreading ground cover of glossy green leaves. Covered in spring with char-

treuse flowers; leaves turn yellow to bright red in fall. See *Rhus trilobata* 'Autumn Amber', p. 237.

Ⓓ **'Blaze' little bluestem** (use 8)
An upright wiry perennial grass bearing fluffy seedheads in

summer. Narrow green blades turn with bright red to tan in fall and look good throughout winter. See *Schizachyrium scoparium*, p. 230.

Ⓔ **Blue gramma grass** (use 13)
Another perennial grass with wispy straw-colored seedheads

that are striking in fall and winter. Green leaves turn tan during the fall. See *Bouteloua gracilis*, p. 230.

Ⓕ **'Burgundy' blanket flower** (use 5)
This perennial wildflower bears striking red daisylike flowers

PLANT PORTRAITS

This bright mix of prairie plants enlivens a hilly entrance with autumnal color displays.
● = First design, pp. 128-129
▲ = Second design, pp. 130-131

'Magnus' coneflower (*Echinacea purpurea* 'Magnus' p. 208) ●

B 'Crandall' clove-scented currant

D 'Blaze' little bluestem

F 'Burgundy' blanket flower

SITE: Sunny

SEASON: Fall

CONCEPT: A low-water-use prairie style planting enlivens a slope.

'Moonshine' yarrow (*Achillea* 'Moonshine', p. 188) ●

'Crandall' clove-scented currant (*Ribes odoratum* 'Crandall', p. 237) ●

atop a mound of gray-green foliage throughout the summer. Remove old flowers as they fade. See *Gaillardia* x *grandiflora* 'Burgundy', p. 214.

See p. 129 for the following:

G **Lydia broom** (use 13)

'Firewitch' dianthus (*Dianthus gratianopolitanus* 'Firewitch', p. 207) ●

Blue gramma grass (*Bouteloua gracilis*, p. 230) ▲

A Pleasant Passage

RECLAIM A NARROW SIDE YARD FOR A STROLL GARDEN

Many residential lots include a slim strip of land between the house and a property line. Usually overlooked by everyone except children and dogs racing between the front yard and the back, this often shady corridor can become a valued addition to the landscape. In this design, a lovely little stroll garden invites adults, and even children, to linger as they move from one part of the property to another.

The wall of the house and a tall, opaque fence on the property line shade the space most of the day and give it a closed-in feeling, like a long empty hallway or a narrow room. The path and plantings create a cozy passage, and like the furnishings of a room, they make a small space seem bigger than it is.

As is common on many residential properties, a gated fence closes off one end of the corridor. At the other, a simple vine-covered arch and low plants mark the transition to a front yard or backyard. In between, small Japanese maples form a graceful arching canopy over a gently curving path. On either side, shrubs, perennials, vines, ferns, and ground covers delight the eye with a mixture of foliage textures and colors, as well as flowers from late winter through the summer.

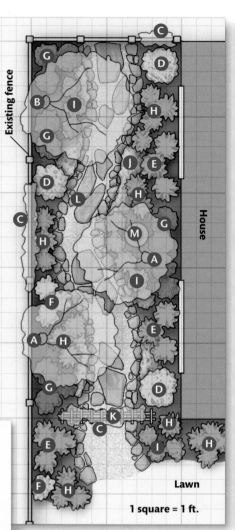

SITE: Shady

SEASON: Summer

CONCEPT: Plants with colorful foliage and pretty flowers make an enticing stroll garden in a frequently neglected area.

Plants & Projects

Lay out and install the path and edging, the arbor, and the irrigation system. Then prepare and plant the beds. As the maples grow, you'll need to prune them so that they arch over the path yet provide headroom for strollers. Once established, the plants require seasonal care as well as pruning to maintain size and shape.

A Coralbark maple
(use 2 plants)
The fine-textured leaves of this small deciduous tree are light green in summer and yellow in fall. In winter and spring, the bright red twigs accent the planting. See *Acer palmatum* 'Sango Kaku', p. 188.

B 'Oshio-Beni' Japanese maple
(use 1)
Similar to coralbark maple in many respects, this small tree has dark red leaves on its arching branches in summer and fall. See *Acer palmatum*, p.188.

C 'Happy Wanderer' hardenbergia (use 4)
Trained on the arbor and fence, this evergreen vine bears pinkish purple flowers in late winter and early spring. The foliage is attractive all year. See *Hardenbergia violacea*, p. 217.

D 'Nikko Blue' hydrangea
(use 3)
This is a smaller form of the popular deciduous shrub. Big clusters of blue flowers are displayed against its bold foliage for months in summer. See *Hydrangea macrophylla*, p. 221.

E Sword fern (use 9)
The shiny dark green fronds of this native fern add interesting form and texture to the planting. See Ferns: *Polystichum munitum*, p. 212.

F Mother fern (use 4)
This fern forms an airy mound of light green fronds that are evergreen where winters are mild. See Ferns: *Asplenium bulbiferum*, p. 212.

G Lenten rose (use 12)
In early spring, pink, rose, green, or white flowers rise on branched stems above this perennial's attractive toothed evergreen leaves. See *Helleborus orientalis*, p. 217.

H 'Big Blue' lilyturf (use 20)
This perennial makes mounds of grassy, dark green foliage. In summer, spikes of small blue flowers float above the leaves. See *Liriope muscari*, p. 226.

I 'Palace Purple' heuchera
(use 11)
A perennial, it is grown primarily for its distinctive purple foliage. Slender stalks bear tiny white flowers in late spring. See *Heuchera*, p.219.

J Ground covers (as needed)
Along the edges of the beds, plant bellflowers and ajuga. Both bloom in late spring and early summer. Serbian bellflower has dark green foliage and spikes of purple flowers. (See *Campanula poscharskyana*, p. 199.) 'Bronze Beauty'

ajuga has purple-bronze foliage and bears short spikes of small bluish flowers (see Ajuga reptans, p. 190). Between pavers and edging stones try annual lobelia, which self-seeds readily.

K Arbor
This shallow arbor can be built easily in an afternoon or two. See p. 283.

L Path
Edged with fieldstones, the path comprises a few large flagstone steppingstones set in crushed rock or decomposed granite. See p. 258.

M Decorative urn
Filled with water (you might use a recycling pump), this makes an effective focal point in the center of the planting.

B 'Oshio-Beni' Japanese maple

'Happy Wanderer' hardenbergia C

K Arbor

A Coralbark maple

M Decorative urn

G Lenten rose

D 'Nikko Blue' hydrangea

E Sword fern

Path L

'Palace Purple' heuchera I

'Big Blue' lilyturf H

F Mother fern

Ground covers J

H 'Big Blue' lilyturf

A sunny corridor

If the side of your house has a sunny exposure and your taste runs to the formal and fragrant, try this design. Here sun-loving vines, shrubs, and perennials are arrayed symmetrically along the passage. A flagstone walkway passes through a vine-draped arch at each end. Neat bushes covered nearly year-round with white roses line the walk, accented by the silvery gray foliage of lavender and snow-in-summer that cascades onto the paving. At the center of the planting, a small courtyard is framed by vine-covered trellises attached to the house and fence.

Enticing scents are supplied by star jasmine on the center trellises, as well as by the roses, lavender, and evergreen clematis. The color scheme is elegantly simple, with flowers in blues, purples, and white, and foliage in shades of green and silvery gray.

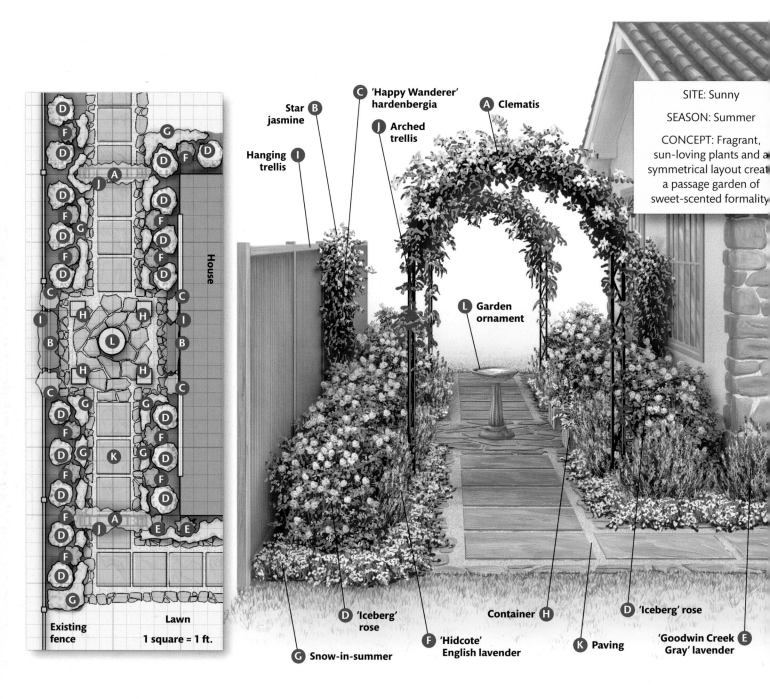

SITE: Sunny

SEASON: Summer

CONCEPT: Fragrant, sun-loving plants and a symmetrical layout creat[e] a passage garden of sweet-scented formality

C 'Happy Wanderer' hardenbergia

B Star jasmine

A Clematis

J Arched trellis

I Hanging trellis

L Garden ornament

Existing fence

Lawn

1 square = 1 ft.

House

D 'Iceberg' rose

G Snow-in-summer

F 'Hidcote' English lavender

H Container

K Paving

D 'Iceberg' rose

E 'Goodwin Creek Gray' lavender

Plants & Projects

Ⓐ Clematis (use 4 plants)
Two different types are used here, one on each arching trellis at the ends of the planting. Evergreen clematis (*Clematis armandii*) bears large clusters of fragrant white flowers in spring against a backdrop of glossy green leaves. C. 'Mme. Le Coultre' is deciduous and produces large white flowers from midsummer through fall. See *Clematis*, p.204.

Ⓑ Star jasmine (use 6)
Trained up the trellises attached to the house and fence, this evergreen vine offers shiny leaves and clusters of fragrant cream-colored flowers in early summer. See *Trachelospermum jasminoides*, p. 246.

Ⓒ 'Happy Wanderer' hardenbergia (use 4)
Plant this evergreen vine at the ends of the house and fence trellises. Pinkish purple flowers dot the dark foliage in late winter and early spring. See *Hardenbergia violacea*, p. 217.

Ⓓ 'Iceberg' rose (use 18)
A mounded deciduous shrub, it is covered nearly year-round with clusters of fragrant white flowers. See *Rosa*, p. 238.

Ⓔ 'Goodwin Creek Gray' lavender (use 2)
This perennial herb forms a large mound of gray-green foliage topped in summer and fall with short spikes of blue flowers. See *Lavandula*, p. 226.

Ⓕ 'Hidcote' English lavender (use 12)
This lavender makes smaller mounds of gray foliage at the feet of the roses. Bears dark purple flowers in summer. See *Lavandula angustifolia*, p. 226.

Ⓖ Snow-in-summer (as needed)
The silvery evergreen foliage of this perennial ground cover will sprawl into the path from the edges of the beds. It is blanketed with small white flowers in early summer. Plant 12 in. apart. See *Cerastium tomentosum*, p. 201.

Ⓗ Containers
Placed at the corners of the courtyard, these pots or wooden boxes can be planted with seasonal annuals and bulbs. Here we show two with lavender and white stocks and two with white freesias. All four are underplanted with alyssum. See Annuals, pg. 190.

Ⓘ Hanging trellises
Attached to the house and the fence, these trellises can be built or bought ready-made. See p. 280

Ⓙ Arched trellises
Framing the entrances, these metal trellises can be purchased in a variety of styles from garden centers.

Ⓚ Paving
Paths of square flagstones lead to a small courtyard of irregular flagstones (see p. 259). Edge the beds with small fieldstones. In the gaps between stones, you can plant creeping thyme (see *Thymus praecox* ssp. *arcticus*, p. 245) and self-seeding annuals such as lobelia and alyssum. See Annuals, pg. 190.

Ⓛ Garden ornament
Place a copper birdbath (as shown), statue, or other ornament as a focal point at the center of the courtyard.

VARIATIONS ON A THEME

A narrow passage is a real design challenge. These examples succeed in creating spaces you want to, rather than have to, walk through.

This side-yard garden features an array of tropical plants, including bird-of-paradise and New Zealand flax.

A geometrical path of cut flagstones set in crushed rock lends an air of formality to this side-yard garden, as does the repetition of plants along the path.

A narrow path overgrown with evergreen plants and accented with playful lighting creates a magical garden in a small space.

A Garden Path

A NEGLECTED SIDE YARD CAN BECOME A SHOWPLACE.

Many side yards are simply narrow strips of land that connect the front and back-yards. But with a little planning, this corridor can become a valued addition to the landscape—a delightful little stroll garden invites adults, and even children, to linger as they move from one part of the property to another.

The wall of the house and a tall fence at the property line create a cozy "room," one that is enhanced by trees, vines, shrubs, and ground covers. Like furnishings in a room, the plantings make the small space seem bigger than it is. To complete the illusion, a gently curving flagstone path widens the passage visually and lengthens the stroll through it.

In spring, scented blossoms of daffodil, wisteria, and Texas mountain laurel will perfume the entire passage. As these flowers fade, the watermelon pink crapemyrtle will begin its long season of bloom, joined by purple verbena along the fence, bushy mounds of baby blue plumbago where the daffodils had been, and a continuous row of pretty pink salvia. As the trees grow, their boughs will arch over the path, creating a bower heavy with blossoms for much of the year.

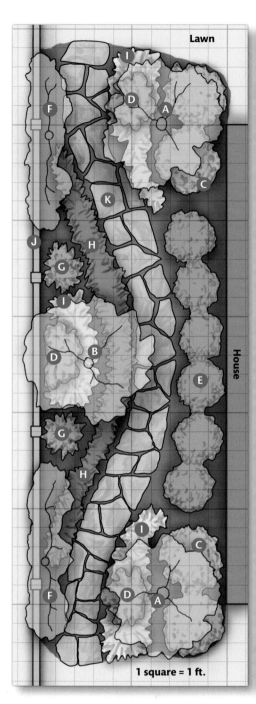

Lawn

House

1 square = 1 ft.

Plants & Projects

Install the fence and flagstone path. Then prepare and plant the beds. You'll need to add sturdy trellises or other strong supports for the vines. As the trees grow, prune them so they arch over the path yet provide headroom for strollers. Once established, the plants require seasonal care as well as pruning to maintain size and shape.

Ⓐ 'Tonto' crapemyrtle (use 2 plants)
A small deciduous tree deserving of its wide popularity. Attractive dark oval leaves showcase spectacular blossoms from summer to frost. This cultivar bears watermelon pink flowers. See *Lagerstroemia* x *fauriei* 'Tonto', p. 224.

Ⓑ Texas mountain laurel (use 1)
Clusters of purple flowers hang from this small glossy evergreen tree in early spring. Passersby on both sides of the fence will appreciate the delightful perfume. Bean pods with bright red seeds follow the

flowers. See *Sophora secundiflora*, p. 243.

Ⓒ Indian hawthorn (use 4)
A mounding evergreen shrub that produces a dense covering of shiny oval leaves. It offers pink or white flowers in spring and purple-black berries in late summer. Choose a pink-flowering cultivar for this spot. See *Rhaphiolepis indica*, p. 236.

Ⓓ Tropical plumbago (use 3)
After the daffodils fade, this perennial emerges apple green and bushy. In summer it spills over with big clusters of clear blue flowers. See *Plumbago auriculata*, p. 234.

Ⓔ 'Pink' autumn sage (use 6)
These low, bushy mounds of tiny oval leaves bristle with spires of bright pink flowers all season. Plant this or any pink cultivar. See *Salvia greggii* 'Pink', p. 241.

Ⓕ Chinese wisteria (use 2)
In spring, this vine will virtually curtain the fence with fragrant violet flowers as large as clusters of grapes. A lacework of

green foliage emerges after fragrant blossoms fade, turning yellowish in fall. See *Wisteria sinensis*, p. 249.

Ⓖ Purple verbena (use 2)
Countless bright clusters of purple flowers rise airily from this perennial's base of dull green leaves. Blooms from midsummer to frost. See *Verbena bonariensis*, p. 246.

Ⓗ 'Big Blue' lilyturf (use 24)
This perennial makes an attractive edge of grassy dark green foliage. In summer, small lavender flowers float among the leaves. See *Liriope muscari*, p. 226.

Ⓘ 'Ice Follies' daffodil (as needed)
Fresh-looking white daffodil flowers with pale yellow centers line the path in early

spring. See Bulbs: *Narcissus pseudonarcissus* 'Ice Follies', p. 196.

Ⓙ Fence
Easy to build, this fence provides privacy and an attractive framework for plants. See p. 274.

Ⓚ Path
Flagstones in random shapes and sizes trace a graceful curve through the planting. A neutral gray would complement any house. See p. 259.

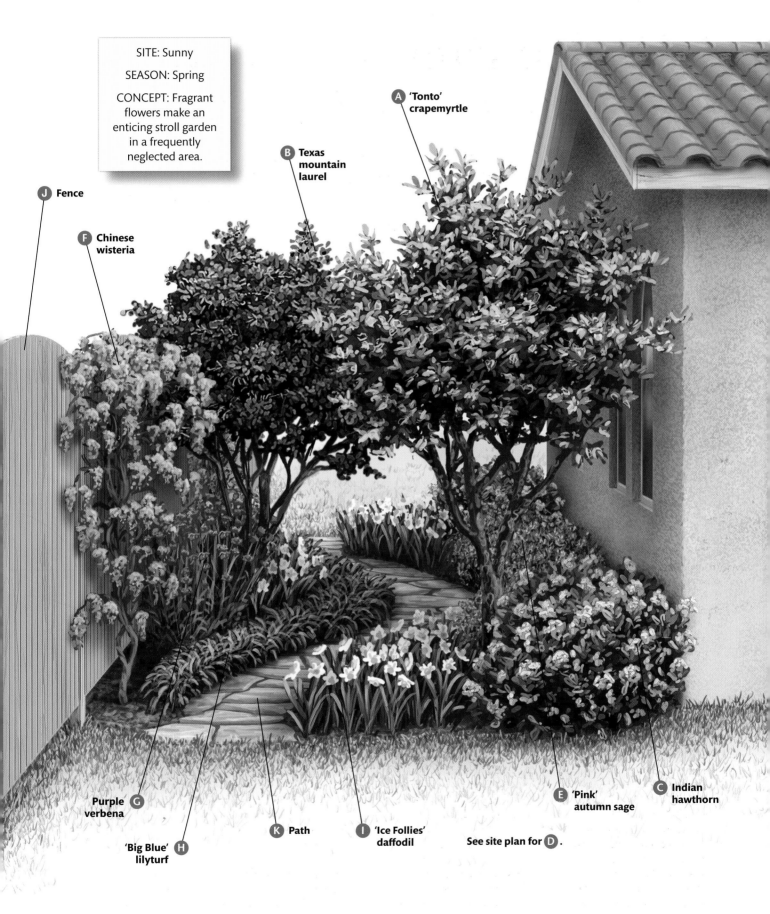

SITE: Sunny

SEASON: Spring

CONCEPT: Fragrant flowers make an enticing stroll garden in a frequently neglected area.

J Fence

F Chinese wisteria

B Texas mountain laurel

A 'Tonto' crapemyrtle

G Purple verbena

H 'Big Blue' lilyturf

K Path

I 'Ice Follies' daffodil

E 'Pink' autumn sage

C Indian hawthorn

See site plan for **D**.

PLANT PORTRAITS

Eye-catching plants for an overlooked spot, here are flowers, foliage, and fragrance to make your side-yard stroll garden a favorite.

● = First design, p. 136-137

▲ = Second design, pp. 138-139

Gold dust aucuba (*Aucuba japonica* 'Variegata', p. 194) ▲

'Ice Follies' Daffodil
(Bulbs: *Narcissus pseudonarcissus*, p. 196) ●

'Pink' Autumn sage
(*Salvia greggii*, p. 241) ●

Indian hawthorn
(*Rhaphiolepis indica*, p. 236) ●

'Tonto' Crapemyrtle (*Lagerstroemia* x *fauriei*, p. 224) ●

Chinese wisteria (*Wisteria sinensis*, p. 249) ●

A shady corridor

If the side of your house has a shady exposure, try this design. Shade-loving shrubs and ground covers are arrayed in colorful layers along the passage. These "furnishings" are selected primarily for their foliage, ranging from light green to purple black, fine-textured to coarse, dull to glossy, and low-growing to large and bold. The big leaves of the fatsia and aucuba combine well with ground covers, soft fern fronds, and stiff, swordlike aspidistra. In this evergreen garden, flowers and berries are added enticements. Fragrant jasmine scents the air in spring and purple berries brighten a winter stroll.

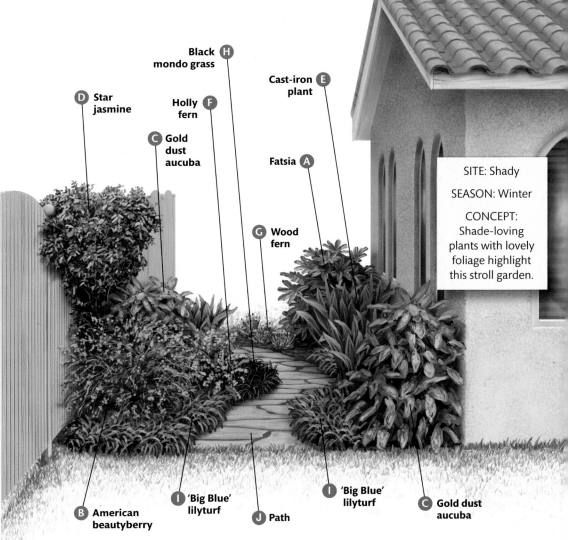

SITE: Shady

SEASON: Winter

CONCEPT: Shade-loving plants with lovely foliage highlight this stroll garden.

Labels in illustration:
- **H** Black mondo grass
- **E** Cast-iron plant
- **D** Star jasmine
- **F** Holly fern
- **A** Fatsia
- **C** Gold dust aucuba
- **G** Wood fern
- **B** American beautyberry
- **I** 'Big Blue' lilyturf
- **J** Path
- **I** 'Big Blue' lilyturf
- **C** Gold dust aucuba

Existing fence
Lawn
House
1 square = 1 ft.

Plants & Projects

Ⓐ Fatsia (use 1 plant)
A handsome evergreen shrub. Leaves like big hands look wonderful above feathery ferns and other fine-textured plants. See *Fatsia japonica*, p. 211.

Ⓑ American beautyberry (use 1)
This shrub has an open, slightly sprawling habit. Purple berries are showy on bare branches in fall and winter. See *Callicarpa americana*, p. 198.

Ⓒ Gold dust aucuba (use 3)
Speckled and shiny, this evergreen shrub is a striking accent plant, made more so by borders of dark green lilyturf and purple-black mondo grass. See *Aucuba japonica* 'Variegata', p. 194.

Ⓓ Star jasmine (use 3)
This vine's stiff oval foliage will "wallpaper" the fence with year-round color and texture. Clouds of tiny white flowers cover the vine in spring. They'll fill the passage with fragrance. See *Trachelospermum jasminoides*, p. 246.

Ⓔ Cast-iron plant (use 12)
This unusual evergreen plant forms a patch of long leathery leaves that jut from the ground like fence pickets. See *Aspidistra eliator*, p. 193.

Ⓕ Holly fern (use 6)
An evergreen fern distinguished by leathery fronds. It contrasts nicely with the mondo grass and other evergreens. See

Ferns: *Cyrtomium falcatum*, p. 212.

Ⓖ Wood fern (use 3)
This is a deciduous fern with a soft shaggy look. Cut back after frost for an attractive brown flat-top. See Ferns: *Thelypteris kunthii*, p. 213.

Ⓗ Black mondo grass (use 12)
Plant this perennial along the path for its unusual color and neat habit. Shear off tops in early spring for new growth. See *Ophiopogon planiscapus* 'Ebony Knight,' p. 229.

See p. 136 for the following:

Ⓘ 'Big Blue' lilyturf (use 24)

Ⓙ Path

An Island Retreat

CREATE A FREESTANDING PATIO GARDEN

Patios and outdoor entertainment areas are often right next to the house. While this proximity has many advantages, it isn't always practical or most effective to graft a patio onto the house. The landscaped freestanding patio shown here offers more flexibility in planning and using your landscape. Place it to take advantage of a view or a particularly private spot on your property. Use it as a retreat from household hubbub. If you already have a deck or patio off the family room or kitchen, a free-standing area can help accommodate large gatherings, perhaps as an area for quiet conversation away from more raucous activities.

In this design, a small multitrunked tree and mid-height shrubs provide a sense of place and enclosure without walling out the surroundings. The wispy foliage of the gaura, artemisia, and rosemary, along with the blue fescue grass and the silvery lamb's ears, gives the planting a Mediterranean look. And there are flowers year-round.

A freestanding patio garden like this one looks self-contained on paper, but like all landscape features, it looks and functions best when carefully correlated with other elements on your property. Transitions, both physical and visual, between major landscape features are particularly important. An expanse of lawn, changes of level that separate one area from another, or a planting that screens sight lines can all help different elements in your landscape coexist effectively.

'Marina' **A** arbutus

Japanese **F** anemone

'Palace Purple' **H** heuchera

Paving **L**

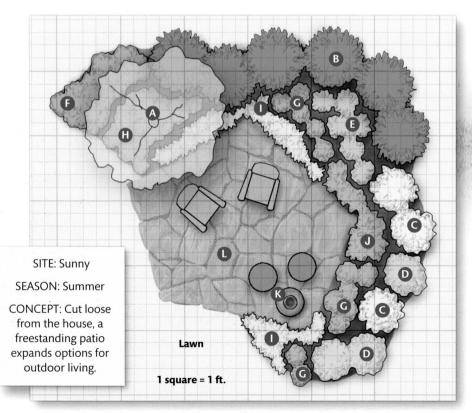

Lawn

1 square = 1 ft.

SITE: Sunny

SEASON: Summer

CONCEPT: Cut loose from the house, a freestanding patio expands options for outdoor living.

Plants & Projects

Installing the patio and preparing the planting beds are strenuous but not difficult work. (Install the patio first.) The plants can be set out in a weekend. Once the plants are established, you'll have very little to do beyond seasonal pruning, division when the perennials get crowded, and cleanup.

A **'Marina' arbutus** (use 1 plant)
This small multitrunked tree offers bell-shaped pink flowers in fall, red berries, and glossy evergreen leaves. Shiny, reddish bark is eyecatching, too. See *Arbutus*, p. 192.

B **'Majorca Pink' rosemary** (use 6)
An evergreen shrub with fragrant deep green foliage, it bears lavender-pink flowers in late winter and early spring. See *Rosmarinus officinalis*, p. 240.

C **'Iceberg' rose** (use 3)
This shrub rose displays fragrant white flowers against attractive green foliage. Blooms nearly all year. See *Rosa*, p. 238.

D **'Powis Castle' artemisia** (use 3)
A billowy mass of silver foliage makes this perennial a striking garden accent. See *Artemisia*, p. 193.

E **Gaura** (use 6)
Another wispy perennial, it forms a loose clump of small lance-shaped green leaves on arching stems. Pale pink-and-white flowers dot the foliage from spring through fall. See *Gaura lindheimeri*, p. 215.

F **Japanese anemone** (use 10)
This perennial forms a low clump of large, dark green leaves. Tall stems carry small daisylike flowers from late summer into fall. See *Anemone* x *hybrida*, p. 191.

G **Pincushion flower** (use 13)
Frilly light blue flowers adorn this perennial's neat mounds of airy foliage from late spring through fall. See *Scabiosa caucasica*, p. 242.

H **'Palace Purple' heuchera** (use 18)
A perennial grown for its distinctive purple foliage, which is shaped like small maple leaves. It bears tiny white flowers on tall thin stalks from spring into summer. See *Heuchera*, p. 219.

I **Blue fescue grass** (use 27)
This perennial forms mounds of thin blue-green leaves at the edge of the flagstones. Narrow flower spikes emerge from the clumps in early summer. See *Festuca ovina* var. *glauca*, p. 230.

J **Lamb's ears** (use 9)
Children can't resist touching this perennial's soft silver foliage. Plants form a low mat topped by purple flowers in early summer. See *Stachys byzantina*, p. 244.

K **Container plantings**
Plants in pots brighten up the patio with seasonal plantings of annuals or, as shown here, perennial scented geraniums. See *Pelargonium*, p. 233.

L **Paving**
Irregular flagstone pavers set on a sand-and-gravel base make a durable, informal patio. See p. 264.

B **'Majorca Pink' rosemary**

E **Gaura**

C **'Iceberg' rose**

I Blue fescue grass

K Container plantings

I Blue fescue grass

G Pincushion flower

J Lamb's ears

D **'Powis Castle' artemisia**

Oasis in the shade

This design allows you to make an outdoor living area in a shady spot anywhere on your property. As in the preceding design, this patio is bordered by mid-height shrubs and lower-growing perennials. The plants create a sense of enclosure and provide attractive companions when you're relaxing or entertaining on the patio.

While there are lovely flowers in spring and summer, the enduring attraction of this planting is its foliage. Largely evergreen, the leaves provide a pleasing variety of shapes and textures in a blend of greens that are tinged, at certain times of year, with other hues.

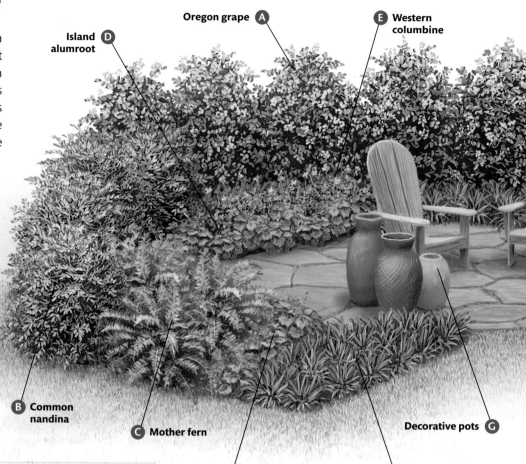

Island alumroot **D**
Oregon grape **A**
Western columbine **E**
B Common nandina
C Mother fern
Decorative pots **G**
D Island alumroot
F 'Big Blue' lilyturf

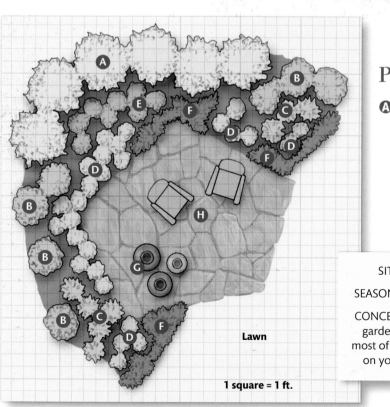

Lawn

1 square = 1 ft.

Plants & Projects

A Oregon grape (use 6 plants)
This spreading evergreen shrub offers distinctive, spiny foliage year-round. In spring it bears showy clusters of yellow flowers, which are followed by dark blue berries. New foliage is tinged with red. See *Mahonia aquifolium*, p. 228.

B Common nandina (use 7)
An evergreen shrub, it has finely cut foliage that changes color with the seasons. Fluffy clusters of white flowers bloom in summer and produce long-lasting red berries. See *Nandina domestica*, p. 229.

C Mother fern (use 8)
The light green fronds of this fern form an attractive airy mound. Evergreen where winters are mild. See Ferns: *Asplenium bulbiferum*, p. 212.

D Island alumroot (use 27)
The dark, heart-shaped evergreen foliage of this native perennial is its main attraction. Tall stems bearing long clusters of tiny white or pink flowers rise above spreading mounds in early spring. See *Heuchera maxima*, p. 219.

SITE: Shady

SEASON: Early spring

CONCEPT: This patio garden makes the most of existing shade on your property.

B **Common nandina**

C **Mother fern**

'Big Blue' lilyturf F

H **Paving**

E **Western columbine** (use 8)
This native perennial produces striking red-and-yellow flowers from spring to early summer. The lacy mounds of foliage look good, too. See *Aquilegia formosa*, p. 192.

F **'Big Blue' lilyturf** (use 27)
Grown as a ground cover for its grassy, mounding evergreen foliage, this perennial also bears pretty spikes of small blue flowers in summer. See *Liriope muscari*, p. 226.

G **Decorative pots**
Place interesting pots or other decorative focal points on the patio, as shown here. Or add planted containers as described for the preceding design.

See p. 141 for the following:

H **Paving**

VARIATIONS ON A THEME

Both of these island retreats owe much of their charm to skillful color coordination between the hardscape and furniture and the plantings.

A cheerful informality pervades this cozy patio setting.

Informal plantings in subdued colors skirt a more formal patio and arbor, a combination that affords a range of entertainment options.

Down to Earth

HARMONIZE YOUR DECK WITH ITS SURROUNDINGS

A backyard deck is a perfect spot for enjoying the outdoors. Too often, however, the deck offers little connection to the outdoor life we most enjoy. Perched on skinny posts above a patch of lawn, it is a lonely outpost rather than an inviting gateway to the world of plants and wildlife.

In the design shown here, a low deck nestles in a planting of trees, shrubs, and perennials. The plants provide shade and privacy as well as lovely flowers and foliage and the birds and other wildlife attracted to them. Conceived for a dry foothills site with a backyard that slopes down from the deck, the planting makes effective use of terrain where play areas are impractical and a manicured lawn or traditional garden beds are difficult to maintain. (The planting can easily be adapted for sites that are steeper or more level than the gradual slope shown here.)

The plants are chosen for their ability to thrive in the hot, dry conditions often found on sloping sites. Western natives such as western redbud, manzanita, and are joined by tough plants from other semiarid regions. There are flowers for much of the year, and a mixture of evergreen and deciduous foliage provides delightful colors and textures year-round. The planting makes a seamless transition to the surrounding cover of native grasses and wildflowers that naturally colonize such hillsides. Mow a path through this "volunteer" ground cover and extend the planting as far as you wish down the hill.

Western redbud **B**

'Twin Peaks' dwarf coyote brush **L**

Mexican bush sage **H**

Autumn sage **J**

Plants & Projects

You'll need to water young plants to get them established. But after a year or two, these durable perennials, trees, and shrubs will require infrequent supplemental watering and a minimum of care. Prune the shrubs (particularly the hop bushes and the butterfly bush) to keep them from overgrowing their neighbors. Shear the dwarf coyote brush each spring. Divide any perennials that become crowded.

A Chitalpa (use 1 plant)
This attractive deciduous tree has a wide crown of airy foliage and bears eye-catching clusters of ruffled pink or white flowers in early summer. See x *Chitalpa tashkentensis*, p. 202.

B Western redbud (use 3)
Tiny magenta flowers line the bare branches of this small multitrunked deciduous tree in spring. Bright green summer foliage turns yellow in fall. See *Cercis occidentalis*, p. 201.

C Purple hop bush (use 3)
Native to the Southwest, this tough evergreen shrub has bronze-green foliage that turns purple in winter. See *Dodonaea viscosa* 'Purpurea', p. 208.

D 'Julia Phelps' (use 4)
This popular evergreen shrub displays clusters of blue flowers against deep green foliage in spring. See , p. 200.

E 'Howard McMinn' manzanita (use 7)
Lining the path, this evergreen shrub forms mounds of shiny dark green foliage. Small white to pink spring flowers produce red berries. See *Arctostaphyllos densiflora*, p. 192.

F 'Black Knight' butterfly bush (use 1)
This deciduous shrub makes a fountain-shaped clump of long arching stems. Clusters of dark purple flowers form from midsummer through fall. See *Buddleia davidii*, p. 196.

G 'Happy Wanderer' hardenbergia (use 1)
The stems and bright green foliage of this evergreen vine twine around the deck railing. Bears pinkish purple flowers in late winter and early spring. See *Hardenbergia violacea*, p.217.

H Mexican bush sage (use 8)
A shrubby perennial, its gray-green foliage contrasts nicely with the dark evergreen leaves of nearby plants. Long spikes of purple-and-white flowers bloom from late spring to fall. See *Salvia leucantha*, p. 241.

I 'Tuscan Blue' rosemary (use 4)
The needlelike dark green leaves of this evergreen shrub add interesting texture to the planting. Small deep blue flowers appear in late winter and early spring. See *Rosmarinus officinalis*, p. 240.

J Autumn sage (use 11)
This bushy perennial's medium green leaves are topped from spring to fall with airy spikes of red flowers. Place two plants in each of the planters on the wide steps leading up to the deck. See *Salvia greggii*, p. 241.

K 'Yellow Wave' New Zealand flax (use 4)
This evergreen perennial's colorful spray of swordlike leaves is topped in summer by tubular red flowers on tall stalks. See *Phormium tenax*, p. 234.

L 'Twin Peaks' dwarf coyote brush (use 10)
The dense foliage of this low, spreading evergreen shrub makes a fine ground cover. See *Baccharis pilularis*, p. 194.

M Path
A path mowed through the native grasses and wildflowers on the hillside will be easier to maintain than a path of wood chips or other loose material.

'Black Knight' butterfly bush **F**

Chitalpa **A**

'Happy Wanderer' hardenbergia **G**

M Path

D 'Julia Phelps'

'Tuscan Blue' rosemary **I**

'Howard McMinn' manzanita **E**

J Autumn sage

H Mexican bush sage

E 'Howard McMinn' manzanita

'Yellow Wave' New Zealand flax **K**

Purple hop bush **C**

House

Deck

Planters

1 square = 1 ft.

Native grasses and wildflowers

SITE: Sunny

SEASON: Early summer

CONCEPT: A pleasing mix of durable plants integrates a low deck with its hillside surroundings.

VARIATIONS ON A THEME

Imaginative plantings completely integrate each of these decks with their surroundings.

This marvelous deck appears to hover above a lush forest glade. Evergreen shrubs create the illusion of a natural setting.

A successful deck-side planting is a treat when viewed from the deck.

Skirting a shady deck

This design also integrates the deck with its surroundings, but it does so in a shadier environment, produced perhaps by large trees nearby. Small western redbud trees and native toyon shrubs create privacy and a comforting sense of enclosure on the deck. Lower-growing shrubs and ferns form an evergreen understory beneath the trees and look good viewed from the deck or the path. Open ground between the massed shrubs, mulched and planted with a scattering of native island alumroot, gives the planting an open, airy feel.

Peak bloom is in spring, but the varied foliage is attractive year-round. As for the preceding design, these plants are chosen for their durability and low water needs once established. (The container plantings will need regular watering.)

Plants & Projects

Ⓐ Toyon (use 4 plants)
This upright evergreen shrub or small tree displays clusters of small white flowers against its glossy deep green foliage in early summer. Bright red berries follow and attract birds. See *Heteromeles arbutifolia*, p. 218.

Ⓑ Oregon grape (use 7)
The distinctive coarse foliage of this evergreen shrub is tinged red when new and turns purplish in cold winters. Clusters of yellow early-spring flowers produce edible blue berries. See *Mahonia aquifolium*, p. 228.

Ⓒ 'Yankee Point' Carmel creeper (use 9)
This evergreen shrub forms a low, spreading mound of dark green foliage. Bears small clusters of blue flowers in spring. See *griseus* var. *horizontalis*, p. 200.

Ⓓ Sword fern (use 10)
An evergreen fern, its dark green fronds are coarsely divided and glossy. They're an effective screen for the space under the deck. See Ferns: *Polystichum munitum*, p. 212.

Ⓔ Feather reed grass (use 10)
This grass forms leafy upright clumps that are evergreen in areas where winters are mild and turn beige in cold weather. Tall stalks are topped by flowers and seeds from late spring on. Planted when the toyon are young, the clumps of grass will die out as the shrubs expand. See *Calamagrostis* x *acutiflora* 'Stricta', p. 230.

Ⓕ Island alumroot (use 21)
This evergreen perennial forms spreading mounds of distinctive foliage. In summer, clusters of small flowers float above the foliage on narrow stalks. Look for a California native cultivar, such as 'Wendy'. See *Heuchera maxima*, p. 219.

Ⓖ 'Palace Purple' heuchera (use 5)
A popular cultivar, its attraction is striking purple-bronze maple-like leaves rather than its tiny flowers. See *Heuchera*, p. 219.

Ⓗ Planters
Large wooden containers on the pads leading up to the deck are planted with small shrubs and perennials. 'Alaska' azalea offers white flowers and evergreen foliage (1 per box; see *Rhododendron*, p. 237). 'Gulf Stream' heavenly bamboo is an upright shrub with lacy colorful evergreen foliage (1 per box; see *Nandina domestica*, p. 229). For color and texture at the feet of these shrubs, plant 'Palace Purple' heuchera in open spaces.

See p. 144 for the following:

Ⓘ Western redbud (use 2)

Ⓙ Path

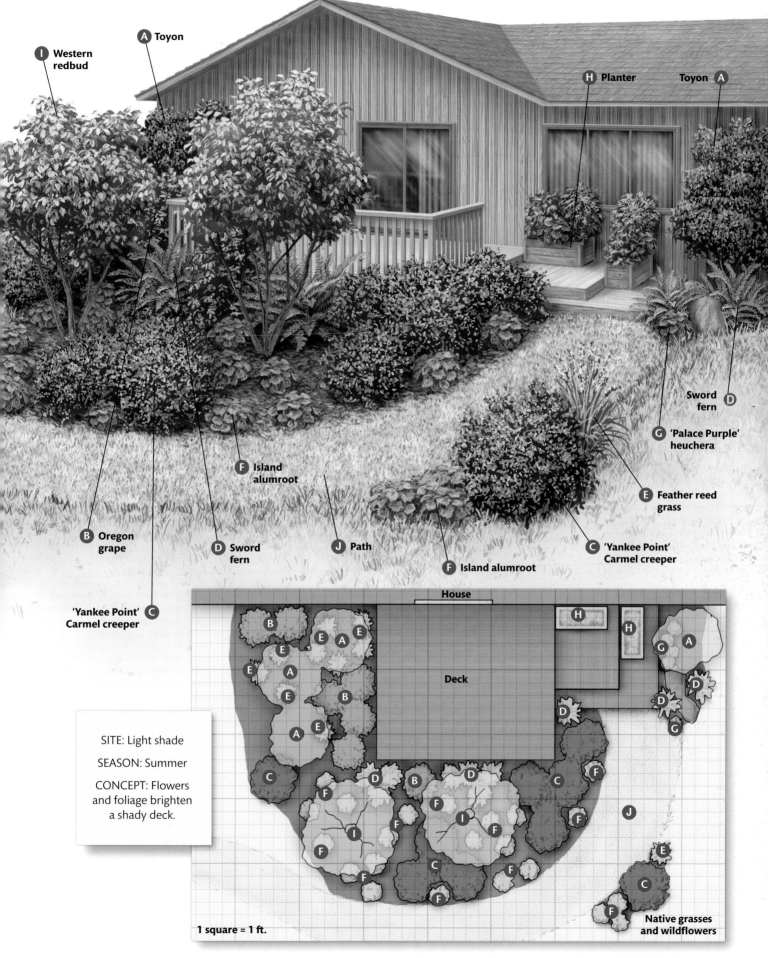

I Western redbud

A Toyon

H Planter   Toyon **A**

B Oregon grape

C 'Yankee Point' Carmel creeper

D Sword fern

F Island alumroot

J Path

F Island alumroot

C 'Yankee Point' Carmel creeper

E Feather reed grass

G 'Palace Purple' heuchera

D Sword fern

House

H   H

Deck

SITE: Light shade

SEASON: Summer

CONCEPT: Flowers and foliage brighten a shady deck.

1 square = 1 ft.

Native grasses and wildflowers

Backyard Enclave

WOODY PLANTS CREATE A PRIVATE RETREAT

If you enjoy open woodlands, you can imagine yourself in one when sitting on your deck surrounded by these trees and shrubs. Though scaled to suit a city or suburban property, these plants are large enough to provide a sense of enclosure similar to that of a woodland.

All but one of the woody plants are deciduous. From spring through fall a leafy wall will enclose the area; in winter, branches make an attractive tracery screen.

Flowers bloom for many months. Beside the deck, fragrant lilacs scent the air in late spring and early summer. Sweet-smelling mock orange perfumes the path for warm-weather strollers. Butterfly bushes will attract their colorful namesakes during the summer. The serviceberries add sustenance to the attraction of shelter for birds.

The planting areas are lawn-free and mulched to conserve water and discourage weeds. The planting may abut a turf-grass lawn or be part of an extended lawn-free landscape of wildflowers, shrubs, and trees.

> SITE: Sunny
>
> SEASON: Early summer
>
> CONCEPT: Provide privacy and multi-seasonal interest around a backyard deck.

'Big Tuna' **D** mugo pine

'Cheyenne' **E** mock orange

Bird **L** bath

K Path

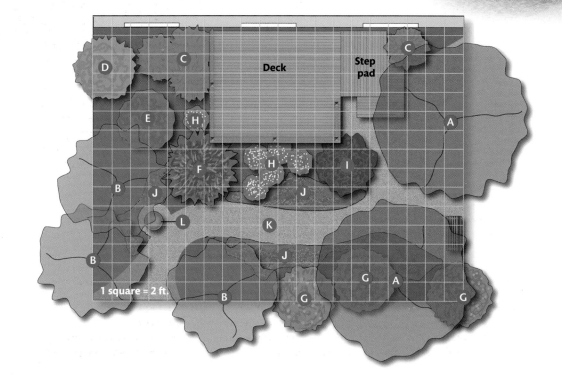

Deck

Step pad

1 square = 2 ft.

Plants & Projects

It will take a few years for the woody plants to grow up (and out). While they're still small, you can fill the open spaces with perennials or annuals that will eventually be shaded out.

Ⓐ **'Newport' purpleleaf plum** (use 2)
This deciduous tree is prized for its deep purple foliage. Bears pinkish flowers in spring; may bear fruit. A small tree, but tall enough to help shade the deck. See *Prunus cerasifera* 'Newport', p. 235.

Ⓑ **Serviceberry** (use 3)
A small deciduous, often multi-trunked tree, it forms an airy, canopy of bright green foliage.

C 'Miss Kim'
dwarf lilac

F 'Black Knight'
buddleia

'Hansa'
rose I

A 'Newport'
purpleleaf
plum

H Shasta
daisy

G Purple rose
of Sharon

J Lemon
thyme

B Serviceberry

Covered with white flowers in spring and bears bluish berries in summer. See *Amelanchier alnifolia*, p. 191.

C **'Miss Kim' dwarf lilac** (use 4) This deciduous shrub bears numerous spikes of fragrant lavender flowers in late spring and early summer. See *Syringa patula* 'Miss Kim', p. 244.

D **'Big Tuna' mugo pine** (use 1) A large evergreen shrub, it has dense fine-textured needles. Slow growing, but worth the time. See *Pinus mugo* 'Big Tuna', p. 234.

E **'Cheyenne' mock orange** (use 1) An early-summer-blooming deciduous shrub, it bears fragrant white flowers on arching branches against a backdrop of green foliage. See *Philadelphus lewisii* 'Cheyenne', p. 233.

F **'Black Knight' butterfly bush** (use 1). This fast-growing deciduous shrub bears spikes of purple flowers for weeks beginning in early summer. Often cut back to the ground in fall, it will grow 6 to 8 ft. tall and wide by frost. See *Buddleia davidii* 'Black Knight', p.196.

G **Purple rose of Sharon** (use 3) An old favorite, prized for its large round flowers that bloom from summer to fall. An upright deciduous shrub, it has lobed, dark green leaves. We've chosen a purple-flowered variety for this design. See *Hibiscus syriacus*, p. 220.

H **Shasta daisy** (use 6) This perennial has bright green foliage topped by yellow-centered, daisylike flowers on sturdy stems for months in summer. See *Chrysanthemum* x *superbum* 'Alaska', p. 226.

I **'Hansa' rose** (use 1) A large, rounded deciduous shrub with crinkled, dark green leaves, it bears fragrant, light purple-red flowers followed by large reddish orange hips. See *Rosa* 'Hansa', p. 238.

J **Lemon thyme** (use 1 to 2 flats) This creeping perennial forms a low mat of semi-evergreen leaves that have a lemony scent when crushed. Bears small clusters of pinkish purple flower for weeks in midsummer. See *Thymus citriodorus*, p. 245.

K **Path** We've shown gray "crusher fines" here. This finely ground stone has sharp edges and compacts into a relatively smooth surface, though it is much more textured and uneven than concrete. See p. 259.

L **Bird bath** Invite birds into your planting and enjoy them from the deck.

Perennial pleasures

Like the previous design, this one creates a shady, private enclosure for the deck. But here, we've used fewer shrubs and more perennials. Tall clumps of ornamental grasses provide screening beneath the canopies of the trees, but the planting is more open on this level.

The perennials offer a balanced mix of colorful flowers and foliage across the seasons. In spring, columbine and bleeding heart join the redbuds and serviceberries in bloom. In summer, hostas and coral bells are of equal interest for their flowers and their foliage, though the foliage comes sooner and lasts longer. The bright flowers of cranesbill and distinctive black leaves of the mondo grass complete the setting.

Like the previous design, this one works well adjacent to a lawn or as part of a large, lawn-free landscape.

J Path

G Bloody cranesbill

I Serviceberry

E Variegated eulalia grass

Plants & Projects

A Eastern redbud (use 3)
This small deciduous tree forms a crown of dark green, heart-shaped leaves. In spring, before it leafs out, bare branches are lined with numerous small red flowers. See *Cercis canadensis*, p. 201.

B White bleeding heart (use 8)
A perennial with rounded clumps of deeply cut blue-green leaves, distinctive for the rows of heart-shaped flowers that hang from arching stems in late spring. See *Dicentra spectabilis* 'Alba', p. 208.

C Rocky Mountain columbine (use 11)
Another perennial with distinctive spring flowers, this bears white-and-blue flowers with long trailing spurs against a backdrop of lobed green leaves. See Aquilegia caerula, p. 192.

D 'Chocolate Ruffles' coral bells (use 8)
Grown primarily for its rich, brownish red crinkled leaves, this perennial also bears a cloud of creamy little flowers in early summer. See *Heuchera* 'Chocolate Ruffles', p. 219.

E Variegated eulalia grass (use 9)
This perennial forms a tall, fountain of green- and white-striped leaves. In late summer, fluffy seed heads rise above the foliage on stiff stalks. Looks good all winter. See *Miscanthus sinensis* 'Variegatus', p. 230.

F Variegated hosta (use 9)
This perennial produces a mound of large, heart-shaped green leaves with white variegations. Large spikes of pale lilac flowers bloom in midsummer. See *Hosta undulata* 'Albo-marginata', p. 220.

G Bloody cranesbill (use 7)
A sprawling perennial with finely cut leaves, it bears round, red-to-purple flowers from early summer to fall. See *Geranium sanguineum*, p. 216.

H Black mondo grass (use 8)
This grasslike perennial forms small, though spreading, clumps of blackish, strap-like leaves. See *Ophiopogon planiscapus* 'Niger', p. 229.

See pp. 148-149 for:

I Serviceberry (use 3)

J Path

SITE: Sunny

SEASON: Summer

CONCEPT: Perennials brighten a woodland understory.

H **Black mondo grass**

C **Rocky Mountain columbine**

A **Eastern redbud**

B **White bleeding heart**

D **'Chocolate Ruffles' coral bells**

F **Variegated hosta**

Deck

Step pad

I I E E B A D C A B D E H F C G H J G H F F A D E

1 square = 2 ft.

PLANT PORTRAITS

A balanced mix of shrubs and perennials brightens up the shade and enhances the view from the deck.

● = First design, pp. 148-149

▲ = Second design, pp. 150-151

Lemon thyme (*Thymus citriodorus*, p. 245) ●

Rocky Mountain columbine (*Aquilegia caerula*, p. 192) ▲

Black mondo grass (*Ophiopogon planiscapus* 'Niger', p. 229) ▲

'Cheyenne' mock orange (*Philadelphus lewisii* 'Cheyenne', p. 233) ●

Variegated hosta (*Hosta undulata* 'Albomarginata', p. 220) ▲

An Entry Oasis

EXTEND A FRIENDLY DESERT WELCOME

A trend in new suburban developments is to crowd larger homes onto smaller and smaller lots. As a consequence, homeowners enjoy spaciousness inside the house but not outside. Making the most of limited space for outdoor living requires expanding the uses of some traditional areas.

This design transforms the entrance of a desert home from a corridor linking the front door and the driveway into a courtyard garden that invites gathering or relaxing outdoors. Shaded by the canopy of a small tree, enclosed by a wall low enough to allow breezes in, and soothed by the trickle of a small fountain, the courtyard can be enjoyed by family and friends year-round.

The design celebrates the desert environment and low-maintenance, low-water use principles. Local materials such as gravel, granite, and boulders provide natural sur-

faces to showcase striking desert plants. To fully integrate the design with the yard and house, you may want to cover the entire yard in gravel as we've shown here. It makes a water-efficient surface that is comfortable for both plants and people. Note the mounded undulating surface around the wall, indicated on the plan by broken lines.

The desert-loving plants featured here contribute distinctive forms, textures, and colors. Grouped together they create a dramatic composition. Spiky agave and ocotillo are boldly paired with the loosely arching bougainvillea and low-spreading lantana. The flowers in the planting bloom in spring, and they are a spectacular sight.

Plants & Projects

Installing the paving, wall, and fountain are the biggest jobs here, though not beyond the means of a resourceful do-it-yourselfer. Once established, the plants will thrive with occasional watering and just seasonal care.

A **Desert willow** (use 1)
From spring to fall this tree's willowy gray-green leaves are decorated with orchid-like flowers in shades of red, purple, pink, and white. The flowers are followed by long dangling seedpods. Leaves drop in winter, exposing attractive twisting branches. See *Chilopsis linearis*, p. 202.

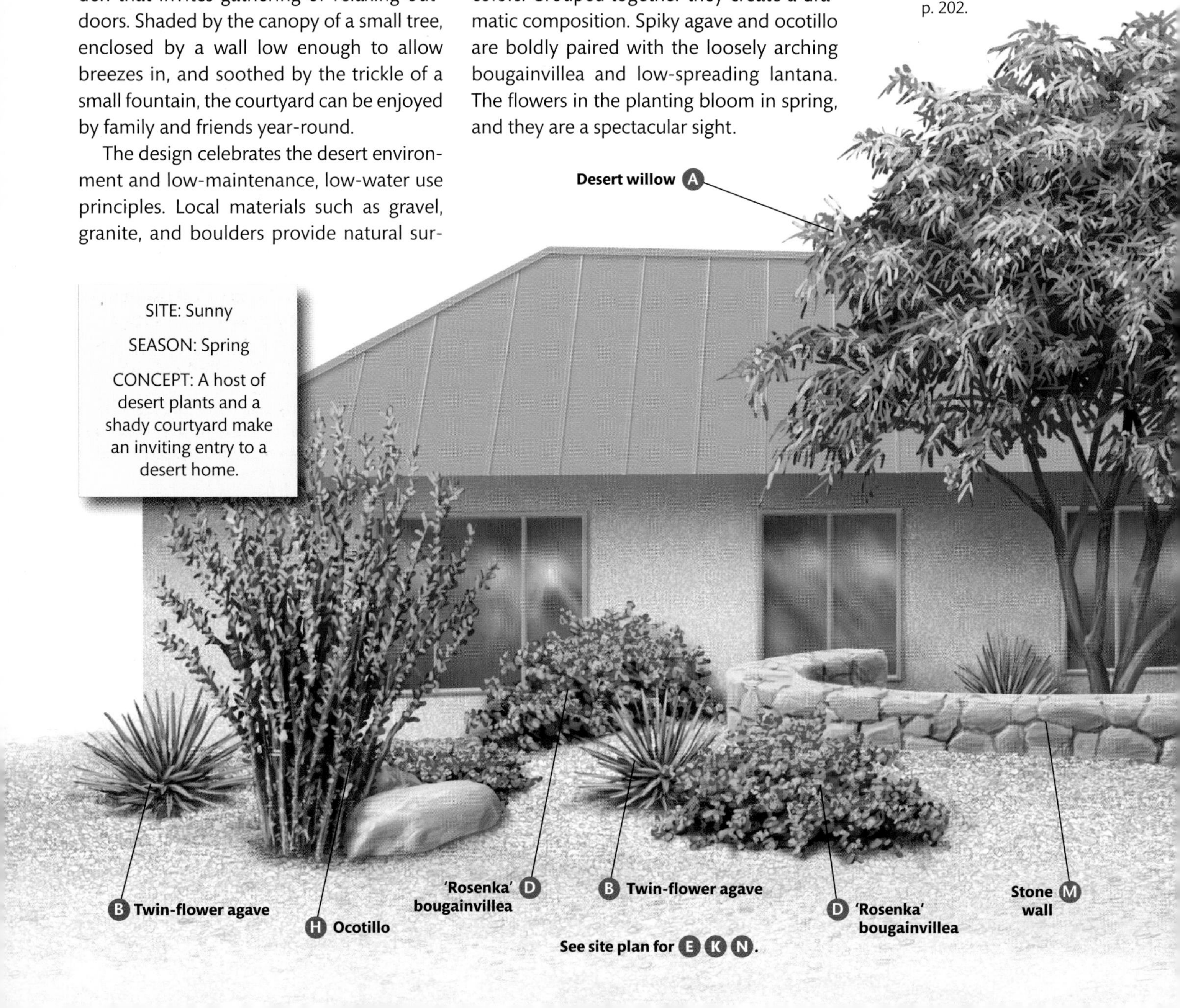

SITE: Sunny

SEASON: Spring

CONCEPT: A host of desert plants and a shady courtyard make an inviting entry to a desert home.

Desert willow **A**

B Twin-flower agave

H Ocotillo

'Rosenka' **D** bougainvillea

B Twin-flower agave

D 'Rosenka' bougainvillea

Stone **M** wall

See site plan for **E** **K** **N**.

B Twin-flower agave (use 4)
An unusually fine-textured agave, with narrow succulent leaves that form a perfect rosette 2 to 3 ft. in diameter. In spring, it sends up double spikes of large, pale yellow, bell-shaped flowers. See *Agave geminiflora*, p. 190.

C 'New Gold' bougainvillea (use 1)
Trained on a trellis, this evergreen vine's lavish display of gold flowers will be eye-catch-

ing from the street or drive. Blooms spring and summer. See *Bougainvillea*, p. 196.

D 'Rosenka' bougainvillea (use 2)
This bougainvillea's arching branches are festooned with papery gold and pink flowers for a long time in spring and summer. It makes a lush green mound in winter. See *Bougainvillea*, p. 196.

E Damianita (use 2)
Fragrant yellow daisies blanket this small shrub in spring and

fall. Needlelike leaves have a pungent but pleasant aroma. Evergreen. See *Chrysactinia mexicana*, p. 202.

F Mexican grass tree (use 1)
This unusual shrub creates a fountain of succulent evergreen foliage. As it matures it forms a central trunk capable of reaching 10 ft. tall and produces long dense clusters of bell-shaped white flowers in summer. See *Dasylirion longissima*, p. 207.

G Euphorbia hybrid (use 2)
Greatly admired for their large showy blossoms, euphorbias have been hybridized into dozens of varieties. Pick a compact one for this entry. Shown here is crown of thorns (*E. milii*), which has bright red flowers all year. See *Euphorbia* hybrids, p. 210.

H Ocotillo (use 1)
This desert shrub is noted for its burst of brilliant orange-red blossoms in spring. Leaves are small, gray-green, and deciduous in dry spells. See *Fouquieria splendens*, p. 214.

I Madagascar palm (use 1)
An eye-stopper by the door, this exotic tree looks like a cross between a cactus and a palm; its plump, spiny trunk is crowned with straplike deep green leaves. See *Pachypodium lamerei*, p. 232.

J Lantana (use 2)
Small lavender flowers brighten this low-spreading perennial's dark green leaves. Evergreen and ever-blooming where winters are mild. See *Lantana montevidensis*, p. 225.

K Annuals (as needed)
A collection of colorful pansies, snapdragons, and marigolds adds a festive look to this desert entry. See Annuals, pg. 190.

L Paving
Flagstones in muted desert tones provide an attractive and level surface for the patio and paths. See p. 259.

M Stone wall
Choose your favorite stone. Shown here is a colorfully veined granite.

N Water feature
Water is a wonderful focal point for a courtyard. Incorporate a small fountain or pool into the wall or have it stand alone. See p. 266.

O Gravel
Gravel emulates a desert surface in lieu of a lawn. Shown here is Desert Tan birdseye gravel.

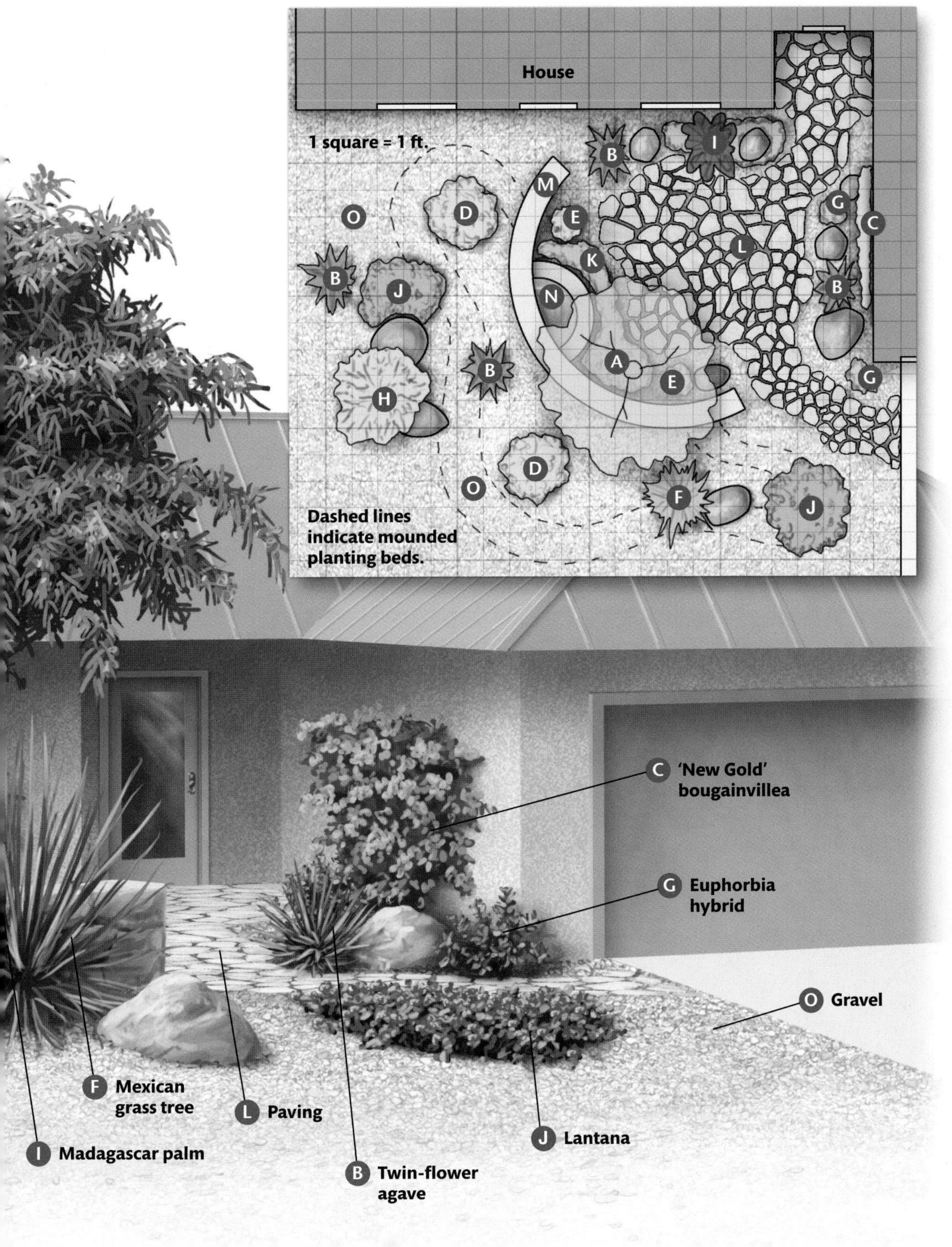

House

1 square = 1 ft.

Dashed lines indicate mounded planting beds.

C 'New Gold' bougainvillea

G Euphorbia hybrid

O Gravel

F Mexican grass tree

L Paving

I Madagascar palm

J Lantana

B Twin-flower agave

VARIATIONS ON A THEME

Here, three different planting styles produce striking entry gardens for Western-style homes.

Loose mounds of foliage and a liberal sprinkling of flowers flank a gravel walk in this "cottage" garden.

This eye-catching front door garden is largely a mix of foliage plants. A few colorful impatiens tucked in here and there add bright accents.

A desert garden is an ideal setting for this modern version of an adobe-style home.

A warm hello

This design creates a front yard entertainment area with a different look and a lower installation expense—there's no wall and it accommodates an existing walkway. The plants require little maintenance but more (low to moderate) supplemental watering than those in the previous design.

This flagstone courtyard is defined by mounded, sweeping planting beds mulched with gravel. A small pool of water adds an oasis-like touch. Under the protective umbrella of the tipu tree, the plants will produce luxuriant foliage all year and a profusion of blossoms in many vibrant colors, sometimes on a single plant. Brunfelsia bears purple, lavender, and white blossoms, and each of the ixora's huge flowers makes an exquisite bouquet of its own.

Plants & Projects

A **Tipu tree** (use 1)
This lovely tree has light green, divided leaves and yellow to apricot flowers in late spring. Woody seedpods follow in fall. See *Tipuana tipu*, p. 245.

B **Pygmy date palm** (use 1)
Crowned with dark green, fine-textured fronds, this is an attractive palm for a small space. Reaches about 6 ft. tall. See *Phoenix roebelenii*, p. 232.

C **Yesterday-today-and-tomorrow** (use 2)
From spring to summer the dark glossy leaves of this bushy evergreen shrub are smothered in pansy-like flowers that age from purple to lavender to white. See *Brunfelsia pauciflora* 'Floribunda Compacta', p. 196.

D **'Thai Dwarf' ixora** (use 4)
A fine ever-blooming tropical shrub. Huge flower clusters in red, orange, pink, or gold are displayed against dark green and glossy leaves. See *Ixora* 'Thai Dwarf', p. 223.

E **Arabian jasmine** (use 1)
Wonderfully fragrant white flowers bloom among this climbing vine's deep green leaves throughout the summer. See *Jasminum sambac*, p. 223..

F **'Flower Carpet Pink' rose** (use 12)
This rose spreads into a beautiful low mat of small glossy leaves topped with clusters of everblooming pink rosettes. See *Rosa*, p. 238.

See p. 153 for the following:
G **Annuals**
H **Mexican grass tree**
I **Paving**
J **Water feature**
K **Gravel mulch**

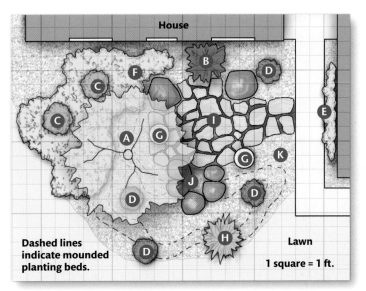

House

Dashed lines indicate mounded planting beds.

Lawn

1 square = 1 ft.

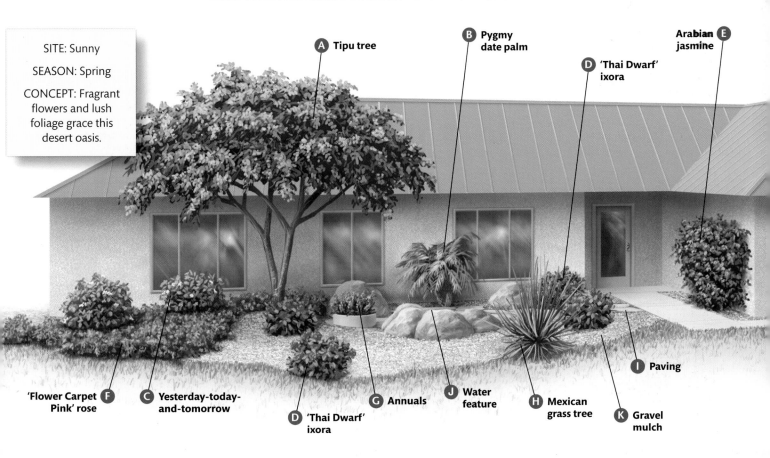

SITE: Sunny

SEASON: Spring

CONCEPT: Fragrant flowers and lush foliage grace this desert oasis.

A Tipu tree

B Pygmy date palm

E Arabian jasmine

D 'Thai Dwarf' ixora

F 'Flower Carpet Pink' rose

C Yesterday-today-and-tomorrow

D 'Thai Dwarf' ixora

G Annuals

J Water feature

H Mexican grass tree

I Paving

K Gravel mulch

A Welcome Respite

GREET VISITORS WITH SHADE, WATER, AND STRIKING PLANTS

This planting can either complement or extend an existing lawn-less landscape. The design focuses more intently on the home's front entrance than do the previous ones, but it shares the same low-water-use goal. Instead of turfgrass, gravel mulches the plants, conserves water, and discourages weeds. A low berm of contoured earth about 3 feet above grade level extends toward the house from the driveway, helping direct visitors down the exposed-aggregate walkway. Farther along the walk, a walled water garden and airy trellis provide an ideal spot for greeting or entertaining visitors. Larger plants across the wall and on the far side of the berm provide additional screening and make a transition to the area adjacent to the entry.

The plants reflect a variety of arid climate forms, from palms to feathery leaved gray-green shrubs and perennials. There are flowers for many months: The striking flowers of bougainvillea, lavender, and lantana are joined by less showy but certainly welcome blooms of cassia and lavender cotton.

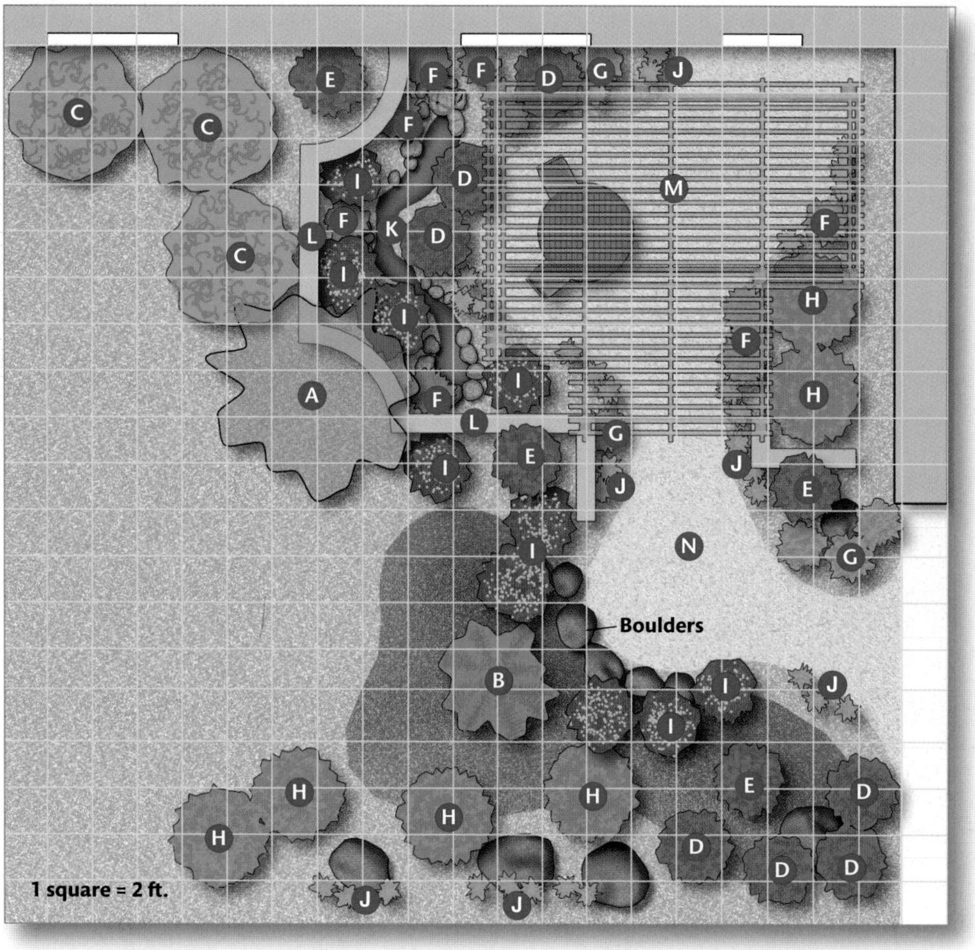

Mediterranean **A** fan palm

Feathery **C** cassia

H 'Powis Castle' artemisia

'Elijah Blue' blue **J** fescue grass

1 square = 2 ft.

Boulders

Plants & Projects

Installing the paving, wall, and fountain are the biggest jobs here, but all are feasible for the energetic do-it-yourselfer.

Ⓐ Mediterranean fan palm (use 1)
This palm has fan-shaped divided blue-green leaves rising from multiple stalks. In spring, long panicles of yellow flowers peek from the foliage. See *Chamaerops humilis*, p.202.

Ⓑ Sago palm (use 1)
Not a true palm, but its long arching featherlike yellow-green leaves look the part. Slow growing but worth the wait. See *Cycas revoluta*, p. 207.

Ⓒ Feathery cassia (use 3)
This evergreen shrub has

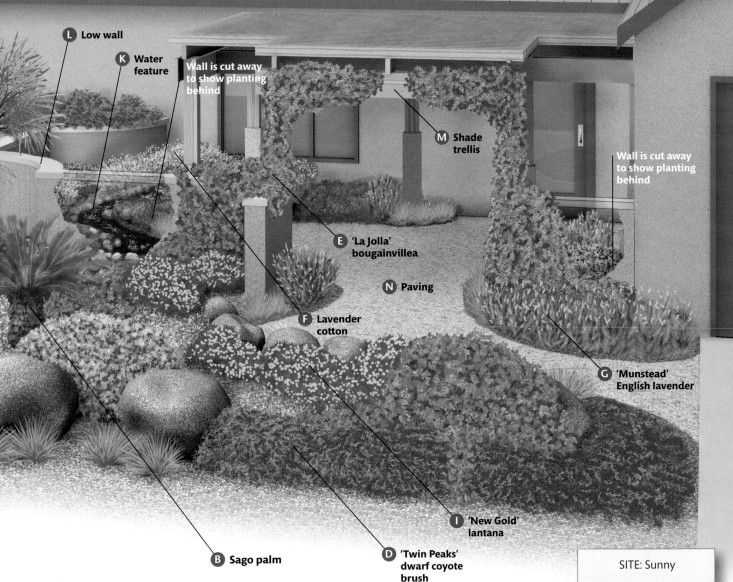

L **Low wall**

K **Water feature**

Wall is cut away to show planting behind

M **Shade trellis**

Wall is cut away to show planting behind

E **'La Jolla' bougainvillea**

N **Paving**

F **Lavender cotton**

G **'Munstead' English lavender**

I **'New Gold' lantana**

B **Sago palm**

D **'Twin Peaks' dwarf coyote brush**

SITE: Sunny

SEASON: Summer

CONCEPT: Arid-climate plants, a shady trellis, and a soothing water feature make this a memorable entry.

needlelike silver-gray foliage. In fall, it bears clusters of yellow flowers followed by abundant seed pods. See *Senna artemisiodes*, p. 243.

D **'Twin Peaks' dwarf coyote brush** (use 7)
A wide-spreading ground cover that is excellent for sunny, dry areas, this evergreen shrub forms a low mound of small bright green leaves. See *Baccharis pilularis* 'Twin Peaks', p. 194.

E **'La Jolla' bougainvillea** (use 4)
An evergreen vine, it forms a sprawling mound of green foliage covered in late spring and summer with spectacular red flowers. See *Bougainvillea* 'La Jolla', p. 196.

F **Lavender cotton** (use 6)
This bushy shrub forms a mound of fine-textured silver-white leaves topped in mid-summer with small, round bright yellow flowers. See *Santolina chamaecyparissus*, p. 242.

G **'Munstead' English lavender** (use 8)
In early summer, countless tall spikes of deep purple flowers cover the very fragrant silver-gray foliage of this bushy evergreen shrub. See *Lavandula angustifolia* 'Munstead', p. 226.

H **'Powis Castle' artemisia** (use 6)
This shrubby perennial forms a mass of lacey silver foliage. See *Artemisia* 'Powis Castle', p. 193.

I **'New Gold' lantana** (use 10)
A low, spreading ground cover, this evergreen shrub bears golden yellow flowers year-round where winters are mild. Grown as an annual in cold-winter areas. See *Lantana* 'New Gold', p. 225.

J **'Elijah Blue' blue fescue grass** (use 31)
This perennial forms grassy mounds of fine gray-blue foliage. Flower spikes turn tan in earlysummer. See *Festuca ovina* var. *glauca* 'Elijah Blue', p. 230.

K **Water feature**
A small water feature is a pleasant addition to arid landscapes. Here we've shown a small waterfall that trickles over rocks into a narrow pond. See p. 266.

L **Low wall**
This wall helps tie the waterscape and plantings to the house. Hire a stone mason, or use precast concrete blocks to make it yourself. See p. 270.

M **Shade trellis**
This simple cedar structure provides shade near the front door. See p. 282.

N **Paving**
The rough texture of this walkway mirrors the stone mulch.

PLANT PORTRAITS

Combining compelling fragrance, lovely flowers, and handsome foliage, these plants create a distinctive oasis.

● = First design, pp. 156-157

▲ = Second design, pp. 158-159

'Munstead' English lavender (*Lavendula angustifolia* 'Munstead', p. 226) ●

'Sundowner' New Zealand flax (*Phormium tenax* 'Sundowner', p. 234.) ▲

Sago palm (*Cycas revoluta*, p. 207) ●

Lavender cotton (*Santolina chamaecyparissus*, p. 242.) ●

'La Jolla' bougainvillea (*Bougainvillea* 'La Jolla', p. 196) ●

'Twin Peaks' dwarf coyote brush (*Baccharis pilularis* 'Twin Peaks', p. 194) ●

Variation on a theme

Here a brick patio shaded by attractive small trees provides a place to sit and relax while enjoying the view of surrounding plantings. By leaving the existing walkway in place and eliminating the trellis, this project is less expensive and time consuming to install than the previous one. However, shrubs and perennials again provide a variety of textures and colors as well as flowers throughout the year. A fragrant flowered vine perfumes the walkway. A small pool in a buried barrel adds the reassuring presence of water.

Plants & Projects

Ⓐ **'Pink Dawn' chitalpa** (use 3) This deciduous tree forms an open spreading crown of narrow green leaves. Bears masses of ruffled, light-pink trumpet-shaped flowers in early summer. See *Chitalpa tashkentensis* 'Pink Dawn', p. 202.

Ⓑ **'Catawba' crape myrtle** (use 2) A small upright deciduous tree, it has bright green leaves, pinkish bark and, for many weeks in summer, large spikes of crinkled, purple flowers. See *Lagerstroemia indica* 'Catawba', p.224.

Ⓒ **Carolina jasmine** (use 3) Trained to a trellis, this climbing evergreen vine can cover a wide area. Its narrow dark green leaves turn maroon in

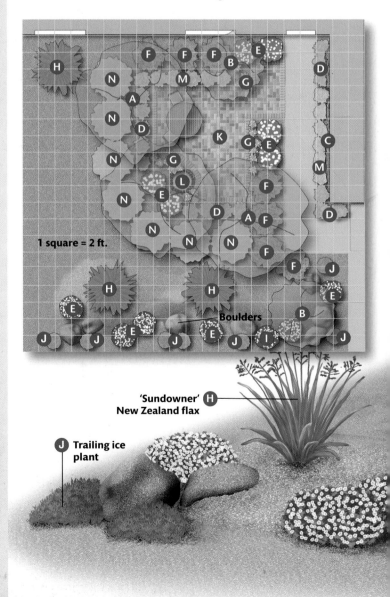

1 square = 2 ft.

Boulders

'Sundowner' Ⓗ **New Zealand flax**

Ⓙ **Trailing ice plant**

winter, but its real appeal is the fragrant bell-shaped yellow flowers it bears from late winter to early spring. See *Gelsemium sempervirens*, p. 215.

D **'Autumn Joy' sedum** (use 15) This perennial forms a mound of succulent gray-green leaves. Sturdy stems carry clusters of tiny flowers that turn from pale pink to rusty red (as seeds) from late summer through fall. See *Sedum* 'Autumn Joy', p. 242.

E **Santa Barbara daisy** (use 6) This mounded, fine-textured perennial with dark green leaves bears small pinkish-white, daisylike flowers from late spring to fall. See *Erigeron karvinskianus*, p. 209.

F **'Furman's Red' autumn sage** (use 7) A perennial, its upright stems bear small green leaves and, from summer into fall, slender spikes of red flowers. See *Salvia greggi* 'Furmans Red', p. 241.

G **Fortnight lily** (use 17) The swordlike green leaves of this perennial are topped from spring to fall with light yellow flowers held singly on tall spikes. See *Dietes bicolor*, p. 208.

H **'Sundowner' New Zealand flax** (use 3) This large evergreen perennial forms a rigid clump of eye-popping swordlike leaves that are a mix red, yellow, cream, and bronze. In summer, tall

spikes bearing creamy yellow flowers rise above the foliage. See *Phormium tenax* 'Sundowner', p. 234.

I **Bush morning glory** (use 7) This perennial's soft-textured mound of silvery foliage is covered with white trumpet-shaped flowers in late spring and early summer. See *Convolvulus cneorum*, p. 204.

J **Trailing ice plant** (use 7) An excellent ground cover, this evergreen perennial has succulent silver-green leaves. Blooms heavily from late winter to spring bearing large pink, red, or purple flowers. See *Lampranthus spectabilis*, p. 224.

K **Patio** Here we've shown a patio-brick surface, which is laid on a sand-and-gravel base with a soldier-course edging surrounding a basket-weave interior. Other designs are possible. See p. 259.

L **Water feature** This simple pool comprises a half barrel buried in the ground and surrounded by various-sized rocks that fade off into the gravel mulch of the surrounding bed. See p. 266.

See p. 157 for the following:

M **Lavender cotton** (use 12)

N **Feathery cassia** (use 7)

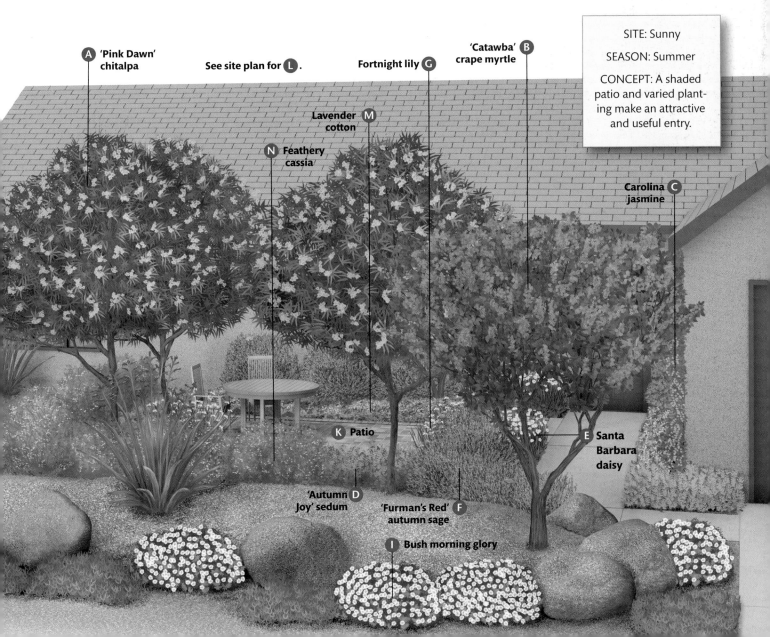

A 'Pink Dawn' chitalpa

See site plan for **L**.

Fortnight lily **G**

'Catawba' crape myrtle **B**

Lavender cotton **M**

N Feathery cassia

Carolina jasmine **C**

SITE: Sunny

SEASON: Summer

CONCEPT: A shaded patio and varied planting make an attractive and useful entry.

K Patio

E Santa Barbara daisy

'Autumn Joy' sedum **D**

'Furman's Red' autumn sage **F**

I Bush morning glory

Backyard Makeover

MAKE THE MOST OUT OF A SMALL, FROST-FREE LOT

Space is at a premium on many suburban lots, but this needn't cramp your outdoor living style. The design shown here makes use of the entire area in a small backyard to provide opportunities for open-air gatherings as well as family relaxation and play. (The rendering is shown as if viewed from the house, which is indicated on the plan.)

At the center is a large flagstone patio bordered by grassy verges where children can play or adults can kick off their shoes and recline. A continuous garden bed meanders along a privacy fence enclosing the lot. As the shade tree matures, its generous canopy will accommodate a table or recliners. To cater outdoor feasts, there's a barbecue. Across the patio, a small pool and fountain provide a cooling presence and the music of bubbling water.

Curving gently around the perimeter, the plantings comprise a pleasing array of trees, shrubs, and trellised vines. Several "boulders" add to the natural composition and provide a few extra places to sit.

Many of the plants originate in exotic parts of the world and are chosen for their proven performance in frost-free areas of the West. South America's native tipu tree is a striking focal point, with long clusters of spring flowers and fine-textured foliage. Equally eyecatching are the diverse and sculptural palms, the extraordinary flowers of the tropical bird of paradise, and the flamboyant blossoms of dwarf ixora.

Plants & Projects

Ambitious do-it-yourselfers can install the entire design. If you're less energetic, have a landscaping service put in the hardscape and do the planting yourself. A layer of small river-washed rocks mulches the beds, complementing the look of the plants and helping to conserve water.

Ⓐ Tipu tree (use 1)
Long clusters of yellow- to apricot-colored blossoms dangle among this small evergreen tree's fine-textured leaves in spring and early summer. Long seedpods add interest in autumn and winter. See *Tipuana tipu*, p. 245.

Ⓑ Mediterranean fan palm (use 1)
This compact palm fits nicely under the tree and thrives in its shade. It forms a clump of trunks crowned with coarse blue-gray fronds, each looking

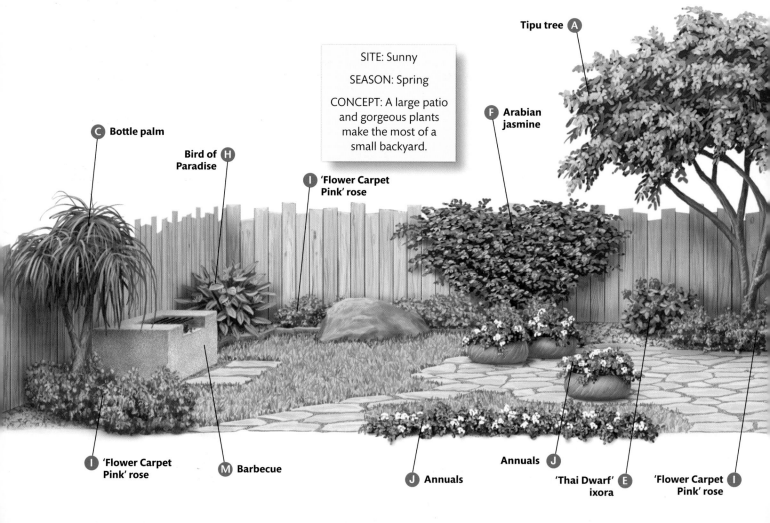

SITE: Sunny

SEASON: Spring

CONCEPT: A large patio and gorgeous plants make the most of a small backyard.

like a giant hand-held fan. See *Chamaerops humilis*, p. 202.

C **Bottle palm** (use 1)
Another palm with great structural appeal. The trunk starts swollen and then narrows before branching into a shaggy bright green crown. See *Nolina recurvata*, p. 229.

D **'New Gold' Bougainvillea** (use 1)
This vigorous climber is clothed in golden flowers spring and summer. Leaves add texture and color in winter. See *Bougainvillea*, p. 196.

E **'Thai Dwarf' ixora** (use 2)
In a sheltered spot, this beautiful shrub promises a bounty of large colorful flowers. Evergreen foliage. See *Ixora* 'Thai Dwarf', p. 223.

F **Arabian jasmine** (use 2)
Two of these white-flowering vines are enough to perfume the entire backyard on summer nights. Evergreen. *Jasminum sambac*, p. 223.

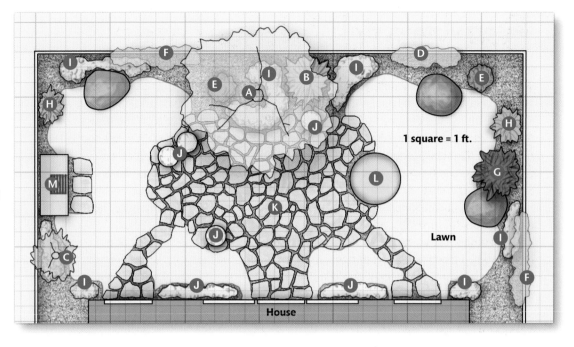

1 square = 1 ft.

Lawn

House

G **Madagascar palm** (use 1)
This shrub produces a single thorned trunk topped with straplike dull green leaves. See *Pachypodium lamerei*, p. 232.

H **Bird of Paradise** (use 2)
An evergreen perennial that forms a wide clump of long-stemmed bluish green leaves and an abundance of large and unusual orange flowers. See *Strelitzia reginea*, p. 244.

I **'Flower Carpet Pink' rose** (use 13)
Shear this ground cover rose once in winter to keep it compact and blooming vigorously. Forms a nearly continuous mass of pink. See *Rosa*, p. 238.

J **Annuals**
Grow in pots and beds next to the house to enliven the patio. Ivy geranium is shown here. See Annuals, pg. 190.

K **Paving**
Choose a flagstone that complements the color of your home. See p. 259.

L **Water feature**
A small fiberglass pool and a simple fountain add interest at a modest cost. See p. 266.

M **Barbecue**
You can install a custom grill of stone or adobe as shown here or use a moveable gas unit.

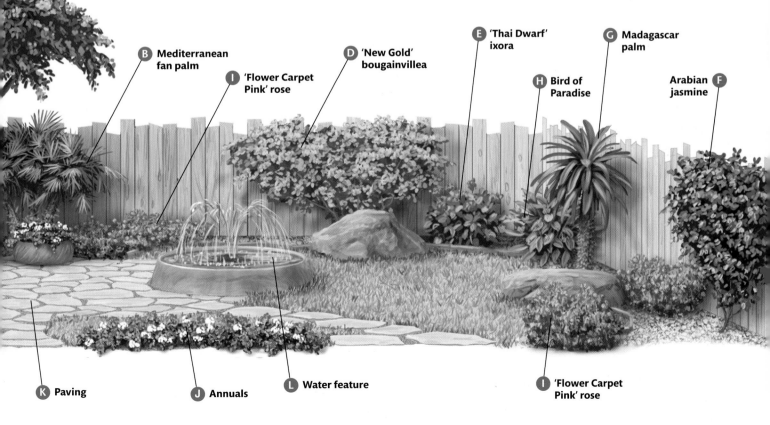

B Mediterranean fan palm

I 'Flower Carpet Pink' rose

D 'New Gold' bougainvillea

E 'Thai Dwarf' ixora

H Bird of Paradise

G Madagascar palm

F Arabian jasmine

K Paving

J Annuals

L Water feature

I 'Flower Carpet Pink' rose

Desert vista

If you live in a dry, nearly frost-free climate, here's a small-backyard design that's as natural as your environment. Inspired by desert landscapes, the design uses striking plants that thrive in desert soils and need less water than the exotic plants too often grown in desert and semi-arid gardens.

The plantings are designed to complement an existing patio or deck off the house, as indicated on the plan. (The rendering shows a view from the house.) In place of a water-thirsty lawn, birds-eye gravel covers the entire area, providing a natural-looking setting for the desert plants.

The plants are grouped on two low, wide mounds, indicated by broken lines on the plan. Thorny ocotillos and cacti top the mounds with tropical bougainvilleas below, where they'll receive runoff from rainfall. Little supplemental watering will be needed after the plants are established.

The garden is at its most colorful in springtime, as shown here, when just about everything is in bloom. If the climate doesn't compel you outdoors, the blossoms will. When the summer heat bleaches most things gray, you'll still be able to enjoy splashes of gold bougainvillea and drifts of lavender lantana from your vantage point in the shade. In winter, the evergreen foliage of the palo verde and Mexican tree grass will contribute lush green color to the landscape.

Plants & Projects

Ⓐ Blue palo verde (use 1)
This native desert tree is prized for its spectacular burst of yellow bloom in spring and its bluish branches and foliage. Evergreen in mild winter areas. See *Cercidium floridum*, p. 201.

Ⓑ Twin-flower agave (use 4)
This succulent forms a single rosette of narrow leaves about 3 ft. high. In spring it bears tall spikes of white flowers. See *Agave gemini-flora*, p. 190.

Ⓒ 'New Gold' bougainvillea (use 2)
Unfazed by desert heat and aridity, this tropical vine covers the fence in a profusion of gold flowers and evergreen foliage. See *Bougainvillea*, p. 196.

Ⓓ 'Rosenka' bougainvillea (use 1)
Masses of flowers open gold and age to pink on this compact evergreen shrub. See *Bougainvillea*, p. 196.

Ⓔ Mexican grass tree (use 1)
This tropical-looking evergreen shrub forms a large fountain of narrow leaves that are completely unarmed, unlike many desert natives. See *Dasylirion longissima*, p. 207.

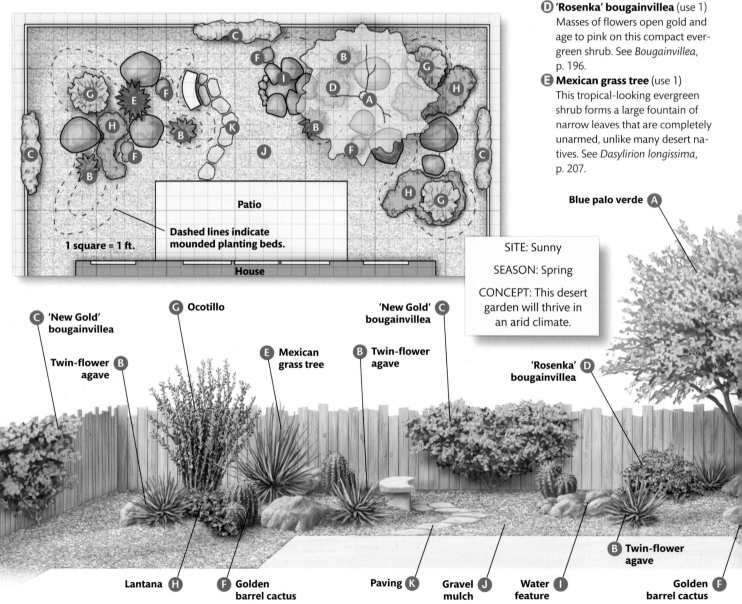

Patio

Dashed lines indicate mounded planting beds.

1 square = 1 ft.

House

SITE: Sunny

SEASON: Spring

CONCEPT: This desert garden will thrive in an arid climate.

Blue palo verde Ⓐ

Ⓒ 'New Gold' bougainvillea

Ⓖ Ocotillo

'New Gold' Ⓒ bougainvillea

Twin-flower Ⓑ agave

Ⓔ Mexican grass tree

Ⓑ Twin-flower agave

'Rosenka' Ⓓ bougainvillea

Ⓑ Twin-flower agave

Lantana Ⓗ Ⓕ Golden barrel cactus

Paving Ⓚ Gravel Ⓙ mulch Water Ⓘ feature

Golden Ⓕ barrel cactus

F Golden barrel cactus (use 4)
Shaped like a barrel and adorned with golden thorns, this small cactus wears a crown of small yellow flowers in summer. See *Echinocactus grusonii*, p. 208.

G Ocotillo (use 3)
Bright orange-red flower clusters bloom from the tips of this shrub's thorny branches from early spring to summer. See *Fouquieria splendens*, p. 214.

H Lantana (use 3)
This low-spreading shrub forms a solid mat of crinkly green leaves and plentiful lavender flowers all year. See *Lantana montevidensis*, p. 225.

I Water feature
A small fiberglass shell or even a barrel surrounded by large stones makes a pleasant little pool. See p. 266.

J Gravel mulch
Shape the planting mounds with soil and then cover the entire area with small-diameter stones such as bird's-eye gravel. See p. 158.

See p. 161 for the following:

K Paving

G Ocotillo

'New Gold' C
bougainvillea

H Lantana   J Gravel
mulch

VARIATIONS ON A THEME

These designs run the gamut from a weekend makeover to projects requiring weeks of work.

It's not quite an instant garden, but containers of tree roses and tulips added character and interest to this patio in short order.

On a steeply sloped backyard, a hillside garden is a lot more fun than a lawn. This one includes a little patio retreat created by a low retaining wall.

Vibrant tropical plants give this lush patio garden some pizzazz.

Creating Garden Rooms

SHRUBS AND TREES CREATE MULTIPLE GARDEN ROOMS

If one outdoor garden room is good, then three must certainly be better. This design creates a whole houseful of rooms within a small backyard. The floor plan is delineated by concrete and flagstone paving, while the walls are a pleasing tapestry of foliage and, for many months, flowers. Three trees provide shade as well as striking foliage.

Texas privet, planted close enough to form solid, loosely-clipped 6-foot-tall hedges, screens neighboring backyards. Standing out against an evergreen background, the shrubs' fragrant white flowers are a welcome attraction in early summer. Along the back property line, an equally tall planting of heavenly bamboo also makes a screen, but with a very dif-

ferent look. Its fluffy white flowers are lovely, but the everchanging colors of the foliage is the real eyecatcher.

Skirting the base of the privet on one end of the planting, a low clipped line of boxwood serves almost as a baseboard to the taller hedge. Strap-leaved agapanthus edges the seating areas, adding a visual

step down from the taller plants to the patio. Roses beside the sliding door mark the entry to the house.

A central area of lawn separates the rooms. At one end, a small fountain provides a focal point for all three areas. If you don't like to mow, you could plant the lawn area with a low ground cover.

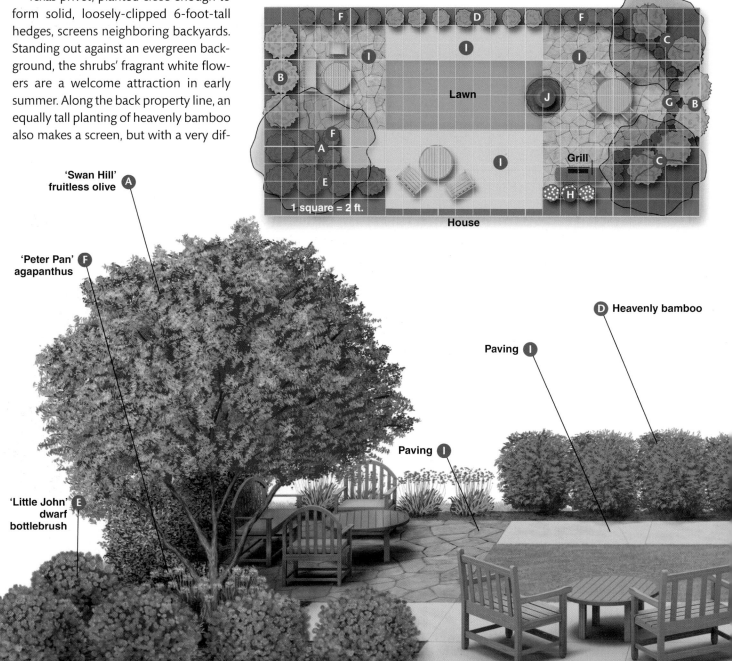

1 square = 2 ft.

Lawn

Grill

House

'Swan Hill' fruitless olive **A**

'Peter Pan' **F** agapanthus

'Little John' **E** dwarf bottlebrush

D Heavenly bamboo

Paving **I**

Paving **I**

Plants & Projects

Installing the hardscape and plants is a big job. Next, you'll need to keep pruning shears at the ready to train the clipped boxwood hedge and to nudge the more loosely pruned hedge plants into the spaces you want. After that, maintenance requires just seasonal cleanup.

Ⓐ 'Swan Hill' fruitless olive (use 1)
This tree forms a wide, spreading crown above multiple trunks. Fine-textured gray-green leaves are evergreen; flowers are inconspicuous and do not produce fruit. See *Olea europaea* 'Swan Hill', p. 229.

Ⓑ Texas privet (use 9)
This fast-growing evergreen shrub forms a solid mass of glossy green foliage. In early summer, it bears scented white flowers that produce long-lasting dark berries. See *Ligustrum japonicum*, p. 226.

Ⓒ 'Krauter Vesuvius' purpleleaf plum (use 2)
A deciduous tree, its bright pink flowers appear in spring before the deep purple foliage emerges. Produces no fruit. See *Prunus cerasifera* 'Krauter Vesuvius', p. 235.

Ⓓ Heavenly bamboo (use 7)
This multi-stemmed evergreen shrub makes a clump of soft, feathery grayish green foliage that is gold, green, or bronzy red depending on the season. In summer, fluffy white flowers are followed by red berries. See *Nandina domestica*, p. 229.

Ⓔ 'Little John' dwarf bottle-brush (use 5)
A dense shrub with arching branches clothed in narrow, light green leaves. Blood-red, brushlike blooms form at ends of branches from fall to spring. See *Callistemon viminalis* 'Little John', p. 198.

Ⓕ 'Peter Pan' agapanthus (use 12)
This perennial makes a compact mound of strap-like, dark green leaves topped in late spring and summer with tall, ball-shaped clusters of blue flowers. See *Agapanthus* 'Peter Pan', p. 189.

Ⓖ 'Green Beauty' Japanese boxwood (use 18)
This little evergreen shrub is the classic hedge plant, forming a solid mass of small, fragrant deep green leaves. See *Buxus microphylla* var. *japonica* 'Green Beauty', p. 198.

Ⓗ 'Iceberg' rose (use 3)
This shrubby rose produces lovely white flowers off and on throughout the year in warm-winter areas. See *Rosa* 'Iceberg', p. 238.

Ⓘ Paving
We used concrete and flag-stones in this design. Given the extent of the paving, hiring a professional will be the best option for many. See p. 264.

Ⓙ Water feature
A simple fountain such as this can be purchased at many gardening centers. Plant a circle of annuals (white sweet alyssum, shown here) to set off the water feature. See Annuals, p. 190.

SITE: Sunny

SEASON: Late spring

CONCEPT: Well screened by attractive hedges, outdoor rooms accommodate several types of gatherings.

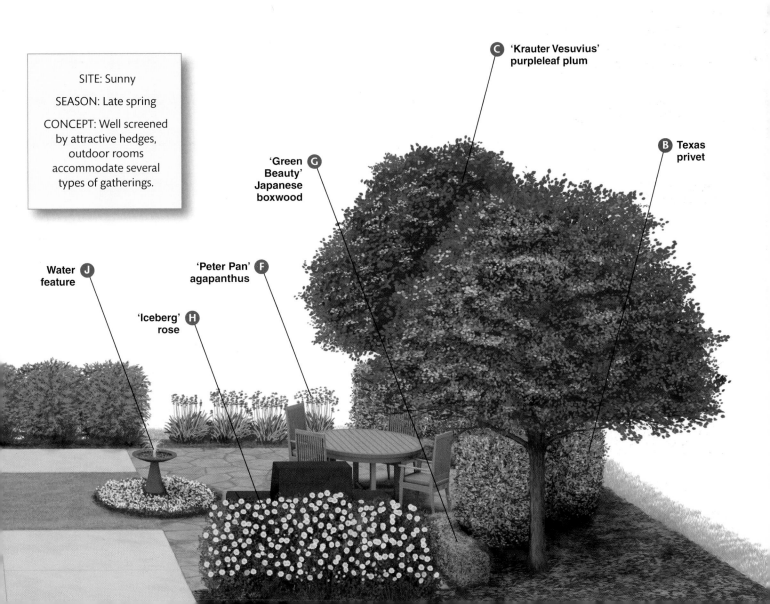

Ⓒ 'Krauter Vesuvius' purpleleaf plum

Ⓑ Texas privet

Ⓖ 'Green Beauty' Japanese boxwood

Ⓙ Water feature

Ⓗ 'Iceberg' rose

Ⓕ 'Peter Pan' agapanthus

PLANT PORTRAITS

A bold mixture of colorful, carefree plants creates or complements a backyard fence in all seasons.

● = First design, pp. 164-165

▲ = Second design, pp. 166-167

'Swan Hill' fruitless olive
Olea europaea 'Swan Hill', p. 229) ●

Candytuft
(*Iberis sempervirens*, p. 221) ▲

'Krauter Vesuvius' purpleleaf plum (*Prunus cerasifera* 'Krauter Vesuvius', p. 235) ●

Lilyturf (*Liriope muscari*, p. 226) ▲

Fenced in

If your backyard is fenced or you'd like to fence it, this design shows how you can create comfortable garden rooms within its confines.

Two paved areas and a grassy semicircle comprise the rooms. They are bordered by attractive shrubs. Because privacy is provided by the fence, these plantings can be more decorative than functional. Including the roses, barberry, kumquat, and two kinds of heavenly bamboo, they offer a wealth of attractive foliage and flowers year-round.

Dressing up the fence itself, star jasmine clothes it in shiny green leaves sprinkled with creamy flowers in spring and early summer. Overhead, one deciduous and two evergreen trees provide shade as well as good looks.

Rectangular beds in the center of the space are home to a variety of low-growing perennials, two of which are evergreen, all of which produce lovely flowers. Nestled in one of the beds, a small "pond" adds the pleasure of water and perhaps a few goldfish or koi.

Plants & Projects

Ⓐ **Golden raintree** (use 1)
This deciduous tree provides interest year round, with fine-textured, divided, green leaves. Doesn't show flowers. See *Koelreuteria paniculata*, p. 224.

Ⓑ **'Saratoga' sweet bay** (use 3)
A small round-headed evergreen tree with deep green leaves, it provides shade but won't outgrow its space. See *Laurus nobilis* 'Saratoga', p. 225.

Ⓒ **'Nagami' dwarf kumquat** (use 2)
This evergreen shrub offers dark green leaves, fragrant yellow spring flowers, and, in winter,

SITE: Sunny

SEASON: Spring

CONCEPT: Ornamented with fine foliage and flowers, a fenced-in yard features attractive garden rooms.

Ⓑ **'Saratoga' sweet bay**

Dwarf heavenly bamboo Ⓒ

'Nagami' dwarf Ⓒ **kumquat**

edible fruit. See *Citrus*, p. 202.

D Lilyturf (use 12)

A grassy evergreen perennial, it bears clusters of lavender flower spikes in summer. See *Liriope muscari*, p. 226.

E Candytuft (use 11)

The slender, glossy evergreen leaves of this perennial are topped in spring with bright white flowers. See *Iberis sempervirens*, p. 221.

F 'Queen Ann' agapanthus (use 12)

Ball-shaped clusters of blue or white flowers float above this perennial's arching narrow leaves in late spring and summer. See *Agapanthus* 'Queen Ann', p. 189.

G Dwarf heavenly bamboo (use 10)

The feathery foliage of this evergreen shrub changes color with the seasons (red, gold, and green). White summer flowers are followed by red berries. See *Nandina domestica* 'Nana', p. 229.

H 'Crimson Pygmy' Japanese barberry (use 12)

This dense, compact, slightly spreading shrub bears small, showy purplish red deciduous leaves that turn bright crimson in fall. See *Berberis thunbergii* 'Crimson Pygmy', p. 194.

I Star jasmine (use 5)

Twining up the fence, this evergreen vine bears clusters of fragrant cream-colored flowers in late spring and early summer atop small glossy green leaves. See *Trachelospermum jasminoides*, p. 246.

J Paving

Precast concrete paving blocks such as these can be laid on a tamped sand-and-gravel base in a couple of weekends. See p. 264.

K Pond

Set into the ground as a half barrel, fiberglass form, or plastic liner with freeform shape, this small pond will take another weekend to install. See p. 266.

L Fence

Made of cedar, the fence shown here provides privacy and a support for flowering vines trained to wires attached to the wood. See p. 274.

See p. 165 for the following:

M Iceberg rose (use 6)

N Heavenly bamboo (use 8)

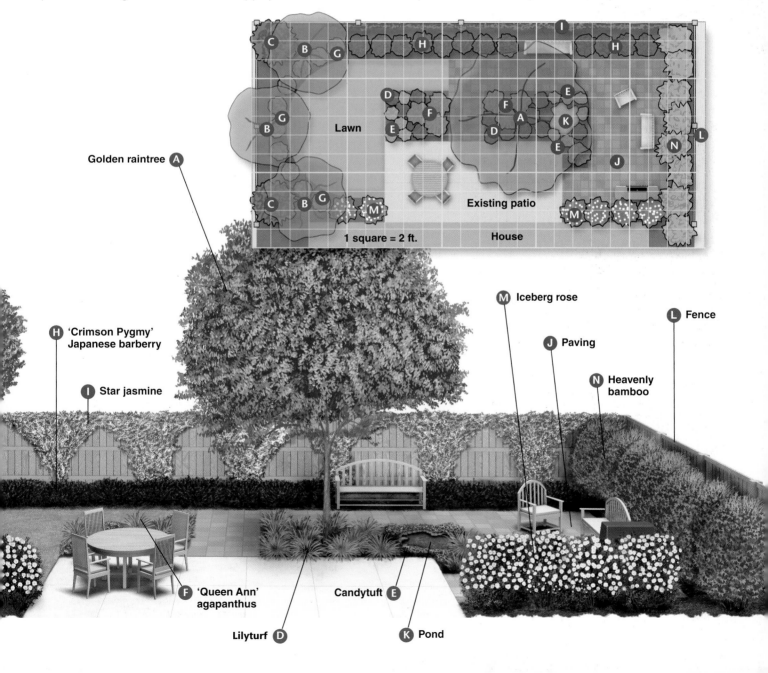

Poolside Pleasures

PLANTINGS ENHANCE YOUR SWIMMING POOL

Where summers are roasting hot, swimming pools are an increasingly common backyard amenity. On an ordinary suburban lot, a pool is often the dominant backyard presence. Too often, however, the backyard pool is little more than an aquatic gym surrounded by a slab of concrete and lawn.

This design shows that a planting of trees, shrubs, and perennials—plus a little hardscaping—can work magic to enhance all your outdoor activities, whether you're escaping with a book, entertaining friends, working in the garden, or playing in the pool. (The rendering shows the design as seen from the house, which is indicated on the plan, opposite.)

Tall shrubs on the perimeter heighten the sense of enclosure and privacy provided by the fence, which building codes usually require around a pool. The paving surrounding the pool extends at each end to accommodate a table and chairs for entertaining and recliners for relaxing. An arbor creates a little niche along one side. Low-growing plants lining the surround add color and texture to the setting. And there's still ample lawn for playing games and lounging.

Plants & Projects

The plants in this design are chosen not only for their year-round good looks, but also because they are well-behaved around a pool. All are low-maintenance evergreens that hold on to their foliage throughout the year, producing as little litter as possible. You won't be fishing leaves out of the water as you would with deciduous trees and shrubs.

Ⓐ 'Majestic Beauty' Indian hawthorne (use 5) Trimmed into small trees with overlapping crowns, these evergreen shrubs are decorated with huge clusters of fragrant pearl pink flowers in spring. Choose single-trunked shrubs for this planting. See *Rhaphiolepis indica* 'Majestic Beauty', p. 236.

SITE: Sunny

SEASON: Spring

CONCEPT: A poolside filled with flowers and foliage lets you go for a swim in the garden.

Fraser photinia Ⓑ

'Majestic Beauty' Indian hawthorne Ⓐ

Ⓒ **'Royal Princess' heavenly bamboo**

Ⓘ **Asian jasmine**

Ⓖ **'Russian Rhapsody' daylily**

Bigleaf hydrangea Ⓓ

B **Fraser photinia** (use 15)
Growing 8 ft. tall and 6 ft. wide, these naturally rounded shrubs overlap to form a coarse dark-leafed hedge. In spring they form a solid bank of white flowers. Note that one is trained flat to the wall as a decorative backdrop for the arbor. See *Photinia x fraseri*, p. 234.

C **'Royal Princess' heavenly bamboo** (use 19)
Airy reddish green foliage covers this narrow, upright evergreen shrub. It bears small pink flowers in spring and summer. See *Nandina domestica*, p. 229.

D **Bigleaf hydrangea** (use 2)
A rounded deciduous shrub clothed in large, deep green leaves and huge, ball-shaped flowers through summer. Varieties abound in blue, pink, or white flowers. See *Hydrangea macrophylla*, p. 221.

E **Sasanqua camellia** (use 3)
This evergreen shrub produces lovely flowers from late fall into winter. Choose from a range of colors. See *Camellia sasanqua*, p. 198.

F **'Gumpo Pink' azaleas** (use 7)
Masses of pink flowers cover this compact, slightly spreading shrub in spring. Small dark green leaves are attractive all year. See *Rhododendron*, p. 237.

G **'Russian Rhapsody' daylily** (as needed)
This grassy perennial is bright green and topped with showy purple flowers in summer. Plant about 12 in. apart for a seamless poolside fringe. See *Hemerocallis*, p. 218.

H **Winter-blooming bergenia** (as needed)
Large round leaves with wavy margins distinguish this evergreen perennial. Pink flowers form on short thick spikes in winter. Plant the clumps 18 in. apart for a continuous border. See *Bergenia crassifolia*, p. 195..

I **Asian jasmine** (as needed)
A dense, sprawling ground cover with small, dull green leaves and star-shaped white flowers. For complete coverage in a season, plant on 12-in. centers. See *Trachelospermum asiaticum*, p. 246.

J **Arbor**
Easily built, this attractive structure provides a central focal point and a welcome sun screen by the pool. See p 282.

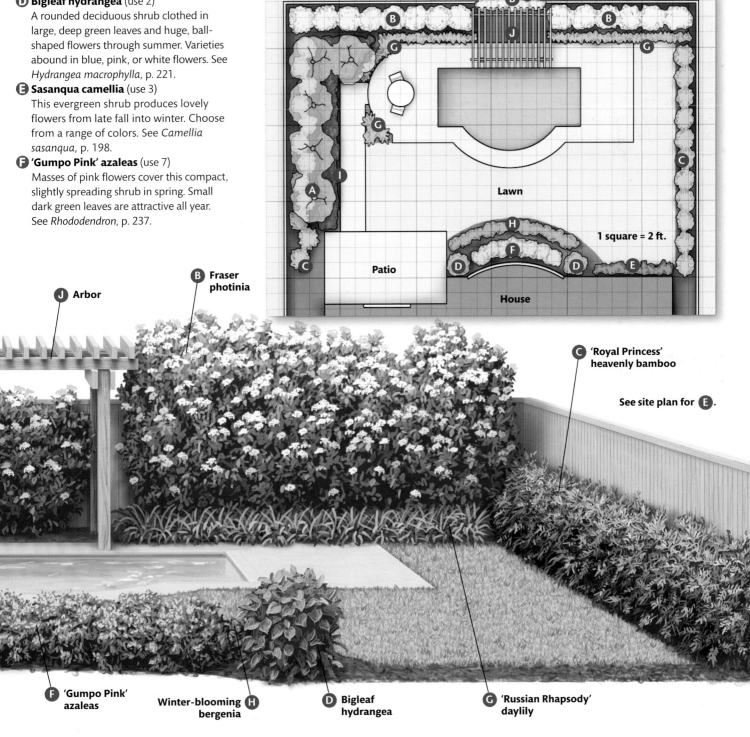

Private haven

This design has a different look than the previous one, but it accomplishes the same goal: integrating a backyard pool into a larger outdoor living space.

Here, spectacular hedges surround the pool like thick, luxuriant drapes. They create a lush backdrop as well as privacy for pool activities; they can also screen an unsightly building from view.

Once again, evergreen foliage predominates. In summer, there are flowers in cool blues and whites. In winter, red camellias and orange kumquats are lively accents. Gardenia, sweet olive, pittosporum, and Asian jasmine ensure lovely fragrance for many months.

SITE: Sunny

SEASON: Spring

CONCEPT: Colorful, lush, and fragrant plants increase poolside pleasures.

Plants & Projects

Ⓐ Fraser photinia (use 3)
These small trees wear a dense canopy of glossy oval leaves. Small white flowers bloom for weeks in spring. See *Photinia* x *fraseri*, p. 234.

Ⓑ Shrubby yew pine (use 21)
This columnar tree makes a fine-textured, fairly dense hedge that may eventually reach 15 ft. tall. Evergreen foliage is flat and needlelike. It grows right to the ground and is soft to the touch. See *Podocarpus macrophyllus*, p. 235.

Ⓒ Pittosporum (use 8)
This fast-growing shrub will quickly form a dense screen of large, glossy, evergreen leaves that showcase clusters of sweetly scented white flowers from spring into summer. See *Pittosporum undulatum*, p. 234.

Ⓓ Sweet olive (use 2)
This evergreen shrub retains its compact, vase-shaped habit as it grows. Leaves are small, glossy, and dark green. Spring flowers are inconspicuous but very fragrant. See *Osmanthus* x *fortunei*, p. 232.

Ⓔ 'Yuletide' sasanqua camellia (use 4)

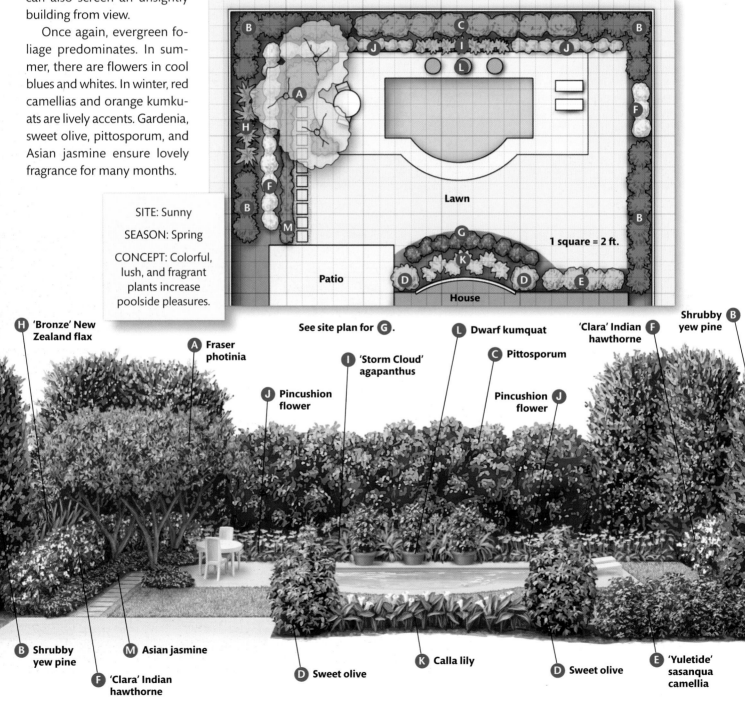

1 square = 2 ft.

Lawn

Patio

House

Ⓗ 'Bronze' New Zealand flax

Ⓐ Fraser photinia

See site plan for Ⓖ.

Ⓙ Pincushion flower

Ⓘ 'Storm Cloud' agapanthus

Ⓛ Dwarf kumquat

Ⓒ Pittosporum

Ⓙ Pincushion flower

'Clara' Indian hawthorne Ⓕ

Shrubby Ⓑ yew pine

Ⓑ Shrubby yew pine

Ⓜ Asian jasmine

Ⓕ 'Clara' Indian hawthorne

Ⓓ Sweet olive

Ⓚ Calla lily

Ⓓ Sweet olive

Ⓔ 'Yuletide' sasanqua camellia

This evergreen shrub has single red flowers that bloom abundantly in winter among lustrous small green leaves. See *Camellia sasanqua*, p. 198.

F **'Clara' Indian hawthorne** (use 16)

A beautiful compact evergreen shrub bearing bright green leaves, red new growth, and clusters of small white flowers in spring, followed by blue berries. See *Rhaphiolepis indica*, 'Clara', p. 236.

G **Gardenia** (use 9)

Sweetly fragrant white flowers open over a long period in spring on this low, spreading, evergreen shrub See *Gardenia jasminoides*, p. 214.

H **'Bronze' New Zealand flax** (use 4)

This bold perennial forms a clump of spiky, bronzy red, straplike leaves and makes a striking backdrop to the photinia. See *Phormium tenax* 'Bronze', p. 234.

I **'Storm Cloud' agapanthus** (use 7)

Big clusters of blue flowers top 4 ft. stalks that rise above this evergreen perennial's fountain of dark foliage. See *Agapanthus* 'Storm Cloud', p. 189.

J **Pincushion flower** (use 13)

This perennial has soft-textured gray-green foliage topped with wiry-stemmed blue flowers from spring through fall. Plant 2 ft. apart for a continuous fuzzy carpet. See *Scabiosa caucasia*, p. 242.

K **Calla lily** (use 7)

Large, pure white flowers unfurl from tall stalks above this perennial's dark glossy foliage. The center of each tubular flower is decorated with an erect yellow spike. See *Zantedeschia aethiopica*, p. 249.

L **Dwarf kumquat** (show 3)

A delightful container plant, this evergreen tree produces a heavy crop of orange, sweet and sour fruit from October to May. See *Citrus*, p. 202.

See p. 169 for the following

M **Asian jasmine** (as needed)

VARIATIONS ON A THEME

These three approaches to landscaping around swimming pools have one thing in common: the designs take their cue from the landscapes in which they are set.

A white-washed wall and gray to deep green foliage plants help to blend this poolside planting with the natural vegetation beyond it.

Plantings and an arbor keep their distance in framing this pool and lawn.

The landscape below can be admired while you're floating in the water.

afy Enclosure

DROUGHT-TOLERANT PLANTS FRAME A BACKYARD OASIS

A swimming pool takes up a lot of space, particularly on a small lot. And most zoning regulations require fencing as a safety measure around a pool. This design uses well-chosen plants and hardscape to make the area inside the fence and outside the pool attractive and useful.

Around the perimeter, three different evergreen shrubs form hedges in front of the fence; their varied leaves and textures make a much more interesting surface than the manmade structure. From fall through spring, the hedges also offer white or pink flowers and, for many of those months, fragrance. Perennials add colorful accents at the feet of the shrubs and edges of the paving.

At three corners, trees invite the eye up above the fence. Near the house, crape myrtles provide interest in every season. Larger Australian willows, with their weeping foliage, add languorous ease—and welcome shade—to hot summer days.

In the final corner, a wooden arbor sun screen covers a large paved patio, an ideal spot to watch swimmers or dine on a balmy evening. If you desire more shade, plant vines at the feet of several arbor posts and train them up and over the top.

Plants & Projects

A substantial undertaking to install, this design requires relatively little maintenance once the plants are established. Other than clipping the hedges as needed to keep them tidy (because you shouldn't shape or shear them), routine seasonal care is all that's needed.

Ⓐ 'Catawba' crape myrtle
(use 4)
This small deciduous tree has multi-season appeal: large spikes of crinkled, purple flowers bloom for weeks in summer; bright green leaves turn orange, red, or purplish in fall; flaky bark is attractive in winter. See *Lagerstroemia indica* 'Catawba', p. 224.

Ⓑ Australian willow (use 3)
Dangling narrow green leaves give this evergreen tree a fine-textured appearance. See *Geijera parviflora*, p. 215.

Ⓒ Compact xylosma (use 12)
This evergreen shrub is prized for its densely mounded, glossy yellow-green foliage. See *Xylosma congestum* 'Compacta', p. 249.

Ⓓ 'Spring Bouquet' laurustinus (use 12)
Another all-season performer, this evergreen shrub bears pink buds that open into

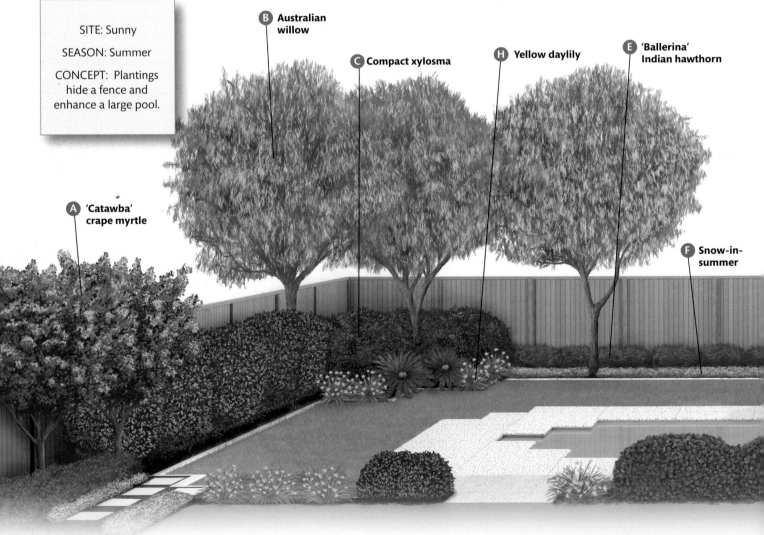

SITE: Sunny

SEASON: Summer

CONCEPT: Plantings hide a fence and enhance a large pool.

fragrant white flowers from late fall to spring. Shiny blue berries speckle the dark-green foliage after the flowers. See *Viburnum tinus* 'Spring Bouquet', p. 246.

E **'Ballerina' Indian hawthorn** (use 13)
In spring, this evergreen shrub bears small pink flowers against a backdrop of thick green leaves. Blue berries persist into the fall. See *Raphiolepis indica* 'Ballerina', p 236.

F **Snow-in-summer** (use 47)
A vigorously spreading perennial, its narrow silvery evergreen foliage is blanketed with small white flowers in early summer. See *Cerastium tomentosum*, p. 201.

G **Sago palm** (use 4)
Long, arching divided yellow-green leaves give this conifer relative a feathery palmlike look. See *Cycas revoluta*, p. 207.

H **Yellow daylily** (use 16)
This popular perennial forms a clump of narrow green leaves topped with trumpet-like flowers. Choose from numerous yellow cultivars. See *Hemerocallis*, p. 218.

I **'Little John' dwarf bottlebrush** (use 3)
A dense shrub, its arching branches bear narrow, light-green leaves. From fall to spring, it produces deep red bottlebrush blooms at the ends of its branches. See *Callistemon viminalis* 'Little John', p. 198.

J **'Wheeler's Dwarf' pittosporum** (use 4)
This dense, mounding evergreen shrub bears distinctive whorls of dark green leaves. In early summer it produces fragrant white flowers. See *Pittosporum tobira* 'Wheeler's Dwarf', p. 234.

K **Arbor sun screen**
This is a large structure, but not a difficult one to build using standard construction-dimension cedar or other weather-resistant wood. See p. 282.

L **Paving**
This design calls for large paved areas. We've shown concrete around the pool, textured concrete by the house doors and under the arbor, and precast pavers at each corner of the house. Separating the lawn and planting beds, a 4-in.-wide concrete mowing curb provides support for mower wheels. Hiring a landscape contractor is your best bet to get this extensive project done correctly. See pp. 258–265.

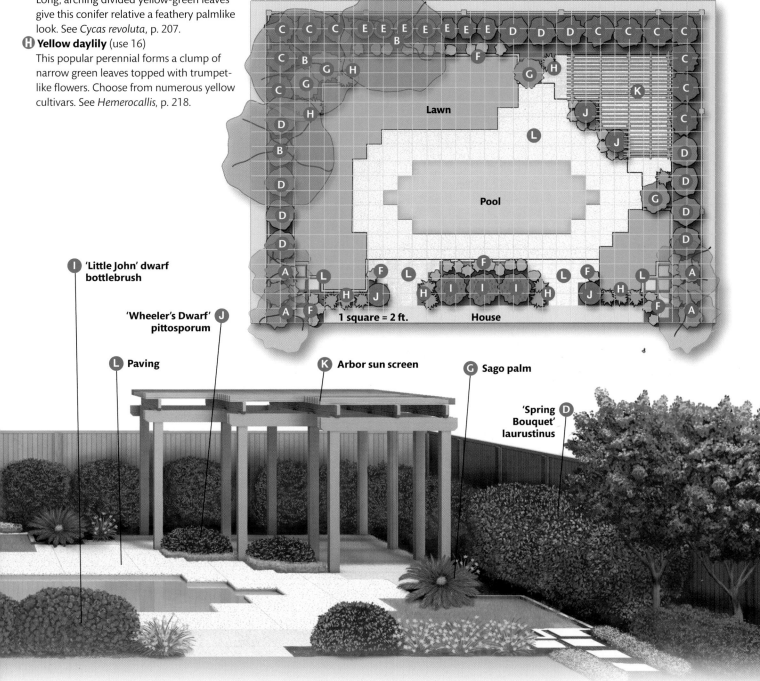

1 square = 2 ft.

I 'Little John' dwarf bottlebrush

J 'Wheeler's Dwarf' pittosporum

L Paving

K Arbor sun screen

G Sago palm

D 'Spring Bouquet' laurustinus

PLANT PORTRAITS

Drought-resistant desert grasses and colorful flowering trees and shrubs create a lovely poolside show.

● = First design, pp. 172-173
▲ = Second design, pp. 174-175

'Regal Mist' deer grass (*Muhlenbergia capillaris* 'Regal Mist', p. 230) ▲

Autumn sage
(*Salvia greggi*, p. 241) ▲

'Abbeville Blue' chaste tree
(*Vitex agnus-castus* 'Abbeville Blue', p. 247) ▲

'Desert Museum' palo verde (*Cercidium* 'Desert Museum', p. 201) ▲

A desert setting

This design creates a distinctive desert flavor while addressing the concerns of the previous design. All of the plants shown here are drought tolerant, and many are natives of Western deserts and arid environs.

Much of the foliage is narrow-leaved and gray-to-silvery green, which is characteristic of drought-tolerant plants. Small trees and good-size shrubs frame the perimeter in front of the fence. Smaller perennials accent the plantings. You will have colorful flowers for many months. Small grassy areas at the corners provide shady spots for a few chairs and a table and, of course, a good vantage point to watch the fun in the pool.

Plants & Projects

Ⓐ 'Desert Museum' palo verde (use 3)
This semi-evergreen tree bears fine-textured foliage on light green, thornless stems. Branches are smothered in striking yellow flowers in spring and off and on through the summer. See *Cercidium* 'Desert Museum', p. 201.

Ⓑ Coolibah (use 3
This tree is grown for its ever-green foliage and upright habit. The leaves are long, narrow and blue-green. Tolerates desert conditions. See *Eucalyptus microtheca*, p. 210.

Ⓒ 'Abbeville Blue' chaste tree (use 2)
A low-branching, open decidu-ous tree, it bears fan-shaped, divided, gray-green leaves. But-terflies love the tall spikes of blue flowers that bloom in sum-mer. See *Vitex agnus-castus* 'Abbeville Blue', p. 247.

'Abbeville Blue' chaste tree Ⓒ

SITE: Sunny

SEASON: Late spring

CONCEPT: Desert plants and a poolful of cool water make a striking combination.

Ⓕ **'New Gold' lantana**

Ⓔ **'Regal Mist' deer grass**

Ⓗ **Variegated century plant**

D **'Rio Bravo' sage** (use 12)
This evergreen shrub bears lavender flowers against blue-green foliage. See *Leucophyllum langmaniae*, 'Rio Bravo', p. 226.

E **'Regal Mist' deer grass** (use 12)
A cloud of pink flowers float above this perennial's dark-green mound of fine-textured foliage in fall and winter. Leaves are evergreen where winters are warm. See *Muhlenbergia capillaris* 'Regal Mist', p. 230.

F **'New Gold' lantana** (use 12)
An excellent spreading ground cover, this evergreen shrub is covered with golden-yellow flowers from late spring to frost. See *Lantana* 'New Gold', p. 225.

G **Autumn sage** (use 8)
This shrubby perennial bears silvery leaves and, from late spring to fall, many slender spikes of light-purple flowers. See *Salvia greggi*, p. 241.

H **Variegated century plant** (use 2)
A striking evergreen succulent, it forms a large rosette of thick arching swordlike silver-green and white leaves. Watch out for the thorns on the margins! See *Agave americana* 'Mediopicta Alba', p. 190.

I **'Winnifred Gilman' Cleveland sage** (use 3)
This perennial forms a large clump of fragrant wispy silver-green leaves topped through the summer with spikes of intensely blue flowers. See *Salvia clevelandii* 'Winnifred Gilman', p. 241.

J **Lavender cotton** (use 13)
A mounding shrub, its fine-textured silver-gray foliage is a backdrop in midsummer for round yellow flowers. See *Santolina chamaecyparissus*, p. 242..

K **'Goblin Yellow' blanketflower** (use 28)
This daisylike perennial provides a summer-long display of yellow flowers. See *Gaillardia* x *grandifora* 'Goblin Yellow', p. 214.

L **Angelita daisy** (use 37)
Bright yellow flowers appear above narrow green leaves from spring to fall. See *Hymenoxys acaulis*, p. 221.

See p. 173 for the following

M **Paving**

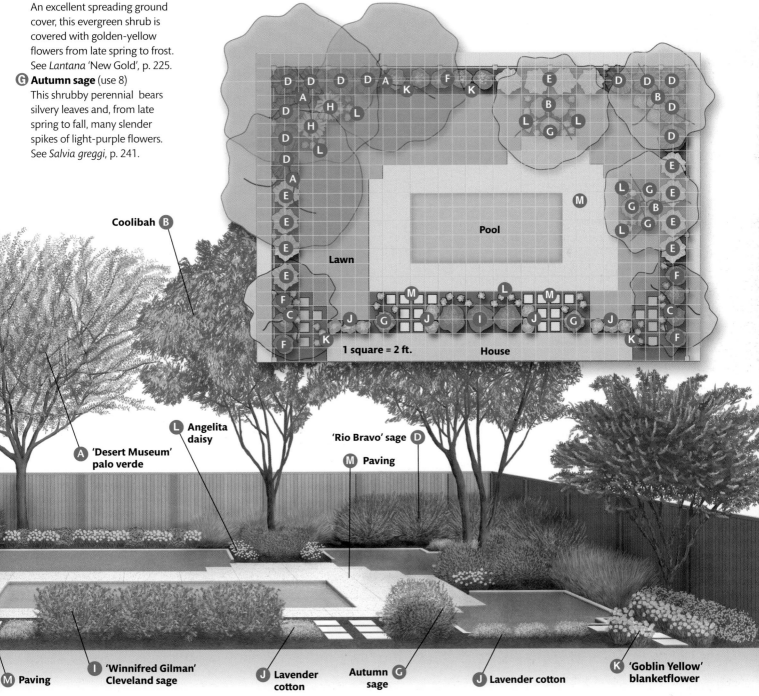

1 square = 2 ft.

Planting in the Pines

A WOODLAND DECK IS SURROUNDED BY SHRUBS

This simple patio planting is intended for a home located on the wooded slopes of the West's mountain ranges. In this type of terrain, residences often feature backyard terraces or decks nestled in the pines, where fresh mountain air, cool evenings, and wildlife can be enjoyed year-round.

Many desirable ornamental plants thrive in the dry mid-elevations of the mountain ranges. This design features drought-tolerant and fire-resistant trees and shrubs that look natural in a setting of mature conifers.

Native western redbuds planted around the deck create a leafy canopy among the bare trunks of taller pines. Around them are a variety of low-growing shrubs displaying contrasting foliage and springtime flowers. The entire planting is edged in a foot-high swath of bright green foliage.

Like the plants on the surrounding hillsides, these planting will be in full bloom in spring, with masses of white, yellow, and pink flowers.

To protect your home from wildfires, keep areas near the house well irrigated and keep vegetation 15 to 20 feet from the house. For more safety tips, contact your local fire department or state Department of Forestry.

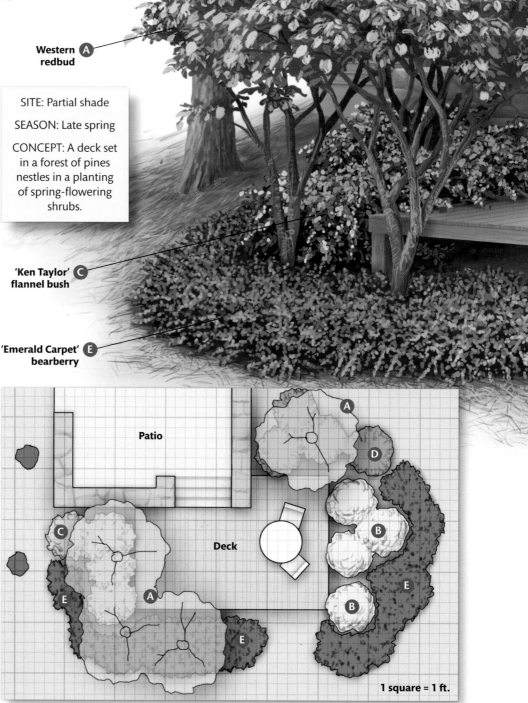

Western **A** redbud

SITE: Partial shade

SEASON: Late spring

CONCEPT: A deck set in a forest of pines nestles in a planting of spring-flowering shrubs.

'Ken Taylor' **C** flannel bush

'Emerald Carpet' **E** bearberry

Patio

Deck

1 square = 1 ft.

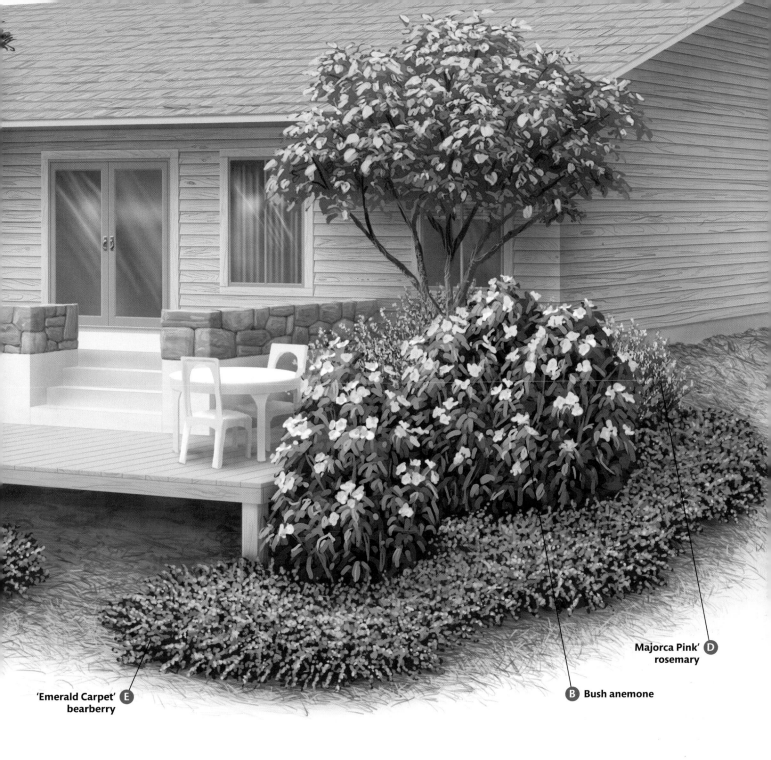

'Emerald Carpet' **E**
bearberry

D Majorca Pink'
rosemary

B Bush anemone

Plants & Projects

Preparing the planting beds and installing the shrubs can be done in a few weekends. Then sit back and enjoy the display. Once established, these plants require little care beyond seasonal pruning.

Ⓐ Western redbud (use 4)
Native to the foothills, this small tree is so vivid in bloom it stops drivers along the roads in spring. The purplish pink flowers give way to bright green deciduous leaves that turn yellow in fall. Purplish seedpods

decorate the bare branches in winter. See *Cercis occidentalis*, p. 201.

Ⓑ Bush anemone (use 4)
One of the loveliest chaparral shrubs in the West. Dark glossy leaves with whitish undersides create a beautiful backdrop in spring for masses of showy white flowers sporting bright yellow centers. See *Carpenteria californica*, p. 200.

Ⓒ 'Ken Taylor' flannel bush (use 4)
Cup-shaped golden yellow-to-orange flowers stand out brightly against this evergreen

shrub's felty, dark green leaves. See *Fremontodendron* 'Ken Taylor', p. 214.

Ⓓ 'Majorca Pink' rosemary (use 4)
Lavender-pink flowers adorn this tough, upright evergreen shrub in late winter and early spring. See *Rosemarinus* 'Majorca Pink', p. 240.

Ⓔ 'Emerald Carpet' bearberry (use 12)
Exceptional as a ground cover, this low-spreading shrub forms a dense, slightly mounding carpet of small oval leaves that are bright green throughout the year. See *Arctostaphylos* 'Emerald Carpet', p. 192.

VARIATIONS ON A THEME

You don't have to live in the foothills or mountains to appreciate these handsome designs.

This playful pattern of paths and planting beds edged in native rock is ideal for a rustic setting in the sun.

This stacked platform deck and plantings would be striking even without the huge boulder that anchors the design.

Pink geraniums and pink-tinged stones make an attractive combination in this hillside patio.

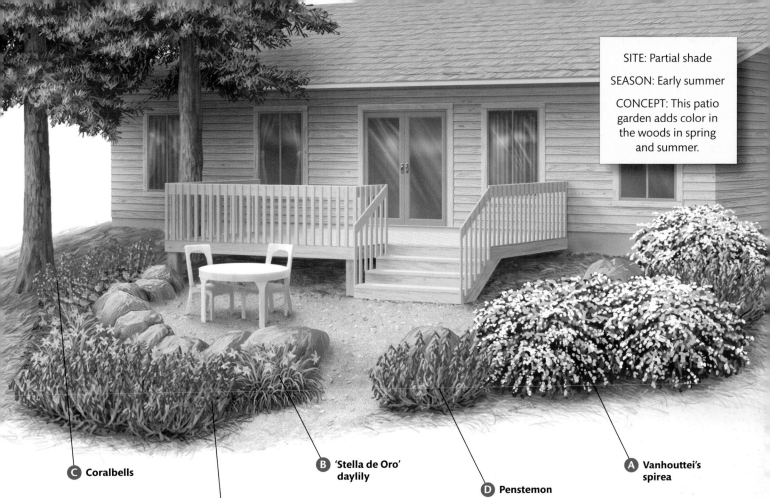

SITE: Partial shade

SEASON: Early summer

CONCEPT: This patio garden adds color in the woods in spring and summer.

C Coralbells

B 'Stella de Oro' daylily

D Penstemon

D Penstemon

A Vanhouttei's spirea

Rustic charm

In this design, a simple ground-level patio augments an existing deck for outdoor entertaining. This design requires only a small initial investment in materials and time and promises years of enjoyment.

The patio is created by an artless (if not effortless) arrangement of large rocks, shrubs, and perennials in a clearing near the deck. Pine needles make a serviceable surface and are in abundant supply.

Chosen for a location at a higher elevation than the previous design, the carefree perennials and shrubs that loosely border the patio are right at home in the shade of tall pines. Relax on a comfortable chair to enjoy the flowers and watch the acrobatics of hummingbirds drawn to the penstemon.

Plants & Projects

A **Vanhouttei's spirea** (use 3) This deciduous shrub forms a large bushy mound of arching branches lined with small dark green leaves. They disappear in spring under a heavy bloom of small white flowers. See *Spiraea x vanhouttei*, p. 243.

B **'Stella de Oro' daylily** (use 11) Golden yellow flowers shaped like trumpets bloom just above this perennial's grassy foliage through the summer. See *Hemerocallis*, p. 218..

C **Coralbells** (use 7) This perennial's beautifully scalloped leaves form neat, almost evergreen mounds. In spring and early summer, the plants send up countless thin flower stalks nodding with clusters of tiny, bright red, bell-shaped flowers. See *Heuchera sanguinea*, p. 219.

D **Penstemon** (use 9) This popular perennial produces a tall clump of wiry spikes that open into sprays of tubular red flowers above a low mat of dark green foliage. Attracts hummingbirds. See *Penstemon*, p. 233.

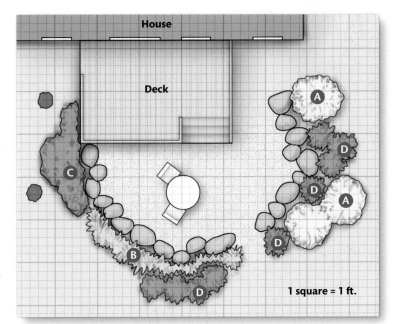

House

Deck

1 square = 1 ft.

Gateway Garden

ARBOR, FENCE, AND PLANTINGS MAKE AN INVITING ENTRY

Entrances are an important part of any landscape. They can welcome visitors onto your property; highlight a special feature, such as a rose garden; or mark the passage between two areas with different character or function. The design shown here can serve in any of these situations.

A picket fence set amid shrubs and perennials creates a friendly and attractive barrier, just enough to signal the boundary of the front yard. The simple vine-covered arbor provides welcoming access.

Uncomplicated elements are combined imaginatively in this design, creating interesting details to catch the eye and an informal, happy-to-see-you effect. The arbor will be covered with cheerful yellow flowers in spring, and the fence with fragrant honeysuckle blossoms in summer. For winter color, both offer evergreen foliage. A multilayered planting in front of the fence offers contrasts in foliage texture as well as pretty flowers, and enough structure to remain inviting even after the blossoms fade.

'Gracillimus' Japanese maiden grass **C**

'Goldsturm' black-eyed Susan **G**

Coral honey-suckle **E**

Russian sage **F**

Mealycup sage **J**

'Stella d'Oro' daylily **I**

Plants & Projects

For many people, a picket fence and vine-covered arbor represent old-fashioned neighborly virtues. The structures and plantings are easy to install. You can extend the fence and plantings as needed.

A Carolina jasmine (use 2 plants)
A lovely evergreen vine for the arbor. Sweetly fragrant clear yellow flowers bloom among the masses of shiny leaves in early spring. The leaves turn maroon in winter. See *Gelsemium sempervirens*, p. 215.

B Firebush (use 1)
Summers set this perennial ablaze with orange-red flowers. New clusters keep coming until frost. Its location lets you catch a glimpse of hummingbirds as you come and go. See *Hamelia patens*, p. 216.

C 'Gracillimus' Japanese maiden grass (use 1)
This fine-textured grass makes an attractive anchor at one end of the planting. Stalks of creamy white flower plumes rise above the foliage in fall. See *Miscanthus sinensis* 'Gracillimus', p. 231.

D 'Radiation' lantana (use 1)
This perennial spreads to form a 3-ft. mound of coarse green leaves topped with many small, round clusters of orange and yellow flowers. Blooms prolifically all season. See *Lantana camara* 'Radiation', p. 225.

E Coral honeysuckle (use 4)
Unlike the more invasive honeysuckles, this native vine is mannerly, climbing up the fence in neat tiers of rounded blue-green leaves. Clusters of coral-colored flowers radiate from the foliage in summer and

sometimes fall. See *Lonicera sempervirens* p. 227.

F Russian sage (use 4)
These perennials make a big splash when planted together. They offer silvery foliage and blue flowers to cool down the border's many hot colors. See *Perovskia atriplicifolia*, p. 233.

G 'Goldsturm' black-eyed Susan (use 1)
A popular perennial companion of ornamental grasses. It forms a robust stand of dark leaves that are blanketed in summertime with bright gold

Carolina jasmine Ⓐ

Cigar plant Ⓗ

Ⓚ Arbor and fence

Ⓑ Firebush

Ⓔ Coral honey-suckle

Ⓓ 'Radiation' lantana

Ⓙ Mealycup sage

Mealycup sage Ⓙ

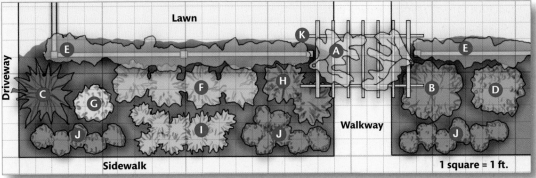

Lawn

Driveway

Ⓔ

Ⓚ Ⓐ

Ⓔ

Ⓒ

Ⓖ

Ⓕ

Ⓗ

Ⓑ

Ⓓ

Ⓙ

Ⓘ

Ⓙ

Ⓙ

Walkway

Sidewalk

1 square = 1 ft.

flowers. See *Rudbeckia fulgida* 'Goldsturm', p. 240.

Ⓗ **Cigar plant** (use 2)
An upright perennial with the look of a dwarf oleander. Forms a dense bush bearing multiple branches of narrow foliage that terminate in small tubelike orange and yellow flowers in autumn. See *Cuphea micropetala*, p. 206.

Ⓘ **'Stella d'Oro' daylily** (use 9)
Trumpet flowers the color of ripe pineapples crown these grassy perennials in summer. One of the best ever-blooming

daylilies. When planting, space about 1 ft. apart as they will gradually fill in. See *Hemerocallis* 'Stella d'Oro', p. 218.

Ⓙ **Mealycup sage** (use 18)
Beautiful in front of a border, this upright perennial bears spikes of small blue flowers above gray-green leaves. See *Salvia farinacea*, p. 241.

Ⓚ **Arbor and fence**
Thick posts give this simple arbor a sturdy visual presence, and the low picket fence adds character. Both can be stained or painted. If made of cedar or redwood they can be left to age with the weather, as shown here, reducing maintenance. See p. 284.

SITE: Sunny

SEASON: Summer

CONCEPT: Shrubs, perennials, and flowering vines accent a traditional picket fence and simple entry arbor.

Say hello with roses

Not every entry calls for a fence. This design offers a traditional welcome with a rose garden. A border of tea roses and other flowering shrubs and perennials serves as a fragrant and colorful barrier on each side of a rose-covered entry arbor. The formal symmetry (an element often associated with rose gardens) is enhanced by boxwoods trimmed into pyramids at the foot of the arbor. The roses will bloom for many months. In spring they're joined by pink dianthus and blue iris, and in late summer and fall by purple asters and sage. The boxwood's evergreen foliage provides green in winter.

Tea roses are not as difficult as many people fear, but they do require regular attention.

SITE: Sunny

SEASON: Fall

CONCEPT: Fragrant roses and other flowers provide a sweet welcome.

Plants & Projects

A **'Climbing Old Blush' China rose** (use 2 plants)
This delicate-looking rose is nonetheless a vigorous climber. It bears apple green foliage and a steady bloom of baby pink semi-double flowers, especially in spring. See *Rosa chinensis* 'Climbing Old Blush', p. 238.

B **'Gilbert Nabonnand' tea rose** (use 2)

The silky flowers of this bushy rose are pale pink and very fragrant all season. Petals are semi-double. See *Rosa x odorata* 'Gilbert Nabonnand', p. 238.

C **'Martha Gonzales' rose** (use 6)
Wine red flowers cover this reliable dwarf rose in spring and fall. New shoots and leaves are also red. See *Rosa chinensis* 'Martha Gonzales', p. 238.

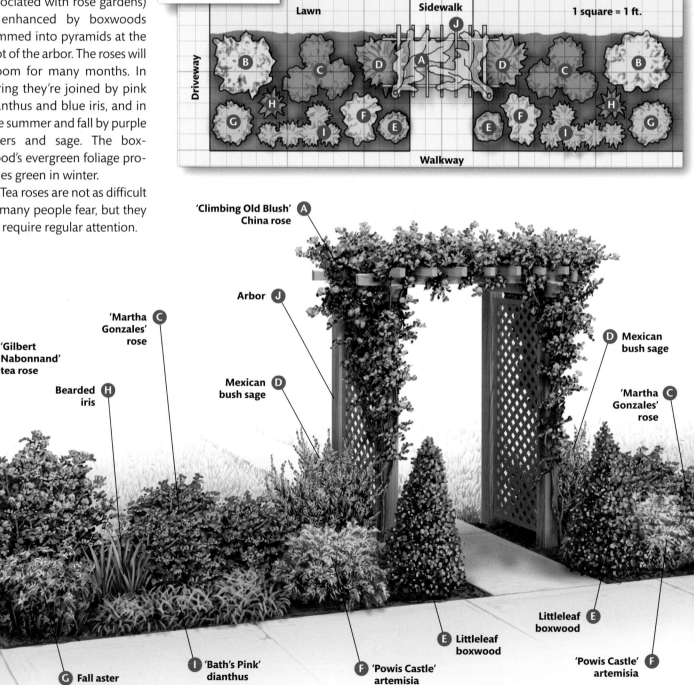

'Climbing Old Blush' China rose **A**

Arbor **J**

'Martha Gonzales' rose **C**

B 'Gilbert Nabonnand' tea rose

Bearded iris **H**

Mexican bush sage **D**

D Mexican bush sage

'Martha Gonzales' rose **C**

Littleleaf boxwood **E**

E Littleleaf boxwood

G Fall aster

I 'Bath's Pink' dianthus

F 'Powis Castle' artemisia

'Powis Castle' artemisia **F**

D **Mexican bush sage** (use 2)
This tall perennial adds height at the trellis. Bears spikes of purple and white flowers in fall. See *Salvia leucantha*, p. 241.

E **Littleleaf boxwood** (use 2)
Plant these evergreen shrubs in front of the arbor, and trim them into pyramids to enhance the formal look of the entry. See *Buxus microphylla*, p. 198.

F **'Powis Castle' artemisia** (use 2)
Prized for its foliage texture and color, this perennial forms silvery pillows beside the boxwoods. See *Artemisia* x 'Powis Castle', p. 193.

G **Fall aster** (use 2)
This gray-green perennial complements the boxwoods. In autumn it bursts into eye-catching lavender-purple bloom. See *Aster oblongifolius*, p. 193.

H **Bearded iris** (use 2)
This perennial's foliage adds a spiky presence to the planting as well as showy blue flowers in spring. *Iris* x *germanica*, p. 222.

I **'Bath's Pink' dianthus** (use 10)
This perennial spreads to form low, wide tufts of very fine-textured foliage. Delicate pink flowers blanket the gray-green leaves in spring. See *Dianthus* 'Bath's Pink', p. 207.

See p. 181 for the following:

J **Arbor**

B **'Gilbert Nabonnand' tea rose**

G **Fall aster**

H **Bearded iris**

I **'Bath's Pink' dianthus**

PLANT PORTRAITS

Combining compelling fragrance, lovely flowers, and handsome foliage, these plants create a distinctive entry.
● = First design, pp. 180-181
▲ = Second design, pp. 182-183

'Martha Gonzales' rose
(*Rosa chinensis*, p. 238) ▲

'Gilbert Nabonnand' Tea rose
(*Rosa* x *odorata*, p .238) ▲

'Climbing Old Blush' China rose
(*Rosa chinensis*, p. 238) ▲

Littleleaf boxwood
(*Buxus microphylla*, p. 198) ▲

Plant Profiles

Plants are the heart of the designs in this book. In this section you'll find descriptions of all the plants used in the designs, along with information on planting and maintaining them. These trees, shrubs, perennials, grasses, bulbs, and vines have all proved themselves as dependable performers in the region. They offer a wide spectrum of lovely flowers and fruits, handsome foliage, and striking forms. Most contribute something of note in at least two seasons. You can use this section as an aid when installing the designs in this book and as a reference guide to desirable plants for other home landscaping projects.

Using the plant profiles

This section of the book includes a description of each of the plants featured in the Portfolio of Designs on pp. 14–183. These profiles outline the plants' basic preferences for soil, moisture, sun, or shade, and provide advice about planting and ongoing care.

Working with the book's landscape designers, we selected plants carefully, following a few simple guidelines: Every plant should be a proven performer in the region; once established, it should thrive without pampering. All plants should be available from a major local nursery or garden center; if they're not in stock, they could be ordered, or you could ask the nursery staff to recommend suitable substitutes.

In the Portfolio of Designs section, you'll note that plants are referred to by their common name but are also cross-referenced by their Latinized scientific name. While common names are familiar to many people, they can be confusing. Distinctly different plants can share the same common name, or one plant can have several different common names. Scientific names, therefore, ensure the greatest accuracy.

All of these plants are proven performers in many of the soils, climates, and other conditions commonly found in the West. But they will perform best if planted and cared for as described in the Guide to Installation, beginning on p. 250.

In the following descriptions and recommendations, the term "full sun" means a site that gets at least eight hours a day of direct sun throughout the growing season. "Partial sun" and "partial shade" both refer to sites that get direct sun for part of the day but are shaded the rest of the time by a building, fence or tree. "Full shade" means sites that don't receive direct sunlight.

The plants are organized here alphabetically by their scientific name. While many plants are sold by common name, scientific names help ensure that you get what you want. Page references direct you to the designs in which the plants appear.

Western hardiness zones

This map is based on one developed by the U.S. Department of Agriculture. It divides the West into hardiness zones based on average minimum winter temperatures. Plants described in this book are given a hardiness designations corresponding to a USDA Hardiness Zone on the map. A Zone 7 plant, for example, can be expected to survive winter temperatures as low as 0 degrees F. and it can usually be used with confidence in zones 7 through 11 but not in the colder Zone 6. However, cold hardiness is not the only climate factor that determines whether a plant is adapted to specific western climates. Most notably, high summer temperatures, intense sunlight, and aridity, often limit plant adaptation in desert areas. Consequently, where appropriate, plant descriptions also include comments when plants cannot grown in various desert climates and other specific areas of the West. These regions include low elevation desert areas, such as the Coachella Valley in California and Phoenix, Arizona, and higher elevation desert areas, such as Tucson, Arizona and Las Vegas, Nevada. If a plant is described as not adapted to the Southwest, that means it is not recommended for desert areas, southern California or western Texas.

Even when USDA Zone designations seem to indicate a plant will do well in your area, it is always good advice to double check final plant lists with a knowledgeable local nurseryman. Your local water department and cooperative extension service are also good sources of information on plant adaptation.

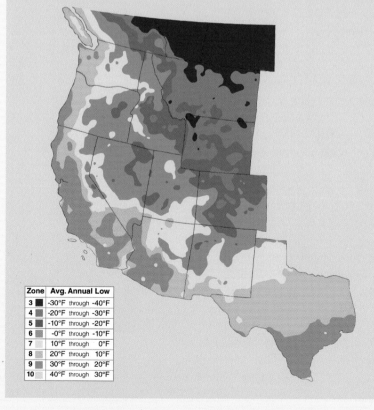

Zone	Avg. Annual Low		
3	-30°F	through	-40°F
4	-20°F	through	-30°F
5	-10°F	through	-20°F
6	-0°F	through	-10°F
7	10°F	through	0°F
8	20°F	through	10°F
9	30°F	through	20°F
10	40°F	through	30°F

Abelia x *grandiflora*
'Edward Goucher'
GLOSSY ABELIA

Abelia x *grandiflora*
GLOSSY ABELIA

Abelia x *grandiflora*

GLOSSY ABELIA. This easy-to-grow semievergreen shrub bears countless small white flowers from early summer until frost and attracts many butterflies. The lustrous, small, pointed leaves are dark green in summer and purple-bronze in winter. It grows a sprawling 5 ft. wide and tall. **Hardy to Zone 6.** The cultivar 'Edward Goucher' (pp. 22, 83, 114) has showy pink flowers, grows a smaller 3 to 4 ft. tall and wide, and is slightly less hardy than the species (Zone 7). Both need full sun to partial shade and grow with an arching habit. To keep the plants compact, in summer cut new shoots in half. Then in late winter to early spring cut a third of the old stems close to the ground. Page: 38.

Acacia aneura

MULGA. A roundheaded, evergreen tree with thin, pendulous, silvery green leaves and yellow rod-like blooms in late winter to early spring. Grows 12 to 20 ft high and equally as wide. Makes a nice, small evergreen shade tree, especially in hot dry areas. Needs little water. **Hardy to Zone 9.** Page 98.

Acanthus mollis
BEAR'S BREECHES

Acanthus mollis

BEAR'S BREECHES. A perennial with bold, deeply lobed, dark green leaves that grow up to 2 ft. long. Tall spikes of white to pinkish purple flowers bloom in late spring, reaching 2 to 3 ft. above the foliage. Grows best in moist shade but can take some sun. Cut back flowers after bloom. Divide crowded plants in spring. A vigorous plant, it can be invasive. **Hardy to Zone 7.** Pages: 89, 105.

Acer circinatum
VINE MAPLE

Acer palmatum
JAPANESE MAPLE

Acer ginnala
AMUR MAPLE

Acer circinatum

VINE MAPLE. This Western native can be a large, spreading, bushy, multi-stemmed deciduous shrub or a small single-stemmed tree growing 25 ft. tall. Leaves are green in summer and turn yellow, red, and purple in fall. Grows in full sun to shade. Plants in sunnier spots have more intense fall color. Tolerant of a wide range of soils, vine maples thrive in moist areas but also adapt to very dry soils. Can be shaped as a large multitrunked shrub or tree. Pages: 30.

Acer palmatum

JAPANESE MAPLE. A neat, small deciduous tree with delicate-looking leaves that have jagged edges. There are many kinds, with leaves that are green, bronze, or red in summer. You can buy seed-grown plants or named cultivars. Most turn red or scarlet in fall. 'Oshio-Beni' (p. 132) stays dark red all season. Coralbark maple, *A. p.* 'Sango Kaku' (pp. 18, 68, 132), is an upright tree with foliage that is reddish in spring, light green in summer, and yellow in fall. Bark is bright red. 'Atropurpureum' (p. 26) has purplish green leaves. All grow best in partial shade and rich, moist soil covered with a layer of mulch. In cooler climates they can take more sun. Leaf burn is common in hot-summer areas, especially southern California. Not well adapted to low elevation desert areas. Tends to get leaf burn in hot, dry climates. Water deeply at least once a week during dry weather. Japanese maples grow slowly, so buy the biggest tree you can afford to start with. Plants are sold in containers or balled-and-burlapped. Prune trees to open and highlight branching. Plants grow 10 to 20 ft. tall and wide. **Hardy to Zone 5.** Pages: 26.

Acer ginnala

AMUR MAPLE. A deciduous shrub or small tree growing to about 20 ft. tall, often sold with multiple trunks. Bears clusters of small, very fragrant yellow flowers in early spring. Bright clusters of red-winged seeds follow. In fall, the glossy green lobed leaves turn yellow, red, and purple. Full or partial sun. Leaves color best in full sun. Tolerant of a wide range of soil conditions. Not adapted to Southern California or desert areas. **Hardy to Zone 3.** Page: 28.

Achillea

YARROW. A long-blooming perennial with flat clusters of small flowers on stiff stalks and finely di-

Achillea
A. mille-
folium
'Apple-
blossom'
YARROW

Acorus
gramineus
'Variegatus'
VARIEGATED
SWEET FLAG

Acer palmatum 'Oshio-Beni'
JAPANESE MAPLE

vided gray-green leaves that have a pungent aroma. Spreads to form an irregular patch. 'Moonshine' (pp. 47, 59, 128) grows about 2 ft. tall and has lemon yellow flowers. A. *millefolium* 'Appleblossom' (p. 22) reaches up to 3 ft. tall and bears clear pink flowers; if it isn't available, a good substitute is 'Rosea'. 'White Beauty' (p. 61) has pure white flowers. Yarrow needs full sun and well-drained soil. Thrives with little water. Cut off old flower stalks when the blossoms fade; they're often used in dried-flower arrangements. Divide clumps every few years in spring or fall. **Hardy to Zone 3.**

Acorus gramineus 'Variegatus'

VARIEGATED SWEET FLAG. A perennial grasslike plant that grows 1 ft. tall and spreads by rhizomes. Looks good near water. Leaves are striped creamy white and green. Flowers bloom in midsummer but are inconspicuous. Prefers constantly moist soil in full or partial shade but will adapt to drier, fertile soils. **Hardy to Zone 6.** Not adapted to desert areas. Page: 111.

Agapanthus

AGAPANTHUS, LILY-OF-THE-NILE. Very useful flowering perennials with arching, straplike leaves and ball-shaped clusters of blue or white flowers in late spring and summer. A. *orientalis* (pp. 19, 127) grows 2 to 3 ft. tall and bears flower clusters on stalks up to 5 ft. tall. A. 'Storm Cloud' (p. 171) grows 3 to 4 ft. tall and is topped with blue-violet flowers. A. 'Midnight Blue' has captivating, deep blue flowers. A. 'Peter Pan' (pp. 24, 84, 97, 165) is a dwarf variety with leaves reaching only 12 in. tall and blue flowers on stalks up to 18 in. tall. A. 'Queen Ann' (p. 167) is a little wider and taller. Plant in full sun or light shade and well-drained soil. All grow best with regular water but can take dry periods. Evergreen in mild-winter climates, they go dormant in cold winters. Divide only when very crowded—every 5 to 7 years. Excellent in pots. **Hardy to Zone 8.**

Agapanthus
LILY-OF-THE-NILE

Agave A. americana
CENTURY PLANT

Agave A. americana 'Marginata'
CENTURY PLANT

Ajuga reptans
'Bronze Beauty'
BUGLEWEED

Ajuga reptans
'Burgundy Glow'
BUGLEWEED

Agave

CENTURY PLANT. These are bold evergreen succulents with thick spiny leaves in fantastic architectural rosettes. (Be careful to avoid the sharp spines on the tips of the leaves.) Rare flowering stalks occur after many years, giving rise to the popular name, century plant. Mother plants die upon flowering, followed by new suckers at their base. *A. americana* has striking blue-green foliage and grows 5 ft. tall and wide. Yellow variegated agave (*A. americana* 'Marginata') has green and yellow leaves and is slightly smaller than the species. *A. americana* 'Mediopicta Alba' (p. 175) has silver-green and white leaves. *A. victoriae-reginae* (pp. 122, 123) is a bold perennial with green and white leaves that resemble an artichoke bud. This small succulent grows only 1 ft. tall and wide. Twin-flower agave (*A. geminiflora*, pp. 153, 162) forms a tight rosette 2 to 3 ft. round of stiff, narrow green leaves with yellow bell-shape flowers. Agaves require full sun and good drainage. **Agaves vary in hardiness but are generally well adapted to hot, dry climates.**

Annuals

Western gardeners use annuals generously to provide bright patches of color throughout the seasons. They're fast-growing plants that bloom abundantly for months; when they're finished, they are easy to replace with something else. One of the fun things about growing annuals is that you can try different kinds from year to year, choosing varieties that have colorful flowers or foliage in sizes ranging from 6-in.-tall alyssum to 6-ft.-tall castor beans. Annual flowers are also mainstays in pots.

Annuals in the West can be divided into two groups. The first are winter, or cool-season, annuals, which are planted when the weather starts to cool in the fall or in early spring. In mild winter areas, they bloom through the winter and put on a good show in spring. This group includes pansies, snapdragons, violas, sweet alyssum, dusty miller, and dianthus. Pages 19, 37, 43, 135, 165,

Warm-season annuals are planted in spring after the danger of frost. They bloom throughout the summer and into fall. In warm-winter areas, such as low-elevation desert areas, they can bloom on into winter. This group includes petunias, begonias, verbena, ageratum, nicotiana, marigolds, zinnias, impatiens, and salvia. Pages: 17, 19, 27, 75, 87, 89, 153,

In addition to warm- and cool-season annuals, many free-blooming perennials are treated as annuals. These include salvias, geraniums, and daisies. Pages: 19, 161.

Ajuga reptans

AJUGA, BUGLEWEED. A low-growing, mat-forming perennial, used as a ground cover. The glossy leaves are evergreen. Erect, 6-in. spikes densely packed with small flowers are very showy for a few weeks in spring and early summer. 'Bronze Beauty' (pp. 19, 91, 132) has dark purplish bronze foliage and blue flowers. 'Burgundy Glow' has glossy leaves with purple, green, and white markings. Both grow best in full sun or partial shade and rich, moist soil. After flowers fade, cut them off with a string trimmer, or hedge shears. Plants spread quickly and will invade a lawn unless you keep cutting along the edge or install a mowing strip. **Hardy to Zone 3.** Page: 26.

Alstroemeria
MEYER HYBRID

Amelanchier x grandiflora 'Autumn Brilliance'
SERVICEBERRY

Alstroemeria

ALSTROEMERIA. Colorful perennials with tall stalks bearing azalea-like flowers in a rainbow of speckled and striped shades. White, pink, red, yellow, orange, or purple flowers open from late spring to midsummer and make great cut flowers. Plants grow 2 to 5 ft. tall and eventually form large clumps. Evergreen types such as the Cordu and Meyer hybrids (p. 90,) bloom for the longest period. Plant in full sun or partial shade and rich, well-drained soil. Water regularly. Pull out flower stalks after blooming. Divide infrequently. **Hardy to Zone 8.** Not well adapted to desert areas.

Amelanchier

SERVICEBERRY. *A.* x *grandiflora* 'Autumn Brilliance' (p. 53) is a deciduous tree up to 25 ft. tall. White flowers in early spring are followed by edible blue or purplish berries, and bright red-orange fall foliage. Smooth gray bark adds winter interest. Full or partial sun. *A. alnifolia* (p. 149), is a similar western native that is usually grown as a multi-trunked shrub or small tree to 12 to 15 ft. high and 8 to 10 ft. wide. It makes an excellent background plant. **Both serviceberries are very hardy (to at least Zone 4) and are best adapted to the Pacific Northwest and high elevation areas of the West.**

Anemone x hybrida

JAPANESE ANEMONE. A perennial with small daisylike flowers on branching stalks above a clump of large dark green leaves. Blooms for several weeks in late summer into fall. Most varieties have white flowers, some pink. All need partial shade and rich,

Anemone x hybrida
JAPANESE ANEMONE

Anisodontea x hypomandarum
CAPE MALLOW

moist soil. Divide every few years in fall or early spring. Plants grow 3 to 4 ft. tall and spread at least as wide. **Hardy to Zone 4.** Pages: 19, 141.

Anisodontea x hypomandarum

CAPE MALLOW. Fast-growing evergreen shrub with a long season of bloom. Small pink hollyhocklike flowers appear almost year-round in mild-winter areas. (Bloom time is shorter in inland and foothill areas.) Grows 6 ft. tall. Full sun. Needs little water once established. **Hardy to Zone 9.** Page: 114.

Aquilegia formosa
COLUMBINE

Arbutus A. unedo
STRAWBERRY TREE

Antigonon leptopus

CORAL VINE. A vigorous vine that climbs by tendrils, it bears airy panicles of coral pink heart-shaped flowers among apple green foliage in summer and autumn. Grows best in full hot sun. Grow it as an annual in northern areas. Also known as queen's crown and Mexican love vine. **Hardy to Zone 10.** Page: 103.

Aquilegia

COLUMBINE. A large group of wonderfully delicate flowering perennials with lovely spurred flowers in many single and multicolored shades. They bloom in spring and early summer and form neat mounds of blue-green, scalloped leaves that range from 12 to 48 in. high. There are many hybrids and species to choose from. The western columbine, *A. formosa* (p. 143), is native to California. It grows 18 to 36 in. tall and bears lovely red-and-yellow flowers. Rocky Mountain columbine, *A. caerulea* (pp. 76, 150), grows to a similar height but has blue-and-white blooms. The yellow columbine, *A. chrysantha* (p. 45), grows 36 in. high by 24 in. wide and has yellow flowers. The native Texas gold columbine, *A. chrysantha hinckleyana* (pp. 21, 66), bears fra-grant golden flowers with long spurs. Columbines grow best in light shade but can also take full sun where summers are cool. Water regularly. Carefree. Individual plants live only a few years, but replacements will pop up here and there if you let the seeds mature and scatter naturally. **Generally hardy to Zone 7, but not well adapted to low-elevation desert areas.**

Arbutus

ARBUTUS. Striking evergreen trees with shiny red to orange bark and small, bell-shaped flowers followed by red fruits. Leaves are shiny green. Usually grown with multiple trunks. Strawberry tree, *A. unedo* (p. 125), grows 10 to 25 ft. tall and has distinctive, gnarly branches and white flowers in fall and winter. *A . 'Marina'* (pp. 16, 141) can grow to 40 ft. but is usually smaller, with larger leaves and pinkish flowers in fall. It's a perfect substitute for the California native madrone, *A. menziesii*, which is hard to grow in gardens. Plant in full sun or partial shade and well-drained soil. Arbutus gets by on little water. Prune to expose branches. **Hardy to zones 7 or 8.** Not well adapted to desert areas.

Arctostaphyllos

MANZANITA. Western native evergreen shrubs with shiny red bark, lustrous deep green foliage, and small white-to-pink flowers in spring followed by red berries. *A. densiflora* 'Howard McMinn' (p. 144) grows 5 to 6 ft. tall and spreads a little wider. *A. uva-ursi* 'Point Reyes' is an excellent ground cover less than a foot high but spreading up to 15 ft. wide. *A. uva-ursi* 'Massachusetts' (p. 105) is also a fine ground cover less than a foot tall and spreading to 8 ft. wide. The same is true of *A. 'Emerald Carpet'* (p. 177) which grows 8 to 14 in. high by 5 ft. wide and has brilliant green leaves. Manzanitas are best used in dry areas and on slopes where there is infrequent watering. Plant in fall in full sun to partial shade. **Hardiness varies.** Not adapted to desert areas.

Armeria maritima

THRIFT. A perennial that forms a neat tuft of grassy evergreen leaves and bears spherical flower heads on stiff stalks about 1 ft. tall. Blooms generously in spring, with scattered blossoms throughout the summer and fall in shades of rose, pink ('Sea Pink', p. 125), or white ('Alba'). *A. 'Victor Ruter'* (p. 47) grows only 4 in. high by 4 in wide. Thrifts need full sun and well-drained soil. Look best with occasional watering. Remove flowers as they fade, and shear off old foliage in early spring. **Hardy to Zone 3.** Not adapted to desert areas. Pages 32, 91.

Artemisia

ARTEMISIA. Shrubby perennials, woody at the base, with fragrant, gray-green, finely divided leaves. Beautiful accent plants. Rarely flower. *A.* 'Powis Castle' (pp. 23, 39, 53, 61, 112, 123, 129, 141, 157, 183) grows 3 to 4 ft. tall and spreads up to 6 ft. wide. Lovely lacy, silver foliage. *A. schmidtiana* 'Silver Mound' grows only 1 to 2 ft. high and wide and has feathery silver leaves. It is a good alternative where space is limited. *A. versicolor* 'Seafoam' (p. 47) grows 12 in high by 24 in. wide, producing an airy mound of silver, curly foliage. **Hardiness varies but generally widely adapted.**

Aspidistra elatior

CAST-IRON PLANT. An unusual evergreen perennial valued for its tolerance of deep shade. It forms a dense patch of stiff, dark, pointed leaves that grow directly from the ground and reach 3 ft. tall. Spreads slowly into a weed-proof colony about 2 ft. wide. Purple to gray-white flowers are solitary and mostly hidden in the foliage. Cast-iron plant grows well in full or partial shade with occasional summer watering. Cut back the old growth in early spring before the new leaves emerge. The bold foliage is often used in floral arrangements. **Hardy to Zone 7.** Pages 66, 117, 139.

Aster

ASTER. Carefree perennials that bloom over a long season from late spring to fall, bearing thousands daisylike flowers in shades of white, blue, lavender, purple and pink. *A.* x *frikartii* 'Wonder of Stafa' and 'Mönch' are popular purple varieties, which make good cut flowers (p. 114). *A. lateriflorus* 'Lady in Black' (p. 45) is an upright, mound-shaped plant with purplish to blackish stems and purplish pink flowers. *A. oblongifolius*, the fall aster (pp. 22, 37, 60, 64, 95, 183), is a carefree Texas native with showy lavender-purple flowers from early fall until the first hard freeze. It is drought tolerant. Plant asters in full sun and well-drained soil. Most prefer regular water. Cut stems back by a third in late spring if the plant has gotten floppy. Divide every year or two in fall or early spring. Most grow 2 to 3 ft. tall and wide. Adaptation varies.

Arctostaphyllos A. uva-ursi 'Massachusetts' MANZANITA

Arctostaphyllos A. uva-ursi 'Point Reyes' MANZANITA

Aspidistra elatior CAST-IRON PLANT

Aster A. oblongifolius ASTER

Astilbe

ASTILBE. Among the best perennials for shady or partly shady sites. In early to midsummer, fluffy plumes of tiny flowers stand high above glossy compound leaves. Foliage is attractive all season. There are many hybrids that grow from 6 to 42 in. tall and bear white, pale pink, rose, purple, or deep red flowers. *A.* x *arendsii* 'Cattleya', reaching 3 ft. tall, has large open crimson-pink flowers. *A.* x *japonica* 'Peach Blossom' (p. 111) grows about 2 ft. tall and has peach-pink flowers. All astilbes prefer rich, moist, well-drained soil. Grow in full or partial shade, or in full sun if you can water them regularly. **Generally hardy to zones 3 or 4 but are short lived in areas with hot dry summers.**

Aucuba japonica

AUCUBA. These are showy evergreen shrubs with thick erect stems sporting large, lustrous, leathery leaves. They generally grow around 4 ft. tall and 3 ft. wide. The cultivar 'Variegata', also known as gold dust aucuba (pp. 138, 139), has green leaves sprinkled with yellow dots. The leaves of 'Picturata' are splashed with yellow blotches. Aucubas are some of the best shrubs for dark shady areas. They will not tolerate hot, exposed, sunny sites. Provide monthly watering during dry summers. Plants are generally pest free. Prune lightly in late winter to control size. **Hardy to Zone 6.**

Aurinia saxatilis

BASKET-OF-GOLD. A tough flowering perennial that forms a spreading mound of gray-green foliage, 10 in. high by 18 in. wide. Covered with bright yellow flowers in spring and early summer. Plant in full sun. Water occasionally. Lightly cut back after bloom to maintain a compact habit. **Hardy to Zone 4.** Page: 45.

Baccharis pilularis 'Twin Peaks'

'TWIN PEAKS' DWARF COYOTE BRUSH. California native evergreen shrub valuable as a ground cover for sunny, dry, low-maintenance areas. Grows 10 to 24 in. high and spreads about 6 ft. wide, forming a dense cover of small green leaves. 'Twin Peaks' is a male selection that doesn't produce seeds. Shear back and fertilize in early spring. Needs little water near the coast, once a month in warmer areas. Pages: 144, 157, 158. **Hardy to Zone 7.**

Berberis thunbergii

JAPANESE BARBERRY. A deciduous shrub with stiff, spiny stems and small leaves. Small red berries hang on most of the fall and winter. Can grow into a broad mound 6 ft. tall and 8 ft. wide but is typically kept smaller by shearing. 'Atropurpurea' has purple-red foliage through the summer and fall. 'Crimson Pygmy' (pp. 24, 26, 56, 62, 63, 97, 125, 167) is a dwarf form grown for its colorful foliage and com-

Astilbe x *japonica* 'Peach Blossom'
ASTILBE

Acuba japonica 'Picturata'
GOLD DUST ACUBA

Baccharis pilularis 'Twin Peaks'
DWARF COYOTE BRUSH

Bergenia B. crassifolia
BERGENIA

pact, spreading habit. The small leaves are showy purplish red all summer, bright crimson in fall. Can grow into a broad mound 2 ft. tall and 3 to 5 ft. wide or trimmed as a low hedge. It makes an excellent ground cover. Barberries need full sun, well-drained soil, and occasional water. Shear any time, as desired. **Hardy to Zone 5.**

Bergenia

BERGENIA. Low-growing perennials with large, dark green, wavy-edged leaves that are evergreen except in cold-winter areas. In late winter to spring, they bear tall stems bear clusters of pink, red or white flowers. *B. crassifolia* (p. 169) bears pink flowers in late winter. *B. cordifolia* 'Bressingham White' (pp. 74, 75) has white flowers in spring. Plant in partial shade (or full sun where summers are cool). Will withstand poor conditions but looks best grown in good soil and with regular watering. **Hardy to Zone 3.** Not adapted desert areas.

Bignonia capreolata 'Tangerine Beauty'

'TANGERINE BEAUTY' CROSS VINE. This vigorous evergreen vine grows to a generous 15 ft. tall and wide. In spring the entire plant turns into a mass of beautiful trumpetlike orange flowers with yellow throats. Scattered bloom continues through the growing season. Excellent for covering walls, trellises, and fences. Cross vine is a Texas native and requires little care or water. It is rarely plagued by insects or disease. **Hardy to Zone 6.** Not adapted desert areas. Page: 39.

Bignonia capreolata 'Tangerine Beauty'
CROSS VINE

Bougainvillea 'Barbara Karst'
BOUGAINVILLEA

Buddleia davidii
'Black Knight'
BUTTERFLY BUSH

Bougainvillea

BOUGAINVILLEA. One of the most spectacular flowering plants, bougainvillea blooms in spectacular shades of white, pink, red, orange, yellow, or purple in late spring and summer. Foliage is evergreen. Habit varies by variety, of which there are many. Most are sprawling vinelike plants that can spread over 20 ft. wide and thus need lots of room. Others are smaller and more shrublike. 'Barbara Karst' is one of many vigorous types that need the support of a strong fence or trellis but can be used as ground covers on banks. It has red to crimson flowers. 'La Jolla' (pp. 157, 158) makes sprawling, mounding vines 4 ft high and twice as wide, with bright red flowers. 'New Gold' (pp. 153, 161, 162) has bronzy yellow flowers and grows 5 to 6 ft. tall provided it has the support of a trellis. The shrublike 'Rosenka' (pp. 153, 162) forms an arching mound 4 ft. tall and 5 ft. wide and bears gold flowers that become pinkish as they age. 'Gold' bears yellow-gold blooms and is more vigorous.

Bougainvilleas are reliably hardy only in mild-winter climates (Zone 9). Widely grown elsewhere, they may lose leaves or die back partially in colder areas. Can also be grown in pots or treated as summer annuals in cold climates. Plant in spring in full sun, or light shade in hot areas. Be careful not to damage roots when planting. Plants get by with little water once established but bloom better with summer irrigation. In spring, fertilize and prune as necessary to keep within bounds. Pages: 70, 97.

Brunfelsia pauciflora 'Floribunda Compacta'

YESTERDAY-TODAY-AND-TOMORROW. A very floriferous evergreen shrub, named for its changing flower colors, from purple (yesterday) to lavender (today) to white (tomorrow). Blooms spring to summer. Large, attractive, oblong leaves are dark green above and light green below. Grows best in partial shade and with regular water. Reaches a compact, bushy 3 to 4 ft. tall. Leaves and seeds are poisonous. **Hardy to Zone 9.** Page: 155.

Buddleia davidii

BUTTERFLY BUSH. A fast-growing shrub that blooms from midsummer through fall and is sometimes evergreen where winters are mild. Arching shoots make a vase-shaped clump reaching 5 to 8 ft. tall and wide by the end of the summer. Spikes of small white, pink, lilac, blue, or purple flowers form at the end of each stem. The flowers have a sweet fragrance and really do attract butterflies. 'Black Knight' (pp. 43, 144, 149) has purple flowers. 'Nanho Blue' (p. 127) with lavender flowers, and 'Adonis Blue' (p. 45), with blue blooms, reach only 4 to 5 ft. tall and are better choices for small spaces. 'Pink Delight' (p. 109) has medium pink flowers. All need full sun and well-drained soil. Cut old stems down to 1-ft. stubs in late winter to early spring to promote vigorous growth and maximum flowering. Requires regular watering. **Hardy to Zone 5.**

Bulbs

The bulbs recommended in this book are all perennials that come up year after year and bloom in late winter, spring, or early summer. After they flower, their leaves continue growing until sometime in summer, when they gradually turn yellow and die down to the ground. To get started, buy bulbs from a garden center or catalog in late summer or fall. Plant them promptly in a sunny or partly sunny bed with well-prepared, well-drained soil, burying them to a depth two to three times the bulb's height. In subsequent years, all you have to do is pick off the flowers after they fade and remove (or ignore) the old leaves after they yellow in summer. Most bulbs can be divided every few years. Dig them up as the foliage is turning yellow, shake or pull them apart, and replant them right away in a different spot in your landscape. For more information on specific bulbs, see the box on page 197.

Recommended bulbs

Allium, Ornamental onion

Dependable onion relatives with grassy or straplike foliage and eye-catching, ball-shaped flower clusters in late spring to early summer. Blue allium (*A. caeruleum*, p. 57) produces 2-in.-wide bright blue flowers on 12-in. stems. Star of Persia (*A. christophii*, p. 71) bears large clusters of glistening lilac-colored, star-shaped blooms on 12- to 15-in. stems. Leaves are hairy white underneath. Golden garlic (*A. moly*, p. 59) has bright clusters of yellow flowers on 9- to 18-in. stems. Round-headed garlic (*A. sphaerocephalum*, p. 71) has reddish purple flowers on 24-in. stems. Alliums grow best in full sun or partial shade and well-drained soil. Plant the bulbs at a depth 2 to 3 times their width. Water while bulbs are growing. Flowers are great for bouquets and look good on the plant even after they dry. **Most alliums are hardy (at least Zone 2) and widely adapted.**

Leucojum aestivum, Snowflake

This dependable perennial bulb delights with clusters of tiny white bells on 1 ft. stalks in early spring. The healthy green foliage emerges in early winter and goes dormant in summer. Snowflakes are great for introducing bright patches of early bloom among ground covers and landscaped beds. They grow in sun or shade and in moist or dry conditions. This foolproof bulb is pest free and requires no supplemental watering. **Hardy to Zone 3.** Not adapted to lower elevation desert areas. Page: 119.

Muscari armeniacum, Grape hyacinth

Grapelike clusters of sweet-scented purple flowers last for several weeks in April and May. Plant bulbs 3 in. deep, 3 in. apart. Don't be surprised to see the grassy foliage appear in fall; it lasts through winter. Blooms best in full sun. Naturalizes and blooms on forever. **Hardy to Zone 4.** Page: 57.

Narcissus, Daffodil

The most popular spring bulb. There are hundreds of cultivars and species, with flowers in shades of yellow or white on stalks 6 to 24 in. tall, blooming in sequence from early to late spring. Some kinds have a lovely fragrance. 'February Gold' and 'Tête-à-Tête' (p. 57) are two of the first to bloom. Both have yellow flowers on stalks under 12 in. tall and, like all daffodils, are good for interplanting in flower beds because their flowers are large enough to be showy, but their leaves are short enough to be inconspicuous after the flowers bloom. 'Ice Follies' (pp. 21, 136) is one of the few daffodils that does well in Texas. It has wide, ruffled, yellow trumpets fading to creamy white. *N. tazetta* 'Grand Primo' (pp. 82, 83, 117) is a southern heirloom with creamy white flowers and pale yellow cups. Paperwhites (*N. tazetta papyraceous*) bloom late fall and early spring. They bear extremely fragrant white flowers in dense clusters. Plant the bulbs 4 to 6 in. deep, 6 in. apart. **Daffodils are generally very hardy and widely adapted.**

Tulipa, Tulip

Large flowers in bright or pastel shades of all colors but blue, held on stalks 6 to 20 in. tall. Different kinds bloom between February and April. Plant bulbs 4 to 6 in. deep, 4 to 6 in. apart. For the best display, every fall divide and replant existing bulbs, add new ones, and fertilize. Page: 29

Allium, A. sphaerocephalum
ORNAMENTAL ONION

Leucojum aestivum
SNOWFLAKE

Muscari armeniacum
GRAPE HYACINTH

Narcissus pseudonarcissus
'Ice Follies' DAFFODIL

Buxus microphylla
'Winter Gem'
LITTLELEAF BOXWOOD

Callicarpa americana
AMERICAN BEAUTYBERRY

Buxus microphylla

LITTLELEAF BOXWOOD. This shrub forms a dense mass of neat, small, glossy evergreen leaves that make it ideal for shearing. (p. 183) The leaves, and also the small flowers in spring, have a distinct fragrance. *B. m.* var. *japonica*, Japanese boxwood, forms soft 4- to 6-ft.-high mounds if left alone. It can be sheared into formal globes, cones, hedges, or topiary. Leaves turn brownish in cold winters. 'Green Beauty' (pp. 34, 87, 89, 165) has small leaves that stay bright green in winter. It forms a compact globe up to 4 ft. tall. 'Winter Gem' (pp. 16, 41,) is a similar hybrid. Boxwoods need well-drained soil and grow best in full or partial sun. Use mulch to protect their shallow roots. Water regularly. Shear in late spring. **Hardy to Zone 6.**

Callicarpa americana

AMERICAN BEAUTYBERRY. This native deciduous shrub has a lax habit, spreading 4 ft. wide and tall. Tapered dull green leaves line the slightly arching branches. In fall they give way to profuse clusters of vivid violet-purple berries. Beautyberry is pest free and drought tolerant. Irrigation may be needed during periods of drought to maintain attractive foliage. Thin one-third of the older branches to the ground each spring to promote a denser appearance. **Hardy to Zone 5.** Not adapted to desert climates. Pages: 37, 66, 119, 139.

Callistemon viminalis 'Little John'

'LITTLE JOHN' DWARF BOTTLEBRUSH. A compact, dense evergreen shrub 2 to 3 ft. high and wide. Arching branches are clothed in narrow, light green leaves. Bears blood-red, bottlebrushlike blooms at ends of branches from fall to spring. Useful informal hedge or container plant. Full sun and regular water. **Hardy to Zone 8.** Pages: 24, 34, 35, 165, 173.

Calluna vulgaris

SCOTCH HEATHER. An evergreen shrub that is often confused with heath. Ranging from a few inches to 3 ft. tall, its many ascending branches bear tiny scalelike leaves. Depending on cultivar, summer and winter foliage can be colorful. Small bell-shaped flowers bloom on new wood in summer. Because the dried flowers remain on the stems, heathers can appear to be in bloom through the winter. 'Robert Chapman' (pp. 105, 106) grows to 10 in. tall, has bright red new growth that turns golden as it matures, and bears purple flowers in summer. 'Silver Knight' grows to 18 in. and bears mauve-pink flowers and silvery gray foliage. Heathers prefer full sun to partial shade and moist, well-drained soil with lots of organic matter. To ensure that you get plants with the winter foliage color you want, shop for plants in winter. Shear in late winter to encourage new growth. **Hardy to Zone 5.** Not adapted to hot, dry areas of the southwest.

Camellia

CAMELLIA. Evergreen shrubs with glossy foliage and large, lovely white, pink or rose flowers. There are hundreds of cultivars, differing mostly in flower color, size, and form (single or double) as well as in overall plant habit, mature size and hardiness. Japanese camellia (*C. japonica*) is the most popular, usually ranging in height from 6 to 12 ft. and blooming in late winter to early spring. Reliable varieties include 'Debutante' (p. 68), a vigorous plant with pink, peonylike flowers; 'Eleanor McCown', with white flowers streaked red and pink; 'Kramer's Supreme', with deep red, lightly fragrant blooms; and 'Tom Knudson', sporting deep red flowers marked with deeper red veins. Sasanqua camellias (*C. sasanqua*, pp. 74, 169) are smaller plants that generally range from 2 to 3 ft. upward to 10 ft. and are useful as ground covers or hedges. They bloom in late fall and winter and can take more sun than Japanese camellias. Favorite varieties include 'Apple Blossom' (pp. 54, 55), a spreading plant with single white flowers that are blushed with pink; 'Cleopatra' (p. 110), a more upright, compact plant and bears rose-pink flowers; 'Hana Jiman' (pp.117,

Calluna vulgaris 'Robert Chapman'
SCOTCH HEATHER

118), which grows 6 ft. tall and 4 ft. wide and bears semi-double white flowers edged in pink; 'Shi Shi Gashira' (p. 82) with rose-colored semi-double flowers and a more compact habit; 'Setsugekka' (pp. 30, 31, 76), with white flowers borne on an upright plant; 'White Doves', producing white flowers on a low, spreading plant; and 'Yuletide' (pp. 21, 22, 170), with single red flowers on an upright plant. Camellias need moist, well-drained, acid soil with a layer of mulch, and shade from midday sun. They are excellent choices for containers. Prune and fertilize immediately after flowering, if desired. **Hardy to Zone 7.** Difficult in desert areas.

Camellia 'Shi Shi Gashira'
CAMELLIA

Campanula

BELLFLOWER. A large group of useful flowering perennials (a few are annuals) that vary in plant habit and flower form. Plant them in flower beds, rock gardens or containers. Spreading types are useful as small-scale ground covers. Italian bellflower (*C. isophylla*) is a low-growing, sprawling plant that reaches 6 in. tall but can spread up to 2 ft. wide. Small white or blue flowers appear in late summer to fall. Serbian bellflower (*C. poscharskyana*, pp. 89, 132) is spreading and has flower stalks about 1 ft. tall. Blooms in spring to early summer in shades of blue to lavender. All grow best in partial shade but can take full sun near the coast. Water regularly. Cut back after bloom. Divide as necessary in fall. Most do well in cold winter climates. Not long-lived in desert areas.

Carex buchananii
FOX RED CURLY SEDGE

Campsis x *tagliabuana* 'Mme. Galen'
TRUMPET VINE

Campsis x *tagliabuana* 'Mme. Galen'

'MME. GALEN' TRUMPET VINE. A vigorous deciduous vine with a woody trunk and thick stems, large leaves, and very showy clusters of salmon flowers in late summer. Needs full sun, room to grow, and regular water. Once started, it can climb and cover a trellis, wall, or fence with no further assistance or care. Can reach 30 to 40 ft. Prune in winter to control size. **Hardy to Zone 5.** Pages: 92, 94, 112

Campanula
C. isophylla
BELLFLOWER

Carex buchananii

FOX RED CURLY SEDGE. A grasslike plant that grows in clumps 2 to 3 ft. tall. Leaves curl at the tip and keep their reddish bronze color all year, providing texture and color contrast in the garden through the seasons. Summer flowers are insignificant. Grow in full sun or partial shade. Does well in hot sun and well-drained soil. Self-sows to form a patch. **Hardy to Zone 6.** Not adapted to desert areas. Page: 105.

Cassia artemisioides
FEATHERY CASSIA

Carissa macrocarpa
'Tuttle'
NATAL PLUM

Ceanothus 'Julia Phelps'
WILD LILAC

Carissa macrocarpa 'Tuttle'

'TUTTLE' NATAL PLUM. A colorful evergreen shrub best adapted to coastal areas of southern California. Rich, shiny green leaves on spiny stems. Wonderfully fragrant, star-shaped white flowers appear throughout the year and are followed by bright red, edible fruits. Grows 2 to 3 ft. tall, spreading up to 5 ft. Useful as a ground cover or short hedge. Full sun or partial shade. Needs little water near the coast; more inland. Prune at any time. **Hardy to Zone 9.** Page: 90.

Carpenteria californica

BUSH ANEMONE. Native to California's foothills, this evergreen shrub is grown for its lovely, lightly fragrant white flowers with yellow centers, which are displayed in late spring and early summer against handsome, glossy dark green leaves. Grows upright 4 to 6 ft. high and wide. Plant in full sun except in the hottest areas, where partial shade is best. Needs little water once established. Prune to shape after flowering. Sometimes gets aphids or mites. **Hardy to Zone 8.** Not adapted to desert areas. Page: 177.

Cassia artemisioides

FEATHERY CASSIA. An airy, light-textured evergreen shrub well adapted to hot, dry conditions. Small yellow flowers bloom in winter and spring, sometimes longer. Leaves are gray green and needlelike. Requires full sun and well-drained soil. Water occasionally during summer for best appearance. Will be damaged by a hard freeze. Spreads 3 to 5 ft. tall and wide. Prune after bloom if necessary. Sometimes sold as *Senna artemisioides*. **Hardy to Zone 9.** Page: 156.

Ceanothus

CEANOTHUS, WILD LILAC. California native evergreen shrubs useful in dry landscapes, especially on slopes. Blue or (rarely) white flowers appear in early spring. Leaves are deep green. 'Julia Phelps' (pp. 78, 144) reaches 4 to 7 ft. tall and up to 9 ft. wide and has deep blue flowers. 'Victoria' (p. 53) grows 5 ft. tall and wide, with deep blue flowers. Carmel creeper (*C. griseus* var. *horizontalis*) is low-growing to 2 to 3 ft. tall and 5 to 10 ft. wide. The cultivar 'Yankee Point' (p. 146) has dense, darker green foliage and slightly darker blue flowers than the species. Plant ceanothus in full sun in fall. Do not water once established. **Most are hardy to Zone 7 and not adapted to desert climates.**

Cerastium tomentosum

Snow-in-summer. A perennial often used as a ground cover, with silvery evergreen foliage and masses of white flowers in early summer. Forms a low mat 6 to 8 in. high, with stems that trail 2 to 3 ft. wide. Requires full sun or partial shade and well-drained soil. Water regularly. Shear off the top of the plant, cutting it back right after it blooms. **Hardy to Zone 3.** Pages: 56, 71, 89, 135, 173.

Cerastostigma plumbaginoides

Dwarf plumbago. A perennial ground cover with indigo blue flowers in summer and fall and dark green foliage that turns maroon or crimson after a frost. Deciduous in cold winters and late to emerge in spring, it looks good with early-spring bulbs. Adapts to full or partial sun. Looks best with regular water. Cut old stems to the ground in early spring. Stays under 1 ft. high, spreads 2 to 3 ft. wide or more. **Hardy to Zone 5.** Not well adapted to low-elevation desert areas. Pages: 77, 115, 125.

Cercidium floridum

Blue palo verde. A fast-growing deciduous desert tree prized for its toughness, its blue-tinged foliage and branches, and its stunning display of small yellow flowers in spring. Useful as a shade tree, it grows 30 to 35 ft. tall and almost as wide at the crown. Needs little water once established. Prune in winter to enhance form. The variety 'Desert Museum' (p. 174) is an improved hybrid with more upright, tree form (to 25 ft. high and wide) and better bloom. **Hardy to Zone 8.** Page: 162, 174.

Cercis

Redbud. Small, early-spring-flowering, deciduous trees. Eastern redbud (*C. canadensis*, pp. 21, 43, 117, 128, 150) is native to the Mid-Atlantic region but does well in all of the West. Clusters of bright pink-purple flowers line the twigs in early spring, before the leaves unfold. Heart-shaped leaves are medium green all summer, turn gold in fall. Available with single or multiple trunks. May reach 20 to 25 ft. tall and wide. Eastern redbuds require well-drained soil with regular water. 'Forest Pansy' (p. 76) has purple foliage and grows best in partial shade. Western redbud (*C. occidentalis*, pp. 127, 144, 177) is native to California and is a good choice for dry or natural landscapes. Less refined than its eastern relative, it is often grown as a large multi-trunked shrub. Magenta flowers are followed by seedpods some people find unsightly. Leaves turn yellow in fall. Grows 10 to 20 ft. tall. Thrives in poor, dry soils. In hot-summer climates, it looks best if given some water. Prune to maintain shape and to open canopy. Texas redbud (*C. texensis*) is adapted to drier areas with alkaline soils but performs well throughout the West. **Redbuds are generally hardy throughout the west except in the very coldest areas.**

Cercocarpus ledifolius

Curl leaf mountain mahogany. Evergreen shrub or small tree native to arid, high elevation areas of the West. Grows 4 to 12 ft. high and wide with leathery dark green leaves, white underneath. Makes a fine hedge or background plant. Plant in full sun. Needs little water where adapted. **Hardy to Zone 6.** Not adapted to desert areas. Page: 45.

Ceratostigma plumbaginoides
Dwarf plumbago

Cerastium tomentosum
Snow-in-summer

Cercis occidentalis
Redbud

Chamaecyparis obtusa
'Nana Gracilis'
DWARF HINOKI CYPRUS

Chitalpa tashkentensis
'Pink Dawn'
CHITALPA

Chamaecyparis obtusa 'Nana Gracilis'

DWARF HINOKI CYPRESS. A slow-growing conifer with graceful, glossy, emerald green foliage. Its habit is naturally open and sculpted with short sprays of scalelike foliage. No pruning necessary. Prefers full to partial sun and moist, well-drained soil. Buy the largest plant you can afford. It may someday reach 8 ft. or taller and spread 3 to 4 ft. wide. **Hardy to Zone 4.** Not adapted to southern California, desert areas or southern Texas. Page: 28.

Chamaerops humilis

MEDITERRANEAN FAN PALM. A bushy palm with coarse, blue-green, palm-shaped leaves arising from the tops of multiple stalks. Yellow flowers are borne in long panicles in spring but are mostly hidden in the dense foliage. Grows 6 to 12 ft. or more tall or and half as wide. This adaptable palm does well in full sun to partial shade and in moderately fertile to poor soils. **Hardy to Zone 7.** Pages: 156, 160.

Chilopsis linearis

DESERT WILLOW. Native to desert areas, this small deciduous tree has an open, twisting, multitrunked habit and willowy green-gray leaves. From spring to fall, fragrant clusters of trumpetlike flowers bloom in shades of red, purple, pink, and white, sometimes with yellow and purple throat streaks. Flowers are followed by many long, thin seedpods. It survives on little water once established. Prune to keep it open and to expose its attractive branching habit. Extremely drought tolerant and has few pests. Desert willow may reach 15 to 30 ft. tall and about half as wide at the crown. 'Bubba' (pp. 92, 94) has greener leaves and dark wine-purple flowers. 'Rio Salado' (p. 98) is a roundheaded tree, 12 to 15 ft. high and wide, with deep burgundy flowers. **Hardy to Zone 8.** Page: 152.

x *Chitalpa tashkentensis*

CHITALPA. A deciduous tree, sun-loving with narrow leaves that quickly grows 20 to 30 ft. tall. Large clusters of ruffled, trumpet-shaped flowers bloom in early summer and continue until frost. 'Pink Dawn' (pp. 102, 103, 158) produces pink blooms with yellow throats. 'Morning Cloud' has white flowers. Grows best with occasional water in hot-summer climates. Can be messy, dropping flowers and leaves in summer. Subject to pest problems if overwatered. Plant in full sun. Prune in winter to maintain shape. **Hardy to Zone 6.** Page: 144.

Choisya ternata

MEXICAN ORANGE. An evergreen shrub reaching 6 ft. tall with glossy leaves that are very aromatic in the hot sun. Blooms in the spring and sporadically throughout the summer with terminal white clusters of flowers that smell somewhat like an orange-tree blossom. Plant in full sun to partial shade. It is not picky about soil conditions but will not tolerate standing water on its roots. Prune after flowering to encourage a full bushy look. May die back in cold winters but will usually resprout from the roots. **Hardy to Zone 8.** Not adapted to desert areas. Page: 110.

Chrysactinia mexicana

DAMIANITA. This tough little evergreen shrub stands up well to desert heat and is useful for lining walkways and borders. It forms a densely branched 2 ft. mound of highly aromatic dark green needlelike leaves. Small, fragrant gold-yellow "daisies" are borne in spring and fall, and sometimes through the summer where temperatures are mild. Grows in full sun. Needs little water but will bloom more with occasional irrigation. Shear lightly in early spring to promote dense new growth. **Hardy to Zone 7.** Page: 153.

Chrysanthemum leucanthemum

OX-EYE DAISY. This vigorous cool-season perennial produces loads of white daisies on 2-ft. stems in spring; the flowers are a great addition to bouquets. Prefers full sun and adequate moisture and has few pest problems. Remove flowers after they finish blooming to encourage more of them. To produce more plants, divide the leafy clumps in fall. Ox-eye daisy is a good substitute for Shasta daisies in hot, dry climates. Can be weedy. **Hardy to Zone 5.** Pages: 23, 121.

Cistus x *pulverulentus* 'Sunset'

'SUNSET' ROCKROSE. A compact evergreen shrub reaching 2 ft. tall and 3 ft. wide, with interesting wavy gray-green leaves. Bears many magenta-pink flowers for a long period in summer. Plant in full sun and well-drained soil. Very little pruning is needed. **Hardy to Zone 8.** Not adapted to desert areas. Page: 109.

Citrus

CITRUS. One of the most useful ornamental and edible plants for mild-winter landscapes, these evergreen trees offer handsome dark green leaves, fragrant spring flowers, and colorful, edible fruits in winter. The many varieties vary in adaptation **(generally hardy to Zone 9),** tree height, and form. Check with local nurseries for the best varieties for your area. Good landscape varieties include 'Meyer' lemon (p. 89), which forms a compact tree seldom over 8 ft. tall; 'Washington' navel orange, which grows 12 to 16 ft. tall; 'Satsuma' and 'Clementine' dwarf tangerines (p. 78; also sold as 'Algerian' tangerine), neat-looking trees 8 to 12 ft. tall; and 'Bearss' lime, a productive plant 8 to 10 ft. tall. 'Nagami' kumquat (dwarf kumquat, pp. 84, 166, 171) makes a fine container plant. It grows slowly to 10 ft. tall and 5 ft. wide and bears fragrant white flowers in spring, miniature orangelike fruits in fall, and small leathery bright green leaves year-round. Citrus trees will be at least 50 percent smaller if grown on 'Flying Dragon' rootstock. Plant in full sun and well-drained soil. Water and fertilize frequently for quality fruit. Prune to keep the center of the tree open or to maintain size. Protect trees if temperatures drop below 30°F for prolonged periods of time.

Chrysanthemum leucanthemum
Ox-eye daisy

Choisya ternata
Mexican orange

'Clementine'
Citrus

'Meyer' lemon
Citrus

Clematis armandii
EVERGREEN CLEMATIS

Clematis x jackmanii
'Comtesse de Bouchaud'
CLEMATIS

Coleonema pulchrum
'Sunset Gold'
BREATH OF HEAVEN

Clematis

CLEMATIS. Deciduous or evergreen vines that climb or sprawl, forming a tangle of leafy stems adorned with masses of flowers, which can be tiny or large. Evergreen clematis (*C. armandii*) produces large clusters of fragrant white flowers in spring. Anemone clematis (*C. montana*, p. 76) bears numerous spring flowers that turn from white to pink. The cultivar 'Rubens' (p. 114) has red-bronze foliage and fragrant pink to rosy red flowers.

Large-flowered hybrids, of which there are many, produce flowers up to 10 in. across in single and multicolored shades of white, pink, red, purple, and blue. 'Mme. Le Coultre' (p. 135) bears large white flowers in midsummer and fall. 'Comtesse de Bouchard' bears rosy pink flowers in summer. 'Elsa Spath' (pp. 109, 111) has mauve-blue flowers from late spring into fall.

Clematis need partial or full sun, consistent moisture, and soil rich in organic matter. Plant where the branches can reach sunlight but the roots are shaded and cool. Mulch heavily. Unlike most plants, clematis needs a hole deep enough to cover the root ball and base of the stem with about 2 in. of soil. Cut the stem back to the lowest set of healthy leaves to encourage the plant to branch out near the base. Guide the new stems into position and use twist-ties or other fasteners to secure them as soon as they reach the trellis, wire or other support. Prune annually. It takes most clematis a few years to cover a fence or trellis 6 to 8 ft. tall, but many can eventually climb 15 to 20 ft. **Hardiness varies.** Ask at your nursery about local adaptation. Page: 72.

Coleonema pulchrum 'Sunset Gold'

BREATH OF HEAVEN. Wispy evergreen shrub with fragrant small yellow leaves and pink flowers over a long period in winter and spring. Grows 2 ft. tall but spreads 4 ft. Plant in full sun and well-drained soil. Needs regular water but suffers if overwatered or planted in poorly drained soil. Shear after bloom. **Hardy to Zone 8.** Not adapted to desert areas. Page: 16.

Convolvulus cneorum

BUSH MORNING GLORY. Evergreen shrub that forms a soft-textured mound of silvery foliage covered with white to pink, trumpet-shaped flowers in late spring and early summer. Grows 2 to 3 ft high and 3 to 4 ft. wide. Best in full sun and with regular water. Shear to keep compact. **Hardy to Zone 8.** Page 159.

Convolvulus mauritanicus

GROUND MORNING GLORY. An evergreen, creeping perennial 1 to 2 ft. high but spreading up to 3 ft. Soft, gray-green leaves are a backdrop for lavender-blue flowers summer to fall. Makes a good small-scale ground cover. Plant in full sun or light shade and well-drained soil. Can take periods of drought but does best with occasional water. Shear after bloom to keep plants compact. Pages: 49, 56.

Coreopsis lanceolata

COREOPSIS. A native wildflower, coreopsis explodes each spring with long-blooming masses of golden yellow daisylike flowers. Forms a clump 1 ft. tall and 1½ ft. wide of bright green, lance-like leaves and slender flower stalks. A warm-season, fast-growing perennial, coreopsis grows best in full sun with modest irrigation. Seeds are a favorite food of goldfinches. Tolerates most soil types and has very few pest problems. Looks best if the spent blossoms are sheared off after bloom. **Hardy to Zone 4.** Pages: 95, 121.

Coreopsis verticillata 'Moonbeam'

'MOONBEAM' COREOPSIS. Long-blooming perennial that bears hundreds of small lemon yellow daisy-like blossoms from summer to fall. The dark green leaves are short and threadlike. Spreads to form a patch 2 to 3 ft. tall and wide. Needs full sun. Gets by with little water once established. Remove spent flowers to extend bloom. Cut back to a few inches aboveground in fall. **Hardy to Zone 3.** Page: 71, 72, 74.

Cornus alba 'Elegantissima'

VARIEGATED SIBERIAN DOGWOOD. A deciduous shrub with four-season interest. It has bright red stems in winter, white flowers in spring, variegated green-and-white leaves from spring through fall, and white berries in late summer. Forms a vase-shaped clump 6 to 8 ft. tall with many erect or arching stems. Plant in full sun or partial shade. Does well in most soils and thrives in soils that stay wet. Cut all the stems down close to the ground every few years (or every year, if you prefer) in early spring. After a few weeks, the plant will send up vigorous new shoots. In fall, these young shoots sport brightly colored bark. **Hardy to Zone 2.** Best in cold winter areas. Not adapted to desert areas. Page: 105.

Cortaderia selloana 'Pumila'

DWARF PAMPAS GRASS. An evergreen clumping grass growing 5 ft. tall and 4 ft. wide with long linear leaves that have very sharp margins. In the summer, plumes of white flowers rise above the foliage. They make excellent dried flowers. Dwarf pampas grass thrives in hot sun and in almost all soil types. Irrigation is only neccessary during prolonged summer droughts. In early spring, you can cut the grass low to the ground to eliminate the old, unsightly foliage. **Hardy to Zone 7.** Considered a noxious weed by some. Page: 121.

Corylopsis pauciflora

WINTER HAZEL. A deciduous shrub known for its early-spring show of pendulous, primrose-yellow flower clusters blooming on bare wood. New leaves start out bronze and turn green. Grows to 8 ft. tall and has a delicate and open habit. Blooms best in full sun to partial shade. Prune right after flowering. **Hardy to Zone 6.** Winter hazel ins not well adapted to hot, dry climates of the southwest. Page: 105.

Coreopsis lanceolata
COREOPSIS

Convolvulus mauritanicus
GROUND MORNING GLORY

Cornus alba 'Elegantissima'
VARIEGATED SIBERIAN DOGWOOD

Cortaderia selloana 'Pumila'
DWARF PAMPAS GRASS

Corylopsis pauciflora
WINTER HAZEL

Cotoneaster horizontalis
ROCK COTONEASTER

Crocosmia x 'Lucifer'
CROCOSMIA

Cryptomeria japonica
'Elegans'
PLUME CEDAR

Cuphea C. micropetala
CIGAR PLANT

Cotoneaster horizontalis

ROCK COTONEASTER. One of a varied group of useful evergreen and deciduous shrubs. This is a wiry deciduous shrub with dark green leaves that turn orange and red in fall. Clusters of small white or pinkish flowers in spring are followed by colorful berries. Grows 2 to 3 ft. tall and 10 to 15 ft. wide. It is an excellent, low-maintenance ground cover. Plant in full sun or light shade. Requires little care once established. Prune as necessary to maintain size and shape. **Hardy to Zone 4.** Not adapted to low-elevation desert areas. Page: 127.

Crataegus phaenopyrum

WASHINGTON HAWTHORN. A small, well-behaved tree that grows upright with a rounded crown, reaching about 20 to 25 ft. tall and 15 to 20 ft. wide. It has very thorny twigs, decidous leaves that are glossy green all summer and turn red in fall, clusters of white flowers in late spring, and small bright red fruits that ripen in early fall and last into winter. Needs full or partial sun. Requires only minimal pruning. Best kept on the dry side. **Hardy to Zone 4.** Not adapted to low-elevation desert areas. Page 44, 47.

Crocosmia 'Lucifer'

'LUCIFER' CROCOSMIA. A perennial with long sword-like leaves. Red-orange flowers bloom from summer into fall. Hummingbirds love them. Takes full sun to partial shade and needs little water once established. Grows to 3 ft. **Hardy to Zone 6.** Pages: 29, 53.

Cryptomeria japonica 'Elegans'

PLUME CEDAR. A slow-growing conifer that forms a cone-shaped tree with soft needlelike foliage that is blue-green in summer and bronzy red in winter. The cinnamon-colored bark peels off in strips. Grows to 60 ft. tall. If height will eventually be a problem, 'Elegans Compacta' grows only 12 ft. tall. Both cultivars need full sun. **Hardy to Zone 6.** Not adapted to desert areas. Pages: 28, 105.

Cuphea

CUPHEA. These are showy plants from the tropics that are often grown as perennials or annuals in western gardens. Cigar plant (*C. micropetala*, pp. 80, 181) is a warm-season perennial that covers itself with yellow-and-orange tubular flowers each fall as the days grow short. It makes a bold clump

4 ft. tall and 3 ft. wide. The hybrid 'David Verity' (pp. 93, 94) grows a more compact 2½ ft. tall and wide and blooms all summer with smaller orange flowers. Both attract hummingbirds in profusion. Mexican heather (*C. hyssopifolia*, p. 39) is a tender perennial that is usually treated as an annual. It grows 1 ft. tall and wide and bears lavender-pink flowers all summer long. Cupheas are tough plants that prefer full sun and tolerate most soil conditions. They are drought tolerant as well, requiring water only during periods of prolonged drought or in areas with dry summers. **Hardy to Zone 10.**

Cycas revoluta

SAGO PALM. Though not a true palm (it is a relative of conifers), this distinctive evergreen plant has the overall appearance of a small palm. Its long arching leaves are shiny dark green. The slow-growing plants are usually sold 1 to 2 ft. tall but take years to reach maximum height of 10 ft. Plant in partial shade and water regularly. A great container subject and perfect for a tropical touch near pools or water features. Separate small new plants that grow near the base whenever they appear. **Hardy to Zone 9.** Pages: 156, 158, 173.

Cyperus alternifolius

UMBRELLA SEDGE. This evergreen perennial forms bold clumps 4 ft. tall and 3 ft. wide, topped with lacy green leafy umbrellas. It grows extremely well in sun or shade in any soil type including poorly drained. It is often grown as an aquatic. Umbrella plant has no known pests and can become invasive in mild-winter areas. In northern areas or during severe winters it may die back to the ground or not return. Consider using it as an annual. **Hardy to Zone 9.** Page: 101.

Daphne odora 'Aureomarginata'

VARIEGATED WINTER DAPHNE. A compact, mound-shaped evergreen shrub with glossy leaves that have an irregular thin gold stripe around the edges. In late winter and early spring purple buds open into small, rose-tinged white flower clusters that have a powerful sweet fragrance. Grows 4 ft. tall and wide. Ideal for an entry because of its fragrance. Also good for woodland paths or informal shrub borders. Plant in a location with morning sun, afternoon shade, and well-drained soil. Prune after flowering if desired. **Hardy to Zone 7.** Not well adapted to desert areas. Pages: 31, 76.

Dasylirion longissima

MEXICAN GRASS TREE. An evergreen shrub forming a grassy fountain of narrow, olive green, succulent leaves. With age it bears spikes of tiny white flowers in early summer and develops a treelike trunk. Usually reaches 4 to 5 ft., but may get as tall as 10 ft. Grows best in full sun or light shade and needs good drainage. Its tropical appearance is especially attractive in desert areas, where it survives on little water. **Hardy to Zone 9.** Pages: 153, 162.

Dianthus gratianopolitanus

CHEDDAR PINK DIANTHUS. This low-growing perennial forms a dense, grassy mat of gray-green foliage 6 in. tall and 1 to 2 ft. wide. Fragrant flowers like tiny pink carnations carpet the plant during the spring. Needs full sun and well-drained soil. After blooming, shear off the flower stalks and cut the plants back halfway to encourage new foliage. Divide every few years during the fall. 'Bath's Pink' (pp. 21, 39, 62, 63, 83, 183) and 'Firewitch' (pp. 129, 131) are common varieties. **Hardy to Zone 4.**

Dianthus plumarius

COTTAGE PINK. Low-growing perennial with fragrant flowers resembling small carnations. Blooms in shades of pink and white from late spring into fall. The evergreen foliage forms a dense mat about 4 to 6 in. high and 1 to 3 ft. wide. Flower stalks are about 1 ft. tall. Needs full sun, well-drained soil, and regular water. After they bloom, shear off the flower stalks and cut the leaves back halfway to encourage new foliage. Divide every few years in early spring. **Hardy to Zone 4.** Page: 115.

Cyperus alternifolius
UMBRELLA SEDGE

Daphne odora 'Aureomarginata'
VARIEGATED WINTER DAPHNE

Dianthus plumarius
COTTAGE PINK

Dicentra

BLEEDING HEART. Perennials that form rounded clumps of soft-textured, lacy blue-green foliage. In late spring heart-shaped flowers dangle from delicate stalks. Leaves will die down in summer heat. Common bleeding heart, *D. spectabilis* is a large, showy plant growing 2 to 3 ft. tall and wide with rose-pink flowers. *D. s.* 'Alba' (p. 150) has white flowers. *D.* 'Luxuriant' (p. 107) is smaller and bears rose-red flowers on 18-in. stalks rising above a 1-ft.-tall mass of foliage. Bleeding hearts need partial shade and fertile, moist, well-drained soil. **Hardy to Zone 3.** Not adapted to desert areas.

Dietes iridioides

FORTNIGHT LILY. Grassy, evergreen perennial with lovely white flowers marked with orange, brown, and purple. Blooms appear every two weeks or so atop airy stalks 3 to 4 ft. tall from spring to fall (also called *D. vegeta*). *D. bicolor* (p. 159) is similar but slightly shorter. Plant in full sun or light shade. Can take dry periods but blooms best with regular water. Snap off individual seed heads to prolong bloom. Divide large clumps in fall or winter. **Hardy to Zone 8.** Pages: 70, 84, 87, 125.

Dodonaea viscosa 'Purpurea'

PURPLE HOP BUSH. A tough evergreen shrub valuable for its ability to withstand difficult conditions, including poor soil, heat, wind, and drought. Narrow leaves are bronzy green, picking up a stronger purplish tone in winter. Flowers are inconspicuous, but seedpods are interesting late in summer. Grows 10 to 15 ft. tall, about 8 ft. wide. Ideal hedge or screen. Prune as necessary to maintain size. Best foliage color when planted in full sun. **Hardy to Zone 8.** Page: 144.

Echinacea purpurea

PURPLE CONEFLOWER. A summer-blooming perennial that attracts bees and butterflies. Large daisylike blossoms with large center "cones" are held high on stiff branching stalks above a basal mound of dark green foliage. Grows about 3 ft. tall and 2 ft. wide. Normally this plant has pink-purple flowers, but there are a few cultivars with white flowers. 'White Swan' (p. 45) grows 18 in tall and wide with white blooms. 'Bright Star' has burgundy flower heads and grows about 30 in. tall. 'Magnus' (pp. 109, 129, 131) bears large purple flowers with orange cones. Plants need full sun. **Hardy to Zone 3.** Page: 125.

Echinocactus grusonii

GOLDEN BARREL CACTUS. Popular in southwestern gardens, this barrel-shaped cactus grows slowly to

Dicentra D. 'Luxuriant'
BLEEDING HEART

Dodonaea viscosa 'Purpurea'
PURPLE HOP BUSH

about 4 ft. tall and half as wide. Its pale green body sports neat rows of showy yellow thorns 3 in. long. In summer, small yellow flowers bloom in a circle near the top of the dome. Offshoots at the base eventually form clumps of new plants. This cactus needs well-drained soil, partial shade in the hottest areas, protection from hard frosts, and occasional water in summer. **Hardy to Zone 9.** Page: 163.

Enkianthus campanulatus

RED-VEIN ENKIANTHUS. This deciduous shrub bears clusters of reddish pink flowers with creamy streaks that hang bell-like beneath the leaves in late spring. Foliage turns a brilliant orange-red in the fall. Plant in partial shade. Likes well-drained soil amended with compost and then mulched. Grows up to 8 ft. in 10 years. **Hardy to Zone 5.** Not adapted to desert areas. Page: 106.

Epimedium

BARRENWORT, BISHOP'S HAT. A long-lived perennial with heart-shaped foliage. Excellent ground cover under trees or shrubs. Leaves change from coppery to green to maroon over the course of the summer. Small flowers bloom in spring on thin stems above the foliage in red, pink, yellow, or white. A number of species and cultivars are known by the common name "barrenwort" (pp. 74, 75). *E. x per-ralchicum* 'Fröhnleiten' has long spiny leaflets and 1-in. yellow flowers. *E. pinnatum* 'Colchicum' (p. 55) is a shorter plant with less-spiny leaflets and yellow flowers. *E. x rubrum* 'Sulphureum' (pp. 106, 107) blooms dark yellow above many-leafleted compound leaves. All epimediums need partial or full shade. Provide regular water to get them started. Shear off all foliage to the ground in early spring to encourage a good show of flowers and new foliage. **Generally hardy to at least Zone 5.** Not adapted to the hot, dry southwest.

Erigeron karvinskianus

SANTA BARBARA DAISY. Attractive, sprawling perennial well suited for low-water-use gardens and as a ground cover. Bears smallwhite to pinkish daisy-like flowers from late spring to fall. Pink buds are pretty, too. Grows 1 to 2 ft. high, spreading 2 to 3 ft. or more. Plant in full sun and well-drained soil. Naturalizes easily but can spread into unwanted areas if given too much water. Shear off faded flowers. **Hardy to Zone 9.** Pages: 59, 90, 159.

Enkianthus campanulatus
RED-VEIN ENKIANTHUS

Epimedium E. x rubrum 'Sulphureum'
BARRENWORT

Erigeron karvinskianus
SANTA BARBARA DAISY

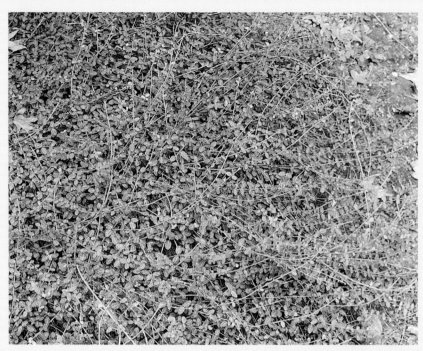

Euonymus E. japonicus 'Microphyllus' Euonymus

Euonymus E. kiautschovicus 'Manhattan' Euonymus

Escallonia rubra 'Newport Dwarf'

'Newport Dwarf' escallonia. A compact evergreen shrub densely clothed in shiny dark green leaves edged in red. In summer, small upright clusters of red flowers bloom at the ends of the branches. Prefers hot sun and well-drained soil. In cold winters it may freeze to the ground but will usually resprout from the base. Needs very little pruning. Grows about 2 to 3 ft. tall. **Hardy to Zone 8.** Not adapted to desert areas. Page: 72.

Eucalyptus microtheca

COOLIBAH. Evergreen tree, typically 20 to 30 ft. tall by 15 to 20 ft. wide but can get bigger. Upright with long narrow, blue-green leaves. Flowers not showy. Tolerates wind and desert conditions. Plant in full sun. Needs little water. **Hardy to Zone 8.** Page 174.

Euonymus

EUONYMUS. A large group of evergreen and deciduous shrubs and vines. *E. fortunei* is a versatile small shrub or ground cover with glossy evergreen leaves. There are many fine cultivars. 'Coloratus' (p. 62), the purple wintercreeper, grows 1 to 2 ft. tall and spreads 5 to 6 ft. wide. Its leaves turn purplish red in winter. 'Silver Queen' (p. 55) is similar size and bears white-edged bright green leaves that also turn pinkish in winter. *E. kiautschovicus* 'Man-

hattan' (p. 118) is an evergreen shrub with thick, glossy, rounded medium green leaves and small but showy pink-and-orange fruits that ripen in the fall. It grows naturally as an upright shrub, reaching about 5 ft. tall and wide, but it can be sheared, pruned, or trained as you choose. *E. japonicus* 'Microphyllus', the boxleaf euonymus (pp. 43, 127), is a tough, dependable evergreen shrub with a compact habit and small shiny leaves. Has a refined look as a clipped hedge or planted closely as a ground cover. Grows 1 to 2 ft. tall and roughly a foot wide. Euonymus adapt to sun or shade and need well-drained soil. Best with regular water. **Generally hardy to at least Zone 6,** but its usefulness in mild winter climates is often limited due to insects and disease, especially scale and powdery mildew.

Euphorbia hybrids

EUPHORBIA. These evergreen shrubs come in a wide variety of sizes, shapes, and colors; some have the appearance of thorny palm trees; others are bushy and thornless. Greatly admired for their oversized blossoms. Crown of thorns (*E. milii*) is a compact shrub growing 18 in. tall and wide. Evergreen leaves cluster at ends of thorny stems and are topped with bright red flower bracts all year. Carefree. **Hardy to Zone 9.** Page: 153.

Euryops pectinatus

EURYOPS. Reliable spring-flowering perennial with an open, mounded habit and finely cut gray-green leaves. Heavy, long-lasting bloom of yellow, daisy-like flowers mainly from late winter into summer, but one and off all year in many areas. Plant in full sun. Needs occasional water and well drained soil. Cut back in summer after main bloom to maintain compact habit. **Hardy to Zone 9.** Page 32.

Fatsia japonica

FATSIA. This bold evergreen shrub grows around 4 ft. tall and wide and prefers shade to prevent leaf burn. It sports large shiny tropical-looking leaves all year and small rounded clusters of white flowers in early spring; the flowers become black berries. Fatsia requires well-drained soil and regular watering. It has no common pest problems. It may get leaf burn during severe winters. **Hardy to Zone 8.** Not adapted to desert areas. Pages: 66,139.

Felicia amelloides

BLUE MARGUERITE. Dependable perennial covered with small blue daisylike flowers for a long season, usually starting in late winter and spring. Some bloom year-round in warm-winter areas. Grows about 18 in. tall and 3 to 4 ft. wide. Plant in full sun and water regularly. Often grown as an annual. Great in pots. Remove spent flowers to promote more bloom. Cut back by half in late summer. Page: 113. **Hardy to Zone 9.** Grown as an annual anywhere.

Ferns

Ferns provide distinctive, lush foliage for shady sites. Despite the delicate appearance of their lacy leaves, they are among the most durable and trouble-free plants you can grow. Most perform best in soil that has been amended with extra organic matter and is kept moist. However, some ferns adapt to dry conditions. Divide them every few years if you want more plants, or leave them alone for years. See the box on page 212 for specific ferns.

Fatsia japonica
FATSIA

Felicia amelloides
BLUE MARGUERITE

Recommended ferns

Asplenium bulbiferum, **Mother fern**
Delicate fern with lacy, light green fronds up to 4 ft. tall. Small plantlets on fronds can be planted. Likes water and shade. Where temperatures regularly drop below 26°F, use sword fern (see below). **Hardy to Zone 10.** Not adapted to desert areas. Pages: 132, 142.

Athyrium nipponicum **'Pictum,' Japanese painted fern**
A colorful fern that forms rosettes of finely cut fronds marked in shades of green, silver and maroon. They look almost iridescent. Deciduous, but can be evergreen when planted in spots where conditions are mild in winter. Grows about 1 ft. tall, 2 ft. wide. **Hardy to Zone 5.** Not adapted to desert areas. Page: 107.

Cyrtomium falcatum, **Holly fern.**
A showy evergreen fern with fronds divided into large glossy hollylike leaflets. It forms dense clumps about 2 ft. tall and wide. In more northern areas mulch well during cold winters. **Hardy to Zone 8.** Not adapted to desert areas. Pages: 21, 66, 93, 139.

Dicksonia antarctica, **Tasmanian tree fern**
Spectacular, almost prehistoric-looking fern with arching, 3- to 6-ft.-long fronds emerging from a thick, fuzzy trunk. Grows slowly but can eventually reach 15 ft. tall. Keep moist. Can take some sun near the coast, otherwise plant in shade. **Hardy to Zone 9.** Not adapted to desert areas. Page: 18.

Dryopteris x *complexa* **'Robust' male fern**
A thick, lush evergreen fern growing over 3 ft. tall. Divided fronds with slightly arched tips give it a lacy look. Once established it can take some drought. **Hardy to Zone 6.** Best adapted to Northern California and the Pacific Northwest. Page: 55.

Dryopteris filix-mas **'Barnesii', Barnes' narrow male fern**
A narrowly upright semievergreen fern with slightly ruffled pinnules (small leaflets). Can reach over 3 ft. tall over time. Does best in well-drained soil. **Hardy to Zone 5.** Best adapted to Northern California and the Pacific Northwest. Page: 29.

Polystichum munitum, **Sword fern**
Native fern with shiny, 2- to 4-ft.-long fronds. One of the most dependable ferns for shady areas, but it will also tolerate quite a bit of sun in cool summer areas. Needs little water once established but looks better if watered occasionally. **Hardy to Zone 4.** Not adapted to desert areas. Pages: 68, 132, 146.

Polystichum polyblepharum, **Tassel fern**
An evergreen fern with stiff, glossy, finely divided fronds. Needs moist soil. Forms a clump about 2 ft. tall, 3 to 4 ft. wide. **Hardy to Zone 6.** Not adapted to desert areas. Pages: 75.

Asplenium bulbiferum
MOTHER FERN

Athyrium nipponicum 'Pictum'
JAPANESE PAINTED FERN

Cyrtomium falcatum
HOLLY FERN

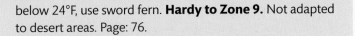

***Polystichum setiferum,* Soft shield fern**

An evergreen fern with soft gray-green to green fronds that can form a dense crown. It grows 2 ft. tall by 2 ft. wide and prefers morning sun. **Hardy to Zone 6.** Not adapted to desert areas. Pages: 31, 106.

***Rumohra adiantiformis,* Leatherleaf fern**

Coarse-textured, finely cut, glossy deep green fronds grow up to 3 ft. long. Best in light or partial shade. Water regularly. (Often sold as Aspidium capense.) Where temperatures drop below 24°F, use sword fern. **Hardy to Zone 9.** Not adapted to desert areas. Page: 76.

***Thelypteris kunthii,* Wood fern**

Without a doubt the toughest, most versatile fern for Texas; it prefers some shade but will also perform fairly well in full sun. The lacy apple-green fronds grow in clumps 2 ft. tall and wide. Like most ferns, this one requires regular watering during the summer to look its best. **Hardy to Zone 6.** Best adapted to Texas. Pages: 119, 139.

Dicksonia antarctica
TASMANIAN TREE FERN

Polystichum munitum
SWORD FERN

Polystichum polyblepharum
TASSEL FERN

Polystichum setiferum
SOFT SHIELD FERN

Rumohra adiantiformis
LEATHERLEAF FERN

Thelypteris kunthii
WOOD FERN

Galium odoratum SWEET WOODRUFF

Gardenia augusta
'August Beauty'
GARDENIA

Fouquieria splendens

OCOTILLO. This distinctive desert shrub forms a wiry clump of upright, gray-green, thorned and furrowed branches. Very showy clusters of tubular orange-red flowers form quickly at branch tips after spring rains and attract hummingbirds. The deciduous gray-green leaves are small and fleshy, and drop during dry spells. Ocotillo can reach 20 to 25 ft. tall. It makes an attractive silhouette in desert gardens or an impenetrable barrier. Grows in full sun and well-drained soil. **Hardy to Zone 8.** Pages: 153, 163.

Fremontodendron 'Ken Taylor'

'KEN TAYLOR' FLANNEL BUSH. A smaller cultivar of a large showy evergreen shrub found in California's dry woodlands and mountain slopes. Golden yellow cup-shaped flowers bloom continuously from spring to fall among dark green, lobed leaves,

leathery above and downy below. Flowers are followed by bristly seedpods. Grows 4 to 6 ft. tall and about twice as wide. Requires full sun and excellent drainage, making it ideal for a hillside location. **Hardy to Zone 8.** Page: 177.

Fuchsia

FUCHSIA. Evergreen and deciduous shrubs in a variety of flower colors, often with different-colored sepals and petals. The petals may be single or double (many ruffled layers). Hummingbirds are attracted to the single-petaled flowers because they can reach the nectar better. Fruits are purple and edible. The fuchsia selected for this book is hardy in the West and may remain evergreen in mild winters. It can also be used as an annual or grown in pots and protected in winter. *F.* 'Maiden's Blush' (p. 110) has small pink flowers covering an upright shrub that grows 3 ft. tall. Fuchsias love partial shade but will do fine in full sun with some summer watering. **Hardy to Zone 9.**

Gaillardia x grandiflora

BLANKETFLOWER. A perennial wildflower with cheerful red-and-yellow flowers all summer long. Forms a clump 2 to 4 ft. tall. 'Goblin' grows about 1 ft. high. 'Goblin Yellow' (p. 175) has yellow flowers. 'Burgundy' (pp. 47, 130) has red blooms. Plants need full sun and well-drained soil but can get by on little water. Remove old flowers as they fade. Divide every year or two in fall or early spring. **Hardy to Zone 3.** Page: 51.

Galium odoratum

SWEET WOODRUFF. A deciduous perennial ground cover that spreads quickly, needs no care, and lasts for decades in the Pacific Northwest. Fine-textured foliage is bright green throughout the growing season and turns beige or tan in late fall. Thousands of tiny white flowers sparkle above the fresh new foliage in spring. Adapts to most soils, prefers partial or full shade. Water regularly in dry summer areas. Shear or mow close to the ground in early spring and rake away the old foliage. Grows about 6 in. tall, spreads indefinitely. **Hardy to Zone 5.** Not adapted to hot, dry areas of the southwest. Pages: 106, 107.

Gardenia augusta

GARDENIA. An evergreen shrub with intensely fragrant white flowers in summer. 'August Beauty'

(p. 68) is a popular cultivar with double flowers up to 4 in. wide and an upright or rounded habit, reaching 5 ft. or taller and 3 to 5 ft. wide. 'Veitchii' (pp. 26, 41) is 3 to 4 ft. tall and wide and blooms in summer or from late spring through fall where winters are mild. 'Daisy' (p. 21) is a hardy selection that grows 2 to 3 ft. high and bears single white flowers. All need full or partial sun, acid soil, and regular water. They bloom best in warmer areas. Great in pots. Feed with acid-type fertilizer and apply iron to improve yellowed foliage. Prune in winter to control size and shape. **Hardy to at least Zone 9.** Sometimes listed as *G. jasminoides.* Page: 171.

Gaura lindheimeri

GAURA. A perennial wildflower that forms a loose clump of graceful arching stems and bears pale pink-and-white flowers from spring through fall. Gaura normally reaches about 3 ft. tall and wide. 'Whirling Butterflies' (pp. 94, 95) is slightly more compact. 'Dauphin' (pp. 60, 63) is more upright. Needs full sun, well-drained soil, and just a little water. Too much shade or moisture makes the stems floppy. Cut to the ground in winter. **Hardy to Zone 6.** Pages: 112, 141.

Gazania 'Burgundy'

'BURGUNDY' GAZANIA. Clumping evergreen perennial with showy daisylike flowers. 'Burgundy', with wine-colored flowers, is just one of many varieties that bloom in festive shades of yellow, orange, red and purple. They make excellent small-scale ground covers. Upright blooms reaching 6 to 10 in. high appear mostly in spring and early summer. Can bloom year-round in mild-winter areas. Dark green leaves have hairy, gray-green undersides. Tough plants that adapt to most soils but look best with occasional water in summer. Plant in full sun. Divide every three to four years. **Hardy to Zone 8.** Page: 113.

Geijera parviflora

AUSTRALIAN WILLOW. Fine-textured, open evergreen tree with dangling narrow green leaves; looks very much willowlike. Can reach 25 to 30 ft. tall and nearly as wide. Tough tree with few problems. Good shade tree. Best in full sun, it can get by with little water. **Hardy to Zone 9.** Page: 172.

Gelsemium sempervirens

CAROLINA JASMINE. An evergreen vine beloved for its showy display of bell-shaped fragrant yellow flowers in late winter to early spring. The neat small leaves are dark green all summer and turn maroon in winter. Can climb trees but is usually trained against a fence, trellis or post and pruned annually (right after it blooms) to keep it under 10 ft. tall. Can also be used as a ground cover; prune annually to keep it within bounds and about 3 ft. tall. Needs full or partial sun. Looks best with regular water. **Hardy to Zone 7.** Pages: 49, 66, 78, 98, 99, 158, 180.

Gardenia augusta
'Daisy'
GARDENIA

Gaura lindheimeri
GAURA

Gaura lindheimeri 'Dauphin'
GAURA

Gaura lindheimeri 'Whirling Butterflies'
GAURA

Genista pilosa 'Vancouver Gold'
SILKY LEAF WOADWAXEN

Geranium 'Johnson's Blue'
CRANESBILL GERANIUM

Geranium x *riversleaianum* 'Mavis Simpson'
CRANESBILL GERANIUM

Genista pilosa 'Vancouver Gold'

'VANCOUVER GOLD' SILKY LEAF WOADWAXEN. A low deciduous ground cover that forms a mat of green twiggy stems with tiny dark green leaves. In late spring and early summer, a profusion of bright yellow pealike flowers cover the entire mass. Likes full sun and tolerates drought once established. Needs very little care. Lydia broom (*G. lydia*, p. 129) is similar but almost leafless. **Both are hardy to Zone 5,** but 'Vancouver Gold' is better adapted to mild winter and desert areas. Page: 53.

Geranium

GERANIUM, CRANESBILL. Unlike the common geraniums that are grown as bedding plants and in pots, these are hardy perennials that form a compact or sprawling mound of attractive leaves with jagged edges. They bloom in spring or early summer and sporadically until fall with clusters of flowers in various shades of pink, purple, blue-purple, and white. *G. sanguineum* var. *striatum*, bloody cranesbill (pp. 19, 129, 150), forms a low mound or mat of small, very finely cut leaves, topped with pale pink flowers in spring and early summer. Can spread several feet wide. **Hardy to Zone 3.** Not adapted to desert climates. *G.* 'Johnson's Blue' (p. 72), popular and dependable, forms a large sprawling mound, about 1 ft. tall and 2 ft. wide, with medium-size leaves and blue-purple flowers from late spring to fall. **Hardy to Zone 4.** Not adapted to desert climates. *G. macrorrhizum*, bigroot geranium (p. 55) is a short, compact plant that forms bushy clumps of fragrant, light green semievergreen foliage, with magenta or pink flowers in late spring. Makes a good ground cover for partial shade and dry soil. Grows up to 1 ft. tall, 18 to 24 in. wide. **Hardy to Zone 4.** Not adapted to desert climates. *G.* x *riversleaianum* 'Mavis Simpson' (p. 109) is a sprawling plant with gray-green leaves and light pink flowers in summer. **Hardy to Zone 6.** Not adapted to desert climates.

Plant geraniums in full sun or partial shade and well-drained soil. Cut off flower stalks when the blossoms fade. If plants look tattered or get floppy in midsummer, cut them back partway and they will bush out again. Otherwise wait until late fall or early spring and cut them to the ground.

Hamelia patens

FIREBUSH. This colorful tropical shrub is often grown as a tender perennial, usually reaching around 3 to

4 ft. tall and wide. In milder areas it can grow even larger. Firebush bears red-orange trumpet-shaped flowers from summer to frost against red-tinged leaves that turn maroon as cool temperatures set in. Hummingbirds adore this plant. Extremely heat and drought tolerant. Cut to the ground after the first frost. In cold winter areas, mulch the crown heavily or consider growing it as a wonderful summer annual. **Hardy to Zone 10.** Pages: 80, 92, 180.

Hardenbergia violacea 'Happy Wanderer'

'HAPPY WANDERER' HARDENBERGIA. A useful evergreen that can be grown as a vine or a shrub. It produces clusters of pretty pinkish purple flowers in late winter and early spring. Grown as a vine, it will twine around a trellis or up a fence, reaching about 10 ft. high. As a shrubby ground cover, it forms a mound 1 to 2 ft. high and spreads about 10 ft. wide. Plant in full sun or, in hot climates, partial shade. Needs well-drained soil and occasional water (but don't overdo it). Prune to keep within bounds. **Hardy to Zone 9.** Pages: 51, 132, 135, 144

Helianthemum nummularium

SUNROSE. Cheerful flowering evergreen shrublets with small bright-colored spring flowers in shades of white, yellow, orange, pink, and red. Grows 6 to 8 in. high, 2 to 3 ft. wide. Plant in full sun and well-drained soil. Needs little water. Good on dry banks. Cut back after bloom. **Hardy to Zone 6.** Not adapted to desert areas. Page: 113.

Helleborus

HELLEBORE. A clump-forming evergreen perennial with dark leathery leaves and round flowers that bloom for many weeks in late winter and early spring. Christmas rose (*H. niger*, p. 75) has white flowers 3 to 4 in. wide that open some years as early as Christmas. Lenten rose (*H. orientalis*, pp. 31, 68, 75, 79, 105, 111, 132) has pink, purple, white, or greenish flowers 2 to 3 in. wide in early spring. All need partial shade and rich, well-drained soil. Hellebores are slow-growing, but they self-sow, gradually spreading to form a patch. Once established, all are carefree and long-lived. Groom once a year by cutting off any dead leaves when the flower buds appear. Established clumps are typically about 18 in. tall, 18 to 24 in. wide. **Hardiness and adaptation varies.** Generally widely adapted except to desert areas.

Hamelia patens
FIREBUSH

Hardenbergia violacea
'Happy Wanderer'
HARDENBERGIA

Helianthemum nummularium
SUNROSE

Helleborus H. niger
CHRISTMAS ROSE

Hemerocallis
'Lavender Bonanza'
DAYLILY

Hemerocallis
'Stella d'Oro'
DAYLILY

Heteromeles arbutifolia
TOYON

Hemerocallis

DAYLILY. Among the most popular of perennials, daylilies display large lilylike flowers above dense clumps of narrow arching leaves. Almost all daylilies today are hybrids sold as named cultivars. There are many thousands to choose from. Some are evergreen; others die back in winter. Some are low growing, while others have flower stalks reaching 3 ft. tall. Flowers last only a day but are replaced daily. They come in many shades of white, yellow, orange, red and purple, and bloom from a few weeks to several months. Mix early-blooming, midseason, and late-blooming varieties to ensure months of color. 'Stella d'Oro' has golden yellow flowers (pp. 101, 125, 179, 181) on compact plants 1½ ft. tall and wide. 'Black-Eyed Stella' has gold flowers with a dark reddish eye and grows 1½ ft. tall and wide. Both Stellas bloom for months. 'Texas Sunlight' has larger gold flowers and grows 2 ft. tall and wide. 'Russian Rhapsody' (p. 169) has large purple flowers. All daylilies prefer full sun and well-drained soil. Water regularly during bloom. Pinch off spent flowers and then cut off flower stalks after blooming is finished. Divide in fall or late winter if you wish to propagate more plants. When planting, space shorter daylilies about 1 ft. apart and taller kinds 2 ft. apart. They will gradually fill in. Daylilies can occasionally be plagued with aphids in the spring and rust disease during humid summers. **Hardy to Zone 3.** Pages: 22, 34, 35, 41, 51, 90, 173.

Hesperaloe parviflora

RED YUCCA. This native southwestern shrub grows in clumps of spiky gray-green succulent foliage. Attractive coral pink trumpet flowers line graceful 3-ft. stalks from late spring to frost. Very heat and drought tolerant, red yucca is adapted to any well-drained soil in full sun. Generally requires no supplemental watering and attracts very few pests. **Hardy to Zone 6.** Not well adapted to cool coastal areas of the Pacific Northwest. Pages: 92, 98, 123.

Heteromeles arbutifolia

TOYON. A dependable California native evergreen shrub with shiny dark green leaves, clusters of white flowers in early summer, and bright red berries in fall and winter. Birds love the berries. Withstands dry periods but looks best with occasional water. Usually grown as a dense shrub 6 to 12 ft. tall but can also be trained as a multi- or single-trunked tree to almost twice that height. **Hardy to Zone 7.** Not adapted to desert areas. Page: 146.

Heuchera

ALUMROOT, CORALBELLS, HEUCHERA. Perennials that form low clumps of almost evergreen foliage and bloom spring into summer, bearing clouds of tiny red, coral, pink, or white flowers on slender stalks about 18 in. tall. Their handsome, lobed leaves make them fine accent plants or small-scale ground covers. Often sold as *H. x brizoides* or *H. sanguinea*; there are a number of other species and a variety of hybrids. 'Palace Purple' (pp. 132, 141, 146) has large purplish brown leaves and tiny white flowers. 'Velvet Night' (p. 107) has deep purple leaves and brownish green flowers in spring. 'Chocolate Ruffles' (p. 150) has large purplish brown, ruffled leaves. 'Wendy' (p. 146) has bright pink flowers. Island alumroot (*H. maxima*, p. 142), has hairy leaves and white-to-pink flowers. It is best adapted to coastal areas of California. All heucheras prefer full to partial sun, well-drained soil, and some summer water. Remove flower stalks as the blossoms fade. Divide every few years, replanting the divisions an inch or two deeper than before. **Generally hardy to at least Zone 4.** Not adapted to desert areas. Pages: 26, 89, 179.

Heuchera maxima
ISLAND ALUMROOT

Heuchera sanguinea
HEUCHERA

Heuchera 'Wendy'
HEUCHERA

Hibiscus coccineus

TEXAS STAR HIBISCUS. A tall striking perennial that bears large brilliant red star-shaped flowers above leafy stalks from early summer to frost. Foliage is medium green and deeply lobed. Plant can reach 6 ft. tall and 4 ft. wide with the right conditions. Prefers full sun and regular watering. Cut back after bloom cycle to promote bushy plants. It has no common insect or disease problems. **Hardy to Zone 6.** Not adapted to desert areas. Pages: 80, 92, 117.

Hibiscus syriacus

ALTHEA. Also known as rose of Sharon, this is a showy deciduous shrub when in full summer-to-fall bloom. Flowers may be white, pink, or lavender and single or double. Medium-size leaves are dull green and slightly lobed. Altheas grow 6 to 8 ft. tall and 3 to 4 ft. wide. They need full sun and well-drained soil. They have few pest problems but are subject to cotton root rot in alkaline areas. Prune in early spring to give desired shape and size. **Hardy to Zone 5.** Pages: 22, 149.

Hosta

HOSTA. A long-lived carefree shade-tolerant perennial with beautiful leaves in a wide variety of colors and sizes. Plants form dome-shaped clumps or spreading patches of foliage that look good from spring to fall and die down in winter. Lavender, purple or white flowers bloom on slender stalks in mid to late summer. There are many species and hybrids. 'Krossa Regal' (p. 106) has medium-size powdery blue-green leaves and forms vase-shaped clumps 3 ft. tall, 2 ft. wide, with pale lilac flowers on stalks 5 ft. tall. Variegated hostas make striking accents. 'Green Gold' (p. 111) forms a mound about 2 ft. tall and wide of large dark green leaves with yellow borders fading to cream and

Hibiscus coccineus
TEXAS STAR HIBISCUS

Hosta
'Krossa Regal'
HOSTA

Hydrangea macrophylla
BIGLEAF HYDRANGEA

lavender flowers. *H. undulata* 'Albomarginata' (pp. 150, 151) grows 1 to 2 ft. high by 12 to 18 in. wide with large, heart-shaped green leaves, variegated white and large spikes of pale lilac flowers. Some hostas tolerate full sun, but most grow best in partial or full shade. All need fertile, moist, well-drained soil. Cut off flower stalks before seedpods ripen. Clumps can be divided in late summer or early spring if you want to make more plants; otherwise leave them alone. Talk to nursery staff about which varieties are most resistant to snails and slugs. **Generally hardy to Zone 3.** Not adapted to desert areas. Pages: 26, 31, 68, 105.

Hydrangea macrophylla

BIGLEAF HYDRANGEA. A medium-size deciduous shrub with large round leaves and very showy clusters of papery-textured blue, pink, or white flowers in summer. Grows 6 to 10 ft. tall and equally

Hypericum calycinum
ST. JOHNS WORT

Iberis sempervirens 'Little Gem'
EVERGREEN CANDYTUFT

wide. There are many varieties. 'Tricolor' has light green-and-white leaves. 'Nikko Blue' (pp. 110, 132) is a popular cultivar with blue flowers. It grows only 4 to 6 ft. wide. Hydrangeas are usually grown in partial shade but can be planted in full sun near the coast. Need fertile, moist, well-drained soil. Stalks grow one year, bloom the next year. In fall, cut to the ground stalks that have bloomed. Head back others if you need to control size. Plants may require application of aluminum sulfate to produce blue flowers. **Hardy to Zone 6.** Not adapted to desert areas. Pages: 27, 169.

Hymenoxys acaulis

ANGELITA DAISY. Neat, rounded perennial with dark green leaves and yellow, daisy-like flowers from spring to fall. Grows 12 in. tall and wide. Especially prized in dry-summer, desert areas where it gets by on little water. Plant in full sun. Useful ground cover. **Hardy to Zone 5.** Pages: 98, 99, 175.

Hypericum

ST. JOHNS WORT. Shrubs and perennials with neat leaves and five-petaled flowers ranging from pale yellows to golds. There are hundreds of species, many of them evergreen. Aaron's beard, or creeping St. Johns wort (*H. calycinum*, p. 127) is a tough, creeping ground cover that adapts to poor soils and can help control erosion on slopes. Evergreen where winters are mild. Grows about 1 ft. high and bears yellow flowers in summer. Easily planted from rooted stems. Prune or mow close to the ground every year or two in early winter or spring; it regrows quickly. *H.* 'Sungold' (p. 110) is a semievergreen to deciduous shrub that bears clusters of yellow flowers followed by red fruit red in fall. Grows 3 ft. tall and 4 ft. wide. Both need full sun and well-drained soil and look best with regular water. **Hardy to at least Zone 6.** Pages: 62, 66, 100.

Iberis sempervirens

EVERGREEN CANDYTUFT. A bushy perennial that forms a low or sprawling mound, about 1 ft. tall and 2 to 3 ft. wide, of glossy evergreen foliage. Bears clusters of white flowers for several weeks in March or April. 'Little Gem' (pp. 29, 43) is a compact plant growing 6 to 8 in. tall. Candytuft can be used as a ground cover. Needs full or partial sun and well-drained soil. Shear off the top half of the plants after they bloom. Don't try to divide it; buy new plants instead. **Hardy to Zone 3.** Page: 166.

Ilex

HOLLY. An extremely versatile group of shrubs and trees, hollies are used for foundation plantings, hedges, and specimens. The leaves can be small or large, smooth or spiny, dull or glossy. Holly plants are either male or female. If a male is planted within a few hundred yards, females bear heavy crops of small round berries that ripen in fall and last through the next spring. All tolerate sun and partial shade and almost any well-drained garden soil. Hollies are generally pest free. Prune or shear at any season to keep them at the desired size.

I. cornuta 'Burfordii Nana', the dwarf Burford holly (pp. 37, 39) is a smaller cultivar that grows a 5 ft. tall and 3 ft. wide. It has small leaves and berries. **Hardy to Zone 7.** *I. decidua* (pp. 80, 118), the possumhaw holly, is a small Texas native deciduous tree with lustrous dark green leaves. Berries are very showy after the leaves fall. They can be yellow, orange, or red depending on the cultivar. **Hardy to Zone 5.** *I. decidua* 'Warren's Red' (pp. 37, 39) has small, bright red berries and an upright habit to 15 ft. tall and 6 ft. wide. *I. vomitoria* 'Nana' dwarf yaupon holly (pp. 21, 38, 60, 119) reaches only 3 ft. tall and wide. Its Latin name is derived from an early ritual among some Native Americans, who brewed the stems and leaves into a tea that induced a purgative effect. Dwarf yaupon holly is commonly used as a substitute for boxwood in Texas and the south. **Hardy to Zone 7.**

Iris

IRIS. A large family of popular perennials with elegant flowers in shades of white, blue, lavender, purple, pink, and yellow are borne on stalks 1 to 3 ft. tall. Plant the thick fingerlike rhizomes or bulbs in fall or early spring, in full sun or partial shade. Plant bulbs 3 to 4 inches deep. Most irises need good drainage and regular water during periods of growth. Fertilize in spring. Divide when the clumps become crowded. Most iris are widely adapted but check with your nurseryman to find out if they grow well in your area.

Japanese iris, *I. ensata* (p. 111), forms a clump of dark green, swordlike leaves about 2 ft. tall and produces spectacular 3-to-6-in. flowers on stalks about 3 ft. tall in summer. The broad, ruffled petals have a fragile, velvety texture and come in bright shades of blue, purple, yellow, or white. **Hardy to Zone 3.** Gladwin iris, *I. foetidissima* (p. 55), is a vigorous plant with slender shiny leaves and clusters of purple flowers in summer. Large green seedpods split open to reveal bright orange-red seeds that last for months. Grows 2 ft. tall. **Hardy to Zone 4.** Bearded iris, *I.* x *germanica* (pp. 79, 183) is one of the most popular iris, blooming in early spring, with large elegant flowers in shades of blue, lavender, pink, yellow, or white, on stalks 2 ft. tall. Bury the roots, but expose the rhizome on the soil surface. If you live close to the coast, plant heirloom and species types; they perform better because

Ilex decidua 'Warren's Red'
HOLLY

Ilex vomitoria 'Nana'
DWARF YAUPON HOLLY

Iris ensata
JAPANESE IRIS

Iris foetidissma
GLADWIN IRIS

they are less likely to suffer root rot. **Hardy to Zone 6.** Hybrid Louisiana iris, *I.* x *Louisiana* (pp. 66, 101, 117, 118), forms clumps 2 ft. tall and 3 ft. wide and bears large, delicate flowers rise on 3-ft. stalks in almost every color of the rainbow. Tolerates wet soil or a well-drained soil with winter and spring moisture. **Hardy to Zone 5.** Siberian iris, *I. sibirica* (p. 114) grows 2 to 3 ft. tall and bears elegant flowers in shades of white, blue, lavender, purple, and pink. **Hardy to Zone 3.**

Ixora 'Thai Dwarf'

'THAI DWARF' IXORA. Ixoras are frost-tender evergreen shrubs grown for their showy clusters of brightly colored and highly perfumed flowers atop lustrous rounded leaves. Cultivars come in many sizes. 'Thai Dwarf' reaches 4 ft. tall and wide and bears multicolored flower clusters in shades of red, orange, gold, pink, and yellow. Ixoras require full sun, acid soil, and regular watering. They respond well to pruning but don't require it. **Hardy to Zone 10.** Pages: 155, 161.

Jasminum sambac

ARABIAN JASMINE. This tropical evergreen vining shrub bears deep green, glossy leaves and produces intensely fragrant small white flowers in summer. Grown as a vine, Arabian jasmine will reach 10 ft. tall and at least as wide if tied to a trellis for support. Grows well in full sun. Water regularly. Does best where winters are mild. **Hardy to Zone 10.** Pages: 155, 161.

Juniperus

JUNIPER. These needle-leafed evergreens are tough, hardy shrubs for exposed sites. 'Blue Pacific' shore juniper (*J. conferta* 'Blue Pacific', p. 101) stays around 1 ft. tall and spreads 5 to 6 ft. wide. Dwarf Japanese garden juniper (*J. procumbens* 'Nana', p. 103) grows 1 to 2 ft. high, spreads 5 to 6 ft. wide, and has blue-green foliage. Junipers prefer full sun and excellent drainage. Limit pruning to maintain a natural shape and to avoid brown-tipped foliage. Most are widely adapted throughout the West.

Juniperus conferta 'Blue Pacific'
JUNIPER

Lagerstroemia 'Zuni'
CRAPE MYRTLE

Lagerstromia x *fauriei* 'Tonto'
CRAPE MYRTLE

Koelreuteria paniculata

GOLDEN RAINTREE. Round-topped deciduous tree with fine-textured, divided, green leaves, which often turn bright yellow in fall. Eye-catching clusters of yellow flowers in midsummer are followed by unusual seed pods that last into autumn. Grows 20 to 30 ft. tall and equally as wide. Good patio or lawn tree. Takes drought once established. Plant in full sun. **Hardy to Zone 6.** Pages: 47, 166.

Lagerstroemia

CRAPE MYRTLE. A deciduous small tree or large shrub, often grown with multiple trunks. Blooms for many weeks in the heat of summer, with large clusters of papery textured pink, rose, or white flowers at the end of each stem. Leaves typically turn red, orange, or purplish in fall. Flaking bark is attractive in winter. Many varieties to choose from, the best being the mildew-resistant members of the Indian Tribe Series (*L. indica*). They include 'Cherokee', with red flowers; 'Seminole', with pink blooms; and 'Catawba' (pp. 158, 172), with purple flowers. 'Zuni' (p. 16) is a hybrid variety reaching 10 ft. tall that bears large, dark lavender blooms. *L.* x *fauriei* 'Tonto' (pp. 136, 138) is a semi dwarf hybrid that stays less than 10 ft. tall and 5 ft. wide and has watermelon pink flowers. *L.* x *fauriei* 'Natchez' (pp. 38, 39) is a vigorous tree-type cultivar that reaches 25 ft. tall and 15 ft. wide. It has fragrant white flowers, attractive bark and is resistant to powdery mildew. All crape myrtles need full sun, well-drained soil, and only occasional water. Prune in winter, removing weak, broken, and crowded shoots. We discourage the common practice of topping crape myrtles because it ruins their naturally beautiful shape, scars their trunks, causes them to flop over when blooming, and leads to basal suckering. **Hardy to Zone 7.** Pages: 32, 41.

Lamium maculatum

LAMIUM. A creeping perennial that makes an excellent ground cover for shady areas. Can also be used as an annual. Gray-green heart-shaped leaves are marked with silver and topped with clusters of pink flowers in early summer. Plants form low mats less than 6 in. high and spreading 2 ft. or wider. Foliage is evergreen in mild-winter areas. 'White Nancy' has white flowers and silvery leaves edged with green. 'Roseum' is similar but has pink flowers continuously all year. Lamiums grow best in shade but can take more sun in coastal areas. Water regularly. Cut back halfway with hedge shears after bloom and again in late summer if plants look shabby. Divide every few years in spring or fall. **Hardy to Zone 4.** Page: 68.

Lampranthus spectabilis

TRAILING ICE PLANT. Trailing succulent plant with pointed, silver green leaves. Covers itself in late winter to spring with brilliant, 2-in.-wide flowers in glowing shades of pink, red, or purple. Grows up to 1 ft. tall and spreads up to 2 ft. Makes a tough ground cover. Plant in full sun. Needs little water. **Hardy to Zone 8.** Page 159.

Lantana

LANTANA. A colorful, spreading, evergreen shrub widely grown as a ground cover. Can also be used as an annual. Clusters of small flowers top plants in spring, summer, and fall; year-round in mild-winter areas. Varieties available in many colors. Loved by butterflies. *L. montevidensis* (pp. 24, 153) bears small lavender flowers. 'Confetti' (p. 22) has multicolored flowers of yellow, pink, and purple. Generally about 2 to 4 ft. tall but can be taller. Spreads 3 to 6 ft. 'New Gold' (pp. 80, 98, 157, 175) is the most popular of all spreading lantanas, with golden yellow flowers on 3 to 4 ft. wide mounds. Others appearing in our designs include: 'Radiation' (orange and yellow, pp. 117, 180), 'Lemon Drop' (creamy yellow, p. 93), 'Dallas Red' (orange-red, p. 92), 'Trailing Lavender' (lavender-purple, pp. 95, 121, 122) and 'Weeping White' (pure white, pp. 62, 63). Lantanas are excellent ground covers for slopes or poor soils. Will spill over walls. Plant in full sun; mildews otherwise. Needs little water. Shear after bloom to keep compact and to encourage more flowers. **Hardy to Zone 9.** Page: 163

Laurus nobilis 'Saratoga'

'SARATOGA' SWEET BAY. Dense, roundheaded, evergreen tree with deep green leaves. Usually grows 12 to 20 ft. high and wide. Fragrant yellow flowers in spring followed by small black fruit. Looks great in containers. Can be sheared into formal shapes. Plant in full sun and well drained soil. Requires minimal watering. This variety resists psyllids, a common insect problem in some parts of the West. **Hardy to Zone 8.** Pages: 24, 166.

Lamium maculatum 'Roseum'
LAMIUM

Lamium maculatum 'White Nancy'
LAMIUM

Lagerstroemia 'Natchez'
CRAPE MYRTLE

Lantana camara 'Confetti'
LANTANA

Lavandula angustifolia 'Hidcote'
LAVENDER

Lavandula stoechas
'Otto Quast'
LAVENDER

Lavandula

LAVENDER. Choice evergreen shrubs ideal for dry-summer climates. They form bushy mounds of fragrant gray-green foliage topped in early summer with countless long-stalked spikes of very fragrant flowers. English lavender, *L. angustifolia*, generally grows 3 to 4 ft. tall, with 1-to-2-ft. flower spikes. 'Munstead' (pp. 43, 45, 59, 76, 97, 157, 158) reaches about 18 in. and has pale lavender flowers. 'Hidcote' (pp. 72, 135) grows about 1 ft. tall and wide, with gray foliage and rich purple flowers. 'Mitchum Gray' (p. 47) is similar. *L.* 'Goodwin Creek Gray' (pp. 49, 89, 135) has gray foliage and deep blue blooms from early summer into fall, or longer where summers are mild. Grows 2 to 3 ft. tall and wide. 'Otto Quast' (pp. 16, 59), a cultivar of Spanish lavender (*L. stoechas*), has showy, tufted, dark lavender flowers on a 1-to-3-ft. plant. *L. x intermedia* 'Provence' (pp. 72, 74) grows 12 to 18 in. and has very deep purple flowers. All lavenders need full sun, well-drained soil, and little water. Shear flower stalks to foliage height when the petals fade. **Lavenders vary in hardiness with English lavender being the hardiest (Zone 5). Most others are hardy to Zone 7 or 8.**

Leucanthemum x superbum 'Alaska'

SHASTA DAISY. Bright green perennial with tall, white, daisy-like flowers from late spring into summer. Grows 18 to 24 in tall and wide. Best in full sun but can take some shade. Water regularly. Great cut flower. Divide in fall or early spring. Often sold as *Chrysanthemum maximum*. **Hardy to Zone 5.** Page: 149.

Leucophyllum

TEXAS SAGE. The cultivar *L frutescens* 'Compacta' (pp. 64, 95, 102) is a dwarf version of the striking, evergreen, silver-leaved, drought-tolerant Texas native shrub. It has a dense, slightly irregular shape and reaches 3 to 4 ft. tall and wide. Following summer rains, it becomes flushed with orchid pink flowers. Texas sage demands full sun and excellent drainage and requires little, if any, supplemental watering. Expect few if any insect or disease problems. 'Rio Bravo' sage (*L. langmaniae* 'Rio Bravo', pp. 99, 175) is similar but has compact, dark green foliage, lavender flowers, and grows 5 ft. tall and wide. **Both sages are hardy to Zone 8.**

Ligustrum japonicum

JAPANESE PRIVET. A fast-growing evergreen shrub or small tree with very glossy bright green leaves, clusters of heavy-scented white flowers in early summer, and dark blue-black berries in fall and winter. Usually grown as a hedge or screen. Grows 10 to 12 ft. tall but can be clipped lower. 'Texanum', also called wax leaf privet (p. 41) is similar but slightly smaller and often confused with the species. Needs full or partial sun and occasional water. Grows in almost any soil. Prune in spring and summer. **Hardy to Zone 7.** Pages: 41, 87, 165.

Liriope muscari

LILYTURF. This perennial ground cover forms dense tufts of dark green grasslike leaves that stay green throughout the year. Clusters of slender lavender flower spikes bloom among the foliage in summer. Lilyturf makes a fine small-scale ground cover near walks and patios, and is frequently used as an edging around borders. 'Big Blue' (pp. 101, 115, 132, 136, 143) has larger flowers and foliage than the species and grows about 1 ft. tall and wide. 'Majestic' (p. 113) is similar but bears purple flowers. 'Evergreen Giant' (pp. 122, 123) is the largest cultivar. It grows 2 ft. tall and wide and is often used as a specimen clump. Variegated lilyturf 'Variegata', (p. 39) has attractive striped foliage in creamy white and green and normally grows 1 ft. tall and wide. 'Silvery Sunproof' is very similar to 'Variegata,' and may be the same plant. 'Silver Dragon' (p. 19) has lilac flowers and leaves edged with narrow yellow stripes that fade to creamy white. Lilyturf prefers partial shade in hot summer areas, can take more sun near the coast. It has few pest problems, and requires water in dry summers areas. Mow or shear off old foliage in early spring. Can be invasive. **Hardy to Zone 6.** Not adapted to desert areas. Pages: 166, 167.

Lonicera japonica 'Halliana'

HALL'S JAPANESE HONEYSUCKLE. A fast-growing semi-evergreen to deciduous vine with dull green leaves. Blooms for months from late spring with sweet-smelling white flowers changing to yellow. Plant in full sun to partial shade. Prune heavily each year right after flowering to reduce buildup of old wood. Can be invasive and spread over 30 feet. **Hardy to Zone 4.** Pages: 53, 55.

Lonicera sempervirens

CORAL HONEYSUCKLE. This evergreen vine twines around any support, climbing 10 to 15 ft. or higher. The smooth, oval blue-green leaves are arranged in neat pairs on the stems. Blooms heavily in early summer and continues off and on until fall. The slender, tubular red-orange flowers are scentless but attractive to hummingbirds. Songbirds eat the bright red berries that follow the flowers. Grows in shade but blooms best when planted in full or partial sun. Prune in winter if at all, thinning out some of the older stems. Unlike Japanese honeysuckle (*L. japonica*), this species is not aggressive or invasive. **Hardy to Zone 4.** Pages: 80, 119, 180.

Loropetalum chinense rubrum

CHINESE FRINGE FLOWER. This is a popular large evergreen shrub or small tree for a woodland garden or shrub border. It bears lovely, bright pink, fringe-like flowers among layers of small purple-tinged leaves. Blossoms occur during the spring and again in the fall. Doesn't do well where soils are extremely alkaline. Prefers partial shade in hottest areas. There are many varieties with compact habits or darker foliage. **Hardy to Zone 8.** Not adapted to desert areas. Page: 66.

Leucophyllum frutescens compactum 'Compacta'
TEXAS SAGE

Liriope muscari 'Silver Dragon'
LILYTURF

Lonicera sempervirens
CORAL HONEYSUCKLE

Magnolia x soulangiana
SAUCER MAGNOLIA

Mahonia aquifolium
OREGON GRAPE

Magnolia x *soulangiana*

SAUCER MAGNOLIA. Deciduous tree with large bold leaves and huge flowers in shades of white, pink, and purple borne on leafless stems. Many varieties to choose from. Often the inside and the outside of the flower differ in color. Grows 15 to 25 ft. tall and spreads as wide, usually with multiple trunks. Saucer magnolias need full sun, well-drained soil, and regular water. Prune in early summer, removing only weak or crossing limbs. **Hardy to Zone 5.** Page: 41.

Mahonia aquifolium

OREGON GRAPE. Spreading evergreen shrub with handsome deeply divided leaves. Showy yellow flower clusters in spring produce blackish blue berries later in the year. Grows about 6 ft. tall and has glossy green leaves that are tinged red when new, purplish in cold winters. 'Compacta' grows only 2 to 3 ft. tall but spreads to form a mid-height ground cover. Mahonias can be grown in sun or shade but usually look their best with some shelter. They grow well among tree roots. Water occasionally. Prune to open the center and expose the stems. **Hardy to Zone 6.** Not well adapted to low elevation desert areas. Pages: 142, 146.

Malvaviscus arboreus drummondii

TURK'S CAP. A tough perennial, Turk's cap performs well in sun or shade, acidic or alkaline soils, and in wet or dry situations. Plants grow a bushy 2 ft. tall and 3 ft. wide in shade but can reach 5 ft. tall in full sun. The fairly coarse-textured foliage is medium green and slightly lobed. Small red Turk's turban flowers keep on coming from summer until frost, attracting a stream of butterflies and hummingbirds, especially in the fall. Turk's cap has few pest problems and requires little water. Shear throughout the growing season to keep tidy and cut to the ground after the first frost. **Hardy to Zone 9.** Not adapted to desert areas. Pages: 37, 80, 93, 117, 121.

Myrica cerifera

WAX MYRTLE. An evergreen shrub that naturally maintains an upright and bushy profile. It can also be pruned into a small tree. The slender twigs are densely covered with glossy leaves that have a delicious spicy aroma. Historically, the leaves were used as a flavorful subtitute for bay leaf. In fall and winter, clusters of small gray berries line the stems of female plants. Wax myrtle needs full or partial sun and tolerates most soil conditions, including fairly wet ones. It has few pest problems. Regular water in dry summer areas. It grows quickly and can reach up to 20 ft. tall if left alone. Prune in winter if you want to keep it small or control its shape. **Hardy to Zone 6.** Not adapted to desert areas. Pages: 62, 82, 100.

Nandina domestica

HEAVENLY BAMBOO, NANDINA. An evergreen shrub that forms a clump of slender, erect stems. Fine-textured compound leaves change color with the seasons, from gold to green to red. Fluffy clusters of white flowers in summer are followed by red berries that last for months. Common nandina (pp. 142, 165) grows 4 to 6 ft. tall, 2 to 3 ft. wide; 'Royal Princess' (p. 169) and 'Compacta' (p. 84) are smaller, growing 3 to 4 ft. tall and 2 to 3 ft. wide. 'Harbour Dwarf' (pp. 49, 118, 119), 'Gulf Stream' (pp. 18, 37, 119, 146), and 'Nana' (pp. 32, 35, 59, 167) are dwarf varieties, reaching 2 to 3 ft. high. 'Moyers Red' (p. 29) grows to 6 ft. tall and 4 ft. wide and has intense red leaves in fall and winter. 'Plum Passion' (p. 109) has purple-plum new growth and winter color. Nandina adapts well to most soils, in sun or shade. Looks best with regular water. Prune stems at ground level. **Hardy to Zone 6.**

Nerium oleander 'Petite Salmon'

'Petite Salmon' oleander. A dwarf variety of a tough evergreen shrub bearing slender leaves and clusters of showy flowers. Grows 3 to 4 ft. tall and wide. Salmon pink flowers bloom from spring to frost. Performs best in full sun and tolerates most soil conditions. Water only when severely dry. In early spring, cut out dead wood and shape into desired form. In northern areas consider replacing it with a more cold-hardy shrub such as althea. **Hardy to Zone 9.** Page: 122.

Nolina recurvata

BOTTLE PALM. A curious-looking small evergreen tree with a large swollen base, one or more tapering trunks, and drooping clusters of bright green, straplike leaves. Bottle palm grows slowly and may eventually reach 12 to 15 ft. high. It needs full sun and well-drained soil. Does best where frosts are light or nonexistent. Page: 161.

Olea europaea 'Swan Hill'

'SWAN HILL' FRUITLESS OLIVE. Wide spreading, open, multi-trunked, evergreen tree with fine-textured gray-green foliage. Grows slowly to 12 to 15 ft. tall

Myrica cerifera
WAX MYRTLE

Nandina domestica
'Plum Passion'
HEAVENLY BAMBOO

and wide; often larger. Bears no fruit or pollen. Plant in full sun. Gets by with little or no water. **Hardy to Zone 8.** Pages: 165, 166.

Ophiopogon japonicus

MONDO GRASS. This perennial ground cover grows in clumps of narrow shiny dark green leaves 1 ft. tall and wide. Black mondo grass (*O. planiscapus* 'Ebony Knight' or 'Nigerescens') pp. 66, 106, 107, 139, 150,151) has purple-black foliage and grows 1 ft. tall and wide. Does best in full to partial shade; foliage can burn in the sun. Start with a number of small plants; they'll grow more quickly to fill a spot. Mow off the top of old foliage in early spring before new growth appears. **Hardy to Zone 7.** Not adapted to desert areas. Page: 37.

Ophiopogon japonicus
MONDO GRASS

Ophiopogon planiscapus 'Ebony Knight'
BLACK MONDO GRASS

Opuntia lindheimeri
SPINELESS PRICKLY PEAR

Opuntia lindheimeri

SPINELESS PRICKLY PEAR. This popular cactus has smooth, succulent gray-green leaf pads. Called "spineless," the leaves actually have tiny hidden spines, so wear gloves when handling them. The plant grows to 4 ft. tall and wide over time, on occasion producing showy yellow flowers in spring, followed by purple fruit in fall. Spineless prickly pear rarely needs water and has no major insect or disease problems. It makes a great living sculpture in the garden. Sometimes called *O. engelmannii* var. *lindheimeri*. **Hardy to Zone 8.** Page: 121.

Ornamental grasses

A group of perennial plants that are becoming very popular in western gardens. Their narrow leaves provide a soft texture that contrasts beautifully with the foliage of other plants. Leaves come in shades of red, yellow, blue, and green, and striped combinations. In fall and winter, some turn mingled shades of gold, brown, silver, or red. The flowers, often wispy plumes on tall stalks, last long into winter and sway with the slightest breeze. Most ornamental grasses grow best in full sun and with regular water, although some can take partial shade. Divide in fall or spring when the clumps become crowded. Cut back almost to the ground in winter or whenever the plant becomes floppy or unruly. For information on specific types, see "Recommended Ornamental Grasses," right.

Recommended ornamental grasses

Calamagrotis x *acutifolia* 'Stricta'
FEATHER REED GRASS

Chasmanthium latifolium
INLAND SEA OATS

Festuca ovina 'Glauca'
BLUE FESCUE GRASS

Bouteloua gracilis

BLUE GRAMMA GRASS. Upright gray-green grass with red to straw-colored seed-heads. Grows 1 to 2 ft. tall and wide. Well adapted to arid high-elevation areas where it thrives with little care once established. Can be mowed as a lawn. **Hardy to Zone 5.** Not adapted to low-elevation desert areas. Pages: 130, 131.

Chasmanthium latifolium

INLAND SEA OATS. Forms erect leafy clumps about 2 ft. tall, topped with loose clusters of flat seed heads that dance in the breeze from midsummer through winter. All parts are green in summer and russet or tan in winter. Grows in sun or shade and adapts to almost any soil. This vigorous plant can reseed and naturalize prolifically. **Hardy to Zone 5.** Not well adapted to desert areas. Pages: 37, 119.

Calamagrostis x acutiflora 'Stricta'

FEATHER REED GRASS. Forms narrow erect clumps about 2 ft. wide. Slender stalks 5 to 6 ft. tall are topped in late spring to summer with "pipe cleaner" spikes. In cold-winter areas, the whole plant turns beige by fall. Evergreen in mild-winter areas. Full sun or partial shade. **Hardy to Zone 5.** Page: 146.

Helictotrichon sempervirens
BLUE OAT GRASS

Festuca ovina var. glauca

BLUE FESCUE GRASS. A neat compact grass that forms a dense tuft about 1 ft. tall and wide of very slender blue-green leaves. Narrow flower spikes appear in early summer and soon turn tan. (There is considerable confusion over the Latin name, and plants are often sold as *F. cinerea* or *F. glauca*.) 'Boulder Blue' and 'Elijah Blue' are two of several cultivars with especially blue-colored foliage. All make fine-textured ground covers for small areas. Full sun or partial shade; can take some drought. Must be cut to the ground at least once a year. If cut in late summer, fresh new foliage appears in the fall and lasts all winter. **Hardy to Zone 4.** Pages: 24, 45, 79, 97, 129, 141, 157.

Helictotrichon sempervirens

BLUE OAT GRASS. A clump-forming grass with thin, wiry pale blue evergreen leaves. Blooms sparsely, with thin flower spikes that turn beige or tan. Do not cut back. Comb through the clump to pull out any loose dead leaves. Old clumps may die out in the middle; if so, divide them in fall or early spring. Plant in full sun. Grows 2 to 3 ft. tall and wide. **Hardy to Zone 4.** Not adapted to low elevation desert areas. Pages: 17, 45, 47, 53, 56, 79.

Miscanthus sinensis

JAPANESE SILVER GRASS, MAIDEN GRASS. A showy grass that forms vase-shaped clumps of long arching leaves. Blooms in late summer or fall; fluffy seed heads last through the winter. For best flowering results, plant in hot sunny spots. 'Gracillimus' (pp. 64, 66, 100, 180) is a common variety with gray-green leaves. 'Morning Light' (pp. 39, 105, 106, 128), 'Sarabande' (p. 109), and 'Variegatus' (pp. 18, 150) have slender, white-striped leaves that look silvery from a distance. All three form a clump of foliage 4 to 5 ft. tall, with flower stalks about 6 ft. tall. The similar 'Strictus' (p. 37), commonly called porcupine grass, has wide green leaves with yellow horizontal banding. 'Adagio' (pp. 80, 95) is dwarf (2 ft. high and wide with 3-ft. blooms) and has gray-green foliage. All miscanthus need full sun and regular water. Cut to the ground in late winter to early spring. **Hardy to Zone 6.**

Muhlenbergia capillaris 'Regal Mist'

'REGAL MIST' DEER GRASS. Forms a fine, dark green mound 2 to 3 ft, tall and up to and wide. Pink blooms rise 30 in. above the leaves. Evergreen in mild winter climates. Takes drought but best when watered. **Hardy to Zone 7.** Pages: 174, 175.

Pennisetum

FOUNTAIN GRASS. A grass that forms a hassocklike clump of arching leaves, green in summer and gold or tan in fall. Blooms over a long season from midsummer to fall, with fluffy spikes on arching stalks. Purple fountain grass (*P. setaceum* 'Rubrum', pp. 16, 59) has reddish brown leaves in summer and purple flowers. Hardy to Zone 8. *P. alopecuroides* 'Hameln', dwarf fountain grass (pp. 109, 111) has green leaves and buff pink blooms. It grows 24 in. tall and wide. Fountain grass needs full sun. Cut old leaves close to the ground in late winter, or sooner if storms knock them down. **Hardy to Zone 5.**

Schizachyrium scoparium 'Blaze'

'BLAZE' LITTLE BLUESTEM. Upright, wiry grass with bright blue-green leaves which turn bright red in fall. Flowers not eye-catching but turn attractively silver-hued as they dry. Grows 2 to 4 ft. tall and half as wide. Plant in full sun. Water regularly. **Hardy to Zone 3.** Page: 130.

Miscanthus sinensis 'Adagio'
JAPANESE SILVER GRASS

Miscanthus sinensis 'Sarabande'
JAPANESE SILVER GRASS

Pennisetum setaceum 'Rubrum'
FOUNTAIN GRASS

Osmanthus

SWEET OLIVE. A desirable shrub for screening patios and decks, sweet olive has a compact vase-shaped growth habit, polished evergreen leaves (sometimes toothed), and intoxicatingly fragrant, though not showy, white flowers in late spring and early summer, and occasionally throughout the year. Flowers are followed by blue-black berries. Grows 8 to 10 ft. tall and about half as wide. *O. x fortunei* and *O. fragrans* are very similar, with the former slightly shorter. Both do best in full sun, except in hot summer climates, where partial shade is preferable. Needs well-drained soil and regular watering. Can be lightly sheared to keep compact. **Hardy to Zone 8.** Not well adapted to desert areas. Pages: 84, 170.

Pachypodium lamerei

MADAGASCAR PALM. This palmlike succulent shrub makes an exotic specimen in a pot or planted in the ground in frost-free areas. The plump spiny trunk is topped with long, strap-shaped dull green leaves. In summer, mature plants bear fragrant, white crepe-papery flowers with yellow centers, followed by seedpods that resemble long gourds. Grows slowly up to 8 ft. tall. Adapted to full sun or partial shade. A carefree exotic. **Hardy to Zone 10.** Pages: 153, 161.

Palms

Few plants impart the feeling of mild-winter tropical climates like palms. In the landscape, their bold presence and sturdy appearance evoke warm beaches and cool breezes. Among the many available palms, tolerance to winter cold is the most significant limiting factor. Be sure to check with your local nursery to ensure that you get a palm hardy enough for your climate. Large palms survive transplanting as well as small ones do, so if you want instant results, start with large boxed specimens. However, planting bigger palms requires professional help and heavy equipment. When planting your own palm, work lots of organic matter into the soil in and around the planting hole. Most palms need little more care than regular watering, fertilizing and the occasional removal of old leaves. For information on specific palms, see the box at right.

Recommended palms

Phoenix roebelinii

PYGMY DATE PALM. A uniquely soft-textured palm that grows only about 6 ft. tall. Usually grown with several trunks, it has fairly dense dark green foliage. Frost-sensitive and grown only where winters are very mild. Elsewhere it can be grown in pots and protected in winter. Best in partial shade. Page: 155.

Syagrus romanzoffianus

QUEEN PALM. A bold, single-trunk palm that can grow up to 50 ft. tall. Arching, feathery leaves can reach 15 ft. Full sun. Likes lots of water and fertilizer. Leaves damaged below 25°F, but plant will survive 5° to 10° colder. Page: 90.

Phoenix roebelenii
PYGMY DATE PALM

Syagrus romanzoffianum
QUEEN PALM

Pelargonium

GERANIUM. Flowering perennials loved for their round flower clusters and long season of bloom from spring into fall. (For hardy geraniums, see Geranium.) Flowers come in many single and bi-colored shades of white, pink, red and purple. Lady Washington pelargonium, *P.* x *domesticum*, is a shrubby plant about 3 ft. tall and wide bearing ball-shaped flowers above dark green leaves. Common geranium, *P.* x *hortorum*, reaches a similar size and has soft leaves, often with dark markings. Ivy geranium, *P. peltatum*, is a sprawling plant about 1 ft. tall and 2 to 3 ft. wide. With glossy green leaves, it makes a colorful ground cover. All geraniums grow best in full or partial sun. Water regularly. Remove spent flowers. Cut back in fall or early spring if necessary. Geraniums are ideal container plants and are often grown as annuals. Watch for geranium bud worm, which causes plants to stop blooming. Ask at your nursery about controls. **Generally hardy to Zone 8 or 9 but grown as annuals anywhere.** Pages: 79, 141.

Penstemon gloxinioides

GARDEN OR BORDER PENSTEMON. Late spring and summer-flowering perennial with showy tubular flower spikes in shades of white, pink, red and purple. Grown as an annual in cold-winter areas. Forms erect clumps about 3 ft. tall. Many hybrids and varieties available. Needs full or partial sun. Looks best with regular water, but plants must have excellent drainage or they die quickly. Cut down spent flower stalks to encourage second bloom. In colder, high elevations, *P. barbatus* is a good substitute. It bears red flowers from spring into summer. Also check nurseries for locally native species. **Hardy to Zone 7.** Not adapted to desert areas. Pages: 70, 99, 114, 179.

Perovskia atriplicifolia

RUSSIAN SAGE. A shrubby perennial that forms an open, vase-shaped clump of straight, fairly stiff stems with sparse silver-gray foliage and tiny but abundant lavender-blue flowers. Blooms for weeks in summer and into fall. 'Longin' (p. 109) has the same graceful lavender flowers but a more upright form. 'Blue Spice' (p. 129) has darker blue flowers. Grow in full sun and well-drained soil. Needs little water. Cut old stems down to 6-in. stubs in spring. Grows 3 to 5 ft. tall and wide by fall. To control size, cut stems back by one-third in early summer. **Hardy to Zone 6.** Pages: 56, 112, 121, 180.

Philadelphus lewisii 'Cheyenne'

CHEYENNE MOCK ORANGE. Fountain shaped, deciduous shrub with an abundance of small white fragrant flowers in early summer. Grows 4 to 5 ft. high and up to 6 to 8 ft. wide. Plant in full sun in most areas; part shade in warmest, inland areas. Needs only occasional deep watering. **Hardy to Zone 5.** Not adapted to desert areas. Pages: 149, 151.

Penstemon gloxinioides
GARDEN PENSTEMON

Phormium tenax 'Sundowner'
NEW ZEALAND FLAX

Phormium 'Yellow Wave'
NEW ZEALAND FLAX

Phormium tenax

NEW ZEALAND FLAX. A perennial prized for its bold evergreen foliage. Stiff straplike leaves form a fan-like clump about 5 ft. tall and at least as wide. Stalks bearing red or yellow flowers rise high above the leaves. Many varieties with colorful foliage are available. 'Atropurpureum' (p. 112) has reddish purple leaves, 'Bronze' (p. 171) has red-brown leaves, and 'Rubrum' has deep purple-red leaves. Smaller varieties, better suited to small gardens, include 'Yellow Wave' (p. 144), with yellow leaves, and 'Sundowner' (pp. 16, 158, 159), with foliage that is a blazing mix of red, yellow, cream, green, and bronze. Plant New Zealand flax in full sun. Needs little water. Excellent accent plant, but large types need lots of room. In cold foothill areas, substitute an ornamental grass. **Hardy to Zone 9.** Not adapted to desert areas.

Photinia x fraseri

FRASER PHOTINIA. Evergreen shrub with dark green leaves and white spring flowers. New leaves are bronzy red and appear all summer (shearing encourages new growth). Grows 10 to 15 ft. tall and wide. Plant in full sun. Needs to be watered regularly. Pages: 169, 170. **Hardy to Zone 8.**

Picea abies 'Nidiformis'

BIRD'S-NEST NORWAY SPRUCE. A dwarf conifer with sharp, dark green needles. Grows wider than tall, typically reaching about 2 to 3 ft. tall and 3 to 5 ft. wide, and is flat or slightly concave on top—hence its common name. Grow in full sun or light shade and well-drained soil. Grows slowly, so buy the biggest plant you can afford. **Hardy to Zone 3.** Not adapted to mild-winter areas of the southwest. Page: 30.

Pinus mugho 'Big Tuna'

'BIG TUNA' MUGO PINE. A slow-growing pine that forms an irregular shrubby mound, not a conical tree. Needles are deep green. Needs full sun and well-drained soil, occasional water. Doesn't require pruning, but you can shear it in early summer if you want to, cutting new growth back by less than one-half. Typically grows just a few inches a year, but some plants are faster than others. Usually stays under 6 ft. tall and wide. This variety is more upright than the species. **Hardy to 3.** Not adapted to low-elevation desert areas. Pages: 45, 149.

Pittosporum

PITTOSPORUM. Dependable evergreen shrubs and small trees with tufts of glossy leaves and fragrant, usually white flowers in early summer. *P. tobira* 'Cream de Mint' (p. 68) has gray-green leaves with white edging and grows about 1 to 2 ft. tall and wide. Its compact mounded shape makes it useful for a small hedge or as a ground cover. *P. tobira* 'Wheeler's Dwarf' (pp. 97, 173) is similar but slightly bigger with whorls of dark green leaves. *P. undulatum* (p. 170) is a treelike form with a dense rounded shape and creamy white flowers. All adapt to sun or shade and look best with regular water. Prune anytime. **Hardy to Zone 9.**

Plumbago auriculata

TROPICAL PLUMBAGO. A tropical ever-blooming shrub or vine that is often grown as a tender perennial. The term "auriculata" means ear-shaped, and refers to the leaf base. Plumbago sprawls to 2 ft. tall and at least 2 to 3 ft. wide. Plumbago can also be trained to a trellis and grown as a climber. It is smothered with baby-blue flowers from summer to frost and is attractive to butterflies. Only needs occasional watering during dry spells. Cut to the ground after the first hard freeze and mulch well. **Hardy to Zone 9.** Pages: 21, 32, 83, 103, 136.

Podocarpus macrophyllus

SHRUBBY YEW PINE. A fine-textured columnar shrub or tree covered to the ground in bright green flat, needle-thin leaves. It makes a fine specimen or a fairly dense screen. Grows slowly to 50 ft. tall and 20 ft. wide. 'Maki' (p. 18) is more restrained, reaching 6 to 12 ft. tall if left unpruned and does well in pots. Prefers full sun, well-drained soil and regular watering. **Hardy to Zone 7.** Page: 170.

Prunus cerasifera

PURPLELEAF PLUM. Upright deciduous trees with deep purple foliage and bright pink flowers on bare branches in spring. 'Krauter Vesuvius' (pp. 165, 166) grows 15 to 18 ft. tall and 12 ft. wide and is fruitless. 'Newport' (p. 148) is similar but will bear some fruit, and its foliage turns bright red in fall. Both are handsome small trees that make strong purple accents in the landscape. Plant in full sun and water regularly. **Hardy to Zone 5.**

Pyrus fauriei 'Korean Sun'

KOREAN WILD PEAR. Upright single-trunked tree with white spring flowers and orange-red to purple fall color. Grows 10 to 12 ft. tall and up to 15 ft. wide. Fruitless. It is a useful small tree, especially in cold winter areas. **Hardy to Zone 5.** Not adapted to desert areas. Page: 130.

Pulmonaria saccharata

LUNGWORT. A perennial that blooms for many weeks in early spring, with masses of tiny pink, red or violet flowers. The large white-spotted leaves make a good ground cover throughout the summer and fall. There are many cultivars with smaller leaves and other flower colors. Needs partial shade. Prefers rich, moist, well-drained soil but will tolerate drier conditions in shade. Cut off flower stalks when the petals fade. Divide every few years in late summer. **Hardy to Zone 4.** Not adapted to dry-summer areas of the southwest. Page: 75.

Pittosporum tobira 'Cream de Mint' PITTOSPORUM

Photinia x *fraseri* FRASER PHOTINIA

Plumbago auriculata TROPICAL PLUMBAGO

Punica granatum

POMEGRANATE. Very ornamental deciduous fruit tree. 'Wonderful' (p. 49) is widely grown. Its bright orange-red flowers are held among shiny green leaves in spring. Flowers are followed by large bright red edible fruits. New growth is reddish brown. Leaves turn bright yellow in fall. Grows 10 ft. tall, with a wide-topped, fountainlike shape. 'Nana' (pp. 70, 80, 82) is a neat compact dwarf form that grows only 3 ft. tall and wide. It bears small inedible fruits and is an excellent container plant. Plant pomegranates in full sun and well-drained soil. They need little water once established, but fruit quality is better with regular water. Can be sheared and is often grown as a shrub. **Hardy to Zone 7.**

Quercus

OAK. Among the most majestic and long-lived shade trees in western landscapes. The region is home to many deciduous and evergreen species. However, in the designs in this book we feature only oaks widely grown in Texas.

Texas red oak (*Q. buckleyi*, p. 37) is a small deciduous oak native to the Hill Country and adapted throughout Texas. It normally grows a modest 20 to 30 ft. tall and wide. Its pointed multi-lobed leaves turn shades of brilliant red and orange in the fall. Often available in both single and multitrunked forms. Southern live oak (*Q. virginiana*, p. 94) is a slow-growing evergreen oak that achieves a height of 25 ft. and a width of 30 ft. in a person's lifetime but is capable of reaching immense proportions over the centuries. It has gnarled branches and small hollylike deep olive-green leaves that don't drop until the new leaves emerge in the spring. This oak casts dense shade, making it difficult to grow turfgrass underneath. Ground covers are often a better option. **Southern live oak is hardy to Zone 8.**

When buying oaks, ask where the trees were grown. Texas red oaks and live oaks native to central Texas are smaller, more alkaline tolerant, and more drought tolerant than their cousins in east and southeast Texas. All oaks grow best in full sun and well-drained soils. They require supplemental watering only during periods of drought. They have few serious insect or disease problems. In areas of central Texas where oak-wilt disease is a problem, prune the trees only during the dormant period of winter to avoid attracting disease-spreading insects to the freshly cut wounds. Applying a pruning paint is also recommended.

Rhaphiolepis indica

INDIAN HAWTHORN. An evergreen shrub with thick-textured green leaves, small pink or white flowers in spring, and blue berries that last through the

Punica granatum 'Wonderful'
POMEGRANATE

Quercus virginiana
SOUTHERN LIVE OAK

summer and fall. Most varieties grow 2 to 3 ft. tall, 3 to 6 ft. wide. Some larger forms can be trained into small trees. There are many fine cultivars. 'Clara' (p. 171) reaches 3 to 5 ft. tall and wide and has white flowers and red new growth. 'Ballerina' (pp. 41, 173) grows only 2 ft. tall and 4 ft. wide and has pink flowers. 'Jack Evans' (p. 25) grows to 3 ft. and bears pink flowers. 'Pinkie' is slightly lower growing, with light pink flowers (p. 32).'Majestic Beauty' (p. 168) is a large cultivar, growing 20 to 25 ft. tall and bearing light pink flowers in clusters up to 10 in. wide. *R. umbellata* 'Minor' (p. 24) is a similar species, but only grows about 2 to 3 ft. tall and wide and has white flowers. Indian hawthorn needs full sun and, once established, little water. Requires minimal pruning or care. Fungal leaf spot may occur in shady humid sites. **Hardy to Zone 8.** Pages: 16, 136, 138.

Rhododendron

RHODODENDRON AND AZALEA. An especially diverse and popular group of shrubs with very showy flowers between early spring and early summer. The leaves can be small or large, deciduous or evergreen. The plants can be short, medium, or tall, with spreading, mounded, or erect habits. Gardeners in Northern California and the Pacific Northwest can grow a great many rhododendrons and azaleas, including a number of native species. Evergreen azaleas are widely grown and even do well in southern California's hot summers. They produce masses of flowers in mid- to late spring on compact shrubs, usually 2 to 4 ft. tall, with small evergreen leaves. They can be sheared to produce a neat massed effect. Unsheared, they form irregular billowing mounds. 'Gumpo White' (p. 18) and 'Alaska' (p. 146) are among the best white-flowered azaleas for California. For a pink azalea, select 'Gumpo Pink' (p. 169) or 'Cilpinense' (p. 74).

Rhododendrons and azaleas have similar cultural requirements. All do best with partial shade, and they need fertile, moist, well-drained soil. Mix a 3-in. layer of peat moss into the soil when you prepare a bed for these shrubs. Plant rhododendrons and azaleas in spring or early fall. Be sure not to plant them too deep—the top of the root ball should be level with, or a little higher than, the surrounding soil. Azaleas are usually sold in containers. When planting them it's very important that you make a few deep cuts down the outside of the root ball and tease apart some of the roots; otherwise azaleas will not root in the surrounding soil.

Use a layer of mulch to keep the soil cool and damp around your azaleas and rhododendrons, and water the plants regularly. Prune or shear off the flower stalks as soon as the petals fade to prevent seeds from forming and to neaten the plants. Prune or shear to control the size and shape of the plant at the same time (usually in early summer). Adaptation varies greatly. Check local nurseries for species and varieties that grow best in your area.

Rhus trilobata 'Autumn Amber'

'AUTUMN AMBER' CREEPING SUMAC. Forms a beautifully dense, deciduous ground cover of bright green, lobed leaves that turn bright yellow in fall. Bears yellow-green flowers in spring. Grows 18 in. tall and over 6 ft. wide. Tolerates drought in high-elevation areas. **Hardy to Zone 4.** Not adapted to desert areas. Page: 130.

Ribes odoratum 'Crandall'

'CRANDALL' CLOVE CURRANT. Wiry deciduous shrub with bright green lobed leaves that turn mahogany red in fall. Small yellow spring flowers have intense clove scent and are followed by black edible berries. Grows 3 to 5 ft. high and at least as wide. Plant in full sun. Water regularly. **Hardy to Zone 5.** Not adapted to the southwest. Pages: 130, 131.

Raphiolepis indica
INDIAN HAWTHORN

Rhododendron 'Alaska'
RHODODENDRON

Rosa

ROSE. Fast-growing deciduous shrubs with glossy compound leaves, thorny stems or canes, and very showy, often fragrant flowers. See the box at right for descriptions of specific roses. In winter and early spring, many garden centers stock bare-root roses, with the roots packed in moist wood shavings wrapped in a plastic bag. These are a good investment if you buy them right after they arrive in the stores and plant them promptly, but their quality deteriorates as the weather warms and they begin to grow in the bag. Nurseries may sell bare-root roses in the spring, but they usually grow the plants in containers. If you buy a potted rose, you can plant it anytime.

All roses grow best in full sun and fertile, well-drained soil topped with a few inches of mulch. Most will bloom better if fertilized every 4 to 6 weeks during the growing season. Prune them once a year in spring, before new growth starts. (See p. 300 for more on pruning.)

The roses recommended here have good resistance to various fungal diseases but may have problems during years when the weather is especially moist. To control fungus, mix 2 tsp. baking soda and 2 tsp. summer oil (available at nurseries) in 1 gal. of water and spray the rose foliage until it's dripping wet. Repeat every 10 days. Or use an appropriately labeled fungicide. Aphids—soft-bodied insects the size of a pinhead—may attack the new growth on roses but do no serious damage. You can wash them away with soapy water.

When choosing roses, check local rose society or cooperative extension recommendations. For example, the Texas Cooperative Extension program (a branch of Texas A&M University) has conducted extensive research to identify the roses that perform best in Texas without pesticides. Those that pass the test are designated Earth-Kind™ roses. **Hardiness varies greatly, but types or varieties can be grown almost anywhere in the West.**

Recommended roses

Rosa x 'Flower Carpet'

Rosa chinensis 'Climbing Old Blush'

Rosa x 'Belinda's Dream'

'Flower Carpet'

A low spreading rose that forms a mat of dark green leaves topped with pink, white, rose pink, yellow, and red flowers. Grows 2 ft. high by 3 ft. wide. Pages: 72, 155, 161.

'Iceberg'

One of the best white floribunda roses. Blooms off and on almost all year where winters are warm. Upright, 3-to-5-ft. plant with excellent disease resistance. There is also a climbing form. Pages: 32, 35, 41, 51, 87, 135, 141, 165.

'Margaret Merril'

Lovely, fragrant white floribunda rose with a compact habit. Grows about 3 ft. tall and wide. Generous bloom. Excellent low hedge. Page: 76.

'Red Meidiland'

Spreading ground-cover rose. Flowers are red with white centers. Blooms over a long season. Grows 2 to 3 ft. high and about 5 ft. wide. Page: 49.

Rosa chinensis 'Climbing Old Blush'

The climbing form of the wonderful old China rose, 'Old Blush'. It has a heavy flush of loose double-pink blooms in spring and then a scattering of repeat blooms until fall. Grows vigorously up to 15 ft. tall and wide. Pages: 182, 183.

R. chinensis 'Martha Gonzales'

This dwarf China rose has brilliant red semi-double blooms all season. It grows about 3 ft. tall and 2 ft. wide and occasionally larger. The new growth in spring is a brilliant plum color. Pages: 182, 183.

R. chinensis 'Mutabilis', Butterfly rose

This popular landscape rose is a carefree shrub that produces showy single flowers all season in everchanging shades of yellow, orange, red, and pink. Its name derives from its flowers, which resemble a swarm of butterflies hovering about the bush. Grows to a generous 5 ft. tall and wide, and occasionally larger. New growth is plum colored. Designated an Earth-Kind™ rose. Page: 94.

R. x 'Belinda's Dream'

This showy shrub rose produces large, very double pink flowers all season. Generally grows around 4 ft. tall and 3 ft. wide. The fragrant flowers are great for floral arrangements. Designated an Earth-Kind™ rose. Page: 22.

R. x *odorata* 'Gilbert Nabonnand'

This healthy tea rose makes a profusion of loosely double-pink blooms all season, with the heaviest bloom in spring and fall. 'Gilbert Nabonnand' grows 4 ft. tall has thornless stems. Page: 182.

R. x *polyantha* 'Climbing Pinkie'

This is the climbing form of the polyantha, 'Pinkie'. It can be grown as a loose shrub or as a climber to 8 ft. Pink semi-double blooms burst out in spring and repeat the performance in fall. The stems are mostly thornless. Designated an Earth-Kind™ rose. Pages: 38, 39.

R. x *polyantha* 'Marie Daly'

This is the pink sport of the popular polyantha, 'Marie Pavie'. It produces a profusion of very fragrant light pink, semi-double flowers all season. Grows 3 ft. tall and 2 ft. wide, on mostly thornless stem. Designated an Earth-Kind™ rose. Pages: 82, 83.

R. x 'Hansa'

Rounded shrub rose with dark green leaves and light purple-red flowers. Grows 6 ft. high and wide. Very hardy and well adapted to coastal areas. Page: 149.

Rosa chinensis 'Mutabilis'

Rosa x *polyantha* 'Marie Daly'

Rosmarinus officinalis
ROSEMARY

Rudbeckia hirta
GLORIOSA DAISY

*Ruellia
brittoniana* 'Katie'
DWARF MEXICAN
PETUNIA

Rosmarinus officinalis

ROSEMARY. This classic Mediterranean evergreen is a tough and attractive herbal shrub. The gray-green needlelike leaves combine a lovely fragrance with a tasty flavor. Small blue flowers bloom in late winter and early spring and sporadically throughout the year. Most rosemary species grow upright to a dense 3 ft. tall and wide. 'Tuscan Blue' (pp. 43, 53, 56, 72, 74, 89, 127, 144) is upright to 6 ft., has deep blue flowers, and can be grown as a low hedge. 'Majorca Pink' (pp. 141, 177) is upright to 2 to 4 ft. but has lavender-pink blooms. 'Hill's Hardy' (p. 60) is a cold-hardy selection. Trailing rosemary (the low-growing *R. officinalis* 'Prostratus') has curved stems and grows 1 ft. tall and 3 ft. wide (pp. 103, 123). Rosemaries do best in full sun and very well-drained soil. They need little water once established and can be pruned or sheared lightly during any season. **Hardy to Zone 8.** Page: 22.

Rudbeckia

CONEFLOWER, BLACK-EYED SUSAN. A popular perennial wildflower that bears daisylike flowers with bright-colored petals and large conical centers in late summer. *R. fulgida* 'Goldsturm' (pp. 45, 47, 53, 80, 117, 180) bears hundreds of cheerful yellow black-eyed flowers for several weeks in summer and into fall. Forms a robust clump 2 to 3 ft. tall and wide, with large dark green leaves at the base and stiff, erect, branching flower stalks. Gloriosa daisy (*R. hirta*) has large orange-yellow flowers with black centers. Grows 3 to 4 ft. tall, with upright stems. Can be grown as an annual. Some varieties are much smaller. Plant in full sun and well-drained soil. Plants look best with regular watering. Remove spent flowers. Cut down the stalks in fall or spring. **Hardy to at least Zone 4.**

Ruellia brittoniana 'Katie'

DWARF MEXICAN PETUNIA. An extremely durable and attractive perennial ground cover with narrow dark green leaves. Grows in low, dense clumps 1 ft. tall and wide. From spring until frost it offers a profusion of small, pale purple flowers which resemble cultivated petunias but are slightly more cup-shaped and funnel-like. Grows in full sun or partial shade and tolerates most soil types. It is also quite tolerant of both drought and excess moisture. It has few if any pest problems. It self-seeds; pull out unwanted seedlings. Cut to the ground after the first frost. **Hardy to Zone 9.** Pages: 21, 66.

Salvia

SAGE, SALVIA. These shrubby perennials are grown for their long bloom season (from late spring into fall) and tough constitution. Germander sage (*S. chamaedryoides*, p. 113) forms a spreading mound of silvery leaves about 2 ft. tall covered with short spikes of beautiful light blue flowers. Autumn sage (*S. greggii*, pp. 93, 103, 112, 144, 174, 175) grows about 2 to 3 ft. tall and wide and comes in many varieties. Flowers are typically bright red ('Furman's Red', pp. 98, 129, 159; 'Cherry Chief' p. 60), but they can be light purple, pink (pp. 136, 138), salmon, or white ('Alba', pp. 64, 66). Mexican bush sage (*S. leucantha*, pp. 37, 64, 79, 112, 144, 183) has gray-green leaves and produces long spikes of velvety purple-and-white flowers. It grows 3 to 4 ft. tall and usually wider. *S.* x *superba* (pp. 51, 114) forms a patch of dark green foliage that is topped with countless flower spikes. It grows 18 to 24 in. tall and spreads 2 ft. wide. Cultivars include 'May Night' (p. 109), with dark indigo-purple flowers. The mealycup sage (*S. farinacea*, pp. 64, 100, 121, 181) bears clusters of blue flower spikes borne on upright plants that grow vigorously to 3 ft. tall and wide. Foliage is gray-green. Improved cultivars are purple, blue, or white and grow to a compact 1½ ft. tall and wide. 'Winnifred Gilman' Cleveland sage (*S. clevelandii*, p. 175) grows 3 to 4 ft high with wispy spikes of distinctive blue flowers. *Salvia* x 'Indigo Spires' (p. 83) is a vigorous hybrid that grows a bushy 5 ft. tall and 3 ft. wide. It puts out blue spikes all season.

Sages prefer full sun but can tolerate shade in inland areas. They must have well-drained soil, and most like to be on the dry side. Shear old flower stalks to keep the plant blooming. Mexican bush sage should be cut back to the ground in late fall. Others should be lightly sheared back. Divide spreading types every few years in spring or fall. **Most sages are only hardy to zones 8 or 9.** In cold winter climates many are used as annuals.

Salvia greggii 'Cherry Chief' SAGE

Salvia farinacea MEALYCUP SAGE

Salvia x 'Indigo Spires' SAGE

Salvia leucantha MEXICAN BUSH SAGE

Santolina chamaecyparissus
LAVENDER COTTON

Sarcococca ruscifolia
FRAGRANT SARCOCOCCA

Scabiosa caucasica
PINCUSHION FLOWER

Sedum 'Autumn Joy'
SEDUM

Santolina chamaecyparissus

LAVENDER COTTON, GRAY SANTOLINA. A bushy shrub with soft, fragrant, fine-textured silver-gray foliage. It is often sheared to make an edging or a formal specimen. Can also be used as a ground cover. If unsheared, it bears round yellow blossoms in mid-summer. Needs full sun and well-drained, dry soil. Prune every year in early spring, before new growth starts, cutting the old stems back halfway to the ground. Grows 1 to 2 ft. tall, 2 to 3 ft. wide. **Hardy to Zone 6.** Pages: 61, 79, 123, 157, 158, 175.

Sarcococca

SARCOCOCCA. Low sarcococca (*S. humilis*, pp. 55, 75) is a slow-growing evergreen shrub with small leathery pointed leaves that are glossy green all year. Blooms in February and March; the small white flowers cluster at the bases of the leaves and are very sweet-scented. Grows 12 to 18 in. tall and 2 to 3 ft. wide. Spreads by rhizomes and can be used as a ground cover. **Hardy to Zone 6.** Fragrant sarcococca (*S. ruscifolia*, p. 31) has glossy green, wavy leaves. Small white flowers in late winter and early spring are also strongly scented. Grows about 3 ft. tall and wide. **Hardy to Zone 8.** Plant sarcococcas in full or partial shade. Neither sarcococca is adapted to desert areas.

Scabiosa caucasica

PINCUSHION FLOWER. A perennial that forms a clump of gray-green leaves. Thin stalks about 2 ft. tall bear clusters of blue but sometimes white flowers from late spring through fall. Plant in full sun and water regularly. Remove spent flowers. Cut back in fall to promote additional bloom. **Hardy to Zone 4.** Not adapted to desert areas. Pages: 43, 141, 171.

Sedum

SEDUM. Perennials that form clumps of succulent foliage on thick stems topped with flat clusters of tiny flowers. 'Autumn Joy' (pp. 109, 114, 159) grows 2 to 3 ft. tall, with erect stems and gray-green foliage. The flowers change color from pale to deep salmon pink to rusty red over many weeks in late summer and fall as they open, mature and go to seed. 'Vera Jameson' (p. 72) grows about 1 ft. tall, with floppy stems, rounded leaves in an unusual shade of purple-gray, and pink flowers in August. Sedums need full sun. Cut down old stalks in winter or early spring. Divide clumps every few years in early spring. **Hardy to at least Zone 4.** Not adapted to desert areas.

Senecio greyi

GREY'S SENECIO. A mound-forming evergreen shrub with woolly stems and leaves that are soft to the touch. (Also sold as *Brachyglottis greyi*.) New leaves are covered with white hairs and become dark green and hairless. Yellow daisylike flowers bloom from summer to fall. 'Sunshine' (p. 72) grows 3 ft. tall and wide and has leaves with scalloped edges. Grow senecio in full sun or partial shade. Very drought tolerant once established. Most are grown for their gray foliage, so shear off the flowers if the leaf color is what you're after. Every few years prune older stems by two-thirds in the early spring to en-

Senecio greyii
GREY'S SENECIO

Setcreasea pallida 'Purple Heart'
PURPLE HEART

courage new vibrant gray-green growth. **Hardy to Zone 8.** Not adapted to desert areas. Page: 53.

Senna artemisiodes.
FEATHERY CASSIA. Airy evergreen shrub with fine-textured, needlelike silver-gray foliage. Especially useful in low-elevation desert areas where it produces clusters of yellow flowers in fall followed by abundant seed pods. Grows 3 to 5 ft. tall and equally as wide. Rangy; cut back to keep more compact. Plant in full sun or partial shade. Can take drought but looks best with occasional water. **Hardy to Zone 9.** Pages: 56, 156.

Setcreasea pallida 'Purple Heart'
PURPLE HEART. This Mexican perennial is among the easiest of all plants to grow. The thick succulent stems sport showy purple foliage from spring to frost. Small pink flowers throughout the growing season are an added bonus. Purple heart has no insect or disease problems and requires little to no watering. It will grow in sun or shade but has better coloration in full sun. Tolerates almost any soil. It is sometimes sold as purple Jew or Tradescantia pallida. **Hardy to Zone 10.** Page: 66,

Sophora secundiflora
TEXAS MOUNTAIN LAUREL. This native shrub or small tree boasts beautiful blossoms as well as shiny evergreen foliage. It generally grows 10 ft. tall or better and 7 ft. wide. The extremely fragrant flowers hang like clusters of purple wisteria each spring. Requires full sun and good drainage. It may occa-

sionally suffer attack from leaf-eating caterpillars but generally recovers. It requires little to no supplemental irrigation or pruning. Do not prune during the winter because flower buds are present at that time. **Hardy to Zone 7.** Pages: 121, 136.

Spiraea japonica
JAPANESE SPIREA. A deciduous shrub, it creates a low mound of thin, graceful arching stems that bear sharply toothed leaves and, from late spring into summer, round flat clusters of tiny flowers. Sometimes sold as *S.* x *bumulda*. 'Anthony Waterer' (pp. 62, 63) has carmine pink flowers. 'Goldflame' (pp. 117, 118) has bright gold leaves that are tinged with orange in spring and turn red in fall. Flowers are pink. Both cultivars grow about 2 to 3 ft. tall and wide. Plant them in full or partial sun. Prune every year after bloom, removing some of the older stems at ground level and cutting the others back partway. In summer, shear off faded flowers to promote possible reblooming. Water regularly. **Hardy to Zone 4.** Not adapted to desert areas.

Spiraea x vanhouttei
VANHOUTTEI'S SPIREA. An old-fashioned favorite, this deciduous shrub forms a dense clump of arching branches hidden in spring under thick veils of tiny white flowers. Small leaves are dark green in summer, often purple in fall. Grows 5 to 6 ft. high and about 8 ft. wide. Best in full sun but can take some shade. Water regularly. Prune after flowering. **Hardy to Zone 4.** Not adapted to desert areas. Page: 179.

Sophora secundiflora
TEXAS MOUNTAIN LAUREL

Stachys byzantina
LAMB'S EARS

Stachys byzantina

LAMB'S EARS. A mat-forming perennial whose large oval leaves are densely covered with soft white fuzz. Typically the leaves are 3 to 4 in. long, and the plant spreads about 18 in. wide. Blooms in early summer, with small purple flowers on thick stalks about 1 ft. tall. Needs full or partial sun, well-drained soil, and occasional water. Cut off the bloom stalks when the flowers fade, or as soon as they appear. Use a soft rake to clean away the old leaves in early spring. Divide clumps every few years. **Hardy to Zone 4.** Pages: 35, 115, 141.

Strelitzia reginae

BIRD-OF-PARADISE. Beloved, tropical-looking evergreen plant with large eye-catching flowers that look like the head of a bird. Flowers, mostly orange but touched with blue and white, are concentrated in early spring, but some bloom year-round. Large leathery leaves form a dense clump about 5 ft. tall. Best adapted to frost-free areas. Needs protection elsewhere. Or plant in pots and move to a covered spot in winter. Best in full sun. Water and fertilize regularly. Remove spent flowers. **Hardy to Zone 10.** Page: 161.

Strelitzia reginae BIRD-OF-PARADISE

Syringa vulgaris

COMMON LILAC. A large deciduous shrub valued for its sweet-scented flowers in spring. There are dozens of cultivars, with single or double flowers in shades of lilac, purple, pink, and white. Most grow 10 to 20 ft. tall, with many erect stems. Most varieties need winter chilling to bloom well. In southern California and other mild-winter areas, grow Descanso hybrids such as 'Blue Boy', 'Lavender Lady' (p. 125), and 'White Angel'. 'Miss Kim' is a dwarf variety of *S. pubescens patula* (p. 149), growing 5 ft. high and wide with pale lavender flowers. Plant all lilacs in full sun. Water regularly. Remove spent flowers. Prune as needed. **Hardy to Zone 4.** Pages: 32, 41.

Syringa vulgaris
COMMON LILAC

Tagetes lemmonii

SHRUB MARIGOLD, COPPER CANYON DAISY. Shrublike perennial with small aromatic leaves and bright orange marigoldlike flowers in winter and spring (some year-round). Grows 5 to 6 ft. tall, spreads about as wide. Somewhat rangy in appearance, best used in dry gardens or as a background plant. Plant in full sun. Needs little water. Damaged by hard frost. Prune to mantain size and shape. **Hardy to Zone 9.** Pages: 78, 121.

Tagetes lucida

MEXICAN MINT MARIGOLD. This Mexican perennial has aromatic foliage and clusters of small golden yellow marigoldlike flowers in the fall. The scented foliage has a mild anise flavor, and can be used as a culinary substitute for tarragon. Generally grows 1½ ft. tall and wide and requires full to partial sun. Shear the plants back by one-third several times during the growing season to maintain a compact habit and to promote heavier bloom. It has few pests and requires watering only during dry periods. Water regularly. **Hardy to Zone 9;** grown as an annual elsewhere. Pages: 64, 80, 82.

Taxus baccata

YEW. One of a popular group of evergreen shrubs and trees with flat sprays of dark green needlelike foliage. *T. baccata* 'Stricta', Irish yew (p. 90), is a narrow columnar plant eventually reaching 20 ft. tall. It needs room to grow but adds a strong formal look to the landscape. Like other yews, it tolerates repeated pruning and is often sheared to form a hedge. *T. baccatta* 'Repandans', spreading English yew (p. 105), is a low-growing, wide-spreading evergreen shrub with dark green needles. Grows about 2 ft. tall and 6 to 8 ft. wide after many years.

Female yews produce red berries, which are attractive but poisonous. Prune individual branches as needed to maintain the desired shape. **Hardy to Zone 7.** Not adapted to desert areas.

Ternstroemia gymnanthera

JAPANESE CLEYERA. A neat compact evergreen shrub with glossy leaves in changeable colors; they can be red, gold, green, or purple, depending on the stage of growth, season, and light levels. Grows about 4 ft. tall and 3 ft. wide. Needs minimal pruning; trouble free. Hardy to Zone 5. Page 24.

Thymus

THYME. A creeping perennial that forms low mats of wiry stems and tiny semievergreen leaves. *T. praecox* ssp. *arcticus*, mother-of-thyme, or creeping thyme (pp. 57, 89, 135) grows 4 to 6 in. tall, 1 to 2 ft. wide with bright green leaves. Tolerates light foot traffic and smells good when you step on it. Clusters of pink, lavender, or white flowers bloom over a long season in midsummer. There are several other kinds of creeping thymes. *T. praecox* 'Pseudolanginosus', wooly thyme (p. 47) has wooly gray leaves and grows 2 to 3 in. high and up to 3 ft. wide. Lemon thymes, *T.* x *citriodorus* (pp. 17, 149, 151) 'Argenteus' and 'Aureus' have lemon-scented, silver- and yellow-variegated leaves, respectively. The species has small dark green leaves. All thymes make attractive, fragrant, tough ground covers for sites with full sun and well-drained soil. Plants may self-sow and pop up in cracks of pavementor even in the lawn but aren't weedy. **Hardy to Zone 5.**

Tipuana tipu

TIPU TREE. This large semievergreen or deciduous tree makes a useful lawn or shade tree. It grows 25 to 35 ft. tall and spreads twice as wide. Light green finely divided leaves are topped with long clusters of yellow-to-apricot pea-like flowers from late spring to early summer, followed by large seedpods. Best grown where summers are warm and winters are mild. **Hardy warmest parts of Zone 9.** Foliage is damaged at 25°F. Pages: 155, 160.

Tagetes lucida
MEXICAN MINT MARIGOLD

Taxus baccata 'Repandens'
ENGLISH YEW

Thymus praecox arcticus
CREEPING THYME

Trachelospermum asiaticum
JASMINE

Tsuga canadensis 'Pendula'
WEEPING HEMLOCK

Trachelospermum

JASMINE. Asian jasmine, *T. asiaticum* (p. 37), is a common ground cover. Dense and low growing, it forms a thick mat of small shiny evergreen leaves. It produces small fragrant creamy yellow flowers in spring or early summer. Grows less than 1 ft. tall and spreads to about 3 ft. Shear as needed to keep tidy, or mow each spring with the mower on the highest setting. *T. jasminoides*, star jasmine (pp. 84, 87, 92, 135, 139, 167), is an evergreen vine with woody twining stems lined with pairs of small glossy green oval leaves. Bears dangling clusters of cream-colored, sweet-smelling flowers in late spring to early summer. Climbs 10 to 15 ft. tall if given some type of support such as a fence or pillar. Can also be grown as a sprawling ground cover, 1 to 2 ft. high. Prune anytime to keep within bounds. If used as a ground cover, shear in spring to keep compact. Plant in full sun or partial shade. Water regularly. **Hardy to Zone 8.** Page: 169.

Tsuga canadensis 'Pendula'

WEEPING HEMLOCK. Needlelike leaves are green on top and white below. Grows slowly and spreads wider than tall, reaching 2 to 3 ft. tall and 4 to 6 ft. wide. Will eventually grow twice as tall and wide but will take many years to do so. Start with the largest specimen you can afford. Takes sun or shade but needs moist, well-drained soil. **Hardy to Zone 4.** Not adapted to the hot, dry areas of the southwest. Page: 30.

Verbena bonariensis

PURPLE VERBENA. This perennial forms a low mound of basal foliage topped by a thicket of stiff, erect, much-branched but almost-leafless flower stalks that can reach 6 ft. tall. They bear countless little clusters of lavender-purple flowers throughout the season. The heaviest bloom comes before the heat of summer, beckoning butterflies and floral arrangers. Purple verbena needs full sun and tolerates most soil conditions. Shear as needed during the growing season to promote new blooms. Generally self-sows but isn't weedy. Can be grown as an annual. **Hardy to Zone 7.** Pages: 95, 136.

Verbena x hybrida

VERBENA. These are sprawling perennials with evergreen leaves and round clusters of showy flowers. 'Blue Princess' (pp. 39, 64, 83, 103) has lightly fragrant lavender-blue flowers. 'Homestead Purple' (pp. 22, 61, 95, 101) has vibrant purple flowers. Plant them in full sun and they will bloom nonstop from early spring until hard frost if regularly deadheaded. Plants generally grow about 1 ft. tall and spread 3 ft. or wider. Prune any damaged or frosted shoots in early spring, and shear throughout the growing season to keep tidy. Water regularly. **Hardy to Zone 9** but widely used as annuals elsewhere.

Verbena x *hybrida* 'Homestead Purple'
VERBENA

Viburnum bodnantense 'Dawn'
VIBURNUM

Vinca major
PERIWINKLE

Viburnum

VIBURNUM. Deciduous or evergreen shrubs with many outstanding features—showy foliage, flowers, fragrance or fruits, or all of the above. All need full or partial sun and moist, well-drained soil. Prune after flowering. *V.* x *bodnantense* 'Dawn' (pp. 54, 55) is an upright deciduous shrub with dark green leaves—scarlet in fall—and peely brown bark. Clusters of fragrant pink flowers bloom on bare wood in late winter but can begin as early as October. Blooms best in full sun. Grows 8 to 10 ft. tall and 6 ft. wide. **Hardy to Zone 7.** Not adapted to desert areas. *V. davidii*, David viburnum (pp. 29, 54), is a compact evergreen shrub with leathery veined dark green leaves. Flat-topped clusters of white flowers are borne on branch tips in late spring and sporadically into summer. Metallic blue fruit ripens in late fall. Each plant will produce more fruit when there are several plants in the same area. Grows 3 ft. tall in sun, 5 ft. tall in shade. **Hardy to Zone 7.** Not adapted to desert areas. *V. tinus* 'Spring Bouquet' (pp. 22, 82, 117, 173) is a compact evergreen shrub with fragrant white flowers that emerge from pink buds. Blooms late fall to spring. Flowers are followed by shiny blue berries. Dark green leaves are borne on reddish stems. Grows 6 ft. tall and about 4 ft. wide. Can be sheared as a low hedge, but do not prune in the late fall or winter or you'll remove flower buds. Mildew is a problem in coastal areas. **Hardy to Zone 8.**

Vinca

PERIWINKLE. Spreading evergreen ground covers with dark green leaves and five-petaled lavender-purple flowers in the spring. *V. major* (p. 122) normally grows about 1 ft. tall and 2 to 3 ft. wide before rooting to form new plants. **Hardy to Zone 7.** *V. minor*, dwarf periwinkle (p. 41), forms a thick mass of foliage only about 6 in. high. **Hardy to Zone 4.** Both periwinkles grow best in partial or full shade. Can take drought but look better with occasional water. Can be invasive, especially *V. major*. Shear plants to the ground every few years.

Vitex agnus-castus

CHASTE TREE. Tough deciduous shrub or small tree that can reach 20 to 25 ft. Generally grows with multiple trunks and has an open spreading habit. Fan-shaped divided leaves are dark green on top, grayish underneath. Showy flower spikes bear small tubular lavender-blue flowers in summer and attract many butterflies. 'Abbeville Blue' (page 174) is known for its clear blue flowers. All chaste trees bloom best in warm-summer areas. Plant in full sun and water regularly for best flower display. Able to survive dry periods and isn't bothered by pests. Prune in winter to develop a tree shape; otherwise it will be shrubby and dense. **Hardy to Zone 6.** Pages: 16, 122, 174.

Vitex agnus-castus
CHASTE TREE

Water plants

Many garden centers offer a limited selection of water plants. Specialty nurseries and mail-order water-garden specialists often offer dozens of kinds. Most water plants are fast-growing, sometimes even weedy, so you need only one of each to start. Some water plants are tender to frost, but you can overwinter them indoors in a pot or aquarium. There are three main groups of water plants: marginal, floating, and oxygenating. Choose one or more of each for an interesting and balanced effect.

Marginal plants grow well on the edge of the pond or in containers covered with 2 in. or more of water. Their leaves and flower stalks stand above the water surface while their roots stay submerged. Louisiana iris (*Iris* x *Louisiana* hybrids, p. 222) and umbrella sedge (*Cyperus alternifolius*, p. 207) are two common examples that are easy to grow and readily available.

Floating plants have leaves that rest on the water and roots that dangle into it. Water lettuce (*Pistia* species) is a floater that forms saucer-size rosettes of iridescent pale green leaves.

Oxygenating, or submerged, plants grow completely under water. They help keep the water clear and provide oxygen, food and shelter for fish. Anacharis (*Elodea* species) is a popular oxygenator with tiny dark green leaves.

Water lilies (*Nymphaea* species, pp. 101, 103, 106) are the most popular plants for pools and ponds. The best selection is available from specialty nurseries. There are two main groups of water lilies. Hardy water lilies survive outdoors from year to year and bloom in midsummer. They are usually the easiest to grow. Tropical water lilies, such as Dauben water lily (*N.* x *daubenyana*), need warm water and bloom over a longer season from summer through fall but are cold tender and often treated as annuals. Both kinds are available in dwarf-size plants, suitable for small pools, with fragrant or scentless flowers in shades of white, yellow and pink. Tropicals also come in shades of blue and purple. All water lilies need full sun. Plant the roots in a container of heavy rich garden soil, and set the container in the pool, making sure that about 6 in. of water covers the soil. (See p. 267 for more on planting.)

Nymphaea x *daubenyana*
DAUBEN WATER LILY

Nymphaea
WATER LILY

Wisteria sinensis

CHINESE WISTERIA. A vigorous woody vine with deciduous compound leaves. Dangling clusters of very fragrant purple, lavender or white flowers bloom in spring. It climbs by twining around a trellis, tree or other support and can exceed 30 ft. Needs full sun to flower well, and well-drained soil. A young plant needs regular water and fertilizer. Older plants are less demanding. May not flower for several years after you plant it, but the lacy foliage is attractive meanwhile. Prune anytime to keep within bounds. Prune heavily in winter to keep open and to encourage large flowers. Wisteria can be invasive in East Texas. **Hardy to Zone 5.** Pages: 89, 136, 138.

Xylosma congestum 'Compacta'

COMPACT XYLOSMA. A beautiful evergreen shrub usually grown for its dense glossy yellow-green leaves. Grows 4 to 5 ft. high and wide in mounded fashion. Great background plant or informal hedge. Plant in full sun or partial shade. Water regularly. **Hardy to Zone 8.** Pages: 97, 98 172.

Yucca

YUCCA. These are bold architectural plants with pointed swordlike leaves and tall stalks of showy creamy white flowers. *Y. filamentosa* (pp. 121, 122) has narrow leaves with hairy filaments along the margins and generally grows 3 ft. tall and wide. **Hardy to Zone 4.** Soft-tip yucca (*Y. gloriosa*, pp. 64, 66) has somewhat flexible gray-green leaves and grows 4 to 5 ft. tall and 3 ft. wide. **Hardy to Zone 7.** Yuccas require full sun and good drainage and no supplemental irrigation. Maintenance is limited to removing dead leaves at their base and cutting down dead flower stalks. Yuccas have few if any pest problems.

Zantedeschia aethiopica

CALLA LILY. This showy perennial creates a bright green clump of arrow-shaped leaves punctuated by dramatic, 8-in.-long pure-white flowers for a long period of time in spring and summer. Grows 2 to 4 ft. tall and spreads wider. Calla lilies prefer full sun and rich, moist, slightly acidic soil. In very hot summer climates, plant them where they are protected from the afternoon sun. They can be planted from pots or rhizomes. Divide when clumps become crowded. Evergreen in mild climates. **Hardy to Zone 8.** Page: 171.

Wisteria sinensis
CHINESE WISTERIA

Yucca filamentosa
YUCCA

Yucca gloriosa SOFT-TIP YUCCA

Guide *to* Installation

Welcome to the hard but rewarding work of land-scaping. In this section you'll find the information you need about all the tasks required to install any of the designs in this book, organized in the order in which you'd most likely tackle them. You'll learn how to plan the job; clear the site; construct paths, patios, ponds, fences, arbors, and trellises; prepare the planting beds; and install and maintain the plantings through clearly written text and numer-ous illustrations. Roll up your sleeves and dig in. In just a few weekends you can create a landscape feature that will provide years of enjoyment.

Organizing Your Project

If your gardening experience is limited to mowing the lawn, pruning the bushes, and growing some flowers and vegetables, the thought of starting from scratch and installing a whole new landscape feature might be intimidating. But in fact, adding one of the designs in this book to your property is completely within reach, if you approach it the right way. The key is to divide the project into a series of

steps and take them one at a time. This is how professional landscapers work. It's efficient and orderly, and it makes even big jobs seem manageable.

On this and the facing page, we'll explain how to think your way through a landscaping project and anticipate the various steps. Subsequent topics in this section describe how to do each part of the job. Detailed instructions and illustrations cover all the techniques you'll need to install any design from start to finish.

The step-by-step approach
Choose a design and adapt it to your site. The designs in this book address parts of the home landscape. In the most attractive and effective home landscapes, all the various parts work together. Don't be afraid to change the shape of beds; alter the number, kinds, and positions of plants; or revise paths and structures to bring them into harmony with their surroundings.

To see the relationships with your existing landscape, you can draw the design on a scaled plan of your property. Or you can work on the site itself, placing wooden stakes, pots, or whatever is handy to represent plants and structures.

Lay out the design on site. Once you've decided what you want to do, you'll need to lay out the paths and structures and outline the beds. Some people are comfortable pacing off distances and relying on their eye to judge sizes and relative positions. Others prefer to transfer the grid from the plan full size onto the site, using garden lime (a white powder available at nurseries) like chalk on a blackboard to "draw" a grid or outlines of planting beds.

Clear the site. (See pp. 254–255.) Sometimes you have to work around existing features—a nice big tree, a building or fence, a sidewalk—but it's usually easiest to start a new landscaping project by removing unwanted structures or pavement and killing, cutting down, or uprooting all the plants. This can gener-

DIGGING POSTHOLES

AMENDING SOIL

COMPOST

16-16-16

ate a lot of debris to dispose of, but it's often worth the trouble to make a fresh start.

Make provisions for water. (See pp. 256–257.) In California, most landscape plants require more water than nature provides. A well-thought-out irrigation strategy and system can help you make the most of this increasingly precious natural resource. You'll need to plan its installation carefully. Some permanent parts of most watering systems need to be installed before the other landscape features. Additional parts are installed after the soil is prepared. And the final components are normally placed after planting.

Build the "hardscape." (See pp. 258–285.) Hardscape includes landscape structures such as fences, trellises, arbors, retaining walls, walkways, edging, and outdoor lighting. Install these elements before you start any planting.

Prepare the soil. (See pp. 286–289.) On most properties, it's uncommon to find soil that's as good as it should be for growing plants. Typically, the soil around a new house is shallow, compacted, and infertile. Some plants tolerate such poor conditions, but they don't thrive. To grow healthy, attractive plants, you need to improve the quality of the soil throughout the entire area that you're planning to plant.

Do the planting and add mulch. (See pp. 291–296.) Putting plants in the ground usually goes quite quickly and gives instant gratification. Mulching the soil makes the area look neat even while the plants are still small.

Maintain the planting. (See pp. 297–305.) Most plantings need regular watering and occasional weeding for the first year or two. After that, depending on the design you've chosen, you'll have to do some routine maintenance—watering, pruning, shaping, cutting back, and cleaning up—to keep the plants looking their best. This may take as little as a few hours a year or as much as an hour or two of your time every week throughout the growing season.

TRANSPLANTING

SETTING FLAGSTONES

Clearing the Site

The site you've chosen for a landscaping project may or may not need to be cleared of fences, old pavement, construction debris, and other objects. Unless your house is newly built, the site will almost certainly be covered with plants.

Before you start cutting plants down, try to find someone to identify them for you. As you walk around together, make a sketch that shows which plants are where, and attach labels to the plants, too. Determine whether there are any desirable plants worth saving—mature shade trees that you should work around, shapely shrubs that aren't too big to dig up and relocate or give away, worthwhile perennials and ground covers that you could divide and replant, or healthy sod that you could lay elsewhere. Likewise, decide which plants have to go—diseased or crooked trees, straggly or overgrown shrubs, weedy brush, invasive ground covers, tattered lawn.

You can clear small areas yourself, bundling the brush for pickup and tossing soft-stemmed plants on the compost pile, but if you have lots of woody brush or any trees to remove, you might want to hire someone else to do the job. A crew armed with power tools can turn a thicket into a pile of wood chips in just a few hours. Have them pull out the roots and grind the stumps, too. Save the chips; they're good for surfacing paths, or you can use them as mulch.

Working around a tree

If there are any large, healthy trees on your site, be careful as you work around them. It's okay to prune off some of a tree's limbs, as shown on the facing page, but respect its trunk and its roots. Keep heavy equipment from beneath the tree's canopy, and don't raise or lower the level of the soil there. Try never to cut or wound the bark on the trunk (don't nail things to a tree), because that exposes the tree to disease organisms. Plantings beneath existing native plants, such as California native oaks, that are adapted to dry summers, can endanger their health. Consult a certified arborist on ways to integrate these handsome, but sensitive, trees into your landscape and care for them properly.

Killing perennial weeds

Some common weeds that sprout back from perennial roots or runners are bindweed, blackberry, Bermuda grass, Johnson grass, nutsedge, and poison oak. Garden plants that can become weedy include bamboo, English ivy, ground ivy, pampas grass,

Smothering weeds

This technique is easier than digging, particularly for eradicating large infestations, but much slower. First mow or cut the tops of the weeds as close to the ground as possible ❶. Then cover the area with overlapped sections from a newspaper ❷ or flattened-out cardboard boxes, and top with a layer of mulch, such as straw, grass clippings, tree leaves, wood chips, or other organic material spread several inches deep ❸.

Smothering works by excluding light, which stops photosynthesis. If any shoots reach up through the covering and produce green leaves, pull them out immediately. Wait a few months, until you're sure the weeds are dead, before you dig into the smothered area and plant there.

Where summers are hot, you can also kill weeds through a process called solarization. Till the weeds into the soil and moisten the area. Then cover the soil with a thick sheet of clear plastic, sealing its edges by burying them in a shallow trench. The heat generated underneath the plastic kills the weeds.

SMOTHERING WEEDS

❶ Smothering kills weeds by depriving them of light. Cut the tops off close to the ground.

❷ Cover with thick newspaper or cardboard.

❸ Top with several inches of mulch. Wait a few months to be sure weeds are dead, and then till rotted newspaper and mulch into the soil.

broom, and mint. Once they get established, perennial weeds are hard to eliminate. You can't just cut off the tops, because the plants keep sprouting back. You need to dig the weeds out, smother them, or kill them with an herbicide before you plant a bed.

Digging. You can often do a good job of removing a perennial weed if you dig carefully at the base of the stems, find the roots, and follow them as far as possible, pulling out every bit of root that you find. Some plant roots go deeper than you can dig. Most plants will resprout from the bits that you miss, but these leftover sprouts are easy to pull.

Spraying. Herbicides are fast and effective weed killers. Ask at the nursery for those that break down quickly into more benign substances, and make sure the weed you're trying to kill is listed on the product label. Apply all herbicides as directed by the manufacturer. After spraying, you usually have to wait from one to four weeks for the weed to die. Some weeds need to be sprayed a second or third time before they give up.

Replacing turf

If you're planning to add a landscape feature where you now have lawn, you can recycle the turf to repair or extend the lawn elsewhere on your property.

The drawing below shows a technique for removing relatively small areas of strong, healthy turf for replanting. First, with a sharp shovel, cut it into squares or strips of about 1 to 2 ft. (These small pieces are easy to lift.) ❶ Then slice a few inches deep under each piece and lift them, roots and all, like brownies from a pan ❷. Quickly transplant the squares to a previously prepared site; water them well until the roots are established.

If you don't need the turf, or if it's straggly or weedy, leave it in place and kill the grass. Spraying with an herbicide kills most grasses within one to two weeks, but you may need to spray vigorous turf twice. Or cover it with a tarp or a sheet of black plastic for two to four weeks during the heat of summer (it takes longer in cool weather). Then dig or till the bed, shredding the turf, roots and all, and mixing it into the soil.

Removing large limbs

If there are large trees on your property now, you may want to remove some of the lower limbs so light can reach your plantings. Major pruning of large trees is a job for a professional arborist, but you can remove limbs smaller than 4 in. in diameter and less than 10 ft. above the ground yourself with a simple bow saw or pole saw.

Use the three-step procedure shown below to remove large limbs safely. First, saw partway through the bottom of the limb, approximately 1 ft. out from the trunk ❶. This keeps the bark from tearing down the trunk when the limb falls. Then make a corresponding cut down through the top of the limb ❷—be prepared to get out of the way when the limb drops. Finally, remove the stub ❸. Undercut it slightly or hold it as you finish the cut so that it doesn't fall away and peel bark off the trunk. Note that the cut is not flush with the trunk but is just outside the thick area at the limb's base, called the branch collar. Leaving the branch collar helps the wound heal quickly and naturally. Wound dressing is considered unnecessary today.

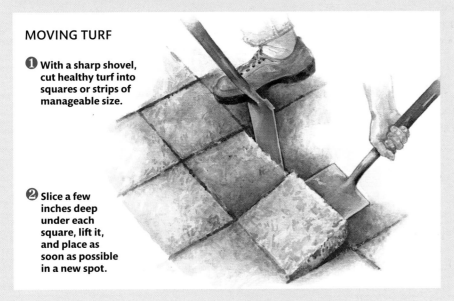

MOVING TURF

❶ **With a sharp shovel, cut healthy turf into squares or strips of manageable size.**

❷ **Slice a few inches deep under each square, lift it, and place as soon as possible in a new spot.**

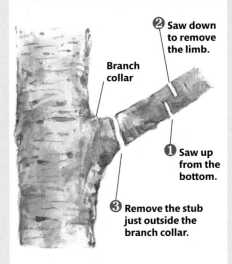

❷ **Saw down to remove the limb.**

Branch collar

❶ **Saw up from the bottom.**

❸ **Remove the stub just outside the branch collar.**

Water for Your Plants

Many areas of the West have long, dry summers and frequent droughts, making water a critical concern of gardeners. Though some plants will survive long dry periods once established, almost all plants will need regular watering the first few years after planting. Most will need summer watering their entire life to look their best.

But there is more at stake than just the survival of plants. Water conservation is a daily obligation in the West, where water is a valuable and limited resource. Outdoor landscapes use a large portion of urban water, so nothing should be wasted.

For the health of your plants and for the preservation of a valuable resource, make water conservation part of your landscape planning from the beginning. The box below outlines effective water-saving practices for home landscapes. (See p. 297 for more on when and how much to water.) You can also consult your local water department for advice about watering gardens and lawns. Many provide incentives for using drought-tolerant plants, reducing the amount of lawn, and installing the most water-conserving irrigation systems. More importantly, some cities, such as Las Vegas, Nevada, have ordinances that restrict where you can install lawns and how often they can be watered.

Watering systems

One of the best ways to conserve water is to use an efficient delivery system. The simplest watering systems—watering cans and handheld hoses—are also the most limited and inefficient. They can be adequate for watering new transplants or widely separated individual plants. But sprinkling plants in an entire bed with a hose and nozzle for even as long as an hour may provide less water than half an inch of rainfall. And wetting just the top few inches of soil this way encourages shallow root growth, making it necessary to water more frequently. To provide enough water to soak the soil to a depth of a foot or more, you need a system that can run untended for extended periods.

Hose-end sprinklers are easy to set up and leave to soak an area. But they're also inefficient: water is blown away by wind. It runs off sloped or paved areas. It is applied unevenly, or it falls too far away from individual plants to be of use to them. And because sprinklers soak leaves as well as soil, the damp foliage may breed fungal diseases.

Low-volume irrigation. For garden beds and landscape plantings, low-volume irrigation systems are the most efficient and offer the most flexibility and control. Frequently called "drip" irrigation systems, they deliver water at low pressure through a network of plastic pipes, hoses, and tubing and a variety of emitters and microsprinklers. Such systems are designed to apply water slowly and directly to the roots of targeted plants, so very little water is lost or wasted on plants that don't need it. Because water is usually applied at soil level, the risk of foliar diseases is reduced. And because less soil is watered, weeds are also reduced.

Water-wise practices

Choose plants carefully. Many plants that require little water, including Western natives, thrive in the state's dry summer climate and are increasingly available from local nurseries and garden centers.

Group plants with similar water needs. Position plants that require the most water near the house, where they can be more easily tended and watered. Use drought-tolerant plants farther from the house.

Plant in fall. This way, new plants will have the cooler, wetter winter and spring seasons to become established before facing the heat of summer.

Mulch plantings. A 2- to 3-in. layer of mulch reduces evaporation by keeping the soil cool and sheltering it from wind.

Create water-retaining basins. Use these to direct irrigation water to large plants. Make a low soil mound around the plant's perimeter, at its drip line. (Basins aren't necessary in drip-irrigated beds.)

Limit lawn size. Lawns demand lots of water. Reduce the size of your lawn by planting beds, borders, and less thirsty ground covers.

Water in the morning. Lower morning temperatures and less wind mean less water is lost to evaporation.

Adjust watering to conditions. Water less during cool weather in the spring and fall. Turn off automatic timers during the rainy season.

Install, monitor, and maintain an irrigation system. Even a simple drip system conserves water. Once it's installed, check and adjust the equipment on a regular basis. Be sure to inspect frequently for clogged emitters.

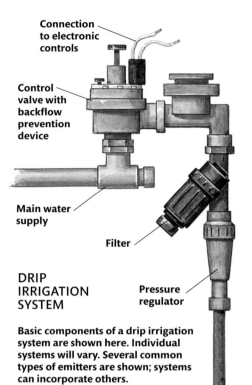

Connection to electronic controls

Control valve with backflow prevention device

Main water supply

Filter

DRIP IRRIGATION SYSTEM

Pressure regulator

Basic components of a drip irrigation system are shown here. Individual systems will vary. Several common types of emitters are shown; systems can incorporate others.

Simple low-volume systems can be attached to ordinary outdoor faucets or garden hoses and controlled manually. More-sophisticated systems include their own attachment to your main water supply, a network of valves and buried pipes that allow you to divide your property into zones, and an electronic control device that can automatically water each zone at preset times for preset durations.

A person with modest mechanical skills and basic tools can plan and install a low-volume irrigation system. Extensive multizone systems (particularly those with their own attachment to the main water supply) are more difficult to install. If you do, have a professional review your plans before you start. You can buy kits or individual system components from garden centers, nurseries, or specialty suppliers. (The main components of low-volume systems are illustrated on this page.) Although most manufacturers provide instructions, choose from among your local suppliers based on their knowledge of system design and installation and their ability to help you with both.

Low-volume-system components. Any irrigation system connected to a domestic water supply needs a ***backflow prevention device*** (also called an "antisiphon device") at the point of connection to the water supply to protect drinking water from contamination. Check with local health or building officials to determine whether a specific type of backflow prevention device is required.

Install a ***filter*** to prevent minerals and flakes that slough off metal water pipes from clogging the emitters. You'll need to clean the filter regularly. All hoses and tubing should be plastic, not metal.

Pressure regulators reduce the mains' water pressure to levels required by the system's low-volume emitters.

Supply lines deliver water from the source to the emitters. Some systems incorporate buried lines of rigid plastic pipe to carry water to plantings anywhere on the property. For aboveground use, you'll need flexible tubing designed specifically for low-volume irrigation.

Emitters and ***soaker hoses*** deliver the water to the plants. Various drip fittings, bubblers, and microsprinklers can be plugged into the flexible plastic tubing. A single emitter or a group of emitters might serve individual or groups of plants. Soaker hoses and "ooze" tubes seep or drip water along their length. Consult with your supplier about which delivery systems best meet your plants' needs.

A ***timer*** or ***electronic controller*** helps ensure efficient water use. A controller won't forget and leave the water on too long. (It may also water during a rainstorm, however.) Used in conjunction with zoned plantings, these devices provide control and flexibility to deal with the specific water needs of groups of plants or even individual specimens.

Newer controllers can be connected (sometimes wirelessly) to on-site or remote weather stations or soil moisture sensors for very precise watering. Many can also be wired to rain sensors, which turn off the sprinklers when it rains.

Installation. Lay underground piping that crosses paths, patios, or similar landscape features after the site is cleared but before installing any of these permanent features. Lay pipes in planting areas after you have prepared the soil. That way, you won't damage the piping when digging or rototilling. Install underground pipe in trenches dug to the appropriate depth, and then temporarily cap the ends. Hook up the aboveground tubing, and position emitters after planting.

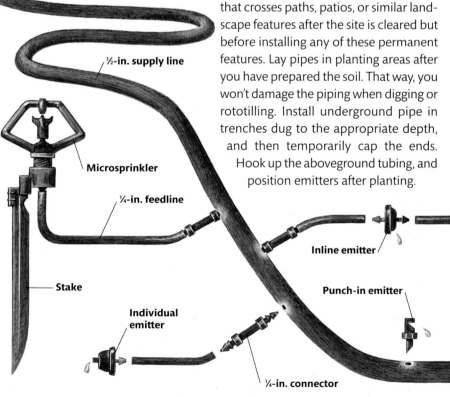

½-in. supply line

Microsprinkler

¼-in. feedline

Stake

Inline emitter

Punch-in emitter

Individual emitter

¼-in. connector

Making Paths and Walkways

Every landscape needs paths and walkways. A path can divide and define the spaces in the landscape, orchestrate the way the landscape is viewed, and even be a key element enhancing its beauty.

Whether it is a graceful curving garden path or a utilitarian slab leading to the garage, a walk has two main functional requirements: durability and safety. It should hold up through seasonal changes. It should provide a well-drained surface that is easy to walk on and to maintain.

A path's function helps determine its surface and its character. In general, heavily trafficked walkways leading to a door, garage, or shed need hard, smooth (but not slick) surfaces and should take you where you want to go fairly directly. A path to a backyard play area could be a strip of soft wood bark, easy on the knees of impatient children. A relaxed stroll in the garden might require only a hopscotch collection of flat stones meandering from one prized plant to another.

Before laying out a walk or path, spend some time observing existing traffic patterns. If your path makes use of a route people already take (particularly children), they'll be more likely to stay on the path and off the lawn or flowers. Avoid areas that are slow to drain. When determining path width, consider whether the path must accommodate rototillers and wheelbarrows or two strollers walking abreast, or just provide steppingstone access for maintaining the plants.

Dry-laid paths

You can make a path by laying bricks or spreading wood chips on top of bare earth. While quick and easy, this method has drawbacks. Laid on the surface, with no edging to contain them, loose materials are soon scattered, and solid materials are easily jostled out of place. If the earth base doesn't drain well, the path will be a swamp after a rainstorm. And in higher-elevation cold-winter areas, repeated freezing and thawing expands and contracts the soil, moving path and walkway materials laid on it. The effect of this "frost heaving" is minimal on loose materials, but it can shift brick and stone significantly out of line.

The method we recommend—laying surface material on an excavated base of sand or gravel, or both—minimizes these problems. Water moves through sand and gravel quickly, and such a base cushions the surface materials from any freeze-thaw movement of the underlying soil. Excavation can place the path surface at ground level, where the surrounding soil or an edging can contain loose materials and keep hard materials from shifting.

The styles and materials discussed in this section can be laid on an excavated base of sand or gravel, alone or in combination.

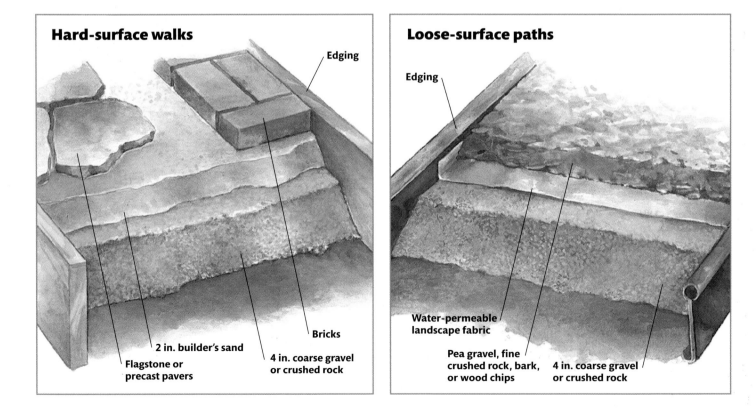

Hard-surface walks

Edging

2 in. builder's sand

Flagstone or precast pavers

Bricks

4 in. coarse gravel or crushed rock

Loose-surface paths

Edging

Water-permeable landscape fabric

Pea gravel, fine crushed rock, bark, or wood chips

4 in. coarse gravel or crushed rock

Choosing a surface

Walkways and paths can be made of either hard or soft material. Your choice of material will depend on the walkway's function, your budget, and your personal preferences.

Soft materials, including bark, wood chips, pine needles, and loose gravel, are best for informal and low-traffic areas. Inexpensive and simple to install, they settle, scatter, or decompose and must be replenished or replaced every few years.

Hard materials, such as brick, flagstone, and concrete pavers, are more expensive and time consuming to install, but they are permanent, requiring only occasional maintenance. (Compacted crushed stone can also make a hard-surface walk.) Durable and handsome, they're ideal for high-traffic, high-profile areas.

Bark, wood chips, and pine needles

Perfect for a natural look or a quick temporary path, these loose materials can be laid directly on the soil or, if drainage is poor, on a gravel bed. Bagged materials from a nursery or garden center will be cleaner, more uniform, and considerably more expensive than bulk supplies bought by the cubic yard. Check with local tree services to find the best prices on bulk material.

Gravel and crushed rock

Loose rounded gravel gives a bit underfoot, creating a soft but messy path. The angular facets of crushed stone eventually compact into a hard and tidier path that can, if the surrounding soil is firm enough, be laid without an edging. Gravel and stone type and color vary from area to area. Buy materials by the ton or cubic yard.

Concrete pavers

Precast concrete pavers are versatile, readily available, and often the least expensive hard-surface material. They come in a range of colors and shapes, including interlocking patterns. Precast edgings are also available. Most home and garden centers carry a variety of precast pavers, which are sold by the piece.

PRECAST PAVERS

Brick

Widely available in a range of sizes, colors, and textures, brick complements many design styles. When carefully laid on a well-prepared sand-and-gravel base, brick provides an even, safe, and long-lasting surface. If you buy used brick, pick the densest and hardest. Avoid brick with glazed faces; the glaze traps moisture and salts, which eventually damage the brick. If you live where it regularly freezes and thaws, buy bricks rated to withstand the weather conditions.

RUNNING BOND

TWO-BRICK BASKET WEAVE

HERRINGBONE

DIAGONAL HERRINGBONE

Flagstone

"Flagstone" is a generic term for stratified stone that can be split to form pavers. Limestone, sandstone, and bluestone are common paving materials. The surfaces of marble and slate are usually too smooth to make safe paving. Cut into squares or rectangles, flagstone can be laid as individual steppingstones or in interesting patterns. Flagstones come in a range of colors, textures, and sizes. Flags for walks should be at least 2 in. thick. Purchased by weight, surface area, or pallet load, flagstones are usually the most expensive paving choice.

CUT FLAGSTONE

CUT AND IRREGULAR FLAGSTONE

IRREGULAR FLAGSTONE

Drainage

Few things are worse than a path dotted with puddles or icy patches. To prevent these from forming, the soil around and beneath the path should drain well. The path's location and construction should ensure that rainwater does not collect on the surface. Before you locate a path, observe runoff and drainage on your property during and after heavy rains. Avoid routing a path through areas where water courses, collects, or is slow to drain.

While both loose and hard paving can sometimes be successfully laid directly on well-drained compacted soil, laying surface materials on a base of sand or gravel will help improve drainage and minimize frost heaving. Where rainfall is scant or drainage is good, a 4-in. base of either sand or gravel is usually sufficient. For most other situations, a 4-in. gravel bed topped with 2 in. of sand will work well. Very poorly drained soils may require more gravel, an additional layer of coarse rock beneath the gravel, or even drain tiles. If you suspect your site has serious drainage problems, consult a landscape architect or contractor.

Finally, keep water from pooling on a walk by making its surface higher in the center than at the edges. The center of a 4-ft.-wide walk should be at least ½ in. higher than its edges. If you're using a drag board to level the sand base, curve its lower edge to create this "crown." Otherwise crown the surface by eye.

Edgings

All walk surfaces need to be contained in some fashion along their edges. Where soil is firm or tightly knit by turf, neatly cut walls of the excavation can serve as edging. An installed edging often provides more effective containment, particularly if the walk surface is above grade. It also prevents damage to bricks or stones on the edges of paths. Walkway edgings are commonly made of 1- or 2-in.-thick lumber, thicker landscaping timbers, brick, or stone.

Wood edging

Wood should be rot-resistant redwood or cedar or some other kind of wood that is pressure-treated for ground-contact use. If you're working in loose soils, fix a deep wooden edging to support stakes with double-headed nails. When the path is laid, pull the nails, and fill and tamp behind the edging. Then drive the stakes below grade. In firmer soils, or if the edging material is not wide enough, install it on top of the gravel base. Position the top of the edging at the height of the path. Dimension lumber 1 in. thick is pliable enough to bend around gradual curves.

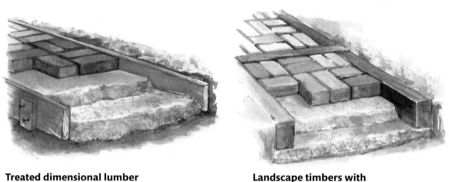

Treated dimensional lumber with support stakes

Landscape timbers with crossties laid on gravel base

Brick and stone edging

In firm soil, a row of bricks laid on edge and perpendicular to the length of the path adds stability. For a more substantial edging, stand bricks on end on the excavated soil surface; add the gravel base; and tamp the earth around the base of the bricks on the outside of the excavation. Stone edgings laid on end can be set in the same way. "End-up" brick or stone edgings are easy to install on curved walks.

Bricks on edge, laid on gravel base

Bricks on end, laid on soil

Preparing the base

Having decided on location and materials, you can get down to business. The initial steps of layout and base preparation are much the same for all surface materials. Before you construct paths or walkways, check your irrigation plans. If underground water lines will cross any paths, be sure to lay the lines first.

Layout

Lay out straight sections with stakes and string ❶. You can plot curves with stakes and "fair" the curve with a garden hose, or you can outline the curve with the hose alone, marking it with lime or sand.

Excavation

The excavation depth depends on how much sand-and-gravel base your soil's drainage calls for, the thickness of the surface material, and its position above or below grade ❷. Mark the depth on a stake or stick and use this to check depth as you dig. Walking surfaces are most comfortable if they are reasonably level across their width. Check the bottom of the excavation with a level as you dig. If the walk cuts across a slope, you'll need to remove soil from the high side and use it to fill the low side to produce a level surface. If you've added soil or if the subsoil is loose, compact it by tamping.

Edging installation

Some edgings can be installed immediately after excavation; others are placed on top of the gravel portion of the base ❸. (See the sidebar "Edgings" on the opposite page.) If the soil's drainage permits, you can now lay soft materials, loose gravel, or crushed stone on the excavated, tamped, and edged soil base. To control weeds, and to keep bark, chips, or pine needles from mixing with the subsoil, you can spread water-permeable landscape fabric over the excavated soil base.

Laying the base

Now add gravel (if required), rake it level, and compact it ❹. Use gravel up to 1 in. in diameter or ¼- to ¾-in. crushed stone, which drains and compacts well. You can rent a hand tamper (a heavy metal plate on the end of a pole) or a machine compactor if you have a large area to compact.

If you're making a loose-gravel or crushed-stone walk, add the surface material on top of the base gravel. (See "Loose materials" page 262.) For walks of brick, stone, or pavers, add a 2-in. layer of builder's sand, not the finer sand masons use for mixing mortar.

Rake the sand smooth with the back of a level-head rake. You can level the sand with a wooden drag board, also called a "screed" ❺. Nail together two 1x4s or notch a 1x6 to place the lower edge at the desired height of the sand, and run the board along the path edging. To settle the sand, dampen it thoroughly with a hose set on fine spray. Fill any low spots; rake or drag the surface level; and then dampen it again.

PREPARING THE BASE

❶ **Lay out the path with stakes, string, garden hose, and lime.**

❷ **Dig out path between layout string and lime lines.**

❸ **Install the edging.**

❹ **Rake out gravel base.**

Lay out free-form curved sections with garden hose and mark with lime.

Mark straight sections with 1x2 stakes and string.

Drag board
Edging

❺ **Level sand base with a drag board.**

Laying the surface

Whether you're laying loose or hard material, take time to plan your work. Provide access so delivery trucks can place material close to the worksite.

Loose materials

Install water-permeable landscape fabric over the gravel base to prevent gravel from mixing with the surface material. Spread bark or wood chips 2 to 4 in. deep. For a pine-needle surface, spread 2 in. of needles on top of several inches of bark or chips. Spread loose pea gravel about 2 in. deep. For a harder, more uniform surface, add ½ in. of fine crushed stone on top of the gravel. You can let traffic compact crushed-rock surfaces, or compact them by hand or with a machine.

Bricks and precast pavers

Take time to figure out the pattern and spacing of the bricks or pavers by laying them out on the lawn or driveway, rather than disturbing your carefully prepared sand base. When you're satisfied, begin in a corner, laying the bricks or pavers gently on the sand so the base remains even ❶. Lay full bricks first; then cut bricks to fit as needed at the edges. To produce uniform joints, space bricks with a piece of wood cut to the joint width. You can also maintain alignment with a straightedge or with a string stretched across the path be-tween nails or stakes. Move the string as the work proceeds.

As you complete a row or section, bed the bricks or pavers into the sand base with several firm raps of a rubber mallet or a hammer on a scrap 2x4. Check with a level or straightedge to make sure the surface is even ❷. (You'll have to do this by feel or eye across the width of a crowned path.) Lift low bricks or pavers carefully and fill beneath them with sand; then reset them. Don't stand on the walk until you've filled the joints.

When you've finished a section, sweep fine, dry mason's sand into the joints, working across the surface of the path in all directions ❸. Wet thoroughly with a fine spray and let dry; then sweep in more sand if necessary. If you want a "living" walk, sweep a loam-sand mixture into the joints and plant small, tough, ground-hugging plants, such as thyme, in them.

Rare is the brick walk that can be laid without cutting some-thing to fit. To cut brick, mark the line of the cut with a dark pen-cil all around the brick. With the brick resting firmly on sand or soil, score the entire line by rapping a wide mason's chisel called a "brickset" with a heavy wooden mallet or a soft-headed steel hammer as shown on the facing page. Place the brickset in the scored line across one face and give it a sharp blow with the hammer to cut the brick.

If you have a lot of bricks to cut, or if you want greater accu-racy, consider renting a masonry saw. Whether you work by hand or machine, always wear safety glasses.

LOOSE MATERIALS

Cover gravel base with water-permeable landscape fabric and add 2 to 4 in. of bark or wood chips.

BRICKS AND PRECAST PAVERS

To turn square corners, align the edging board with a carpenter's square.

❶ **Begin laying in a corner.**

❷ **Check the surface with a level or straightedge. Fill under low bricks; tamp down high ones. Use a plank to distribute your weight if you must work on the path.**

❸ **Sweep fine, dry sand into the joints to fix the bricks or pavers in place.**

Steppingstones

A steppingstone walk set in turf creates a charming effect and is very simple to lay. You can use cut or irregular flagstones or field-stone, which is irregular in thickness as well as in outline. Arrange the stones on the turf; then set them one by one. Cut into the turf around the stone with a sharp flat shovel or trowel, and remove the stone; then dig out the sod with the shovel. Placing stones at or below grade will keep them away from mower blades. Fill low spots beneath the stone with earth or sand so the stone doesn't move when stepped on.

Cut around steppingstone with shovel or trowel.

Remove sod and soil.

Set in place, filling with sand or soil to bed stone firmly.

Cutting bricks

Wear safety glasses.

Scored line

Brickset chisel

Cutting flagstones

Wear safety glasses.

Scored line

Wood batten

Brickset

Flagstones

Install cut stones of uniform thickness as described for bricks and pavers. Working out patterns beforehand is particularly important—stones are too heavy to move around more than necessary. To produce a level surface with cut or irregular stones of varying thickness, you'll need to add or remove sand for each stone. Set the stone carefully on sand; then move it back and forth to work it into place ❶. Lay a level or straightedge over three or four stones to check the surface's evenness ❷. When a section is complete, fill the joints with sand or with sand and loam as described for bricks and pavers.

You can cut flagstone with a technique similar to that used for bricks. Score the line of the cut on the top surface with a brickset and hammer. Prop the stone on a piece of scrap wood, positioning the line of cut slightly beyond the edge of the wood. Securing the bottom edge of the stone with your foot, place the brickset on the scored line and strike sharply to make the cut.

FLAGSTONES

❶ Set flagstones in place carefully to avoid disturbing the sand base.

❷ Extend a straightedge over several stones to check the surface for evenness. Tap high spots to level.

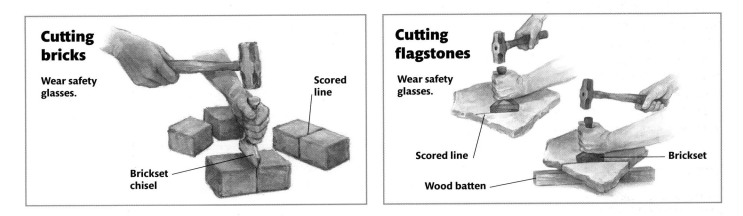

Laying a Patio

You can make a simple patio using the same techniques and materials we have discussed for paths. To ensure good drainage, an even surface, and durability, lay hard surfaces such as brick, flagstone, and pavers on a well-prepared base of gravel, sand, and compacted soil. (Crushed-rock and gravel surfaces likewise benefit from a sound base.) Make sure the surface drains away from any adjacent structure (house or garage); a drop-off of ¼ in. per foot is usually adequate. If the patio isn't near a structure, make it higher in the center to avoid puddles.

Establish the outline of the patio as described for paths; then excavate the area roughly to accommodate 4 in. of gravel, 2 in. of sand, and the thickness of the paving surface. (Check with a local nursery or landscape contractor to find out if local conditions require alterations in the type or amounts of base material.) Now grade the rough excavation to provide drainage, using a simple 4-ft. grid of wooden stakes as shown in the drawings.

Drive the first row of stakes next to the house (or in the center of a freestanding patio), leveling them with a 4-ft. builder's level or a smaller level resting on a straight 2x4. The tops of these stakes should be at the height of the top of the sand base (finish grade of the patio less the thickness of the surface material) ❶. Working from this row of stakes, establish another row about 4 to 5 ft. from the first. Make the tops of these stakes 1 in. lower than those of the first row, using a level and spacer block, as shown below. Continue adding rows of stakes, each

LAYING A SIMPLE PATIO

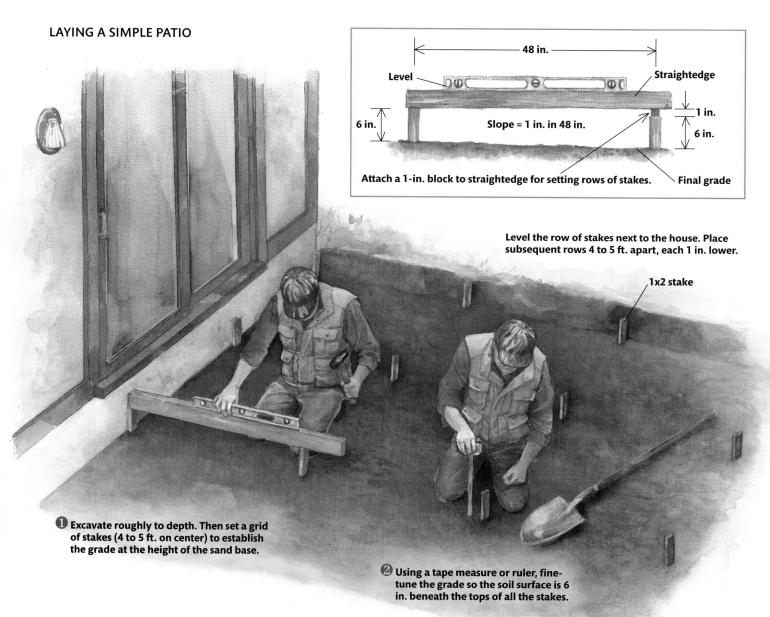

48 in.

Level   Straightedge

6 in.   Slope = 1 in. in 48 in.   1 in.

6 in.

Attach a 1-in. block to straightedge for setting rows of stakes.   Final grade

Level the row of stakes next to the house. Place subsequent rows 4 to 5 ft. apart, each 1 in. lower.

1x2 stake

❶ Excavate roughly to depth. Then set a grid of stakes (4 to 5 ft. on center) to establish the grade at the height of the sand base.

❷ Using a tape measure or ruler, fine-tune the grade so the soil surface is 6 in. beneath the tops of all the stakes.

1 in. lower than the previous row, until the entire area is staked. Then, with a measuring tape or a ruler and a shovel, fine-tune the grading by removing or adding soil until the excavated surface is 6 in. (the thickness of the gravel-sand base) below the tops of all the stakes ❷.

When installing the sand-and-gravel base, you'll want to maintain the drainage grade you've just established and produce an even surface for the paving material. If you have a good eye or a very small patio, you can do this by sight. Otherwise, you can use the stakes to install a series of 1x3 or 1x4 leveling boards, as shown in the drawing below. (Before adding gravel, you may want to cover the soil with water-permeable landscape fabric to keep perennial weeds from growing; just cut slits to accommodate the stakes.)

Add a few inches of gravel ❸. Then set leveling boards along each row of stakes, with the boards' top edges even with the top of the stakes ❹. Drive additional stakes to sandwich the boards in place (don't use nails). Distribute the remaining inch or so of gravel and compact it by hand or machine, then add the 2 in. of sand. Dragging a straight 2x4 across two adjacent rows of leveling boards will produce a precise grade and an even surface ❺. Wet the sand and fill low spots that settle.

You can install the patio surface as previously described for paths, removing the leveling boards as the bricks or pavers reach them ❻. Disturbing the sand surface as little as possible, slide the boards out from between the stakes and drive the stakes an inch or so beneath the level of the sand. Cover the stakes and fill the gaps left by the boards with sand, tamped down carefully. Then continue laying the surface. Finally, sweep fine sand into the joints.

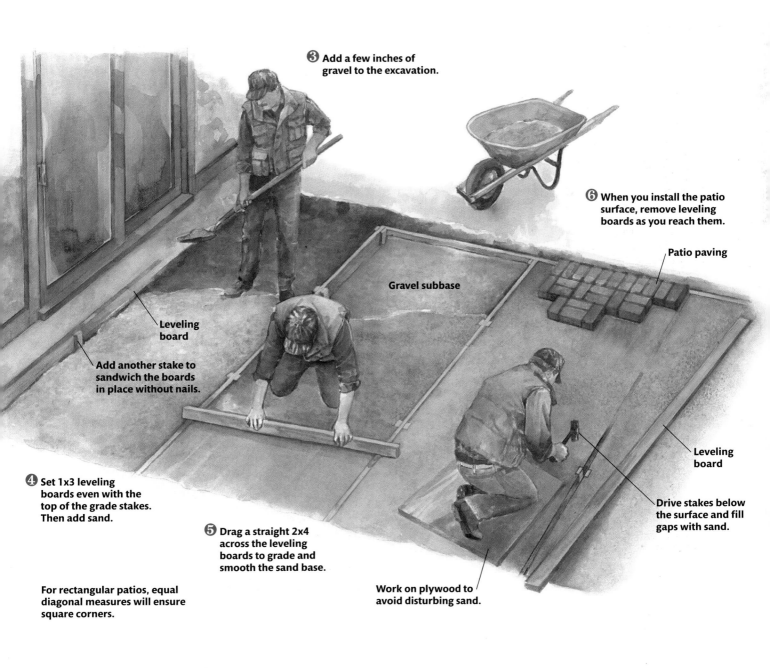

❸ **Add a few inches of gravel to the excavation.**

❻ **When you install the patio surface, remove leveling boards as you reach them.**

Patio paving

Gravel subbase

Leveling board

Add another stake to sandwich the boards in place without nails.

Leveling board

❹ **Set 1x3 leveling boards even with the top of the grade stakes. Then add sand.**

Drive stakes below the surface and fill gaps with sand.

❺ **Drag a straight 2x4 across the leveling boards to grade and smooth the sand base.**

For rectangular patios, equal diagonal measures will ensure square corners.

Work on plywood to avoid disturbing sand.

Installing a Pond

It wasn't so long ago that a garden pond like the one in this book required yards of concrete, an expert mason, and deep pockets. Today's strong, lightweight, and long-lasting synthetic liners and rigid fiberglass shells have put garden pools in reach of every homeowner. Installation does require some hard labor but little expertise: just dig a hole; spread the liner or seat the shell; install edging; and plant. We'll discuss installation of a pond with a liner in the main text; see below for installing a smaller, fiberglass pool.

Liner notes

More and more nurseries and garden centers are carrying flexible pond liners; you can also buy them from mail-order suppliers specializing in water gardens. Synthetic rubber liners are longer lasting but more expensive than PVC liners. (Both are much cheaper than rigid fiberglass shells.) Buy only liners specifically made for garden ponds—don't use ordinary plastic sheeting. Many people feel that black liners look best; blue liners tend to make the pond look like a swimming pool.

Before you dig

First, make sure you comply with any rules your town may have about water features. Then keep the following ideas in mind when locating your pond. Avoid trees whose shade keeps sun-loving water plants from thriving; whose roots make digging a chore; and whose flowers, leaves, and seeds clog the water, making it unsightly and inhospitable to plants or fish. Avoid the low spot on your property; otherwise your pond will be a catch basin for runoff. Select a level spot; the immediate vicinity of the pond

Small fiberglass pool

A fiberglass shell or half barrel 2 to 3 ft. in diameter and 2 to 3 ft. deep is ideal for the small pool on p. 107. Garden centers often stock pond shells in a variety of shapes.

Dig a hole about 6 in. wider on all sides than the shell. Hole depth should equal that of the shell plus 1 in. for a sand base and an allowance for the river rock that mulches the bed and surrounds the pool. To keep rocks out of the water, position the top edge of the shell or barrel so that it will be at the same height as the rock mulch. Compact the bottom of the hole and spread the sand; then lower the shell into place. Add temporary wedges or props if necessary to orient and level the shell. Slowly fill the shell with water, backfilling around it with sand or sifted soil so the fill keeps pace with the rising water level.

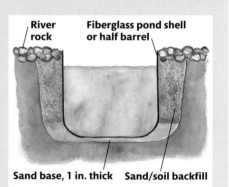

River rock   Fiberglass pond shell or half barrel

Sand base, 1 in. thick   Sand/soil backfill

A patio pond (pp. 104–105)

This pond is integrated with an adjacent patio and incorporates a gently sloping river-rock "shore." Concrete blocks support a flagstone walk and patio paving on three sides. The liner rests on a sand base and is covered with several inches of sand to cushion against, and prevent damage from, the river rock and concrete blocks.

While the techniques on these pages will be useful in the pond's construction, check with your local building-code officials and consult with an experienced pond builder about its details. In particular, you need to ensure that the pond walls supporting the walkway and patio are properly constructed.

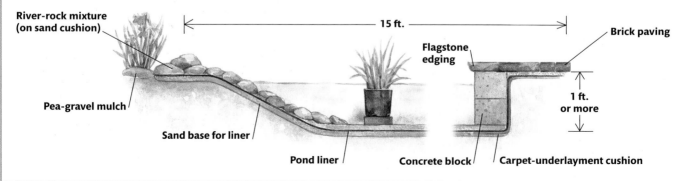

River-rock mixture (on sand cushion)

15 ft.

Brick paving

Flagstone edging

1 ft. or more

Pea-gravel mulch

Sand base for liner

Pond liner

Concrete block

Carpet-underlayment cushion

must be level, and starting out that way saves a lot of work. (Remember that you can use excavated soil to help level the site.)

Using graph paper, enlarge the outline of the pond provided on the site plan on p. 100 or p. 104, altering it as you wish. If you change the size or depth of the pond, or are interested in growing a wider variety of water plants or in adding fish, remember that a healthy pond must achieve a balance between the plants and fish and the volume, depth, and temperature of the water. Even if you're not altering size or pond plants and fish, it's a good idea to consult with a knowledgeable person at a nursery or pet store specializing in water-garden plants and animals.

Calculate the liner width by adding twice the maximum depth of the pool plus an additional 2 ft. to the width. Use the same formula to calculate the length. So, for a 2 x 7 x 15-ft. pond, the liner width would be 4 ft. + 7 ft. + 2 ft. (or 13 ft.). The length would be 4 ft. + 15 ft. + 2 ft. (or 21 ft.).

Water work

Unless you are a very tidy builder, the water you used to fit the liner will be too dirty to leave in the pond. (Spilled mortar can also make the water too alkaline for plants or fish.) Siphon or pump out the water; clean the liner; and refill the pond. If you're adding fish to the pond, you'll need to let the water stand for a week or so to allow any chlorine (which is deadly to fish) to dissipate. Check with local pet stores to find out whether your water contains chemicals that require commercial conditioners to make it safe for fish.

Installing the pond and plants is only the first step in water gardening. It takes patience, experimentation, and usually some consultation with experienced water gardeners to achieve a balance between plants, fish, and waterborne oxygen, nutrients, and waste that will sustain all happily while keeping algae, diseases, insects, and predators at acceptable levels.

Growing pond plants

One water lily, a few upright-growing plants, and a bundle of submerged plants to help keep the water clean are enough for a medium-size pond. An increasing number of nurseries and garden centers stock water lilies and other water plants. For a larger selection, your nursery or garden center may be able to recommend a specialist supplier.

These plants are grown in containers filled with heavy garden soil (not potting soil, which contains ingredients that float). You can buy special containers designed for aquatic plants, or simply use plastic pails or dishpans. Line basketlike containers with burlap to keep the soil from leaking out the holes. A water lily needs at least 2 to 3 gal. of soil; the more, the better. Most other water plants, such as dwarf papyrus, need 1 to 2 gal. of soil.

After planting, add a layer of gravel on the surface to keep soil from clouding the water and to protect roots from marauding fish. Soak the plant and soil thoroughly. Then set the container in the pond, positioning it so the water over the soil is 6 to 18 in. deep for water lilies, 0 to 6 in. for most other plants.

For maximum bloom, push a tablet of special water-lily fertilizer into the pots once or twice a month throughout the summer. Most water plants are easy to grow and carefree, although many are tropicals that die after a hard frost, so you'll have to replace them each spring.

PLANTING WATER PLANTS

Set water plants in a container of heavy garden soil. Then cover the surface with gravel to keep soil from floating away.

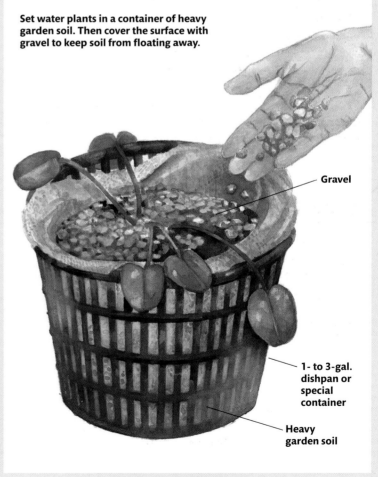

Gravel

1- to 3-gal. dishpan or special container

Heavy garden soil

Excavation

If your soil isn't too compacted or rocky, a good-size pond can be excavated with a shovel or two in a weekend ❶. If the site isn't level, you can grade it using a stake-and-level system like the one described on pp. 264–265 for grading the patio.

Of the two ponds with liners in the Portfolio section, the one on p. 100 is a more common design. The discussion and illustrations on these pages tell how to build a pond like it. The design on p. 104 (shown in cross section in the inset drawing below) is a more demanding construction project.

Outline the pond's shape with garden lime, establishing the curves with a garden hose or by staking out a large grid and plotting from the graph-paper plan. Many garden ponds have two levels. One end, often the widest, is 2 ft. deep to accommodate water lilies and other plants requiring deeper water, as well as fish. The other end is 12 to 16 in. deep for plants requiring shallower submersion. (You can also put plant pots on stacks of bricks to vary heights.) The walls will be less likely to crumble as you dig, and the liner will install more easily, if you slope the walls in about 3 to 4 in. for each foot of depth. Make them smooth, removing roots, rocks, and other sharp protrusions.

Excavate a relief around the perimeter to contain the liner overlap and the width and thickness of the stone edging. To receive runoff after a heavy rain, create an overflow channel, as shown in the drawing on the opposite page. This can simply be a 1- to 2-in. depression a foot or so wide spanned by one of the edging stones. Lengths of PVC pipe placed side by side beneath the stone will keep the liner in place. Position the overflow channel to open onto a lower area of lawn or garden adjacent to the pond or to a rock-filled dry well.

Section through pond

17 ft.

2 ft.

12 to 16 in.

Slope bottom slightly to make draining the pond easier.

5 ft.

Slope in 6 to 8 in.

Slope in 3 to 4 in.

Slope in 3 to 4 in.

INSTALLING A POND WITH A LINER

❶ Dig hole with sloping sides to correct depth. Make sure that perimeter of hole is level.

❷ Spread sand on horizontal surfaces; cushion walls with carpet underlayment.

Excavate shallow relief for edging flagstones.

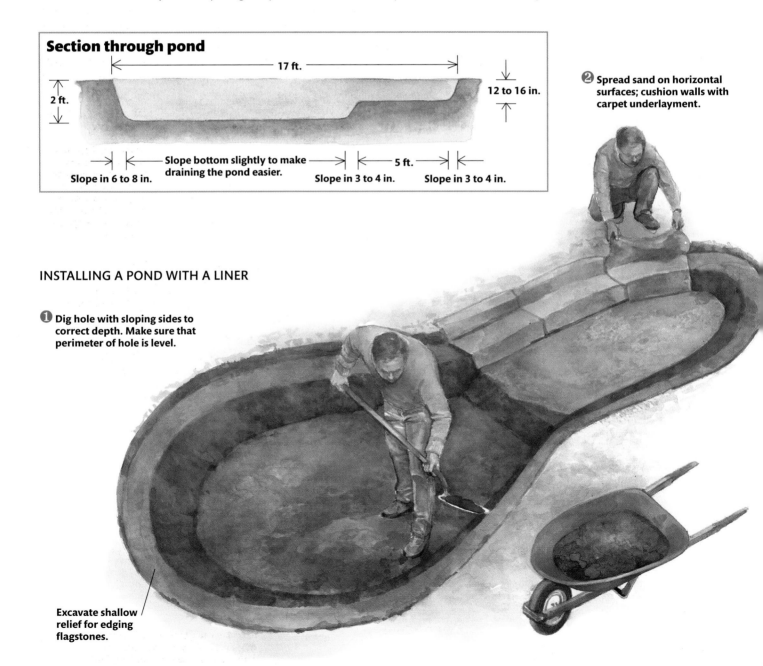

Fitting the liner

When the hole is complete, cushion the surfaces to protect the liner ❷. The drawing shows an inch-thick layer of sand on the bottom surfaces and carpet underlayment on the sloping walls. Fiberglass insulation also works well, as does heavy landscaping fabric.

Stretch the liner across the hole, letting it sag naturally to touch the walls and bottom but keeping it taut enough so it does not bunch up. Weight its edges with bricks or stones; then fill it with water ❸. The water's weight will push the liner against the walls, and the stones will prevent it from blowing around. As it fills, tuck and smooth out as many creases as you can. The weight of the water would make this difficult after the pond is full. If you stand in the pond to do so, take care not to damage the liner. Don't be alarmed if you can't smooth all the creases. Stop filling when the water is 2 in. below the rim of the pond, and cut the liner to fit into the overlap relief ❹. Hold it in place with a few long nails or large "staples" made from coat hangers while you install the edging.

Edging the pond

Finding and fitting flagstones so there aren't wide gaps between them is the most time-consuming part of this task. Cantilevering the stones an inch or two over the water will hide the pond liner somewhat.

The stones can be laid directly on the liner, as shown ❺. Add sand where necessary under the liner to level the surface so that the stones don't rock. Such treatment will withstand the occasional, careful traffic of pond maintenance. If you anticipate heavier traffic, you can bed the stones in 2 to 3 in. of mortar. It's prudent to consult with a landscape contractor about whether your intended use and soil require a footing for mortared stones.

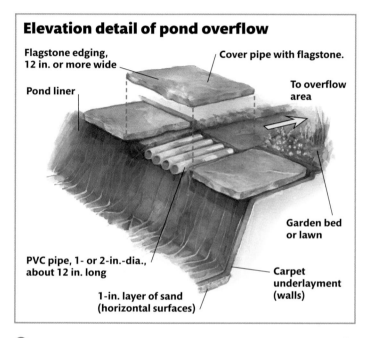

Elevation detail of pond overflow

Flagstone edging, 12 in. or more wide

Cover pipe with flagstone.

Pond liner

To overflow area

Garden bed or lawn

PVC pipe, 1- or 2-in.-dia., about 12 in. long

Carpet underlayment (walls)

1-in. layer of sand (horizontal surfaces)

❸ Spread liner and begin to fill with water. As water rises, tuck and smooth out as many creases as possible. Fill with water to within 2 in. of pond rim.

To overflow area

❺ Fit and lay flagstone edging. Add sand beneath the liner or stones where necessary to create a firm bed. Brush sand into joints when edging is complete.

❹ Trim liner to fit relief for flagstone edging. Fix liner in place with long nails or bent coat-hanger "staples."

Weigh down liner with stones.

Building a Retaining Wall

Contours and sloping terrain can add considerable interest to a home landscape. But you can have too much of a good thing. Two designs in this book employ retaining walls to alter problem slopes. The wall shown on p. 64 eliminates a small but abrupt grade change, producing two almost level surfaces and the opportunity to install attractive plantings and a patio on them. On projects on pp. 120–131, retaining walls help turn steep slopes into a showpieces.

Retaining walls can be handsome landscape features in their own right. Made of cut stone, fieldstone, brick, landscape timbers, or concrete, they can complement the materials and style of your house or nearby structures. However, making a stable, long-lasting retaining wall of these materials can require tools and skills many homeowners do not possess.

For these reasons we've instead chosen retaining-wall systems made of precast concrete for designs in this book.

Readily available in a range of sizes, surface finishes, and colors, these systems require few tools and no special skills to install. They have been engineered to resist the forces that soil, water, freezing, and thawing bring to bear on a retaining wall. Install these walls according to the manufacturer's specifications, and you can be confident that they will do their job for many years.

A number of systems are available through nurseries, garden centers, and local contracting suppliers. (Check the Yellow Pages and online sources.) But they all share basic design principles. Like traditional dry-stone walls, these systems rely largely on weight and friction to contain the soil. In many systems, interlocking blocks or pegs help align the courses and increase the wall's strength. In all systems, blocks must rest on a solid, level base. A freely draining backfill of crushed stone is essential to avoid buildup of water pressure in the retained soil, which can buckle even a heavy wall. (In hilly terrain or where drainage is a concern, experts often recommend installing drainage pipe to remove excess water from behind retaining walls.)

The construction steps shown here are typical of those recommended by most system manufacturers for retaining walls up to 3 to 4 ft. tall; be sure to follow the manufacturer's instructions for the system you choose. For higher walls, walls on loose soil or heavy clay soils, and walls retaining very steep slopes, it is prudent to consult with a landscape architect or contractor. (Some cities and towns have regulations for retaining walls and landscape steps. Be sure to check with local authorities before beginning work.)

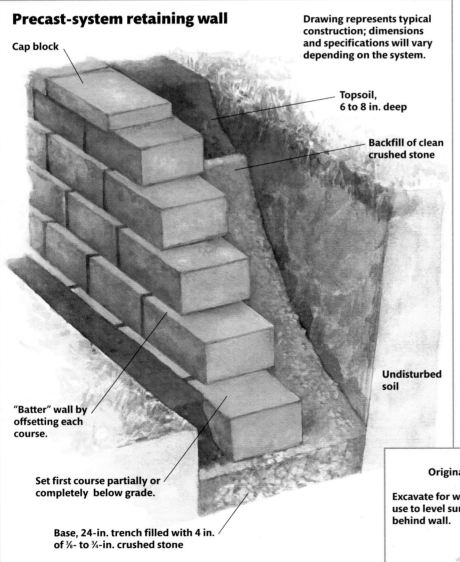

Precast-system retaining wall

Cap block

Drawing represents typical construction; dimensions and specifications will vary depending on the system.

Topsoil, 6 to 8 in. deep

Backfill of clean crushed stone

Undisturbed soil

"Batter" wall by offsetting each course.

Set first course partially or completely below grade.

Base, 24-in. trench filled with 4 in. of ⅜- to ¾-in. crushed stone

Original slope

New grade level

Excavate for wall; use to level surface behind wall.

New grade

30–45° from plumb

Building a wall

Installing a wall system is just about as simple as stacking up children's building blocks. The most important part of the job is establishing a firm, level base. Start by laying out the wall with string and hose (for curves) and excavating a base trench.

As the boxed drawing shows, the position of the wall in relation to the base of the slope determines the height of the wall, how much soil you move, and the leveling effect on the slope. Unless the wall is very long, it is a good idea to excavate along the entire length and fine-tune the line of the wall before beginning the base trench. Remember to excavate back far enough to accommodate the stone backfill. Systems vary, but a foot of crushed-stone backfill behind the blocks is typical. (For the two-wall design, build the bottom wall first, then the top.)

Systems vary in the width and depth of trench and type of base material, but in all of them, the trench must be level across its width and along its length. We've shown a 4-in. layer of ⅜- to ¾-in. crushed stone (blocks can slip sideways on rounded aggregate or pea gravel, which also don't compact as well). Depending on the system and the circumstances, a portion or all of the first course lies below grade, so the soil helps hold the blocks in place.

Add crushed stone to the trench, level it with a rake, and compact it with a hand tamper or mechanical compactor. Lay the first course of blocks carefully ❶. Check frequently to make sure the blocks are level across their width and along their length. Stagger vertical joints as you stack subsequent courses. Offset the faces of the blocks so the wall leans back into the retained soil. Some systems design this "batter" into their blocks; others allow you to choose from several possible setbacks.

As the wall rises, shovel backfill behind the blocks ❷. Clean crushed rock drains well; some systems suggest placing a barrier of landscaping fabric between the rock and the retained soil to keep soil from migrating into the fill and impeding drainage.

Thinner cap blocks finish the top of the wall ❸. Some wall systems recommend cementing these blocks in place with a weatherproof adhesive. The last 6 to 8 in. of the backfill should be topsoil, firmed into place and ready for planting.

BUILDING A WALL

❷ As you add subsequent courses, backfill behind blocks with clean crushed rock.

Stagger joints.

Offset courses so wall leans into retained soil.

❸ Cap blocks complete the wall. Use topsoil for final 6 to 8 in. of backfill.

Rock base

Level

❶ After digging and leveling the trench, spread, level, and compact the base materials; then lay the blocks. Check frequently to see that they are level across their width and length.

Wall parallel with a slope: Stepped base

Construct walls running parallel to a slope in "steps," each with a level base.

Backfill so grade behind finishes level with top of wall.

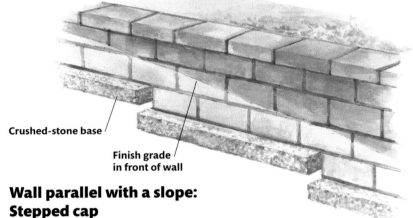

Crushed-stone base

Finish grade in front of wall

Wall parallel with a slope: Stepped cap

Sometimes the top of a wall needs to step up or down to accommodate grade changes in the slope behind.

Cap block

A return corner

Where you want the slope to extend beyond the end of the wall, make a corner that cuts into the slope.

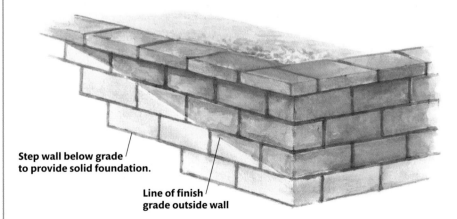

Step wall below grade to provide solid foundation.

Line of finish grade outside wall

Sloped sites

If your slope runs parallel with the length of the wall, you can "step" the bottom of the wall and make its top surface level, as shown in the drawing, top left. Create a length of level trench along the lowest portion of the site. Then work up the slope, creating steps as necessary. Add fill soil to raise the grade behind the wall to the level of the cap blocks.

Alternatively, you can step the top of the wall, as shown in the drawing, middle left. Here, the base of the wall rests on level ground, but the top of the wall steps to match the slope's decreasing height. This saves money and labor on materials and backfill, while producing a different look.

Retaining walls, such as the one shown on p. 120, are frequently placed perpendicular to the run of a slope. If you want to alter just part of the slope or if the slope continues beyond your property, you'll need to terminate the wall. A corner that cuts back into the slope, bottom left, is an attractive and structurally sound solution to this problem.

Constructing curves and corners

Wall-system blocks are designed so that curves, such as the one in the design on p. 124, are no more difficult to lay than straight sections. Corners may require that you cut a few blocks or use specially designed blocks, but they are otherwise uncomplicated. If your wall must fit a prescribed length between corners, consider working from the corners toward the middle (after laying a base course). Masons use this technique, which also helps to avoid exposing cut blocks at the corners.

You can cut blocks with a mason's chisel and mallet or rent a mason's saw. Chiseling works well where the block faces are rough textured, so the faces you cut blend right in. A saw is best for smooth-faced blocks and projects requiring lots of cutting.

Steps

Steps in a low retaining wall are not difficult to build, but they require forethought and careful layout. Systems differ on construction details. The drawing below shows a typical design where the blocks and stone base rest on "steps" cut into firm subsoil. If your soil is less stable or is recent fill, you should excavate the entire area beneath the steps to the same depth as the wall base and build a foundation of blocks, as shown in the boxed drawing.

These steps are independent of the adjacent "return" walls, which are vertical, not battered (stepped back). In some systems, steps and return walls are interlocked. To match a path, you can face the treads with the same stone, brick, or pavers, or you can use the system's cap blocks or special treads.

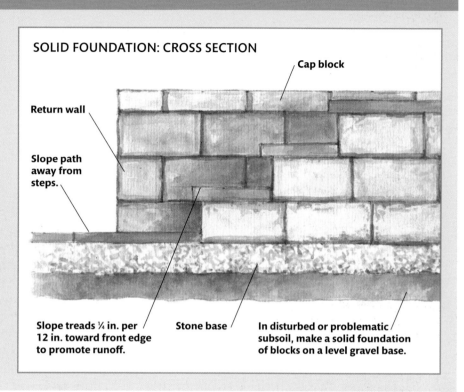

SOLID FOUNDATION: CROSS SECTION

Cap block

Return wall

Slope path away from steps.

Slope treads ¼ in. per 12 in. toward front edge to promote runoff.

Stone base

In disturbed or problematic subsoil, make a solid foundation of blocks on a level gravel base.

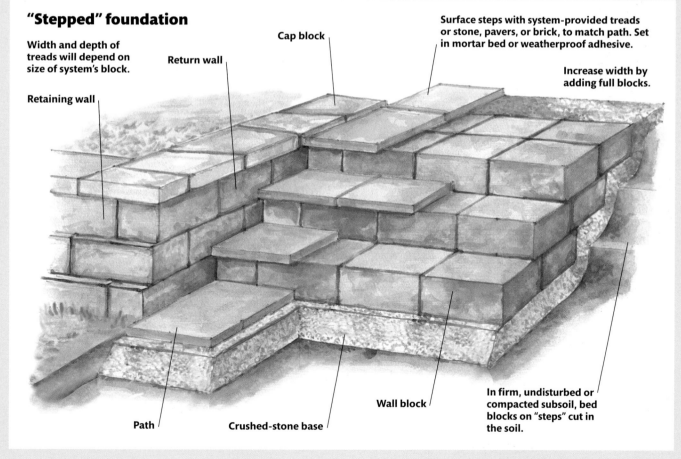

"Stepped" foundation

Width and depth of treads will depend on size of system's block.

Return wall

Cap block

Surface steps with system-provided treads or stone, pavers, or brick, to match path. Set in mortar bed or weatherproof adhesive.

Increase width by adding full blocks.

Retaining wall

Path

Crushed-stone base

Wall block

In firm, undisturbed or compacted subsoil, bed blocks on "steps" cut in the soil.

Fences, Arbors, and Trellises

Novices who have no trouble tackling a simple flagstone path often get nervous when it comes time to erect a fence, an arbor, or even a trellis. While such projects can require more skill and resources than others in the landscape, the ones in this book have been designed with less-than-confident do-it-yourself builders in mind. The designs are simple, the materials are read-ily available, and the tools and skills will be familiar to anyone accustomed to ordinary home maintenance.

First we'll introduce you to the tools and materials needed for the projects. Then we'll present the small number of basic operations you'll employ when building them. Finally, we'll provide drawings and comments on each of the projects.

Tools and materials

Even the least-handy homeowner is likely to have most of the tools needed for these projects: claw hammer, crosscut handsaw, brace-and-bit or electric drill, adjustable wrench, combination square, measuring tape, carpenter's level, and sawhorses. You may even have Grandpa's old posthole dig-ger. Many will have a handheld power circular saw, which makes faster (though noisier) work of cutting parts to length. A cordless drill/screwdriver is invaluable if you're substituting screws for nails. If you have more than a few holes to dig, consider renting a gas-powered posthole dig-ger. A 12-in.-diameter hole will serve for 4x4 posts; if possi-ble, get a larger-diameter digger for 6x6 posts.

Materials
Of the materials offering strength, durability, and attractive-ness in outdoor settings, wood is the easiest to work and affords the quickest results. While almost all commercially available lumber is strong enough for landscape structures, most decay quickly when in prolonged contact with soil and water. Cedar, cypress, and redwood, however, contain natural preservatives and are excellent for landscape use. Alternatively, a range of softwoods (such as pine, fir, and hemlock) are pressure treated with preservatives and will last for many years. Parts of structures that do not come in contact with soil or are not continually wet can be made of ordinary construction-grade lumber, but unless they're reg-ularly painted, they will not last as long as treated or natu-rally decay-resistant material.

In addition to dimension lumber, several of the designs incorporate lattice, which is thin wooden strips crisscrossed to form patterns of diamonds or squares. Premade lattice is widely available in sheets 4 ft. by 8 ft. and smaller. Lattice comes in decay-resistant woods as well as in treated and un-treated softwoods. Local supplies vary, and you may find lat-tice made of thicker or narrower material.

Fasteners
For millennia, even basic structures such as these would have been assembled with complicated joints. Today, with simple nailed, bolted, or screwed joints, a few hours' prac-tice swinging a hammer or wielding a cordless electric screwdriver is all the training necessary.

All these structures can be assembled using nails. But screws are stronger and, if you have a cordless screwdriver, make assembly easier. Buy common or box nails that are galvanized to prevent rust. Self-tapping screws ("deck" screws) require no pilot holes. For rust resistance, buy gal-vanized screws or screws treated with zinc dichromate.

Galvanized metal connectors are available to reinforce the joints used in these projects. For novice builders, con-nectors are a great help in aligning parts and making assem-bly easier. (Correctly fastened with nails or screws, the joints are strong enough without connectors.)

Finishes
Cedar, cypress, and redwood are handsome when left un-finished to weather, when treated with clear or colored stains, or when painted. Pressure-treated lumber is best painted or stained.

Outdoor stains are becoming increasingly popular. Clear or lightly tinted stains can preserve or enhance the rich red-dish browns of cedar, cypress, and redwood. Stains also come in a range of colors that can be used like paint. Because they penetrate the wood rather than forming a film, stains don't form an opaque surface, but stains won't peel or chip like paint and are therefore easier to touch up and refinish.

When choosing a finish, take account of what plants are growing on or near the structure. It's a lot of work to remove yards of vines from a trellis or squeeze between a large shrub and a fence to repaint; consider an unfinished decay-resistant wood or an initial stain that you allow to weather.

Setting posts

Most of the projects are anchored by firmly set, vertical posts. In general, the taller the structure, the deeper the post should be set. Arbor posts should be at least 3 ft. deep. Corner and end posts of fences up to 6 ft. tall and posts supporting gates should also be 3 ft. deep. Intermediate fence posts can be set 2 ft. deep.

The length of the posts you buy depends, of course, on the depth at which they are set and their finished heights. When calculating lengths of arbor posts, remember that the tops of the posts must be level. The easiest method of achieving this is to cut the posts to length after installation. For example, buy 12-ft. posts for an arbor finishing at 8 ft. above grade and set 3 ft. in the ground. The convenience is worth the expense of the foot or so you cut off. The site and personal preference can determine whether you cut fence posts to length after installation or buy them cut to length and add or remove fill from the bottom of the hole to position them at the correct heights.

Arbor posts

When laying out the arbor, take extra care when positioning arbor posts. The corners of the structure must be right angles, and the sides must be parallel with one another. Locating the corners with batter boards and string is fussy but accurate. Make the batter boards by nailing 1x2 stakes to scraps of 1x3 or 1x4, and position them about 1 ft. from the approximate location of each post as shown in the boxed drawing at right. Locate the exact post positions with string; adjust the string so the diagonal measurements are equal, which ensures that the corners of the structure will be at right angles.

At the intersections of the strings, locate the postholes by eye or with a plumb bob ❶. Remove the strings and dig the holes; then reattach the strings to position the posts exactly ❷. Plumb and brace the posts carefully. Check positions with the level and by measuring between adjacent posts and across diagonals. Diagonal braces between adjacent posts will stiffen them and help align their faces ❸. Then add concrete ❹ and let it cure for a day.

To establish the height of the posts, measure up from grade on one post, then use a level and straightedge to mark the heights of the other posts from the first one. Where joists will be bolted to the faces of the posts, you can install the joists and use their top edges as a handsaw guide for cutting the posts to length.

SETTING ARBOR POSTS

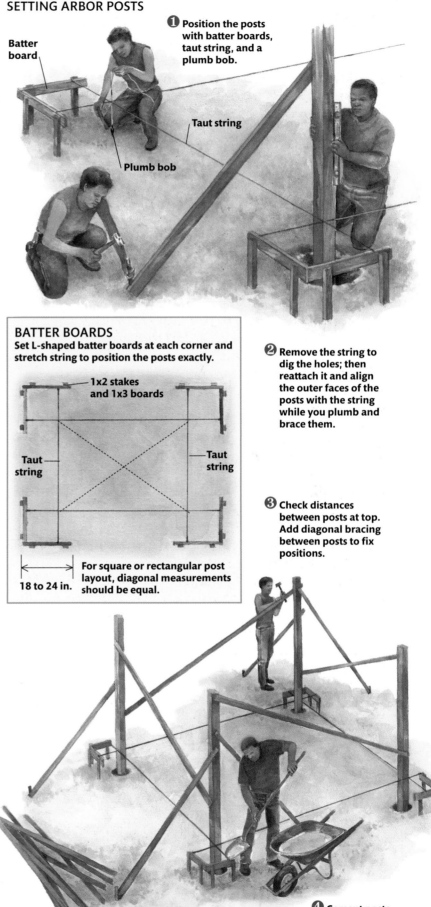

❶ Position the posts with batter boards, taut string, and a plumb bob.

Batter board

Taut string

Plumb bob

BATTER BOARDS
Set L-shaped batter boards at each corner and stretch string to position the posts exactly.

1x2 stakes and 1x3 boards

Taut string

Taut string

18 to 24 in.

For square or rectangular post layout, diagonal measurements should be equal.

❷ Remove the string to dig the holes; then reattach it and align the outer faces of the posts with the string while you plumb and brace them.

❸ Check distances between posts at top. Add diagonal bracing between posts to fix positions.

❹ Cement posts in place.

Fence posts

Lay out and set the end or corner posts of a fence first, then add the intermediate posts. Dig the holes by hand or with a power digger ❶. To promote drainage, place several inches of gravel at the bottom of the hole for the post to rest on. Checking with a carpenter's level, plumb the post vertically and brace it with scrap lumber nailed to stakes ❷. Then add a few more inches of gravel around the post's base.

If your native soil compacts well, you can fix posts in place with tamped earth. Add the soil gradually, tamping it continu-ously with a heavy iron bar or 2x4. Check regularly with a level to see that the post doesn't get knocked out of plumb. This tech-nique suits rustic or informal fences, where misalignments caused by shifting posts aren't noticeable or damaging.

For more formal fences, or where soils are loose or fence pan-els are buffeted by winds or snow, it's prudent to fix posts in con-crete ❸. Mix enough concrete to set the two end posts; as a rule of thumb, figure one 80-lb. bag of premixed concrete per post. As you shovel it in, prod the concrete with a stick to settle it, par-ticularly if you've added rubble to extend the mix. Build the con-

SETTING A FENCE POST

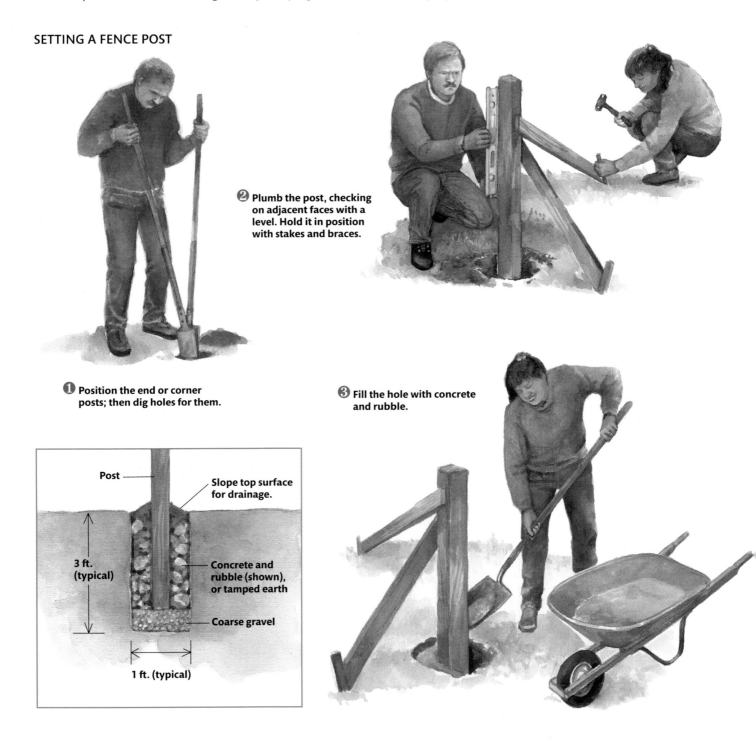

❷ **Plumb the post, checking on adjacent faces with a level. Hold it in position with stakes and braces.**

❶ **Position the end or corner posts; then dig holes for them.**

❸ **Fill the hole with concrete and rubble.**

Post

Slope top surface for drainage.

3 ft. (typical)

Concrete and rubble (shown), or tamped earth

Coarse gravel

1 ft. (typical)

crete slightly above grade and slope it away from the post to aid drainage.

Once the end posts are set, stretch a string between the posts. (The concrete should cure for 24 hours before you nail or screw rails and panels in place, but you can safely stretch string while the concrete is still wet.) Measure along the string to position the intermediate posts; drop a plumb bob from the string at each intermediate post position to gauge the center of the hole below ❹. Once all the holes have been dug, again stretch a string between the end posts, near the top. Set the intermediate posts as described previously; align one face with the string and plumb adjacent faces with the carpenter's level ❺. Check positions of intermediate posts a final time with a measuring tape.

If the fence is placed along a slope, the top of the slats or panels can step down the slope or mirror it (as shown in the drawing below). Either way, make sure that the posts are plumb rather than leaning with the slope.

❹ **Stretch a string between the tops of the two end posts. Then locate positions of intermediate posts with a plumb bob.**

❺ **After digging the holes, stretch a string between the end posts to align intermediate posts. Use a level to plumb adjacent faces.**

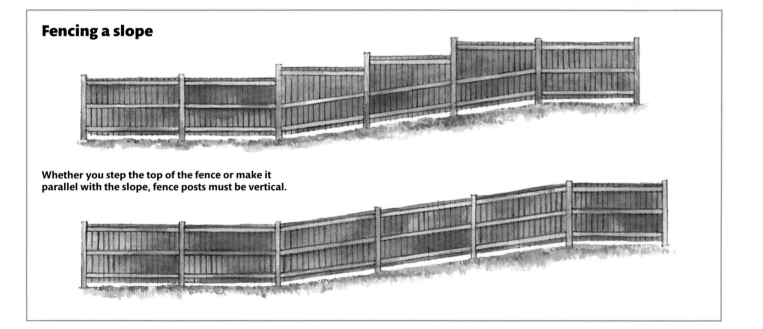

Fencing a slope

Whether you step the top of the fence or make it parallel with the slope, fence posts must be vertical.

Joints

The components of the fences, arbors, and trellises used in this book are attached to the posts and to each other with the simple joints shown below. Because all the parts are made of dimensioned lumber, the only cuts you'll need to make are to length. For strong joints, cut ends as square as you can, so the mating pieces make contact across their entire surfaces. If you have no confidence in your sawing, many lumberyards will cut pieces to length for a modest fee.

Beginners often find it difficult to keep two pieces correctly positioned while trying to drive a nail into them, particularly when the nail must be driven at an angle, called "toenailing." If you have this problem, consider assembling the project with screws, which draw the pieces together, or with metal connectors, which can be nailed or screwed in place on one piece and then attached to the mating piece.

For one of the designs, you need to attach lattice panels to posts. The panels are made by sandwiching store-bought lattice

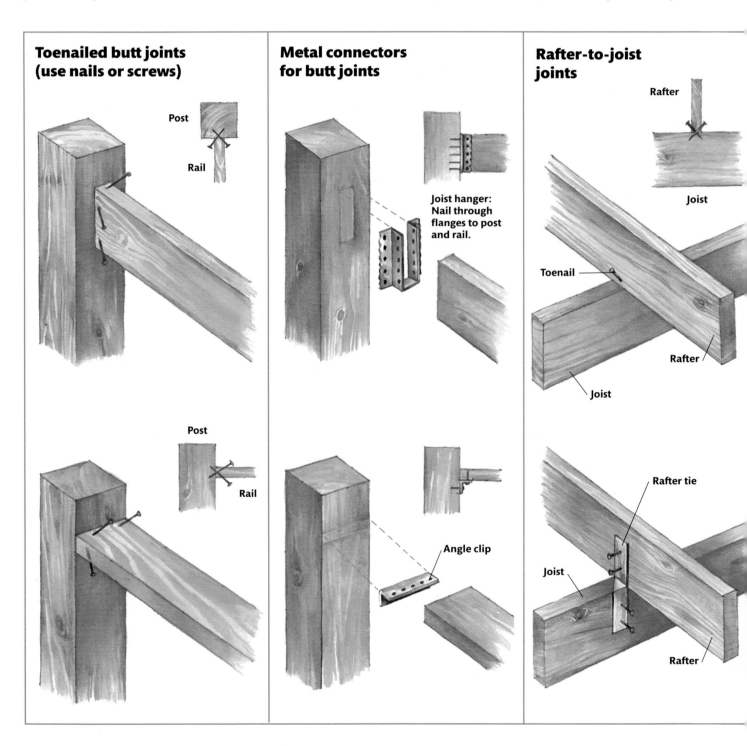

Toenailed butt joints (use nails or screws)

Post

Rail

Post

Rail

Metal connectors for butt joints

Joist hanger: Nail through flanges to post and rail.

Angle clip

Rafter-to-joist joints

Rafter

Joist

Toenail

Rafter

Joist

Rafter tie

Joist

Rafter

between frames of dimension lumber (construction details are given on the following pages). While the assembled panels can be toenailed to the posts, novices may find that the job goes easier using one or more types of metal connector, as shown in the drawing at below right. Attach the angle clips or angle brackets to the post; then position the lattice panel and fix it to the connectors. For greatest strength and ease of assembly, attach connectors using self-tapping screws driven by a cordless or electric screwdriver or drill-driver.

In the following pages, we'll show construction details of the fences, arbors, and trellises presented in the Portfolio of Designs. (The page number indicates the design.) Where the basic joints discussed here can be used, we have shown the parts but left choice of fasteners to you. Typical fastenings are indicated for other joints. We have kept the constructions shown here simple and straightforward. They are not the only possibilities, and we encourage experienced builders to adapt and alter constructions as well as designs to suit differing situations and personal preferences.

Frame corner with metal connector

Attaching framed lattice panels to posts

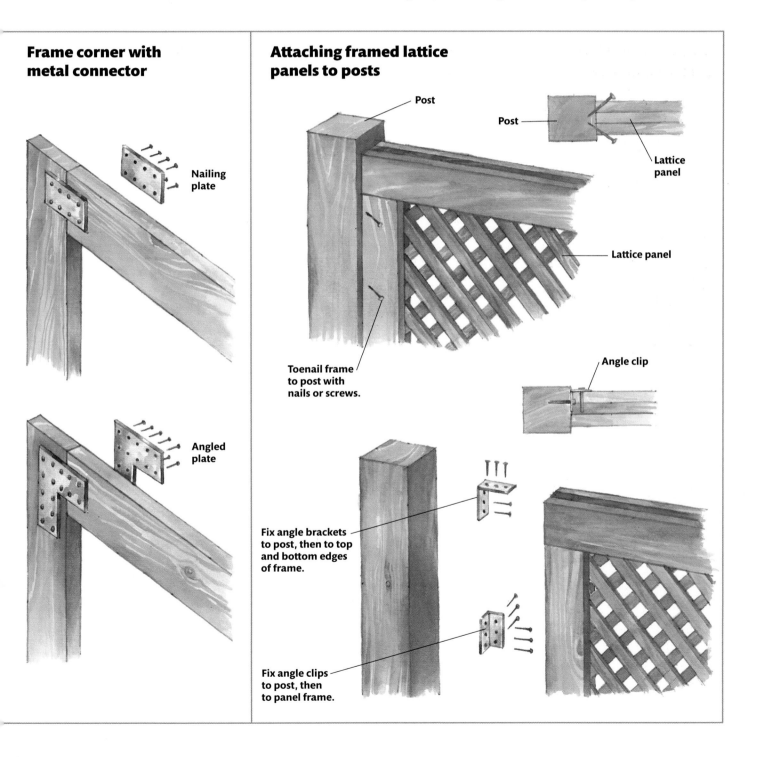

Nailing plate

Angled plate

Post

Post

Lattice panel

Lattice panel

Toenail frame to post with nails or screws.

Angle clip

Fix angle brackets to post, then to top and bottom edges of frame.

Fix angle clips to post, then to panel frame.

Homemade lattice trellis
(pp.46–47, 70–71, and 72–73)

The trellis shown here supports climbing plants to make a vertical garden of a blank wall (or tall fence). The design can be altered to fit walls of different sizes, while keeping its pleasing proportions. The 32-in.-wide modules are simpler to make than a single large trellis. Hung on L-hangers, they're easy to remove when you need to paint the wall or fence behind. For the design on p. 71, the trellis is 8 ft. tall and requires four sections. The design on p. 51 uses six sections (three on the wall and three on the fence) and is 6 ft. tall.

Start by cutting all the pieces to length. (Here we'll call the horizontal members "rails" and the vertical members "stiles.") Working on a large flat surface, nail or screw the two outer stiles to the top and bottom rails, checking the corners with a framing square. The 2x2 rails provide ample material to house the L-hangers.

Carefully attach the three intermediate stiles, then the 1x2 rails. Cut a piece of scrap 6 in. long to use as a spacer. Fix the L-shaped hangers to the wall or fence. Buy hangers long enough to hold the trellis several inches away from the surface, allowing air to circulate behind the foliage.

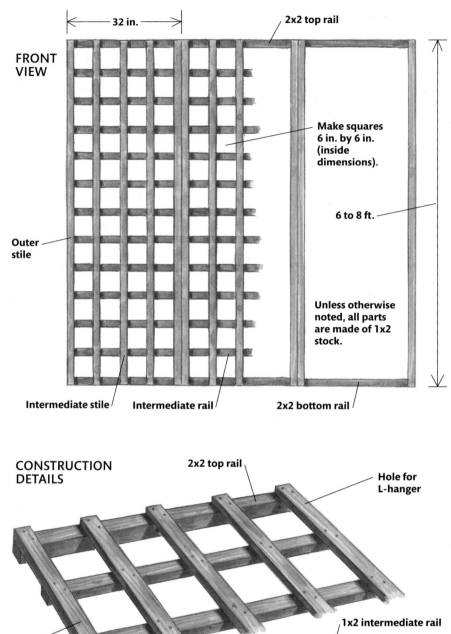

FRONT VIEW

32 in.

2x2 top rail

Make squares 6 in. by 6 in. (inside dimensions).

6 to 8 ft.

Unless otherwise noted, all parts are made of 1x2 stock.

Outer stile

Intermediate stile

Intermediate rail

2x2 bottom rail

CONSTRUCTION DETAILS

2x2 top rail

Hole for L-hanger

1x2 outer stile

1x2 intermediate stile

1x2 intermediate rail

Nail or screw each joint twice for rigidity.

Nail or screw through 1x2 stile into 2x2.

2x2 bottom rail

Hole for L-hanger

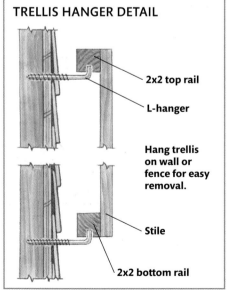

TRELLIS HANGER DETAIL

2x2 top rail

L-hanger

Hang trellis on wall or fence for easy removal.

Stile

2x2 bottom rail

Hideaway arbor
(pp. 76–79)

This cozy enclosure shelters several comfortable chairs or a bench and supports vines to shade the occupants.

Its rustic posts and rafters, made from peeled logs and tree stakes, create a setting of comfortable informality perfectly in tune with the surrounding plantings. Tree stakes are used to support newly planted trees. Peeled posts and tree stakes are available from nurseries, garden centers, or landscape contractors.

The arbor is easy to construct. Set the posts in concrete. (see pp. 274–277.) Then bolt the 4x4 beams to the tops of the posts, boring clearance and pilot holes first. You can toenail 4x4 ties between beams to keep the structure rigid while you add the stake rafters, but the finished arbor would be sturdy enough without them. Fix the stake rafters in place with galvanized spikes or long deck screws, as shown in the detail drawing. Bore pilot holes for spikes and screws to prevent splitting the rafters and to make the fasteners easier to drive.

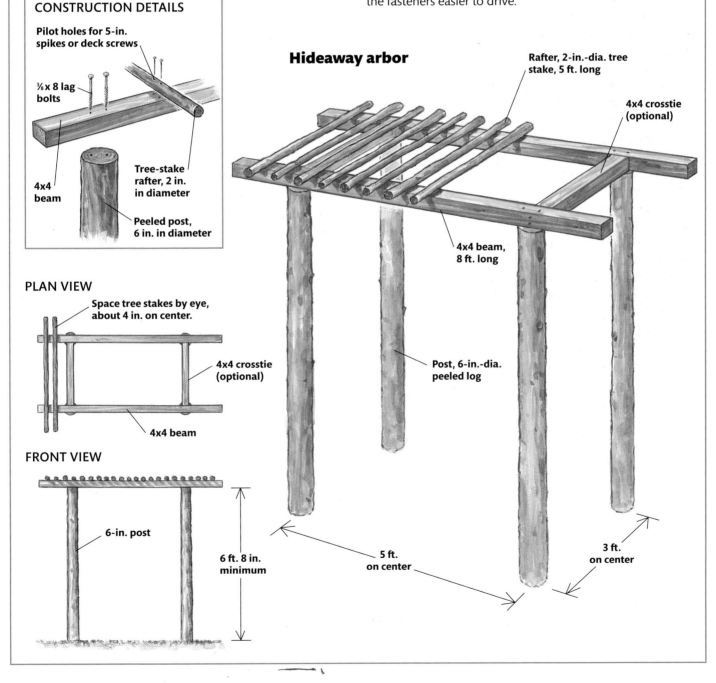

CONSTRUCTION DETAILS

Pilot holes for 5-in. spikes or deck screws

⅜ x 8 lag bolts

4x4 beam

Tree-stake rafter, 2 in. in diameter

Peeled post, 6 in. in diameter

PLAN VIEW

Space tree stakes by eye, about 4 in. on center.

4x4 crosstie (optional)

4x4 beam

FRONT VIEW

6-in. post

6 ft. 8 in. minimum

Hideaway arbor

Rafter, 2-in.-dia. tree stake, 5 ft. long

4x4 crosstie (optional)

4x4 beam, 8 ft. long

Post, 6-in.-dia. peeled log

5 ft. on center

3 ft. on center

Patio arbor and sun screen
(pp. 80–81, 84–86, 88–89, 92–93, 157–158, 168–169, and 172–173)

This simple structure offers relief from the sun on a portion of a backyard patio. The closely spaced 2x4 rafters form a sun screen, while allowing air circulation. Adapt rafter spacing and orientation to accommodate your site. In the design on pp. 88–89, the arbor supports wisteria vines, which provide cooling shade as well as a pleasant leafy ambiance.

If you're building the patio and arbor at the same time, set the 6x6 posts (see pp. 274–277) before you lay the patio surface. If you're adding the arbor to an existing patio, you'll need to break through the paving to set the posts or pour footings to support surface attachments. Consult local building officials or a landscape contractor for advice on how best to proceed.

Once the posts are set, fix the 2x8 beams to pairs of posts with carriage bolts. Nail the 2x8s in place; then make the bolt holes by boring through the 2x8s and the post with a long electrician's bit. Fix the long 2x6 joists and the 2x4 rafters in place with metal connectors. Metal connectors fixed with screws will stand up best to the vigorous growth of wisteria.

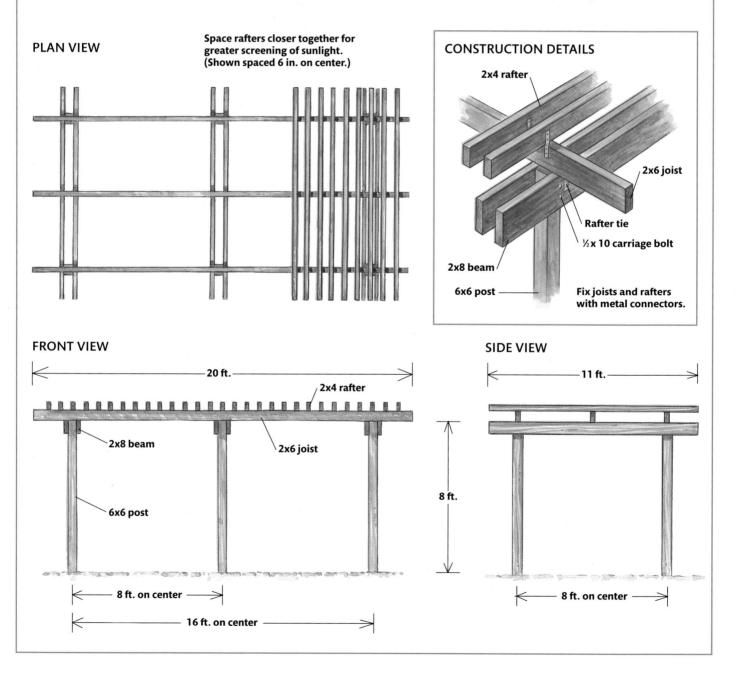

PLAN VIEW

Space rafters closer together for greater screening of sunlight. (Shown spaced 6 in. on center.)

CONSTRUCTION DETAILS

2x4 rafter

2x6 joist

Rafter tie

½ x 10 carriage bolt

2x8 beam

6x6 post

Fix joists and rafters with metal connectors.

FRONT VIEW

20 ft.

2x4 rafter

2x8 beam

2x6 joist

6x6 post

8 ft. on center

16 ft. on center

SIDE VIEW

11 ft.

8 ft.

8 ft. on center

Narrow arbor
(pp. 118–119, 132–133)

Draped with hardenbergia, this shallow arbor welcomes visitors to a small stroll garden situated in a narrow side yard. Once you have gathered the materials together, you should need no more than an afternoon to build the arbor.

Set the posts first, as described on pp. 274–277. The hefty 6x6 posts shown here add presence to the arbor, but cheaper, easier-to-handle 4x4s will make an equally sturdy structure. Cut the joists and rafters to length. The 60° angles on their ends can easily be cut with a handsaw. Bolt or nail the joists in place. Then toenail the short rafters to the joists or attach them with metal connectors.

In addition to the posts, you can provide other supports for the hardenbergia to twine around. Strands of coarse rope or cord work well when stretched between the large screw eyes fixed to the rafters and the base of the posts, as shown here. The vines soon hide the rope or cord from view.

PLAN VIEW

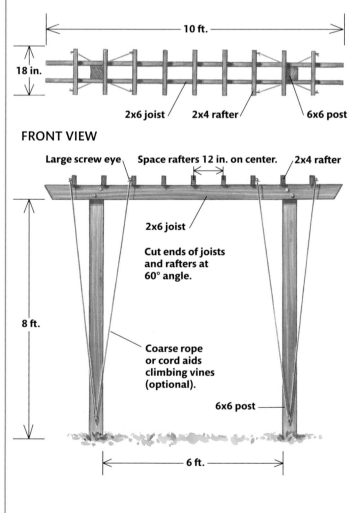

10 ft.

18 in.

2x6 joist   2x4 rafter   6x6 post

FRONT VIEW

Large screw eye   Space rafters 12 in. on center.   2x4 rafter

2x6 joist

Cut ends of joists and rafters at 60° angle.

8 ft.

Coarse rope or cord aids climbing vines (optional).

6x6 post

6 ft.

CONSTRUCTION DETAILS

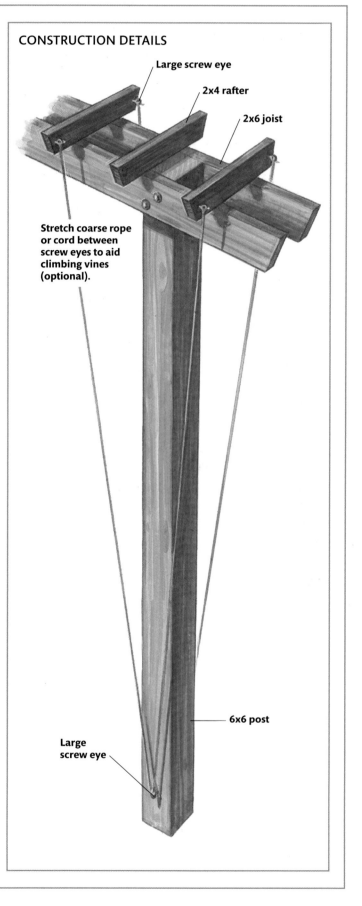

Large screw eye
2x4 rafter
2x6 joist

Stretch coarse rope or cord between screw eyes to aid climbing vines (optional).

6x6 post

Large screw eye

Entry arbor and fence
(pp. 180–183)

This arbor makes an event of the passage from sidewalk to front door or from one part of your property to another. Two versions are shown in the Portfolio. One features the arbor alone; the other adds a picket fence.

Hefty 6x6 posts provide real presence here; the 12-footers you'll need are heavy, so engage a couple of helpers to save your back. As with the previous arbor, once the posts are set, the job is easy. You can toenail the 3x6 beams to the tops of the posts and the 2x4 rafters to the beams. (Or you can fix them with long spikes or lag screws, 10 in. and 8 in. long, respectively. This job is easier if you drill pilot holes, with bits slightly thinner than the spikes.) Attach the 2x2 cross rafters with screws or nails. If you can't buy 3x6s, you can nail two 2x6s together face to face.

Sandwich lattice between 1x3s to make the side panels and fix them between posts with nails, screws, or metal connectors. Alternating the corner overlap, as shown on the drawing, makes a stronger frame.

The fence forms small enclosures on either side of the arbor before heading off across the property. To match the arbor, use 6x6 posts for the enclosures; then switch to 4x4s if you wish, spacing them no farther apart than 8 ft.

You can purchase ready-made lengths of picket fence, but it is easy enough to make yourself. Set the posts; then cut and fit 2x4 rails on edge between them. Space 1x3 picket slats 1½ in. apart. The drawing on the facing page shows large round wooden finials atop the fence posts; you can buy various types of ready-made finials, or you could work a heavy bevel around the top end of the posts themselves.

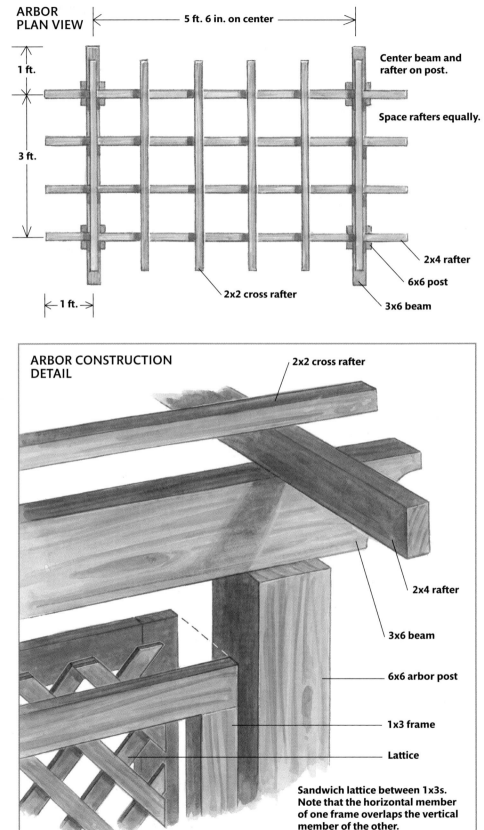

ARBOR PLAN VIEW

5 ft. 6 in. on center

1 ft.

3 ft.

1 ft.

Center beam and rafter on post.

Space rafters equally.

2x4 rafter

6x6 post

3x6 beam

2x2 cross rafter

ARBOR CONSTRUCTION DETAIL

2x2 cross rafter

2x4 rafter

3x6 beam

6x6 arbor post

1x3 frame

Lattice

Sandwich lattice between 1x3s. Note that the horizontal member of one frame overlaps the vertical member of the other.

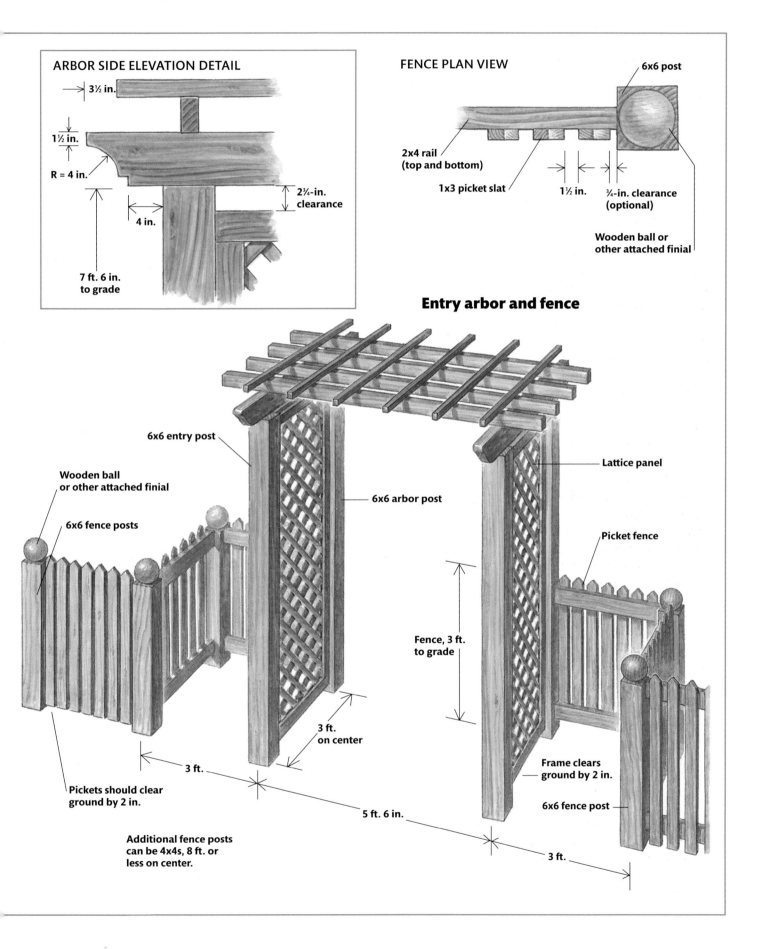

ARBOR SIDE ELEVATION DETAIL

3½ in.

1½ in.

R = 4 in.

2¾-in. clearance

4 in.

7 ft. 6 in. to grade

FENCE PLAN VIEW

6x6 post

2x4 rail (top and bottom)

1x3 picket slat

1½ in.

¾-in. clearance (optional)

Wooden ball or other attached finial

Entry arbor and fence

6x6 entry post

Lattice panel

Wooden ball or other attached finial

6x6 arbor post

6x6 fence posts

Picket fence

Fence, 3 ft. to grade

3 ft. on center

Frame clears ground by 2 in.

3 ft.

6x6 fence post

Pickets should clear ground by 2 in.

5 ft. 6 in.

3 ft.

Additional fence posts can be 4x4s, 8 ft. or less on center.

Preparing the Soil for Planting

The better the soil, the better the plants. Soil quality affects how fast plants grow, how big they get, how good they look, and how long they live. But on many residential lots, the soil is shallow and infertile. Unless you're lucky enough to have a better-than-average site where the soil has been cared for and amended over the years, perhaps for use as a vegetable garden or flower bed, you should plan to improve your soil before planting in it.

If you were planting just a few trees or shrubs, you could prepare individual planting holes for them and leave the surrounding soil undisturbed. However,

for nearly all the plantings in this book, digging individual holes is impractical, and it's much better for the plants if you prepare the soil throughout the entire area that will be planted. (The major exception is when you're planting under a tree, which is discussed on p. 288.)

For most of the situations shown in this book, you could prepare the soil with hand tools—a spade, digging fork, and rake. The job goes faster, though, if you use a rototiller, and a rototiller is better than hand tools for mixing amendments into the soil. Unless you grow vegetables, you probably won't use a rototiller often enough to justify buying one yourself, but

you can easily rent one or hire someone to come and prepare your site.

Loosen the soil

After you've removed any sod or other vegetation from the designated area (see pp. 254–255), the first step is digging or tilling to loosen the soil ❶. Do this on a day when the soil is moist—not so wet that it sticks to your tools or so dry that it makes dust. Start at one end of the bed and work back and forth until you reach the other end. Try to dig down at least 8 in., or deeper if possible. If the ground is very compacted, you'll have to make repeated passes with a tiller to reach 8 in. deep. Toss aside any large rocks, roots, or debris that you encounter. When you're working near a house or other buildings, watch out for buried wires, cables, and pipes. Most town and city governments have a number you can call to request that someone help you locate buried utilities.

After this initial digging, the ground will likely be very rough and lumpy. Whump the clods with the back of a digging fork or make another pass with the tiller until you've reduced all the clumps to the size of apples.

Once you've loosened the existing soil and dug it as deeply as possible, you may need to add topsoil to fill in low spots, refine the grade, or raise the planting area above the surrounding grade for better drainage or to make it easier to see a favorite plant. Unless you need just a small amount, order topsoil by the cubic yard. Consult the staff at your local nursery to find a reputable supplier of topsoil.

In some areas—central Texas, for example—only a thin layer of soil covers limestone bedrock, making digging or tilling impossible. In these areas, the best option is to bring in topsoil or landscape mix. Mound it to create a low berm or contain it in a raised bed enclosed in wood or stone.

Common fertilizers and soil amendments

The following materials serve different purposes. Follow soil-test recommendations or the advice of an experienced gardener in choosing which amendments and fertilizers would be best for your soil. If so recommended, you can apply two or three of these at the same time, using the stated rate for each one.

Material	Description	Amount for 100 sq. ft.
Compost	Amendment. Decomposed or aged plant parts and animal manures	1 cu. yd.
Wood by-products	Amendment. Finely ground bark or sawdust, composted or not. Add nitrogen to non-composted material.	1 cu. yd.
All-purpose fertilizer	Synthetic fertilizer containing various amounts of nitrogen, phosphorus, and potassium	According to label
Organic fertilizer	Derived from a variety of organic materials. Provides nutrients in slow-release form.	According to label
Composted manure	Weak nitrogen fertilizers. Bagged steer manure is common.	6–8 lb.

Add organic matter

Common soil (and purchased topsoil, too) consists mainly of rock and mineral fragments of various sizes. One of the best things you can do to improve any kind of soil for landscape and garden plants is to add some organic matter.

Organic materials used in gardening and landscaping are derived from plants and animals and include ground bark, peat moss, compost, and composted manures. Organic matter can be bought in bags or in bulk at nurseries and many municipal recycling centers. If possible, purchase only composted or aged material to amend your soil. Fresh manure can "burn" plant roots. Fresh bark and sawdust can "steal" nitrogen from the soil as they decay. If you buy uncomposted materials, ask at your nursery how best to use them as amendments (some require supplemental nitrogen).

PREPARING THE SOIL FOR PLANTING

Compost or aged material can be spread 2 to 3 in. thick across the entire area you're working on ❷. At this thickness, a cubic yard (about one heaping pickup-truck load) of bulk material will cover 100 to 150 sq. ft. If you're working on a large area and need several cubic yards of organic matter, have it delivered and dumped close to your project area. You can spread a lot of material in just a few hours if you don't have to cart it very far. Composted and aged manures contain higher concentrations of nitrogen and should be applied at much lower rates than other composts. They are more commonly used as slow-release fertilizers than as soil-improving amendments.

Add fertilizers and mineral amendments

Organic matter improves the soil's texture and helps it retain water and nutrients, but these materials usually lack essential nutrients. To provide the nutrients that plants need, you typically need to use organic or synthetic fertilizers and powdered miner-

als. It's most helpful if you mix these materials into the soil before you do any planting, putting them down into the root zone as shown in the drawing ❸. But you can also sprinkle them on top of the soil in subsequent years to maintain a planting.

Getting a sample of soil tested is the most accurate way to determine how much of which nutrients is needed. (Ask your Cooperative Extension Service.) Less precise, but often adequate, is seeking the advice of nursery staff. Test results or a good adviser will point out any significant deficiencies in your soil, but large deficiencies are uncommon. Most soil needs a moderate, balanced dose of nutrients.

The key thing is to avoid using too much of any fertilizer or mineral. Don't guess at this; measure and weigh carefully. Calculate your plot's area. Follow your soil-test results or instructions on a commercial product's package. If necessary weigh out the appropriate amount, using a kitchen or bathroom scale. Apply the material evenly across the plot with a spreader or by hand.

❶ Use a spade, digging fork, or tiller to dig at least 8 in. deep and break the soil into rough clods. Discard rocks, roots, and debris. Watch out for underground utilities.

❷ Spread a 2- to 3-in. layer of organic matter on top of the soil.

❸ Sprinkle measured amounts of fertilizer and mineral amendments evenly across the entire area, and mix thoroughly into the soil.

Mix and smooth the soil

Finally, use a digging fork or tiller and go back and forth across the bed again until the added materials are mixed thoroughly into the soil and everything is broken into nut-size or smaller lumps ❹. Then use a rake to smooth the surface ❺.

At this point, the soil level may look too high compared with adjacent pavement or lawn, but don't worry. It will settle a few inches over the next several weeks and end up close to its original level.

Working near trees

Plantings under the shade of stately old trees can be cool lovely oases, like the ones shown on pp. 76–77. But to establish the plants, you'll need to contend with the tree's roots. Contrary to popular belief, most tree roots are in the top few inches of the soil, and they extend at least as far away from the trunk as the limbs do. Always try to disturb as few roots as possible when planting beneath established trees. To do so, it's often best to dig individual planting holes. Avoid cutting large roots. To start ground covers and perennials, you can add up to 6 inches of soil under the canopy of many established trees. Keep the new soil and any mulch away from the trunk. Covering roots with too much soil can starve them of oxygen, damaging or killing them; soil or mulch next to the trunk can rot the bark.

Plantings beneath existing native oaks and madrones are normally problematic because the additional water needed to maintain the planting may damage or kill these trees. If you're uncertain about whether or how to plant beneath any established tree, or if your landscape plans call for significant grade changes beneath them, consult with a certified arborist.

❹ Use a tiller or digging fork to mix everything together, again working as deep as possible.

❺ Finish by smoothing the surface with a rake.

All but the most informal landscapes look best if you define and maintain neat edges between the lawn and any adjacent plantings. There are several ways to do this, varying in appearance, effectiveness, cost, and convenience. Attractive, easy-to-install edges include cut, brick or stone, and plastic strip. If you plan to install an edging, put it in after you prepare the soil but before you plant the bed.

Cut edge

Lay a hose or rope on the ground to mark the line where you want to cut. Then cut along the line with a sharp spade or edging tool. Lift away any grass that was growing into the bed (or any plants that were running out into the lawn). Use a rake or hoe to smooth out a shallow trench on the bed side of the cut. Keep the trench empty; don't let it fill up with mulch.

Pros and cons: Free. Good for straight or curved edges, level or sloped sites. You have to recut the edge every four to eight weeks during the growing season, but you can cut 50 to 100 ft. in an hour or so. Don't cut the trench too deep; if a mower wheel slips into it, you may scalp the lawn. Crabgrass and other weeds may sprout in the exposed soil; if this happens, hoe or pull them out.

Brick mowing strip

Dig a trench about 8 in. wide and 4 in. deep around the edge of the bed. Fill it halfway with sand; then lay bricks on top, setting them level with the soil on the lawn side. You'll need three bricks per foot of edging. Sweep extra sand into any cracks between the bricks. In cold-winter areas, you'll probably need to reset a few frost-heaved bricks each spring. You can substitute cut stone blocks or concrete pavers for bricks.

Pros and cons: Good for straight or curved edges on level or gently sloped sites. Looks good in combination with brick walkways or brick houses. Fairly easy to install and maintain. Some kinds of grass and plants will grow under, between, or over the bricks.

Plastic strip edging

Garden centers and home-improvement stores sell heavy-duty plastic edging in strips 5 or 6 in. wide and 20 or 50 ft. long. To install it, use a sharp tool to cut straight down through the sod around the edge of the bed. Hold the edging so the round lip sits right at soil level, and drive the stakes through the bottom of the edging and into the undisturbed soil under the lawn. Stakes, which are supplied with the edging, should be at least 8 in. long and set about 3 ft. apart.

Pros and cons: Good for straight or curved edges, but only on relatively level sites. Neat and carefree when well installed, but installation is a two- or three-person job. If the lip isn't set right on the ground, you're likely to hit it with the mower blade. Liable to shift or heave unless it's very securely staked. Hard to drive stakes in rocky soil. Some kinds of grass and ground covers can grow across the top of the edging.

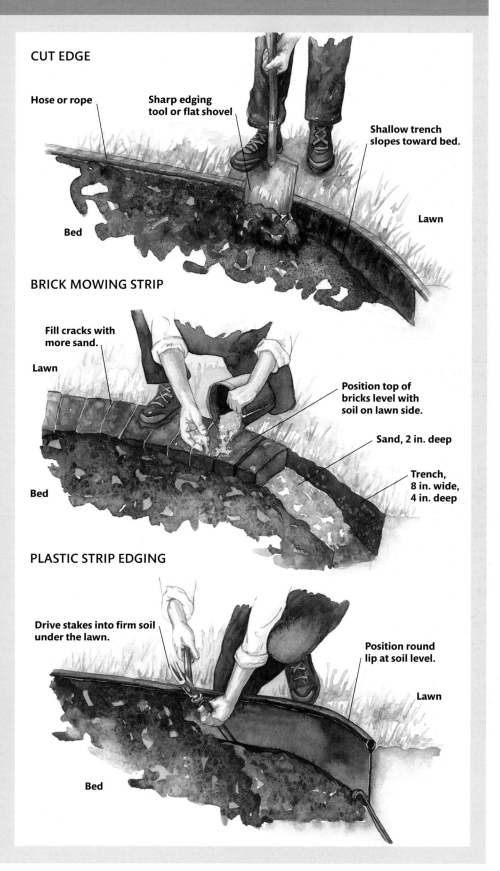

CUT EDGE

Hose or rope

Sharp edging tool or flat shovel

Shallow trench slopes toward bed.

Lawn

Bed

BRICK MOWING STRIP

Fill cracks with more sand.

Lawn

Position top of bricks level with soil on lawn side.

Sand, 2 in. deep

Trench, 8 in. wide, 4 in. deep

Bed

PLASTIC STRIP EDGING

Drive stakes into firm soil under the lawn.

Position round lip at soil level.

Lawn

Bed

Buying Plants

Once you have chosen and planned a landscape project, make a list of the plants you want and start thinking about where to get them. You'll need to locate the kinds of plants you're looking for, choose good-quality plants, and get enough of them to fill your design area.

Where and how to shop

You may already have a favorite place to shop for plants. If not, look online or in the Yellow Pages under the headings "Nurseries," "Nurserymen," and "Garden Centers," and choose a few places to visit. Take your shopping list, find a salesperson, and ask for help. The plants in this book are commonly available in most parts of the West, but you may not find everything you want at one place. The salesperson may refer you to another nursery, offer to special-order plants, or recommend similar plants that you could use as substitutes.

If you're buying too many plants to carry in your car or truck, ask about delivery—it's usually available and sometimes free. Some nurseries offer to replace plants that fail within a limited guarantee period, so ask about that, too.

The staff at a good nursery or garden center will normally be able to answer most of the questions you have about which plants to buy and how to care for them. If you can, go shopping on a rainy weekday when business is slow so staff will have time to answer your questions.

Don't be lured by the low prices of plants for sale at supermarkets or stores that sell plants for only a few months unless you're sure you know exactly what you're looking for and what you're looking at. The staff at these stores rarely have the time or knowledge to offer you much help, and the plants are often disorganized, unlabeled, and stressed by poor care.

If you can't find a plant locally or have a retailer order it for you, you can always order it yourself from a mail-order nursery. Most mail-order nurseries produce good plants and pack them well, but if you haven't dealt with a business before, be smart and place a minimum order first. Judge the quality of the plants that arrive; then decide whether or not to order larger quantities from that firm.

Timing

It's a good idea to plan ahead and start shopping for plants before you're ready to put them in the ground. That way, if you can't find everything on your list, you'll have time to keep shopping around, place special orders, or choose substitutes. Most nurseries will let you "flag" an order for later pickup or delivery, and they'll take care of the plants in the meantime. Or you can bring the plants home; just remember to check the soil in the containers every day and water if needed.

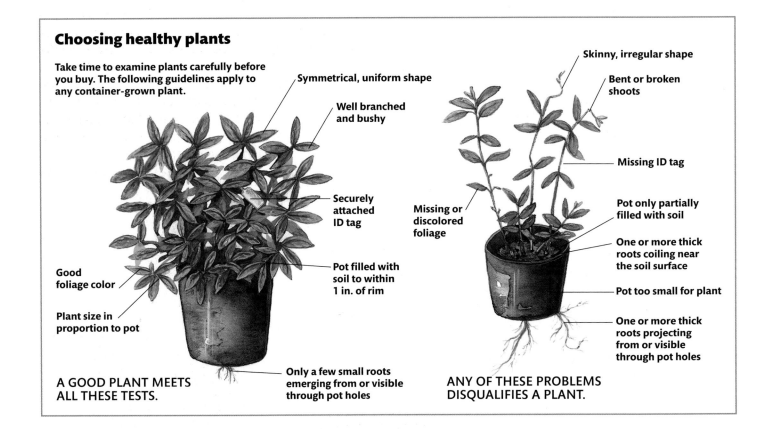

Choosing healthy plants

Take time to examine plants carefully before you buy. The following guidelines apply to any container-grown plant.

Symmetrical, uniform shape

Well branched and bushy

Securely attached ID tag

Pot filled with soil to within 1 in. of rim

Good foliage color

Plant size in proportion to pot

Only a few small roots emerging from or visible through pot holes

A GOOD PLANT MEETS ALL THESE TESTS.

Skinny, irregular shape

Bent or broken shoots

Missing ID tag

Missing or discolored foliage

Pot only partially filled with soil

One or more thick roots coiling near the soil surface

Pot too small for plant

One or more thick roots projecting from or visible through pot holes

ANY OF THESE PROBLEMS DISQUALIFIES A PLANT.

Choosing particular plants

If you need, for example, five azaleas and the nursery or garden center has a whole block of them, how do you choose which five to buy? Because the sales staff may be too busy to help you decide, you may need to choose by yourself.

Most plants today are grown in containers, so it's possible to lift them one at a time and examine them from all sides. Following the guidelines shown in the drawings below, evaluate each plant's shape, size, health and vigor, and root system.

Trees and shrubs are sometimes sold "balled-and-burlapped," that is, with a ball of soil and roots wrapped tightly in burlap. For these plants, look for strong limbs with no broken shoots, an attractive profile, and healthy foliage. Then press your hands against the burlap-covered root ball to make sure that it feels firm, solid, and damp, not loose or dry. (If the ball is buried within a bed of wood chips, carefully pull the chips aside; then push them back after inspecting the plant.)

To make the final choice when you're considering a group of plants, line them up side by side and select the ones that are most closely matched in height, bushiness, and foliage color. If your design includes a hedge or mass planting where uniformity is very important, it's a good idea to buy a few extra plants as potential replacements in case of damage or loss. It's easier to plan ahead than to find a match later. Plant the extras in a spare corner so you'll have them if you need them.

Sometimes a plant will be available in two or more sizes. Which is better? That depends on how patient you are. The main reason for buying bigger plants is to make a landscape look impressive right away. If you buy smaller plants and set them out at the same spacing, the planting will look sparse at first, but it will soon catch up. A year after planting, you can't tell if a perennial came from a quart- or gallon-size pot: they will look the same. For shrubs, the difference between one pot size and the next larger one usually represents one year's growth.

The Planting Process

Throughout most of the West, the cooler weather of fall or early spring makes those times best for planting. In fall, new plants have the upcoming wet season to become established before the onset of hot summer weather. Frost-tender plants such as citrus, on the other hand, are best planted in spring after the threat of cold temperatures has passed. Most nurseries also have a wider selection of perennials, trees, and shrubs in fall and spring.

Although it's handy to plant a whole bed at once, you can divide the job, setting out some plants in fall and adding the rest in spring, or vice versa. If possible, do the actual planting on a cloudy day or evening when rain is forecast. On the following pages, we'll give an overview of the process and discuss how to handle individual plants. If you're installing an irrigation system, remember that some of the components may need to be put in place after the soil is prepared but before planting.

Try to stay off the soil

Throughout the planting process, do all you can by reaching in from outside the bed. Stepping on the newly prepared bed compacts the soil and makes it harder to dig planting holes. Use short boards or scraps of plywood as temporary steppingstones if you do need to step on the soil. As soon as you can decide where to put them, lay permanent steppingstones for access to plants that need regular maintenance.

Check placement and spacing

The first step in planting is to mark the position of each plant. It's easy to arrange most of the plants themselves on the bed; use empty pots or stakes to represent plants too heavy to move easily. Follow the site plan for the design, checking the spacing with a yardstick as you place the plants.

Then step back and take a look. What do you think? Should you make any adjustments? Don't worry if the planting looks a little sparse. It *should* look that way at first. Plants almost always get bigger than you can imagine when you're first setting them out. And it's almost always better to wait for them to fill in rather than having to prune and thin a crowded planting in a few years. (You might fill between young plants with low-growing annuals, as suggested in the box on p. 292.)

PLANTING POINTERS

When working on top of prepared soil, kneel on a piece of plywood to distribute your weight.

Use empty pots or stakes to mark positions of plants not yet purchased or too heavy to move frequently.

Moving through the job

When you're satisfied with the arrangement, mark the position of each plant with a stake or stone, and set the plants aside out of the way, so you won't knock them over or step on them as you proceed. Start planting in order of size. Do the biggest plants first, then move on to the medium-size and smaller plants. If all the plants are about the same size, start at the back of the bed and work toward the front, or start in the center and work to the edges.

Position trees and shrubs to show their best side

Most trees and shrubs are slightly asymmetric. There's usually enough irregularity in their branching or shape that one side looks a little fuller or more attractive than the other sides do. After you've set a tree or shrub into its hole, step back and take a look. Then turn it partway, or try tilting or tipping it a little to one side or the other. Once you've decided which side and position looks best, start filling in the hole with soil. Stop and check again before you firm the soil into place.

The fine points of spacing

When you're planting a group of the same kind of plants, such as perennials or ferns, it normally looks best if you space them informally, in slightly curved or zigzag rows, with the plants in one row offset from those of the next row. Don't arrange plants in a straight row unless you want to emphasize a line, such as the edge of a bed. After planting, step back and evaluate the effect. If you want to adjust the placement or position of any plant, now is the time to do so.

Rake, water, and mulch

Use a garden rake to level out any high and low spots that remain after planting. Water enough to settle the soil into place around the roots. Mulch the entire planting area with 1 to 3 in. of composted bark, wood chips, or other organic matter. Mulch is indispensable for controlling weeds and regulating the moisture and temperature of the soil. If you're running out of time, you don't have to spread the mulch right away, but try to get it done within a week or so after planting.

Using annuals as fillers

The plants in our designs have been spaced so they will not be crowded at maturity. Buying more plants and spacing them closer may fill things out faster, but in several years (for perennials; longer for shrubs) you'll need to remove plants or prune them frequently.

If you want something to fill the gaps between young plants for that first year or two, use some annuals. The best annual fillers are compact plants that grow only 6 to 10 in. tall. These plants will hide the soil or mulch and make a colorful carpet. Avoid taller annuals, because they can shade or smother your permanent plantings. And don't forget, filler plants will need water.

The following annuals are all compact, easy to grow, readily available, and inexpensive. Seeds of those marked with a symbol (✿) can be sown directly in the garden. For the others, buy six-packs or flats of plants. Thin seedlings or space plants 8 to 12 in. apart.

Annual phlox ✿: Red, pink, or white flowers. Good for hot dry sites.

China pink ✿: Red, pink, white, or bicolor flowers. Blooms all summer.

Dusty miller: Silvery foliage, often lacy-textured. No flowers.

Edging lobelia: Dark blue, magenta, or white flowers. Likes afternoon shade.

Flossflower: Fluffy blue, lavender, or white flowers. Choose dwarf types.

Garden verbena: Bright red, pink, purple, or white flowers.

Globe candytuft ✿: Pink or white flowers. Best in cool weather.

Moss rose: Bright flowers in many colors. Ideal for hot dry sites.

Pansy and viola: Multicolored flowers. Grow best in cool weather.

Sweet alyssum ✿: Fragrant white or lilac flowers. Blooms for months. Prefers cool weather.

Wax begonia: Rose, pink, or white flowers. Good for shady sites but takes sun if watered regularly.

Planting Basics

Most of the plants that you buy for a landscaping project today are grown and sold in individual plastic containers, but large shrubs and trees may be balled-and-burlapped. Mail-order plants may come bare-root. And ground covers are sometimes sold in flats. In any case, the basic concern is the same: be careful what you do to a plant's roots. Spread them out; don't fold or coil them or cram them into a tight hole. Keep them covered; don't let the sun or air dry them out. And don't bury them too deep; set the top of the root ball level with the surrounding soil. Make sure the young plants don't dry out. Even drought-tolerant plants need water for at least the first year.

Planting container-grown plants

The steps are the same for any plant, no matter the size of the container. Dig a hole that's a little wider than the container but not quite as deep ❶. Check by setting the container into the hole—the top of the soil in the container should be slightly higher than the surrounding soil. Dig several holes at a time, at the positions that you've already marked out.

Remove the container ❷. With one hand, grip the plant at the base of its stems or leaves, like pulling a ponytail, while you tug on the pot with the other hand. If the pot doesn't slide off easily, don't pull harder on the stems. Try whacking the pot against a hard surface; if it still

doesn't slide off, use a strong knife to cut or pry it off.

Examine the plant's roots ❸. If there are any thick, coiled roots, unwind them and cut them off close to the root ball, leaving short stubs. If the root ball is a mass of fine, hairlike roots, use the knife to cut three or four slits from top to bottom, about 1 in. deep. Pry the slits apart and tease the cut roots to loosen them. This cutting or slitting may seem drastic, but it's actually good for the plant because it forces new roots to grow out into the surrounding soil. Work quickly. Once you've taken a plant out of its container, get it in the ground as soon as possible. If you want to prepare several plants at a time, cover them with an old sheet or tarp to keep the roots from drying out.

Set the root ball into the hole ❹. Make sure that the plant is positioned right, with its best side facing out, and that the top of the root ball is level with or slightly higher than the surface of the bed. Then add enough soil to fill in the hole, and pat it down firmly.

PLANTING CONTAINER-GROWN PLANTS

❶ **Dig a hole a little wider than the container but not as deep.**

❷ **Remove the plant from the container.**

❸ **Unwind any large, coiled roots and cut them off short. Cut vertical slits through masses of fine roots.**

❹ **Position the plant in the hole and fill in around it with soil.**

Planting a balled-and-burlapped shrub or tree

Nurseries often grow shrubs and trees in fields, and then dig them with a ball of root-filled soil and wrap a layer of burlap snugly around the ball to keep it intact. The problem is that even a small ball of soil is very heavy. A root ball that is a foot wide is a two-person job. For larger root balls, ask the nursery to deliver and plant it. Here's how to proceed with plants that are small enough that you can handle them.

Dig a hole several inches wider than the root ball but not quite as deep as the root ball is high. Firm the soil so the plant won't sink. Set the plant into the hole, and lay a stick across the top of the root ball to make sure it's at or a little higher than grade level. Be sure to cut or untie any twine that wraps around the trunk. Fold the burlap down around the sides of the ball. Don't try to pull the burlap out altogether—roots can grow out through it, and it will eventually decompose. Fill soil all around the sides of the ball and pat it down firmly. Spread only about 1 in. of soil over the top of the ball.

The top of the ball should be level with the surrounding soil. Cut twine that wraps around the trunk. Fold down the burlap, but don't remove it.

Planting bare-root plants

Mail-order nurseries sometimes dig perennials, roses, and other plants when the plants are dormant, cut back the tops, and wash all the soil off the roots, to save space and weight when storing and shipping them. If you receive a plant in bare-root condition, unwrap it, trim away any roots that are broken or damaged, and soak the roots in a pail of water for several hours.

To plant, dig a hole large enough that you can spread the roots across the bottom without folding them. Start covering the roots with soil, then lay a stick across the top of the hole and hold the plant against it to check the planting depth, as shown in the drawing. Raise or lower the plant if needed in order to bury just the roots, not the buds. Add more soil, firming it down around the roots, and continue until the hole is full.

Dig a hole wide enough that you can spread out the roots. A stick helps position the plant at the correct depth as you fill the hole with soil.

Planting ground covers from flats

Sometimes ground covers are sold in flats of 25 or more rooted cuttings. Start at one corner, reach underneath the soil, and lift out a portion of the flat's contents. Work quickly because the roots are exposed. Tease the cuttings apart, trying not to break off any roots, and plant them individually. Then lift out the next portion and continue planting.

Remove a clump of little plants, tease their roots apart, and plant them quickly.

Planting bulbs

Plant spring-blooming bulbs from September to November. If the soil in the bed was well prepared, you can use a trowel to dig holes for planting individual bulbs; where you have room, you can dig a wider hole or trench for planting a group of bulbs all at once. The perennials, ground covers, shrubs, and trees you planted earlier in the fall or in the spring will still be small enough that you won't disturb their roots. As a rule of thumb, plant small (grape- or cherry-size) bulbs about 2 in. deep and 3 to 5 in. apart, and large (walnut- or egg-size) bulbs 4 to 6 in. deep and 6 to 10 in. apart.

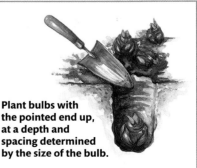

Plant bulbs with the pointed end up, at a depth and spacing determined by the size of the bulb.

Basic Landscape Care

The landscape plantings in this book will grow increasingly carefree from year to year as the plants mature, but of course you'll always need to do some regular maintenance. This ongoing care may require as much as a few hours a week during the season or as little as a few hours a year. You'll have to control weeds, use mulch, water as needed, and do spring and fall cleanups. Trees, shrubs, and vines may need staking or training at first and occasional pruning or shearing afterward. Perennials, ground covers, and grasses may need to be cut back, staked, deadheaded, or divided. Performing these tasks, which are explained on the following pages, is sometimes hard work, but for many gardeners it is enjoyable labor, a chance to get outside in the fresh air. Also, spending time each week with your plants helps you identify and address problems before they become serious.

Mulches and fertilizers

Covering the soil in all planted areas with a layer of organic mulch does several jobs at once: it improves the appearance of your garden while you're waiting for the plants to grow, reduces the number of weeds that emerge, retards water loss from the soil during dry spells, moderates soil temperatures, and adds nutrients to the soil as it decomposes. Inorganic mulches such as landscape fabric and gravel also provide some of these benefits, but their conspicuous appearance and the difficulty of removing them if you ever want to change the landscape are serious drawbacks.

Many materials are used as mulches; the box on p. 296 presents the most common, with comments on their advantages and disadvantages. Consider appearance, availability, cost, and convenience when you're comparing different products. Most garden centers have a few kinds of bagged mulch materials, but for mulching large areas, it's easier and cheaper to have a nursery or other supplier deliver a truckload of bulk mulch. A landscape looks best if you see the same mulch throughout the entire planting area, rather than a patchwork of different mulches. You can achieve a uniform look by spreading a base layer of homemade compost, hay, or other inexpensive material and topping that with a neater-looking material such as bark chips or shredded bark.

It takes at least a 1-in. layer of mulch to suppress weeds, but there's no need to spread it more than 3 in. deep. As you're spreading it, don't put any mulch against the stems of any plants, because that can lead to disease or insect problems. Put most of the mulch between plants but not *around* them. Check the mulch during your spring and fall cleanups. Be sure it's pulled back away from the plant stems. Rake the surface of the mulch lightly to loosen it, and top it up with a fresh layer if the old material appears to have decomposed.

Fertilizer

Decomposing mulch frequently supplies enough nutrients to grow healthy plants, but using fertilizer helps if you want to boost the plants—to make them grow faster, get larger, or produce more flowers. Young plants or those growing in poor soils also benefit from occasional applications of fertilizer. There are dozens of fertilizer products on the market—liquid and granular, fast-acting and slow-release, organic and synthetic. All give good results if applied as directed. And observe the following precautions: Don't overfertilize, don't fertilize when the soil is dry, and don't fertilize tender plants after late summer, because they need to slow down and finish the season's growth before cold weather comes.

Planting on a hillside

Successful planting on a hillside depends on keeping the bare soil and young plants from blowing or washing away while they establish themselves. Here are some tips. Rather than amending all the soil, prepare individual planting holes. Work from the top of the slope to the bottom. Push one or more wooden shingles into the slope just below a plant to help hold it in place. Mulch with heavier materials, such as wood chips, that won't wash or blow away. If the soil is loose, spread water-permeable landscape fabric over it to help hold it in place; slit the fabric and insert plants through the openings. Water with drip irrigation, which is less likely to erode soil than sprinklers are.

Confining perennials

Yarrow, bee balm, artemisia, and various other perennials, grasses, and ferns are described as invasive because they spread by underground runners. To confine these plants to a limited area, install a barrier when you plant them. Cut the bottom off a 5-gal. or larger plastic pot, bury the pot so its rim is above the soil, and plant the perennial inside. You'll need to lift, divide, and replant part of the perennial every second or third year.

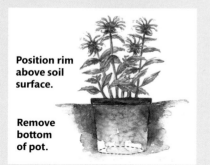

Position rim above soil surface.

Remove bottom of pot.

Mulch materials

Bark products

Bark nuggets, chipped bark, shredded bark, ground bark, and composted bark, usually from conifers, are available in bags or in bulk. All are attractive, long lasting, medium-price mulches.

Chipped tree trimmings

The chips available from utility companies and tree services are a mixture of wood, bark, twigs, and leaves. These chips cost less than pure bark products (you may be able to get a load for free), but they don't look as good and you have to replace them more often, because they decompose fast.

Sawdust and shavings

These are cheap or free at sawmills and woodshops. They make good path coverings, but they aren't ideal mulches, because they tend to pack down into a dense, water-resistant surface. Sawdust can also blow around.

Hulls and shells

Ground coconut hulls, cocoa hulls, and nut shells can be picked up at food-processing plants and are sometimes sold at garden centers. They're all attractive, long lasting mulches. Price varies from free to quite expensive, depending on where you get them.

Tree leaves

A few big trees may supply all the mulch you need, year after year. You can just rake the leaves onto a bed in fall, but it's better to chop them up with the lawn mower, pile them in compost bins for the winter, and spread them where needed in late spring. Pine needles likewise make good mulch, especially for rhododendrons, azaleas, and other acid-loving shrubs. You can spread pine needles in fall, because they cling together and don't blow around.

Grass clippings

A 1- to 2-in. layer of dried grass clippings makes an acceptable mulch that decomposes within a single growing season. Don't pile clippings too thick, though. If you do, the top surface dries and packs into a water-resistant crust, and the bottom layer turns into nasty slime.

Hay and straw

Farmers sell hay that's unsuitable for fodder as "mulch" hay. Hay is cheap but likely to include weed seeds. Straw—the stems of grain crops such as wheat—is usually seed free but more expensive. Both hay and straw are more suitable for mulching vegetable gardens than landscape plantings because they decompose quickly and must be renewed each year. They also tend to attract rodents.

Gravel

A mulch of pea gravel or crushed rock, spread 1 to 2 in. thick, helps keep the soil cool and moist, and many plants grow very well with a gravel mulch. However, compared with organic materials, such as bark or leaves, it's much more tiring to apply a gravel mulch in the first place; it's harder to remove leaves and litter that accumulate on the gravel or weeds that sprout up through it; it's annoying to dig through the gravel if you want to replace or add plants later; and it's tedious to remove the gravel itself, should you ever change your mind about having it there. Gravel mulches also reflect heat and can make a yard hotter than normal.

Landscape fabrics

Various types of synthetic fabrics, usually sold in rolls 3 to 4 ft. wide and 20, 50, or 100 ft. long, can be spread over the ground as a weed barrier. Unlike plastic, these fabrics allow water and air to penetrate into the soil. A topping of gravel, bark chips, or other mulch can anchor the fabric and hide it from view. If you're planting small plants, you can spread the fabric and insert the plants through X-shaped slits cut in the fabric where needed. You can plant larger plants first, then cut and snug the fabric around them. Drip irrigation is best laid on top of the fabric, to make it easier to see clogs and leaks. It's also useful to lay fabric under paths, although it can be difficult to secure the fabric neatly and invisibly along the edges of adjacent planting beds. Removing fabric—if you change your mind—is a messy job. However, there are newer biodegradable fabrics that break down after a few years.

Clear or black plastic

Don't even think about using any kind of plastic sheeting as a landscape mulch. The soil underneath a sheet of plastic gets bone-dry, while water accumulates on top. Any loose mulch you spread on plastic won't stay in an even layer. No matter how you try to secure them, the edges of plastic sheeting always pull loose, appear at the surface, degrade in the sun, and shred into tatters.

Watering

To use water efficiently and effectively it is helpful to know how to gauge when and how much your plants need and how to ensure that your system supplies it.

Deciding whether water is needed

Many experienced gardeners can judge whether a plant needs water simply by looking at its leaves. But drooping or dull leaves can be caused by pests, disease, and overwatering as well as by water stress. A surer way to decide whether you need to water is to examine the soil. If the top 3 to 4 in. is dry, most annuals, perennials, and shallow-rooted shrubs such as azaleas will need to be watered. Most trees and larger shrubs need water if the top 6 to 8 in. is dry. To check soil moisture, you can get down on your hands and knees and dig. But digging in an established planting can be awkward as well as harmful to crowded roots.

A less invasive method of checking moisture is to use a paint stirrer or similar piece of unfinished, light-colored wood. Push it down through the mulch and 6 to 8 in. into the soil. Leave it there for an hour or so; then pull it out to see whether moisture has discolored the wood. If so, the soil is moist enough for plants. It is also helpful to make a habit of monitoring rainfall. Also, listen to the weather reports, marking a calendar to keep track of rainfall amounts.

Pay attention to soil moisture or rainfall amounts all year long because plants can suffer from dryness in any season, not just in the heat of summer. Water whenever the soil is dry. As for time of day, it's best to water early in the morning when the wind is calm, evaporation is low, and plant foliage will have plenty of time to dry off before nightfall (wet leaves at night can promote some foliar diseases). Early morning (before 5 a.m.) is also when most urban and suburban neighborhoods have plenty of water pressure.

How much to water

Determining how much water to apply and how often to apply it is one of gardening's greatest challenges. Water too much and plants drown. Water too little and they dry out and die. For most gardeners, gauging how much water a plant or bed needs is an art more than a science. The key to watering enough but not too much is to be a good observer. Examine your soil often, keep an eye on your plants, and make adjustments with the weather.

New plantings, even those of drought-tolerant plants, require frequent watering during the first year until the plants are established. In the heat of summer, new plantings may require water twice a week or more.

Established landscape plants vary in their water needs. (The descriptions for most of the plants in the Plant Profiles include water requirements.) When you do water, it is always best to water deeply, wetting a large portion of the plant's root zone. Shallow watering encourages shallow rooting, and shallow-rooted plants dry out fast and need watering more frequently. Furthermore, a water-stressed plant is also more susceptible to disease and insect damage. As a rule of thumb, water most perennials to a depth of 12 to 18 in.; water most shrubs 2 to 3 ft. deep and most trees 3 to 4 ft. deep. (Lawns, by contrast, should be watered 6 to 8 in. deep, but they require frequent watering.)

Determining how much water will be required to penetrate to these depths depends on your soil. Water moves through different soils at different speeds. In general, 1 in. of water will soak about 4 to 5 in. deep in clay soil, 6 to 7 in. deep in loam, and 10 to 12 in. in sandy soil.

Different watering systems, from hose-end sprinklers to automated drip systems, deliver water at different rates. Manufacturers often provide these rates in the product descriptions. You can determine the delivery rate for a sprinkler by setting tuna-fish cans in the area it covers and timing how long it takes to deposit an inch of water in one or more cans.

Whatever your system, you'll need to know how long it has to run for water to penetrate to the desired depths in your soil. As we've said, digging to determine water penetration is often impractical. To gauge penetration to a foot or so deep, you can use wooden "dipsticks" as described previously. (Insert the sticks after you've watered.) For a rough gauge of deeper penetration, you can push a ¼- to ½-in.-diameter iron bar into the soil. The bar will move easily through wet soil. When it encounters dry soil, it will become harder to push or it will feel different as you push. Run your system and time it as you check penetration depths.

CHECKING SOIL MOISTURE

Stick a paint stirrer or similar piece of light-colored, unfinished wood down through the mulch and into the soil. Pull it up after an hour. If the bottom of the stick looks and feels damp, the soil is moist enough for plants.

Controlling weeds

Weeds are not much of a problem in established landscapes. Once the "good" plants have grown big enough to merge together, they tend to crowd or shade out all but the most persistent undesirable plants. But weeds can be troublesome in a new landscape unless you take steps to prevent and control them.

There are two main types of weeds: those that mostly sprout up as seedlings and those that keep coming back from perennial roots or runners. Try to identify and eliminate any perennial weeds before you start a landscaping project (see p. 254). Then you'll only have to deal with new seedlings later, which is a much easier job.

Annual and perennial weeds that commonly grow from seeds include Bermuda grass, bindweed, crabgrass, dandelions, oxalis, plantain, purslane, and spurge. Trees and shrubs such as cherry laurel, Chinese elm, privet, mimosa, cottonwood, and Scotch broom produce weedy seedlings, too. For any of these weeds that grow from seeds, the strategy is twofold: try to keep the weed seeds from sprouting, and eliminate any seedlings that do sprout as soon as you see them, while they are still small.

Almost any patch of soil includes weed seeds that are ready to sprout whenever that soil is disturbed. Preparing the soil for planting will probably cause an initial flush of weeds, but you'll never see that many weeds again if you leave the soil undisturbed in subsequent years. You don't have to hoe, rake, or cultivate around perennial plantings. Leave the soil alone, and fewer weeds will appear. Using mulch helps even more; by shading the soil, it prevents weed seeds from sprouting. And if weed seeds blow in and land on top of the mulch, they'll be less likely to germinate there than they would on bare soil.

Pull or cut off any weeds that appear while they're young and small, just a few inches tall. Don't let them mature and go to seed. Most weed seedlings emerge in late spring and early summer. If you get rid of them then, you won't see many more seedlings for the rest of the growing season.

Using herbicides

Two kinds of herbicides can be very useful and effective in maintaining home landscapes, but only if used correctly. Follow the directions on the label.

Preemergent herbicides. Sold in granular or liquid form, these herbicides are designed to prevent weed seeds, particularly crabgrass and other annual weeds, from sprouting. For annual winter weeds, such as chickweed, annual bluegrass, and henbit, make the first application in early fall before the first signs of rain and cooler weather. For annual summer weeds, such as crabgrass and spurge, you'll need to make another ap-

WEEDS THAT SPROUT FROM SEEDS

Simple root systems can be easily pulled while still small.

Spurge

Oxalis

WEEDS THAT SPROUT BACK FROM PERENNIAL ROOTS OR RUNNERS

Connected by underground runners, the shoots of these weeds need to be pulled repeatedly, smothered with a thick mulch, or killed with an herbicide.

Bermuda grass

Runner

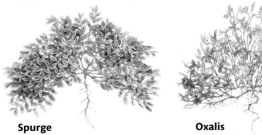

Use a disposable, sponge-type paintbrush to apply the herbicide selectively, painting only the weeds. Prepare the solution as directed for spray application. Use only enough to wet the leaves, so none drips off.

USING HERBICIDES ON PERENNIAL WEEDS

Ready-to-use spot-weeder sprays are convenient, but you must aim carefully. Try using a sheet of cardboard as a backdrop to protect desirable plants from herbicide drift.

Caring for Woody Plants

plication in spring. Your cooperative extension service can provide exact timing.

Make sure the herbicide you buy is registered for use around the plants you have. Granular forms are often used in smaller areas, liquid in larger areas. Apply them exactly as described on the product label. Wear heavy rubber gloves that are rated for use with farm chemicals, not household rubber gloves.

Postemergent herbicides. These chemicals are used to kill growing plants. Some kill only the aboveground parts of a plant; others are absorbed into the plant and kill it, roots and all. Postemergent herbicides are typically applied as sprays, which you can buy ready-to-use or prepare by mixing a concentrate with water. Look for those that break down quickly; read the label carefully for specific directions and safety instructions.

Postemergent herbicides work best if applied when the weeds are growing vigorously. You usually have to apply enough to thoroughly wet the plant's leaves, and do it during a spell of dry weather. Applying an herbicide is an effective way to get rid of a perennial weed that you can't dig or pull up, but it's really better to do this before you plant a bed, as it's hard to spray herbicides in an established planting without getting some on your good plants. (Some postemergent herbicides are more selective, affecting only certain types of plants.) Aim carefully, shielding nearby plants as shown in the drawing, left, and don't spray on windy days. Brushing or sponging the herbicide on the leaves is slower than spraying, but you're sure to avoid damaging adjacent plants.

Using postemergent herbicides in an established planting may be the only way to get rid of a persistent perennial weed. For young weed seedlings, it's usually easier to pull them by hand.

A well-chosen garden tree, such as the ones recommended in this book, grows naturally into a pleasing shape, won't get too large for its site, is resistant to pests and diseases, and doesn't drop messy pods or other litter. Once established, these trees need very little care from year to year.

Regular watering is the most important concern in getting a tree off to a good start. Don't let it suffer from drought for the first few years. To reduce competition, don't plant ground covers or other plants within 2 ft. of the tree's trunk. Just spread a thin layer of mulch there.

Arborists now dismiss other care ideas that once were common practice. According to current thinking, you don't need to fertilize a tree when you plant it (in fact, unless they show obvious signs of deficiency or grow poorly, most landscape trees never need fertilizing). Keep pruning to a minimum at planting time; remove only dead or damaged twigs, not healthy shoots. Finally, research has shown that tree trunks grow stronger when they're not supported by stakes. However, most newly planted trees need some support, usually for no more than a year. It is very important that the supported trunk be allowed a certain amount of movement. Be sure to ask your nursery about proper staking for your tree.

Pruning basics

Proper pruning keeps plants healthy and looking their best. There are two basic types of pruning cuts: heading and thinning. Heading cuts are made along the length of a branch or stem, between its tip and its base. These cuts induce vigorous growth in the dormant buds below the cut. Such growth is useful for filling in hedges and rejuvenating shrubs and perennials. But heading can drastically change the appearance of a plant, even destroying its natural shape. Heading can also produce weakly attached branches in trees and shrubs.

Thinning cuts remove stems and branches at their origin (the plant's crown or where the branch attaches to the trunk or a larger limb). Unlike heading, thinning does not produce vigorous growth. Instead, thinning opens the plant's interior to light and air, which improves its health. And, by reducing congested growth, thinning often enhances the natural appearance of the plant. In most cases, thinning is the preferred pruning technique, especially for trees and shrubs.

BUSHIER GROWTH

For many plants, simple heading cuts can produce fuller, bushier growth. Cut off the ends of stems to induce growth from lower buds.

Pruning roses

Roses are vigorous, fast-growing shrubs that need regular pruning to keep them shapely and attractive. Most of this pruning is done in winter to early spring, just as the buds start to swell but before the new leaves start to unfold. Always use sharp pruning shears and cut back to a healthy bud, leaving no stub. Right after pruning is a good time to add fresh mulch around the plant.

Prune hybrid tea roses to keep them neat, compact, and continuously producing long-stemmed flowers. Remove skinny or weak stems plus a few of the oldest stems (their bark is tan or gray instead of green) by cutting them off at their base. Prune off any shoots that got frozen or broken during the winter, remove old or weak shoots and crossing or crowded stems, and trim back any asymmetric or unbalanced shoots. Don't be afraid of cutting back too hard; it's better to leave just a few strong shoots than a lot of weak ones. If you cut old stems off at ground level, new ones will grow to replace them. Cut damaged or asymmetric stems back partway and they will branch out.

Hybrid tea roses bloom on new growth, so if you prune in early spring you aren't cutting off any flower buds. During the growing season, make a habit of removing the flowers as soon as they fade. This keeps the plant neat and makes it bloom longer and more abundantly. At least once a week,

locate each faded flower, follow down its stem to the first or second five-leaflet leaf, and prune just above one of those leaves. (Follow the same steps to cut roses for a bouquet.)

Climbing roses are pruned differently than hybrid teas. In late winter, remove weak, dead, or damaged shoots by cutting them back to the ground or to healthy wood. Select the healthiest stems for a main framework, and tie them securely to a support. Shorten all side shoots on these stems to two buds. Shoots growing from these buds will produce flowers.

Climbing roses need regular attention throughout the summer, because their stems (also called canes) can grow a foot or more in a month. Check regularly and tie this new growth to the trellis while it's still supple and manageable. When the canes grow long enough to reach the top of the trellis or arbor, cut off their tips and tie the canes horizontally to induce production of flowering side shoots. Remove spent roses by cutting the stems back to the nearest healthy five-leaflet leaf.

Shrub roses, floribundas, and other landscape roses can be pruned with hedge shears. Simply cut back one-third to one-half the growth in winter and remove diseased or damaged canes. You can also remove spent flowers with hedge shears.

PRUNING A HYBRID TEA ROSE

In late winter or early spring, remove old, weak, or damaged shoots; stems that are crossing or crowded; and stems that stick out too far and look asymmetric. Don't be afraid to cut a lot away.

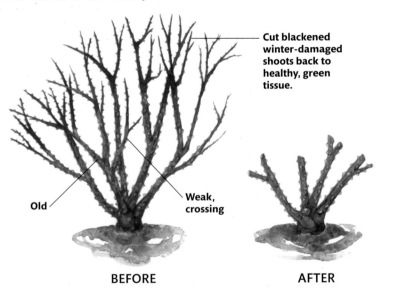

Cut blackened winter-damaged shoots back to healthy, green tissue.

Old

Weak, crossing

BEFORE

AFTER

REMOVING FLOWERS

Roses can look messy as they fade. Cut off by pruning the stem back to the first healthy five-leaflet leaf.

Five-leaflet leaf

Shaping young trees

As a tree grows, you can affect its shape by pruning once a year, usually in winter. Take it easy, though. Don't prune just for the sake of pruning; that does more harm than good. If you don't have a good reason for making a cut, don't do it. Follow these guidelines:

▍ **Use sharp pruning shears, loppers, or saws,** which make clean cuts without tearing the wood or bark.
▍ **Cut branches back** to a healthy shoot, leaf, or bud, or cut back to the branch collar at the base of the branch, as shown at right. Don't leave any stubs; they're ugly and prone to decay.
▍ **Remove any dead or damaged** branches and any twigs or limbs that are very spindly or weak.
▍ **Where two limbs cross over or rub** against each other, save one limb—usually the thicker, stronger one—and prune off the other one.
▍ **Prune or widen narrow crotches.** Places where a branch and trunk or two branches form a narrow V are weak spots, liable to split apart as the tree grows. Where the trunk of a young tree exhibits such a crotch or where either of two shoots could continue the growth of a branch, prune off the weaker of the two.

WHERE TO CUT

When removing the end of a branch, cut back to a healthy leaf, bud, or side shoot. Don't leave a stub. Use sharp pruning shears to make a neat cut that slices the stem rather than tears it.

Trunk

Branch

Branch collar

When removing an entire branch, cut just outside the slightly thickened area, called the branch collar, where the branch grows into the trunk.

SINGLE-TRUNK TREES

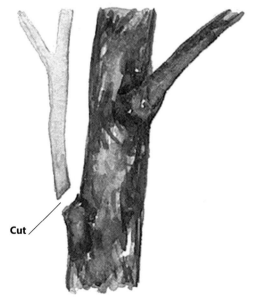

Cut

Correct narrow crotches on a young tree by removing the less desired limb. Choose well-spaced shoots to become the main limbs of a shade tree.

One trunk or several?

If you want a young tree to have a single trunk, identify the leader or central shoot and let it grow straight up, unpruned. The trunk will grow thicker faster if you leave the lower limbs in place for the first few years, but if they're in the way, you can remove them. At whatever height you choose—usually about 8 ft. off the ground if you want to walk or see under the tree—select the shoots that will become the main limbs of the tree. Be sure they are evenly spaced around the trunk, pointing outward at wide angles. Remove any lower or weaker shoots. As the tree matures, the only further pruning required will be an annual checkup to remove dead, damaged, or crossing shoots.

Several of the trees in this book, including crape myrtle, redbud, Japanese maple, and saucer magnolia, are often grown with multiple trunks, for a graceful, clumplike appearance. When buying a multiple-trunk tree, choose one with trunks that diverge at the base. Prune multiple-trunk trees as previously described for single-trunk trees. Remove some of the branches that are growing toward the center of the clump, so the center doesn't get too dense and tangled.

Pruning shrubs

Shrubs are generally carefree plants, but they almost always look better if you do some pruning at least every other year. As a minimum, remove dead twigs from time to time, and if any branches are broken by storms or accidents, remove them as soon as convenient, cutting back to a healthy bud or branch or to the plant's crown. Also, unless the shrub produces attractive seedpods or berries, it's a good idea to trim off the flowers after they fade.

Beyond this routine pruning, some shrubs require more attention. (The entries in Plant Profiles, pp. 184–249, give more information on when and how to prune particular shrubs.) Basically, shrub pruning falls into three categories: selective pruning, severe pruning, and shearing. (See the drawings, below right.)

Selective pruning means using pruning shears to head back or thin individual shoots in order to refine the shape of the bush and maintain its vigor, as well as limit its size. This job takes time but produces a very graceful and natural-looking bush. Cut away weak or spindly twigs and any limbs that cross or rub against each other, and head all the longest shoots back to a healthy, outward-facing bud or to a pair of buds. You can do selective pruning on any shrub, deciduous or evergreen, at any time of year.

Severe pruning means using pruning shears or loppers to cut away most of a shrub's top growth, leaving just short stubs or a gnarly trunk. This kind of cutting back is usually done once a year in late winter or early spring. Although it seems drastic, severe pruning is appropriate in several situations.

It makes certain fast-growing shrubs, such as bigleaf hydrangea and butterfly bush, flower more profusely. It keeps others, such as spirea and 'Powis Castle' artemisia, compact and bushy.

One or two severe prunings done when a shrub is young can make it branch out at the base, producing a bushier specimen or a fuller hedge plant. Nurseries often do this pruning as part of producing a good plant, and if you buy a shrub that's already bushy, you don't need to cut it back yourself. Older shrubs that have gotten tall and straggly sometimes respond to a severe pruning by sprouting out with renewed vigor, sending up lots of new shoots that bear plenty of foliage and flowers. This strategy doesn't work for all shrubs, though—sometimes severe pruning kills a plant. Don't try it unless you know it will work (check with a knowledgeable person at a nursery) or are willing to take a chance.

Shearing means using hedge shears or an electric hedge trimmer to trim the surface of a shrub, hedge, or tree to a neat, uniform profile, producing a solid mass of greenery. Both deciduous and evergreen shrubs and trees can be sheared; those with small, closely spaced leaves and a naturally compact growth habit usually look best. A good time for shearing most shrubs is late spring, after the new shoots have elongated but before the wood has hardened, but you can shear at other times of year. You may have to shear some plants more than once a year.

If you're planning to shear a plant, start when it is young and establish the shape—cone, pyramid, flat-topped hedge, or whatever. Looking at the profile, always make the shrub wider at the bottom than on top; otherwise the lower limbs will be shaded and won't be as leafy. Shear off as little as needed to maintain the shape as the shrub grows. Once it gets as big as you want it, shear as much as you have to to keep it that size.

SELECTIVE PRUNING. Remove weak, spindly, bent, or broken shoots (red). Where two branches rub on each other, remove the weakest or the one that's pointing inward (orange). Cut back long shoots to a healthy, outward-facing bud (blue).

SEVERE PRUNING. In late winter or early spring, before new growth starts, cut all the stems back close to the ground.

SHEARING. Trim with hedge clippers to a neat profile.

Making a hedge

To make a hedge that's dense enough that you can't see through it, choose shrubs that have many shoots at the base. If you can only find skinny shrubs, prune them severely the first spring after planting to stimulate bushier growth.

Hedge plants are set in the ground as described on pp. 293–294 but are spaced closer together than they would be if planted as individual specimens. This helps create the hedge-like look. We took that into account in creating the designs and plant lists for this book; just follow the spacings recommended in the designs. If you're impatient for the hedge to fill in, you can space the plants closer together, but don't put them farther apart.

A hedge can be sheared, pruned selectively, or left alone, depending on how you want it to look. Slow-growing, small-leaved plants such as boxwood and box-leaf euonymus make rounded but natural-looking hedges with no pruning at all, or you can shear them into any profile you choose and make them perfectly neat and uniform. (Be sure to keep them narrower at the top.) Choose one style and stick with it. Once a hedge is established, you can neither start nor stop shearing it without an awkward transition that may last a few years before the hedge looks good again.

Getting a vine off to a good start

Nurseries often sell jasmine, clematis, wisteria, and other vines as young plants with a single stem fastened to a stake. To plant the vine, remove the stake and cut off the stem right above the lowest pair of healthy leaves, usually about 4 to 6 in. above the soil ❶. This forces the vine to send out new shoots low to the ground. As soon as those new shoots have begun to develop (usually a month or so after planting), cut them back to their first pairs of leaves ❷. After this second pruning, the plant will become bushy at the base. Now, as new shoots form, use sticks or strings to direct them toward the base of the support they are to climb ❸.

Once they're started, twining vines such as the ones named above can scramble up a lattice trellis, although it helps if you tuck in any stray ends. The plants can't climb a smooth surface, however. To help them cover a fence with wide vertical slats or a porch post, you have to provide something the vine can wrap around. Screw a few eyebolts to the top and bottom of such a support and stretch wire, nylon cord, or polypropylene rope between them. (The wires or cords should be a few inches out from the fence, not flush against it.)

Clinging vines can climb any surface by means of their adhesive rootlets and need no further assistance or care.

So-called climbing roses don't really climb at all by themselves—you have to fasten them to a support. Twist-ties are handy for this job. Roses grow fast, so you'll have to tie in the new shoots every few weeks from spring to fall.

After the first year, most vines need annual spring pruning to remove any dead, damaged, or straggly stems. If vines grow too long, you can cut them back anytime and they will branch out from below the cut.

STARTING A VINE

❶ At planting, cut just above the first pair of healthy leaves.

❷ Then cut new shoots back to the first pair of leaves.

❸ Severe initial pruning forces the vine to branch at the base. Tie shoots from these branches to cover the trellis fully and evenly.

Caring for Perennials

Perennials are simply plants that send up new growth year after year. A large group, perennials include flowering plants such as daylilies and purple coneflower as well as grasses, ferns, and hardy bulbs. Although some perennials need special conditions and care, most of the ones in this book are adaptable and easygoing. Get them off to a good start by planting them in well-prepared soil, adding a layer of mulch, watering as often as needed throughout the first year, and keeping weeds away. After that, keeping perennials attractive and healthy typically requires just a few minutes per plant each year.

Routine annual care

Some of the perennials that are used as ground covers, such as ajuga, lilyturf, mondo grass, and vinca, need virtually no care. On a suitable site, they'll thrive for decades even if you pay them almost no attention at all.

Most garden perennials, though, look and grow better if you clean away the old leaves and stems at least once a year. When to do this depends on the type of plant. Perennials such as daylily, dwarf fountain grass, hosta, and Siberian iris have leaves and stalks that turn tan or brown after they're frosted in fall. Cut these down to the ground in late fall or early spring; either time is okay.

Perennials such as Shasta daisy, geranium, blue fescue grass, dianthus, coralbells, and phlox have foliage that is more or less evergreen, depending on the severity of the winter. For those plants, wait until after they've bloomed or until the fall; then cut back any leaves or stems that are discolored or shabby-looking. Don't leave cuttings lying on the soil, because they may contain disease spores. To avoid contaminating your compost, send diseased stems or leaves to the dump.

Right after you've cleared away the dead material is a good time to renew the mulch on the bed. Use a fork, rake, or cultivator to loosen the existing mulch, and add some fresh mulch if needed. Also, if you want to sprinkle some granular fertilizer on the bed, do that now, when it's easy to avoid getting any on the plants' leaves. Fertilizing perennials is optional, but it does make them grow bigger and bloom more than they would otherwise.

Remove faded flowers

Removing flowers as they fade (called "deadheading") makes the garden look neater, prevents unwanted self-sown seedlings, and often stimulates a plant to continue blooming longer than it would if you left it alone, or to bloom a second time later in the season. (This is true for shrubs and annual plants as well as for perennial plants.)

Pick large flowers such as daisies, daylilies, irises, and lilies one at a time, snapping them off by hand. Use pruning shears on perennials such as garden penstemon, phlox, and yarrow that produce tall stalks crowded with lots of small flowers, cutting the stalks back to the height of the foliage. Use hedge shears on bushy plants that are covered with lots of small flowers on short stalks, such as salvia, 'Moonbeam' coreopsis, dianthus, evergreen candytuft, and 'Homestead Purple' verbena, cutting the stems back by about one-half their length.

Instead of removing them, you may want to let the flowers remain on purple coneflower, Siberian iris, 'Autumn Joy' sedum, and the various grasses. These plants all bear conspicuous seedpods or seed heads on stiff stalks that remain standing and look interesting throughout the fall and winter.

Pruning and shearing perennials

Some perennials that bloom in summer or fall respond well to being pruned earlier in the growing season. Mexican sage, chrysanthemum, garden phlox, and 'Autumn Joy' sedum all form tall clumps of stems topped with lots of little flowers. Unfortunately, tall stems are liable to flop over in stormy weather, and even if they don't, too-tall clumps can look leggy or top heavy. To prevent floppiness, prune these plants when the stems are about 1 ft. tall. Remove the weakest stems from each clump by cutting them off at the ground; then cut all the remaining, strong stems back by about one-third. Pruning in this way keeps these plants shorter, stronger, and bushier, so you don't have to bother with stakes to keep them upright.

Germander and 'Powis Castle' artemisia are grown more for their foliage than for their flowers. You can use hedge shears to keep them neat, compact, and bushy, shearing off the tops of the stems once or twice in spring and summer.

PRUNING A PERENNIAL

Prune to create neater, bushier clumps of some summer- and fall-blooming perennials, such as garden phlox, chrysanthemums, and 'Autumn Joy' sedum. When the stalks are about 1 ft. tall, cut them all back by one-third. Remove the weakest stalks at ground level.

Dividing perennials

Most perennials send up more stems each year, forming denser clumps or wider patches. Dividing is the process of cutting or breaking apart these clumps or patches. This is an easy way to make more plants to expand your garden, to control a plant that might otherwise spread out of bounds, or to renew an old specimen that doesn't look good or bloom well anymore.

Most perennials can be divided as often as every year or two if you're in a hurry to make more plants, or they can go for several years if you don't have any reason to disturb them. Fall is the best time to divide most perennials, but you can also do it in early spring.

There are two main approaches to dividing perennials, as shown in the drawings at right. You can leave the plant in the ground and use a sharp spade to cut it apart, similar to slicing a pie, and then lift out one chunk at a time. Or you can dig around and underneath the plant and lift it out all at once, shake off the extra soil, and lay the plant on the ground or a tarp where you can work with it.

Some plants, such as ajuga, yarrow, and some ferns, are easy to divide. They almost fall apart when you dig them up. Others, such as agapanthus, daylily, and most grasses, have very tough or tangled roots and you'll have to wrestle with them, chop them with a sharp butcher knife, pry them apart with a strong screwdriver or garden fork, or even cut through the roots with a hatchet or pruning saw. However you approach the job, before you insert any tool, take a close look at the plant right at ground level, and be careful to divide *between*, not *through*, the biggest and healthiest buds or shoots. Using a hose to wash

loose mulch and soil away makes it easier to see what you're doing.

Don't make the divisions too small; they should be the size of a plant that you'd want to buy, not just little scraps. If you have more divisions than you need or want, choose just the best-looking ones to replant and discard or give away the others. Replant new divisions as soon as possible in freshly prepared soil. Water them right away, and water again

whenever the soil dries out over the next few weeks or months, until the plants are growing again.

Divide hardy bulbs, such as daffodils and crocuses, every few years. Dig clumps after bloom but before the foliage turns yellow. Shake the soil off the roots, pull the bulbs apart, and replant them promptly, setting them as deep as they were buried before.

DIVIDING PERENNIALS

You can divide a clump or patch of perennials by cutting down into the patch with a sharp spade, similar to slicing a pie or a pan of brownies, and then lifting out the separate chunks.

Or you can dig up the whole clump, shake the extra soil off the roots, and then pull or pry it apart into separate plantlets.

Problem Solving

Some plants are much more susceptible than others to damage by severe weather, pests, or diseases. In this book, we've recommended plants that are generally trouble free, especially after they have had a few years to get established in your garden. But even these plants are subject to various mishaps and problems. The challenge is learning how to distinguish the problems that are really serious and those that are just cosmetic, and deciding how to solve—or, better yet, prevent—those problems that are serious.

Pests, large and small

Deer and rabbits are liable to be a problem if your property is surrounded by or adjacent to fields or woods. You may not see them, but you can't miss the damage they do—they bite the tops off or eat whole plants of agapanthus, daylilies, and many other perennials. Deer also eat the leaves and stems of maples, azaleas, and many other trees and shrubs. Commercial or homemade repellents that you spray on the foliage may be helpful if the animals aren't too hungry and you use them often. (See the box, below, for thoughts on deer-proof plants.) But in the long run, the only solution is to fence out deer and to trap and remove smaller animals.

Squirrels are cute but naughty. They normally don't eat much foliage, but they do eat some kinds of flowers and several kinds of bulbs. They also dig up new transplants, and they plant nuts in your flower beds and lawns. Meadow voles and field mice can kill trees and shrubs by stripping the bark off the trunk, usually near the ground. Gophers eat the roots of shrubs, trees, and perennials. Moles don't eat plants, but their digging makes a mess of a lawn or flower bed. Persistent trapping is the most effective way to control all of these little critters. (You can protect the roots of some plants from gophers by planting the plants in wire cages sold at many nurseries.)

Aphids, beetles, caterpillars, grubs, grasshoppers, spider mites, scale insects, slugs, snails, weevils, and countless other pests can cause minor or devastating damage in a home landscape. Most plants can afford to lose part of their foliage or sap without suffering much of a setback, so don't panic if you see a few holes chewed in a leaf. However, whenever you suspect that insects or related pests are attacking one of your plants, try to catch one of them in a glass jar and get it identified, so you can decide what to do.

Indentify, then treat

Don't jump to conclusions and start spraying chemicals on a supposedly sick plant before you know what (if anything) is actually wrong with it. That's wasteful and irresponsible, and you're likely to do the plant as much harm as good. Pinpointing the exact cause of a problem is difficult for even experienced gardeners, so save yourself frustration and seek out expert help from the beginning.

If it seems that there's something wrong with one of your plants—for example, if the leaves are discolored, have holes in them, or have spots or marks on them—cut off a sample branch, wrap it in damp paper towels, and put it in a plastic bag (so it won't wilt). Take the sample to the nursery or garden center where you bought the plant, and ask for help. If the nursery can't help, contact the nearest office of your state's Cooperative Extension Service or a public garden in your area and ask if they have a staff member who can diagnose plant problems.

Meanwhile, look around your property and around the neighborhood, too, to see if any other plants (of the same or different kinds) show similar symptoms. If a problem is widespread, you shouldn't have much trouble finding someone who can identify it and tell you what, if anything, to do. If only one plant is affected, it's often harder to diagnose the problem, and you may just have to wait and see what happens to it. Keep an eye on the plant, continue with watering and other regular maintenance, and see if the problem gets worse or goes away. If nothing more has happened after a few weeks, stop worrying. If the problem continues, intensify your search for expert advice.

Plant problems stem from a number of causes: insect and animal pests, diseases, and poor care, particularly in winter. Remember that plant problems are often caused by a combination of these; all the more reason to consult with experts about their diagnosis and treatment.

Deer-proof plants?

Planting from lists of deer-proof plants often results in disappointment. What's deer-proof in one area may not be in another. And if deer are really hungry, they'll eat almost anything. If you live in an area where deer are common, check with local nurseries for planting solutions or stroll through your neighborhood to see what's nibbled and what's not.

DEER-CONTROL FENCING

There are several new kinds of insecticides that are quite effective but much safer to use than the older products. For example, insecticidal soap, a special kind of detergent, quickly kills aphids and other soft-bodied insects, but it's nontoxic to mammals and birds and it breaks down quickly, leaving no harmful residue. Horticultural oil, a highly refined mineral oil, is a good control for scale insects, which frequently infest gardenias, camellias, and other broad-leaved evergreens. Most garden centers stock these and other relatively safe insecticides.

Before using any insecticide, study the fine print on the label to make sure that the product is registered to control your particular pest. Carefully follow the directions for how to apply the product, or it may not work.

Diseases

Several types of fungal, bacterial, and viral diseases can attack garden plants, causing a wide range of symptoms, such as disfigured or discolored leaves or petals, powdery or moldy-looking films or spots, mushy or rotten stems or roots, and overall wilting. As with insect problems, if you suspect that a plant is infected with a disease, gather a sample of the plant and show it to someone who can identify the problem before you do any spraying.

In general, plant diseases are hard to treat, so it's important to take steps to prevent problems. These steps include choosing plants adapted to your area, choosing disease-resistant plants, spacing plants far enough apart so that air can circulate between them, and removing dead stems and litter from the garden.

Perennials that would otherwise be healthy are prone to fungal infections during spells of humid weather, especially if the plants are crowded together or if they have flopped over and are lying on top of each other or on the ground. If your garden has turned into a jungle, look closely for moldy foliage, and if you find any, prune it off and discard (don't compost) it. It's better to cut the plants back severely than to let the disease spread. Plan to avoid repeated problems by dividing the perennials, replanting them farther apart, and pruning them early in the season so they don't grow so tall and floppy again. Crowded shrubs are also subject to fungal problems in the summer and should be pruned so that air can flow around them.

Winter damage

Even though much of the West enjoys mild, if not glorious, winters, occasional cold spells that damage normally hardy plants are not uncommon. After a cold spell, wait until at least midsummer to assess the severity of the damage. At that time, new growth will tell you just how far back a plant has been killed and you can prune out limbs that are brown and dead.

Glossary

Amendments. Organic or mineral materials, such as peat moss, perlite, or compost, that are used to improve the soil.

Annual. A plant that germinates, grows, flowers, produces seeds, and dies in the course of a single growing season; a plant that is treated like an annual and grown for a single season's display.

Antitranspirant. A substance sprayed on the stems and leaves of evergreen plants to protect them from water loss caused by winter winds.

Balled-and-burlapped. Describes a tree or shrub dug out of the ground with a ball of soil intact around the roots; the ball is then wrapped in burlap and tied for transport.

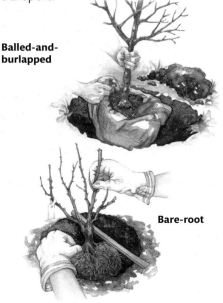

Balled-and-burlapped

Bare-root

Bare-root. Describes a plant dug out of the ground and then shaken or washed to remove the soil from the roots.

Compound leaf. A leaf with two or more leaflets branching off a single stalk.

Container-grown. Describes a plant that is raised in a pot and then removed before planting.

Crown. That part of a plant where the roots and stem meet, usually at soil level.

Cultivar. A cultivated variety of a plant that is often bred or selected for some special trait, such as compact growth, cold hardiness, the production of double flowers, or disease resistance.

Deadheading. Removing old flowers during the growing season to prevent seed formation and to encourage the development of new flowers.

Deciduous. Describes a tree, shrub, or vine that drops its leaves in winter.

Division. Propagation of a plant by separating it into two or more pieces, each of which has at least one bud and some roots. Used mostly for perennials, grasses, ferns, and bulbs.

Drainage. The movement of water down through the soil. With good drainage, water disappears from a planting hole in just a few hours. If water remains standing overnight, the drainage is poor.

Drip line. An imaginary line on the soil around a tree that mirrors the circumference of the canopy above it. Many of the tree's roots are found in this area.

Dry-laid. Describes a masonry path or wall that is installed without mortar.

Edging. A shallow trench or physical barrier of steel, plastic, brick, or boards used to define the border between a flower bed and adjacent turf.

Exposure. The intensity, duration, and variation in sun, wind, and temperature that characterize any particular site.

Feeder roots. Slender branching roots that spread close to the soil surface and absorb most of the nutrients for a tree or shrub.

Formal. Describes a style of landscaping that features symmetrical layouts, with beds and walks related to adjacent buildings, and often with plants sheared to geometric or other shapes.

Foundation planting. Traditionally, a narrow border of evergreen shrubs planted around the foundation of a house. Contemporary foundation plantings often include deciduous shrubs, grasses, perennials, and other plants as well.

Frost heaving. A disturbance or uplifting of soil, pavement, or plants caused when moisture in the soil freezes and expands.

Full shade. Describes a site that receives no direct sun during the growing season.

Full sun. Describes a site that receives at least eight hours of direct sun each day during the growing season.

Garden soil. Soil specially prepared for planting to make it loose enough for roots and water to penetrate easily. Usually requires digging or tilling and the addition of some organic matter.

Grade. The degree and direction of slope on a piece of ground.

Ground cover. A plant such as ivy, liriope, or juniper used to cover the soil and form a continuous low mass of foliage. Often used as a durable substitute for turfgrass.

Habit. The characteristic shape or form of a plant, such as upright, spreading, or rounded.

Hardiness. A plant's ability to survive the winter without protection from the cold.

Hardiness zone. A geographic region where the coldest temperature in an average winter falls within a certain range, such as between 0° and –10°F.

Hardscape. Parts of a landscape constructed from materials other than plants, such as walks, walls, and trellises made of wood, stone, or other materials.

Herbicide. A chemical used to kill plants. Preemergent herbicides are used to kill weed seeds as they sprout, and thus to prevent weed growth. Postemergent herbicides kill plants that are already growing.

Hybrid. A plant resulting from a cross between two parents that belong to different varieties, species, or genera.

Interplant. To combine plants with different bloom times or growth habits, making it possible to fit more plants in a bed, thus prolonging the bed's appeal.

Invasive. Describes a plant that spreads quickly, usually by runners, and mixes with or dominates adjacent plantings.

Landscape fabric. A synthetic fabric, sometimes water permeable, spread under paths or mulch to serve as a weed barrier.

Lime, limestone. White mineral compounds used to combat soil acidity and to supply calcium for plant growth.

Loam. An ideal soil for gardening, containing plenty of organic matter and a balanced range of small to large mineral particles.

Microclimate. Local conditions of shade, exposure, wind, drainage, and other factors that affect plant growth at any particular site.

Mowing strip. A row of bricks or paving stones set flush with the soil around the edge of a bed, and wide enough to support one wheel of the lawn mower.

Mulch. A layer of bark, peat moss, compost, shredded leaves, hay or straw, lawn clippings, gravel, paper, or other material, spread over the soil around the base of plants. During the growing season, a mulch can help retard evaporation, inhibit weeds, and moderate soil temperature. In the winter, a mulch of evergreen boughs, coarse hay, or leaves is used to protect plants from freezing.

Native. Describes a plant that occurs naturally in a particular region and was not introduced from some other area.

Nutrients. Nitrogen, phosphorus, potassium, calcium, magnesium, sulfur, iron, and other elements needed by growing plants. Supplied by the minerals and organic matter in the soil and by fertilizers.

Organic matter. Plant and animal residues, such as leaves, trimmings, and manure, in various stages of decomposition.

Peat moss. Partially decomposed mosses and sedges, mined from boggy areas and used to improve garden soil or to prepare potting soil.

Perennial. A plant that lives for a number of years, generally flowering each year. By "perennial," gardeners usually mean "herbaceous perennial," although woody plants, such as vines, shrubs, and trees, are also perennial.

Pressure-treated lumber. Softwood lumber treated with chemicals that protect it from decay.

Propagate. To produce new plants by sowing seeds, rooting cuttings, dividing plant parts, layering, grafting, or other means.

Retaining wall. A wall built to stabilize a slope and keep soil from sliding or eroding downhill.

Rhizome. A horizontal underground stem, often swollen into a storage organ. Both roots and shoots emerge from rhizomes. Rhizomes generally branch as they creep along and can be divided to make new plants.

Root ball. The mass of soil and roots dug with a plant when it is removed from the ground; the soil and roots of a plant grown in a container.

Rosette. A low, flat cluster of leaves arranged to resemble rose petals.

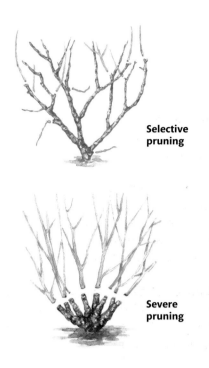

Selective pruning

Severe pruning

Selective pruning. Using pruning shears to remove or cut back individual shoots in order to refine the shape of a shrub, maintain its vigor, or limit its size.

Severe pruning. Using pruning shears or loppers to cut away most of a shrub's top growth, leaving just short stubs or a gnarly trunk.

Shearing. Using hedge shears or an electric hedge trimmer to shape the surface of a shrub, hedge, or tree and produce a smooth, solid mass of greenery.

Specimen plant. A plant placed alone in a prominent position.

Spike. An elongated flower cluster, with individual flowers borne on very short stalks or attached directly to the main stem.

Tender. Describes a plant that is damaged by cold weather.

Underplanting. Growing short plants, such as ground covers, under a taller plant, such as a shrub.

Variegated. Describes foliage that is marked, striped, or blotched with color other than green.

Index

NOTE: Page numbers in **bold italic** *refer to illustrations.*

Landscape Designers

John Ahrens is principal at King's Creek Landscape Management in Austin. His firm has worked throughout the Texas Hill Country, Colorado, and in the Austin and San Antonio areas. The firm specializes in indigenous stone work and water features, as well as in landscapes that include mostly native and "Texas tough" naturalized plantings. Barry Landry, RLA, and Nena Scott assisted John with the designs.

Mark Bowen is a landscape designer and co-founder, in 1987, of the Houston-based landscape design-build firm Living Art Landscapes. He has served as president of the community gardening group Urban Harvest. He writes a weekly column for the Houston Chronicle and is the author of several books.

Michael Buccino has been designing desert landscapes since 1966. A landscape architect and graduate of Cal Poly, Pomona, he and the members of his small Palm Desert firm, Michael Buccino Associates, undertake residential, commercial, and public projects..

Lee Buffington and her husband, Gordon Iwata, operate a design-build landscape company, Arcadia Design, in Mercer Island, Washington. They specialize in residential landscapes.

Laura Crockett, owner and principal of Sylvan Designs of Hillsboro, Oregon, has been designing gardens for clients in the Northwest since 1988. An avid plantswoman, she designs and consults for residential and public-space projects. She is also an instructor at hands-on gardening workshops.

Rosa Finsley founded King's Creek Gardens, a Cedar Hil, Texas, nursery and landscape design firm, in 1970. She has designed residential, public, and commercial gardens throughout Texas, including the Historic River Link for the Riverwalk in San Antonio. She is known for her naturalistic designs. Cheryl Bryant assisted Rosa in the designs.

Lucy Hardiman is the principal of Perennial Partners, a garden-design collective in Portland. A plant enthusiast, she writes for Garden Design and Horticulture magazines, as well as regional publications, and lectures on garden design throughout the United States and Canada. Her own garden has been featured in many magazines and books and has appeared on HGTV's Gardener's Diary and PBS's Victory Garden.

Daniel Lowery is owner of the design-build firm Queen Anne Gardens, Seattle, where he seeks to improve the health and happiness of his clients through garden design. His work has been featured in national magazines and has won a variety of awards. At a recent Northwest Flower and Garden Show, he was joint winner of the Founder's Cup (Best of Show) and the Horticulture Magazine Award for the most interesting use of plants.

Curtis Manning owns Arcadia Desgn Group, which designs and builds landscapes in the greater Boulder-Denver area of Colorado. Curtis has a degree in civil engineering as well as in horticulture. The firm specializes in personalized, functional residential landscapes reflecting the region's environment. He has won several Excellence in Landscape awards from the Associated Landscape Contractors of Colorado.

Richard Marriotti is the founder of Marriotti Landscape Architecture (MLA) of Las Vegas, Nevada. Founded in 1999, MLA specializes in desert-adapted, water-efficient landscapes. Richard has been designing landscapes in the desert southwest since 1984. In addition to residential design, Richard and his firm have designed commercial, institutional, and park projects. They've received several state and local design awards.

Michael Parkey has been a landscape architect and designer of gardens in north Texas since 1983. His special interests are resource-efficient landscapes and the use of native plants in gardens and restored habitats. In addition to his Dallas-based practice, he lectures and writes about design and teaches courses at Southern Methodist University. He has received awards from the City of Dallas and the American Society of Landscape Architects.

Susan Romiti and **Ross Holmquist** are the principal landscape designers in the Landscape Design Division of Mike Parker Landscape in Laguna Beach, California. They work on projects from small beach cottages to large estates and have produced award-winning designs throughout southern California.

Jana Ruzicka operates her own landscape design business in Laguna Beach, California, specializing in residential projects. Trained in Czechoslovakia, she has been a landscape architect in California since 1969. Before establishing her own firm in 1980, she worked on residential, public, and commercial projects. She has won several design awards, and her work has appeared in regional publications.

Carolyn Singer owns Foothill Cottage Gardens, a nursery she developed from her own gardens in the Sierra foothills near Grass Valley, California. Since 1980, she has sold perennials and taught gardening classes at the nursery as well as designed landscapes for foothill and valley residents. She lectures widely and has written about gardening for national and regional publications.

John S. Troy is a landscape architect in San Antonio. His firm, under his own name, was founded in 1981 and specializes in residential landscape design. His designs have appeared in numerous books and magazines and have won several awards from the Texas Chapter of the American Society of Landscape Architects. In 2001, Garden Design magazine presented him with a Golden Trowel Award. His designs are done with his associate designer Anne Solsbery.

John Valentino and **Bob Truxell** are principals in Truxell and Valentino Landscape Development, Inc., founded in 1979 and located in Clovis, California, in the central valley. Their work encompasses private, public, and corporate projects, including a number of award-winning designs. It is regularly featured in regional publications.

Jenny Webber is a self-employed landscape architect in Oakland, California. Also trained in horticulture and fine arts, she specializes in ecologically balanced and creative landscapes. She has won several awards for her designs and has written about gardening and design for national publications.

Richard William Wogisch is a landscape architect and founding partner of Oasis Gardens, a landscape design firm in San Francisco. Since 1989, he has concentrated on designing intimate gardens in the Bay Area. His work has been featured in numerous publications.

Mary Wilhite and **Sharon Lee Smith** are co-owners of Blue Moon Gardens, a nursery near Tyler, Texas. Founded in 1984, the nursery specializes in herbs, perennials, cottage flowers, and Texas natives. Active in numerous professional organizations, Mary also writes a gardening column for the Fort Worth Star-Telegram and articles for regional garden magazines. Sharon, a horticulture graduate of Stephen F. Austin University, features heirloom and native plants in her designs, and she enjoys creating spectacular container gardens.

Phil Wood owns Phil Wood Garden Design in Seattle. His designs have won numerous awards, including gold medals at the Northwest Flower and Garden Show. He is also a board member of the Seattle Chinese Garden Society.

Photo Credits

Front Cover: *bottom (main image)* Saxon Holt; *top left* Jerry Pavia; *top middle* Richard Shiell; *top right* Lance Walheim

Back Cover: *left* Charles Mann, design: Joan Brink; *middle* Richard Shiell; *right* Saxon Holt, design: Jaquie Tomke-Bosch Garden

page 1: Jerry Pavia

page 7: Saxon Holt

pages 14–15: Charles Mann, design: Dulcy Mahar

page 18: *top & center* Saxon Holt; *bottom* Charles Mann, design: Greg Trutza

page 22: *top* Lauren Springer Ogden; *center* Greg Grant; *bottom right* Rita Buchanan; *bottom left* Saxon Holt

page 26: *top* Saxon Holt; *middle left* Rita Buchanan; *middle right* Charles Mann; *bottom* Richard Shiell

page 30: *top left* David McDonald; *top right* Saxon Holt; *middle left* Galen Gates; *bottom right* Jerry Pavia; *bottom left* Charles Mann

page 35: *top* Saxon Holt; *middle both & bottom right* Richard Shiell; *bottom left* Charles Mann

page 39: *top right, top left & middle left* Jerry Pavia; *middle right* Saxon Holt; *bottom right* Greg Grant; *bottom left* Richard Shiell

page 43: *top* Jerry Pavia; *middle & bottom* Saxon Holt

page 47: *top & bottom left* Charles Mann; *middle* Galen Gates; *bottom right* Jerry Pavia

page 50: *top left* Charles Mann, design: Joan Brink; *top right & bottom* Saxon Holt, *bottom* design: Jaquie Tomke-Bosch Garden

page 55: *top left, middle left & bottom left* Richard Shiell; *middle right & bottom right* Charles Mann; *top right* Michael S. Thompson

page 58: *top & bottom right* Saxon Holt; *bottom left* Charles Mann

page 63: *top left* Richard Shiell; *top right & bottom right* Greg Grant; *middle bottom* Charles Mann; *middle left* Milous Chab/Dreamstime.com; *middle right* Karen Bussolini; *bottom left* Galen Gates

page 66: *top both & bottom* Charles Mann; *middle* Greg Gran

page 70: *top & middle* Jerry Pavia; *bottom* Saxon Holt, design: Keeyla Meadows

page 74: *top & middle left* Charles Mann; *bottom right* Rita Buchanan; *bottom left & middle right* Jerry Pavia

page 78: *top left* Jerry Pavia; *top righ* Charles Mann; *bottom* Saxon Holt

page 82: *top* Thomas Eltzroth; *middle both & bottom* Greg Grant

page 87: *top left & bottom right* Jerry Pavia; *top right* Neil Soderstrom; *bottom left* Galen Gates

page 90: *top & middle* Saxon Holt, *top* design: Suzanne Arca; *bottom* Jerry Pavia

page 94: *top left* Jerry Pavia; *top right* Richard Shiell; *middle right* Greg Grant; *bottom right* Charles Mann; *bottom left* Thomas Eltzroth

page 98: *top left, middle left & bottom* Charles Mann; *top right* Jerry Pavia; *middle right* Saxon Holt

page 103: *top left* Jerry Pavia; *top right & middle right* Rita Buchanan; *bottom right* Richard Shiell; *bottom left* Jessamine/Dreamstime.com

page 106: *top left & bottom right* Charles Mann; *top right* Karen Bussolini; *middle left & middle bottom right* David McDonald; *middle top right* Michael S. Thompson

page 111: *top & middle left* Galen Gates; *middle right & bottom right* Jerry Pavia; *bottom left* Richard Shiell

page 115: *top* Jerry Pavia; *bottom* Saxon Holt

page 118: *top left & bottom right* Jerry Pavia; *top right* Greg Grant; *middle right* Carole Ottesen; *bottom left* Galen Gates

page 122: *top left, top right & bottom right* Richard Shiell; *bottom left* Jerry Pavia; *middle left* Rick Mastelli; *middle right* Saxon Holt

page 127: *top* Jerry Pavia; *bottom* Saxon Holt

page 131: *top left & both bottom* Charles Mann; *top right* Galen Gates; *middle right* Saxon Holt

page 135: *top & bottom right* Saxon Holt, *bottom right* design: Sharon Osmund; *bottom left* Jerry Pavia, courtesy of Chozen Garden, design: Roger's Gardens Colorscapes

page 138: *top left* Galen Gates; *top right* Rita Buchanan; *bottom right* Carole Ottesen; *bottom left* Greg Grant; *middle left* Jerry Pavia; *middle center* Charles Mann

page 143: *both* Saxon Holt

page 146: *both* Saxon Holt, *bottom* design: Diana Stratton

page 151: *top & bottom right* Saxon Holt; *middle both & bottom left* Charles Mann

page 154: *top left & bottom* Charles Mann, *top* design: Tina Rousselot, *bottom* design: Steve Martino; *top right* Saxon Holt

page 158: *top left* Rita Buchanan; *top right & bottom right* Jerry Pavia; *middle right both* Charles Mann; *bottom left* Thomas Eltzroth

page 163: *all* Saxon Holt

page 166: *top left* Saxon Holt; *top right & middle* Charles Mann; *bottom* Ruth Rogers Clausen

page 171: *top* Jerry Pavia; *middle & bottom* Saxon Holt

page 174: *top & bottom* Charles Mann; *middle both* Saxon Holt

page 178: *top left & bottom* Saxon Holt; *top right* Charles Mann

page 183: *top left & bottom left* Greg Grant; *top right* Charles Mann; *bottom right* Galen Gates

pages 184–185: Mark Lohman

page 187: *top left* Saxon Holt; *top right* Michael & Lois Warner/Photos Horticultural; *bottom* Charles Mann

page 188: *top left* Richard Shiell; *right both* Galen Gates

page 189: *top left* Richard Shiell; *top right* Rita Buchanan; *middle right* David McDonald; *bottom right* Saxon Holt

page 190: *top left* Richard Shiell; *top right & bottom left* Charles Mann; *middle left* Rita Buchanan

page 191: *top left & bottom right* Jerry Pavia; *top right* Galen Gates; *bottom left* Thomas Eltzroth

page 192: *top left* Saxon Holt; *top right* Thomas Eltzroth

page 193: *top left* Saxon Holt; *top right* Jerry Pavia; *middle* Rita Buchanan; *bottom* Greg Grant

page 194: *left* Jerry Pavia; *right* Richard Shiell

page 195: *top left* Jerry Pavia; *top right* Thomas Eltzroth; *bottom* Charles Mann

page 196: *top* Richard Shiell; *bottom* Jerry Pavia

page 197: *all* Jerry Pavia

page 198: *top* Richard Shiell; *middle* Charles Mann; *bottom* Michael S. Thompson

page 199: *top* Greg Grant; *middle right & bottom* Thomas Eltzroth; *David McDonald*

page 200: *top left* Thomas Eltzroth; *right both* Saxon Holt

page 201: *top & middle* Charles Mann; *bottom* Jerry Pavia

page 202: *top* Rita Buchanan; *bottom* Charles Mann

page 203: *top* Charles Mann; *middle* David McDonald; *bottom right* Jerry Pavia; *bottom left* Lance Walheim

page 204: *top left* Saxon Holt; *top right & bottom* Jerry Pavia

page 205: *top left* Jerry Pavia; *top right* Charles Mann; *middle* Karen Bussolini; *bottom right* Neil Soderstrom; *bottom left* Saxon Holt

page 206: *top left & bottom* Saxon Holt; *top right & middle* David McDonald

page 207: *top* Saxon Holt; *middle* Lauren Springer Ogden; *bottom* Jerry Pavia

page 208: *left* Rick Mastelli; *right* Thomas Eltzroth

page 209: *top* Charles Mann; *bottom right* Jerry Pavia; *bottom left* David McDonald

page 210: *left* Jerry Pavia; *right* Galen Gates

page 211: *top* Richard Shiell; *bottom* Saxon Holt

page 212: *left* Thomas Eltzroth; *middle & right* Jerry Pavia

page 213: *top row & bottom middle all* Jerry Pavia; *bottom left* David McDonald; *bottom right* Greg Grant

page 214: *top* Charles Mann; *bottom* Richard Shiell

page 215: *top & bottom middle* Greg Grant; *bottom right & bottom left* Charles Mann

page 216: *top & middle* Richard Shiell; *bottom* Saxon Holt

page 217: *top left* Jerry Pavia; *top right & bottom* Saxon Holt; *middle* Charles Mann

page 218: *top* Greg Grant; *middle* Charles Mann; *bottom* Saxon Holt

page 219: *all* Saxon Holt

page 220: *top left* Carole Ottesen; *right* Saxon Holt; *bottom left* Galen Gates

page 221: *top* Saxon Holt; *bottom* Charles Mann

page 222: *both* Greg Grant

page 223: *top left* Jerry Pavia; *top right* Richard Shiell; *bottom* Rita Buchanan

page 224: *left* Richard Shiell; *right* Greg Grant

page 225: *top left* Charles Mann; *top right* Lauren Springer Ogden; *bottom right* Jerry Pavia; *bottom left* Richard Shiell

page 226: *both* Jerry Pavia

page 227: *top & bottom* Richard Shiell; *middle* Saxon Holt

page 228: *left* Dency Kane; *right* Saxon Holt

page 229: *top left* Galen Gates; *top right* Michael S. Thompson; *bottom both* Charles Mann

page 230: *top* Greg Grant; *top right & bottom both* Charles Mann; *middle center* Jerry Pavia

page 231: *left* Saxon Holt; *middle & right* Jerry Pavia

page 232: *top* Thomas Eltzroth; *bottom* Richard Shiell

page 233: Charles Mann

page 234: *left* Thomas Eltzroth; *right* Saxon Holt

page 235: *top* Richard Shiell; *middle* Jerry Pavia; *bottom left* Richard Shiell

page 236: *left* Thomas Eltzroth; *right* Greg Grant

page 237: *top* Rita Buchanan; *bottom* Richard Shiell

page 238: *top & bottom right* Richard Shiell; *bottom left* Charles Mann

page 239: *top* Richard Shiell; *bottom* Greg Grant

page 240: *top & middles* Charles Mann; *bottom* Greg Grant

page 241: *top left* Charles Mann; *top right & bottom left* Richard Shiell; *bottom right* Jerry Pavia

page 242: *top left, middle & bottom* Charles Mann; *top right* Jerry Pavia

page 243: *top both* Jerry Pavial; *bottom* Charles Mann

page 244: *top* Charles Mann; *middle* Saxon Holt; *bottom* Susan A. Roth

page 245: *top* Greg Grant; *bottom right* Jerry Pavia; *bottom left* Rita Buchanan

page 246: *top left* Greg Grant; *top right* David McDonald; *bottom* Charles Mann

page 247: *top left* Michael S. Thompson; *top right* Richard Shiell; *bottom* Saxon Holt

page 248: *both* Jerry Pavia

page 249: *top* Carole Ottesen; *middle* Rick Mastelli; *bottom* Greg Grant

pages 250–251: Charles Mann, design: Joan Brink

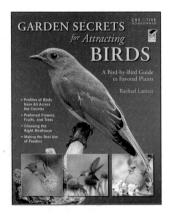

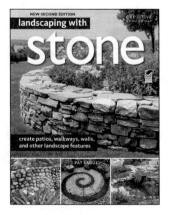
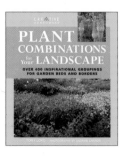